Creative Dissent

Creative Dissent

Psychoanalysis in Evolution

Edited by Alan Roland, Barry Ulanov, and Claude Barbre

PRAEGER

Westport, Connecticut
London

Library of Congress Cataloging-in-Publication Data

Creative dissent : psychoanalysis in evolution / edited by Alan Roland, Barry Ulanov, and Claude Barbre.
p. cm.
Includes bibliographical references and index.
ISBN 0–275–98061–8 (alk. paper)
1. Psychoanalysis. 2. Psychoanalysis—History. I. Roland, Alan, 1930– II. Ulanov, Barry. III. Barbre, Claude.
BF173.C794 2003
150.19′5—dc21 2003053026

British Library Cataloguing in Publication Data is available.

Library of Congress Catalog Card Number: 2003053026
ISBN: 0–275–98061–8

First published in 2003

Praeger Publishers, 88 Post Road West, Westport, CT 06881
An imprint of Greenwood Publishing Group, Inc.
www.praeger.com

Printed in the United States of America

The paper used in this book complies with the Permanent Paper Standard issued by the National Information Standards Organization (Z39.48–1984).

10 9 8 7 6 5 4 3 2 1

Copyright Acknowledgments

A version of Chapter 1 in this volume originally appeared in *The Psychoanalytic Review* 71(1) (1984): 169–177.

A version of Chapter 2 in this volume originally appeared in the *Journal of Religion and Health* 40(1) (Spring, 2001): 41–59.

A version of Chapter 4 in this volume originally appeared in *Psychiatric Times* 14 (1997); 54–55. Reprinted with permission of *Psychiatric Times*. ©1998 by CME, Inc., Irvine, CA 92614-5835.

A version of Chapter 5 in this volume originally appeared in the *Journal of Religion and Health* 40(1) (Spring, 2001): 71–88.

A version of Chapter 7 in this volume originally appeared in *A Psychoanalysis for Our Time: Exploring the Blindness of the Seeing I*. New York: New York University Press, 1998.

A version of Chapter 11 in this volume originally appeared in *Psychoanalytic Psychology* 18 (2001): 729–736. Copyright © 2001 by the Educational Publishing Foundation. Adapted with permission.

A version of Chapter 15 in this volume originally appeared in *Reaching Across Boundaries of Culture and Class: Widening the Scope of Psychotherapy*, RoseMarie Perez Foster, Michael Moskowitz, and Raphael Javier, eds. Northvale, NJ: Jason Aronson, 1996.

A version of Chapter 16 in this volume originally appeared in *Gender and Psychoanalysis*, Claude Barbre, ed. Madison, CT: International Universities Press, 2003.

A version of Chapter 21 in this volume originally appeared in *Heinz Kohut: The Making of an Analyst*. New York: Farrar, Straus & Giroux, 2001.

A version of Chapter 22 in this volume originally appeared in Columbia University's *Journal of the Ancient Near Eastern Society* 5 (1973): 411–20.

To Esther Menaker—
friend and colleague,
psychoanalyst and scholar,
teacher and supervisor

Contents

Acknowledgments

As editors, we are grateful for the patience of our contributors, some of whom submitted papers at least five years ago. Claude Barbre and I deeply regret the death of our third co-editor, Barry Ulanov, a giant of an intellectual with in-depth knowledge in a number of different fields, and a close friend of Esther Menaker. He and Claude selected the various contributors to this volume.

Finally, we are grateful to Jody Cutler for her computer skills and enthusiasm in preparing this manuscript and getting it into final form for printing.

Introduction

Alan Roland

Creative dissent has a long history in psychoanalysis that has played out in diverse ways. The collection of chapters in this book, written in the main by well-known contributors to psychoanalysis, continues in this tradition: critiquing the status quo and exploring new directions in a variety of areas. Rather than formulating still another comprehensive alternative to mainstream psychoanalysis—as has usually been the wont by such figures as Jung, Sullivan, Klein, Winnicott, Kohut, and Mitchell—these essays express a variety of creatively dissenting viewpoints in four different areas: Psychoanalysis and Early Dissidence, the Psychoanalytic Process, Psychoanalysis and Culture, and Psychoanalysis and Religion.

Dissidence today is of another order than in the early period of psychoanalysis when it was paradoxically an avant-garde movement but one that was becoming increasingly orthodox in conformity with Freud's thinking. Today's creative dissidence is in part a reaction to the great popularization and success of Freudian psychoanalysis in the United States after World War II. This occasioned the development of a rigorous orthodoxy in theory and practice, where drive and structural theory and ego psychology held complete sway.

In the last few decades, as intellectuals and others became disillusioned and highly critical of traditional psychoanalysis, creative dissent within psychoanalysis launched an assault on the older orthodoxies. The advent of self psychology and intersubjectivity; the import of British object relations theory with a smattering of Lacan; and the development of relational psychoanalysis, a new integration of interpersonal psychoanalysis with object relations theory and some self psychology, have all changed the face of psychoanalysis in America. Nevertheless, within all of these new models, certain rigidities remain, and other central factors, such as the influence of culture on psychoanalysis, are ignored. It is toward further opening up the psychoanalytic field in theory and practice that the creative dissent of the papers in this volume is oriented.

This book originated in the wish to honor Esther Menaker, an important creative dissident herself, whose humanistic psychoanalytic interests are reflected in these four different sections. The essays have been written more in the broad spirit of psychoanalytic inquiry characteristic of Esther Menaker than around any specific theme. The theories of Otto Rank, an early creative dissident, appear directly in several of the chapters, and are a silent presence in others. This is quite fitting, as Esther Menaker has had a dialectical relationship with Rank, being strongly influenced by his ideas but also clarifying and reviving them to make Rank relevant to a broader psychoanalysis today.

ORGANIZATION OF THE BOOK

Part I, Psychoanalysis and Early Dissidence, first delves into the creative process involved in dissidence with essays by the Kainers on "The Anxiety of Influence in the Creation of Theory" and by Claude Barbre on "The Creative Dilemma: The Influence of Schiller's Aesthetics on the Life and Work of Otto Rank." The first essay cites the necessity of poets and analysts to misread their precursors to clear a space for their own creativity, while they often go on to make similar constructions in their own work. This is illustrated by Leslie Farber's and Erich Fromm's misreading of Otto Rank's theory of the creative will. The second chapter essays the differential effect of Schiller's theory of aesthetics on the theoretical and clinical work of Rank and Freud, with its relevance to therapy today.

Chapters 3 and 4 delve into the historical roots of dissidence in the psychoanalytic movement, particularly the conflicts of Otto Rank and Sandor Ferenczi with Freud, Jones, and Abraham. Robert Kramer's "Why Did Ferenczi and Rank Conclude that Freud Had No More Emotional Intelligence than a Pre-Oedipal Child?" details Ferenczi's and Rank's focus on the earliest mother-child relationship and the need to relate to the patient in the here and now, in contrast to Freud; and why they concluded that Freud's self-analysis was incomplete. E. James Lieberman continues this theme in "The Evolution of Psychotherapy Since Freud," in which he stresses the conflict between Jones and Abraham with Rank and Ferenczi over the Oedipal versus the pre-Oedipal, the scientific versus the artistic, research versus therapy, focusing on the past versus the present, unconscious versus conscious expression, wish versus will and creativity, and understanding versus experience and emotion.

Chapters 5 and 6 are concerned with the maintenance of the Psychoanalytic Movement by both Sigmund and Anna Freud against criticism and dissidence. Paul Roazen gives an example in "What Is a Fact? Eva Rosenfeld and Historiography." By examining Rosenfeld's correspondence, Roazen concluded that as she became more inclined toward Melanie Klein's theories, Rosenfeld was seen as being disloyal to Freud, which resulted in the loss of Anna Freud's friendship. Arnold Wm. Rachman, in Chapter 6, "Freud's Analysis of His Daughter, Anna: A Confusion of Tongues," explores the various implications of one of the best kept secrets in psychoanalysis, only surfacing after 1965, that Sigmund was Anna's analyst.

Part II, The Psychoanalytic Process, is centered on clinical work with illustrative case material. Four of the six chapters challenge monolithic, conventionalized ways of working with patients, whereas three explore working with trauma from a variety of innovative viewpoints. All of the essays highlight therapists' creative and intuitive use of themselves in the intersubjective relationship.

Chapter 7, by Jeffrey B. Rubin, on "The Psychoanalyst and Freedom" explores a hidden enslavement in psychoanalytic practice, where analysts from any persuasion can become overinvested in their favored theories and practices, thus inhibiting their creative work. This theme is continued by Peter L. Giovacchini in "Changing Clinical Orientation, Humor, and the Transitional Space," in which he critiques the humorless, ritualistic orthodoxy in much of American Freudian psychoanalysis. He then argues for a more playful, creative interaction with humor in the transitional space between analyst and patient. Julie Joslyn Brown cites another variant of the creative interaction between analyst and patient in Chapter 9, "In Praise of Small Talk." Small talk in sessions can be pivotal in creating a context and shared experience in which the treatment takes place, rather than having to be avoided or questioned as is customarily the case.

Chapter 10, Spyros D. Orfanos's "Imagining Ithaca: The Impact of the Analyst's Worldview," bridges the themes of analysts' innovative ways of working with the focus on trauma in the last section of Part II. Coming from a Greek heritage, Orfanos drew upon his own selfobject, a Greek composer who reacted to war and death with an affirmation of life and beauty, to work with the trauma of a gay man whose many friends had died of AIDS. Judith L. Alpert's "Beastly Memories Live in Beastly Memory Land" then deals with the enormous complexity of trauma: dissociation and other defense mechanisms, memory, and the development of different selves, all illustrated by case material. Part II concludes with Chapter 12, Doris Brothers's "Cinderella's Gender Trouble: Sadomasochism as the Intersubjective Regulation of Uncertainty," which challenges the traditional psychoanalytic understanding of masochism in women. She rather sees it as a woman's self-restorative efforts in the aftermath of trauma associated with the imposition of gender, illustrated by a reinterpretation of "Cinderella" and case material.

Part III, Psychoanalysis and Culture, focuses in an innovative way on the relationship of culture to psychoanalytic understanding and therapy, an area of psychoanalysis usually observed in the breach regardless of the psychoanalytic orientation. This section starts with Ludwig Janus's and Brigitte Janus

Stanek's Chapter 13 which delineates William and Esther Menaker's work in developing a psychoanalytic psychology that can integrate culture and social change through an evolutionary perspective. Along with Rank and Erikson, the Menakers are among the only psychoanalysts to have attempted this. Daniel Liechty then follows with an uncannily prescient Chapter 14, "Human Fascination with Violence as a Response to Mortality Awareness," that uses Otto Rank's and Ernest Becker's work on immortality for understanding the psychology of war and of suicidal terrorists.

The following four chapters delineate how psychoanalysis is embedded in the modern Western culture of individualism, as well as in the specific cultures of various psychoanalytic institutes. This affects how an analyst thinks and works, the nature of the analyst-patient dialogue, and how analysts treat culturally and ethnically diverse populations. RoseMarie Perez Foster, in Chapter 15, "Considering a Multicultural Perspective for Psychoanalysis," tries to broaden the scope of psychoanalysis to work with patients from different ethnic and culturally diverse national groups, as well as from the lower classes, by examining the cultural influences of Western individualism on psychoanalytic therapy. She then calls for a more pluralistic framework and illustrates her approach with two case examples. The emphasis on broadening psychoanalytic work with race is continued by Dolores O. Morris in "Race in the Analytic Situation: Reflections of an African American Therapist." She assesses the effects of race on the psychoanalytic process when the analytic dyad is composed of women of color, illustrating differential effects. Paul Lippmann, in Chapter 17, "Reflections on Culture and Psychoanalysis," critiques how analysts of all persuasions, including the relational and intersubjective, rarely take into account the importance of the sociocultural identity of their patients and its intrinsic connection to their depth psychology. Contributing to this disconnection are the effects of the American culture of individualism along with the divorce of psychoanalysis from involvement in socioeconomic and political issues. Robert Prince continues the critique of analysts ignoring the influence of culture on psychoanalysis, not only from the surrounding culture but also from the specific cultures of psychoanalytic institutes. Yet he sees it as entering importantly into the dialogue between analyst and patient. He then connects the historical development of psychoanalysis within a changing sociocultural framework.

Part IV, "Psychoanalysis and Religion," starts with a major paradigm shift in contemporary Freudian psychoanalysis by analysts involved in one or another meditative tradition. Alan Roland's Chapter 19, "Psychoanalysts and the Spiritual Quest: Framing a New Paradigm," details this shift from seeing mysticism in the usual psychoanalytic reductionistic way of it being regressive and/or psychopathological; instead, it is now viewed as a valid quest that intersects with the psychoanalytic and with psychopathology in complex ways. The following two chapters also depart from Freud's and mainstream psychoanalysis's reading of religion. Ester Schaler Buchholz's "Freedom to

Choose between Goodness and Badness: Self-Regulation and the Temptation to Be Evil" draws upon Otto Rank and Esther Menaker on issues of choice, decision, free will, and creativity to create a self. Charles B. Strozier's essay on "Kohut and God," Chapter 21, discusses Kohut's view on religion from a self-psychology standpoint, emphasizing various objects of religion as important selfobjects. The book concludes with the late Barry Ulanov's classic essay, "Mysticism and Negative Presence," on the psychology of mysticism and spiritual experiences and how the great mystics must negate everything on their spiritual journey to the transcendent, eventually investing what has been negated with a spiritual presence.

ESTHER MENAKER

To write of Esther Menaker's life (1907–2003) and contributions, I am reminded of Robert Jay Lifton's comments on Erik Erikson. Lifton saw Erikson's creativity as centrally related to his being on the margin of American psychoanalysis. Although highly esteemed by many and a member of the American Psychoanalytic Association, Erikson was not particularly accepted. The same can be said of Esther Menaker. She and her late husband, William, went to Vienna in 1930 for four years of training in psychoanalysis—much more than most other Americans (and also receiving a Ph.D. in psychology at Vienna University)—with the promise of becoming members of the New York Psychoanalytic Institute upon their return to the United States. This promise was withdrawn as the New York Psychoanalytic Institute began restricting itself to those with a medical background. Nor were they made members of the International Psychoanalytic Association. This was a blessing in disguise. They had to make their own way on the margin for many years without being part of a psychoanalytic establishment. It demanded courage and resourcefulness, but they were actually much freer to go their own way in their thinking and to forge their own unique psychoanalytic identities.

The Menakers were certainly two of the most important figures in New York City, along with Theodor Reik and Erich Fromm, from the late 1930s on, in training non-medical psychoanalysts, or what I prefer to call multidiscipline psychoanalysts. Quite a roster of recognized current-day and deceased psychoanalysts were supervisees, analysands, or students of theirs. To name just a few: Ruth Jean Eisenbud, Edmund Weil, Helen Bloch Lewis, and Martin Bergman. In the 1950s they became central figures at the New York University Clinical Psychology Program and played a major role in the formation of its Postdoctoral Program in Psychoanalysis and Psychotherapy in the late 1950s.

As psychologists/psychoanalysts went from being on the margin to gradually building an important establishment of their own with Division 39 of the American Psychological Association, Esther Menaker again experienced being on the margin. The postdoctoral program changed from being one that freely exposed students to a number of different psychoanalytic perspectives, in full accord with the Menakers' vision, to a track system where a student is primarily a traditional Freudian, or an Interpersonalist, or now a Relational Psychoanalyst. Esther eventually resigned from the Freudian track as she was not a traditional Freudian, and she was invited to join the Interpersonal track. But she wasn't really that either. Esteemed and honored with important awards, by Division 39 included, she was once again on the margin. In her subsequent teaching, supervising, and analyzing of students at the National Psychological Association for Psychoanalysis, with its multimodel Freudian orientation, and then at the Training and Research Institute for Self Psychology, she had chosen to be at psychoanalytic institutes more on the margin than centrally located in the medical or psychological psychoanalytic establishments. And once again her creativity flourished; she published two books at age 88.

Two things are striking about Esther Menaker's numerous papers and books. The first is the fluidity and clarity of her writing, even and especially when dealing with complex conceptual discussions, such as differentiating her position from the premises of classical Freudian psychoanalysis. In a field not always known for its felicity of expression, this is no small accomplishment.

Even more striking is that unlike most psychoanalysts who have made contributions, sometimes important ones, Esther Menaker has evolved a broad philosophy and psychology of life that permeates her thinking on many different levels: the conceptual, the therapeutic, and the everyday. It is a broad vision of the human condition in which growth, evolution, self-creation, and affirmation predominate. Even when considering specific psychoanalytic matters, Esther has always been attuned to the larger issue or principle, and by so doing has anticipated psychoanalytic thinking, sometimes by decades.

For instance, in her first paper published in a psychoanalytic journal in 1942, "Masochistic Factors in the Psychoanalytic Situation," she is the first person in Freudian psychoanalysis to openly assert that the psychoanalytic relationship is not only transference but also develops on the reality of the interactions between two people with their own personalities. She thus anticipated by some four decades the current formulations of intersubjectivity.

Another example is her 1953 paper on masochism, "Masochism as a Defense Reaction of the Ego." She focuses on the pre-oedipal relationship with the mother, which was just beginning to occur in Freudian psychoanalysis; and on masochism as being driven not by the pleasure principle and guilt, as hitherto formulated, but rather by primary considerations of the ego. And in her situating masochism in a particular kind of unloving, tenuous early object relationship, she again anticipated much of the contemporary interest in American psychoanalysis in early object relations.

The major way in which Esther, and Esther and William together, expressed their encompassing vision in the 1950s, 1960s, and the first half of the 1970s was through ego psychology, the most innovative theoretical model in American Freudian psychoanalysis at that time. Their vision was expressed in *Ego in Evolution.* But the Menakers' ego psychology differs in marked ways both from classical theory and from other developments in ego psychology; theirs is an ego with muscle. It is *not* an ego that simply mediates between the drives, the superego, and social reality, and activates defense mechanisms when confronted with signal anxiety as in classical theory; or that adapts to the social surround as in Hartmann's formulations. Nor is it the same as developmental ego psychology, although it has some affinities with Margaret Mahler's formulation of separation-individuation and Erikson's ego-identity. Rather, the Menakers' ego is evolving in a life-long striving for autonomy and differentiation; to new levels of individuation, integration, and complexity with its attendant anxiety and guilt; toward self-creation and self-realization of inner potentials—an ego profoundly related to the will and to the human spirit.

Theirs is also an ego integrally related to the sociocultural world of values and social relationships in a dialectical interaction in which each influences the other, rather than the ego being self-contained; and most important, their ego partakes of social change, an arena that only the rarest of psychoanalytic thinkers, such as Rank and Erikson, have dealt with. More specifically, their ego psychology is profoundly related to American society with its more open opportunities for growth, change, mobility, and choice than most other societies, as well as to the rapid social change of the 1960s and 1970s. And even more specifically, they see women's ego evolution as related to the groundswell of social change in the 1960s that spawned the Women's Movement, to which they contributed. Esther was already one of the rare pioneers of American women before the 1960s who combined a high-level career with having a family; and thus served as a model to younger women who have worked with her. Betty Freidan's *The Feminine Mystique*, a seminal work at the very beginning of the Women's Movement, emerged out of an analysis with William.

In the 1960s and particularly in the first half of the 1970s, Esther wrote a number of papers on the evolving ego as being intrinsically related to identifications and the internalization process. Again, she carefully differentiates her position from the classical one. Rather than identifications being seen as defensively motivated by anxiety, as in oedipal resolutions, or compensatory for loss, as in early separation experiences or mourning, Esther views identifications as major building blocks for the growing, developing ego, as well as for the ego ideal and superego. They are integrally related to values, cultural continuity, and social change. She also makes significant clinical contributions around conflicts involving identifications. These papers, together with earlier ones on masochism, appeared in a book edited by Leila Lerner in 1979, *Masochism and the Emerging Ego.*

It was natural for Esther to move toward a more comprehensive consideration of Otto Rank, who had been thoroughly ostracized from the psychoanalytic movement. Rank's work had already influenced the Menakers' thinking in a number of ways. Perhaps it would be more accurate to say that Esther resonated with Rank in her own thinking and in her own life rather than simply being influenced by him. Although there have been other important books and articles written on Rank, I think it is fair to say that for the psychoanalytic community, at least in New York City, Esther Menaker almost single-handedly rescued Rank from oblivion in *Otto Rank: A Rediscovered Legacy* (1982). She made his thinking accessible, clinically and theoretically relevant, and influential to current-day analysts.

After the book was published, Esther was invited to present her work on Rank at a number of meetings in the 1980s. These presentations and other papers she wrote were edited by Claude Barbre in 1996 in *Separation, Will, and Creativity*, in which Esther continues not only her lucid theoretical exposition of Rank, juxtaposing him in relationship to contemporary theorists, including Kohut, but also importantly shows the clinical relevance of Rank's views with a number of case examples.

It is striking that over 80 percent of Esther's more than 45 articles and 6 books were written and published after she was 60. This includes a personal memoir involving her experience of psychoanalytic training in Vienna and her analysis with Anna Freud (*Appointment in Vienna*, 1989). Anyone might well have been content to have staked out a whole point of view with major works on masochism, ego evolution, identifications, the psychology of women, and Otto Rank. Yet in line with her own philosophy and psychology of life, Esther continued to expand her horizons. As Kohut formulated self psychology in the 1970s, Esther resonated with the affirming nature of selfobject relationships, the need for idealizations which she had earlier written about, and the development of the self. Issues of the self as the primary focus of a psychoanalytic psychology seemed more appropriate than the concept of the ego. Esther began fascinating integrations of self psychology with her earlier work on masochism and later work on Rank. Gems of this integration are chapters in a book that Claude Barbre edited in 1995, *The Freedom to Inquire.*

Esther's life has been a remarkable journey of important contributions, of creating and being herself, of careful inquiry, and of thinking freely. Often living on the margins of the psychoanalytic institutional world, her creativity has continued to flourish. At age 95, she has been working for the last few years on still another book—a fascinating memoir, "The Secret and the Shame: Growing Up in the Shadow of a Terrorist."

Jeffrey Rubin's comments are apropos. "I first met Esther Menaker at a friend's book party . . . I was struck by her open spirit, her passion for ideas, her breadth of interests, and her capacity to laugh. Subsequent meetings . . . deepened my initial impressions. Each time we spoke an intellectual spark was ignited and an emotional or intellectual doorway was opened . . . Esther is a rare and vanishing breed, a psychoanalytic humanist . . . I have been touched and inspired by Esther's interest in culture as well as the consulting room, her love of questions no less than answers, and her belief in the wisdom of the visionary." (Personal communication, September 2002)

REFERENCES

Menaker, E. 1942. Masochistic factors in the psychoanalytic situation. *Psychoanalytic Quarterly, 11.*

______. 1953. Masochism as a defense reaction of the ego. *Psychoanalytic Quarterly, 22.*

______. 1979. *Masochism and the emerging ego*, edited by Leila Lerner. New York: Human Sciences Press.

______. 1982. *Otto Rank: A rediscovered legacy.* New York: Columbia University Press.

______. 1989. *Appointment in Vienna.* New York: St. Martin's Press.

______. 1995. *The freedom to inquire*, edited by Claude Barbre. Hillsdale, NJ: Jason Aronson.

______. 1996. *Separation, will, and creativity*, edited by Claude Barbre. Hillsdale, NJ: Jason Aronson.

Menaker, E., and W. Menaker. 1965. *Ego in evolution.* New York: Grove Press.

Part I

Psychoanalysis and Early Dissidence

CHAPTER 1

The Anxiety of Influence in the Creation of Theory

R. G. K. Kainer and S. Kainer

INTRODUCTION: THE ANXIETY OF INFLUENCE AS A THEORY OF LITERARY CREATIVITY

The Anxiety of Influence is a theory of poetry and its originator is Harold Bloom (1973), a poet and professor of literary criticism at Yale University. It is not incidental to this paper that Bloom consider Freud to be the "Poet of the Sublime" (Bloom 1978, 369), and refers to Freud as one of "non-literary fathers" (1982, xiii). Bloom makes many references to the psychoanalytic paradigm throughout the constructions of his theory. In fact, the anxiety of influence refers to oedipal primacy: the unconscious worry of each poet-son that he owes his own begetting to his father—that he is not the originator of his own works and that he has, so to speak, come too late onto the scene. Since every son—or daughter for that matter—must inevitably arrive after the parent, a tragedy built into the creative process is, in Nietzsche's words, the tragedy of "belatedness" (Bloom 1975, 83). We have all come too late. Bloom tells us that even Nietzsche, that great originator, had a "hatred of the perniciousness of his own belatedness" (83).

Now psychoanalysis, in its main thrust, and in Freud's words, has not been concerned with issues of "priority and originality" (Bloom 1978, 363); Bloom is correct in pointing this out. The roots of psychoanalysis are embedded in the matrix of libido theory, in which drives are object seeking. We have therefore paid a great deal of attention to concepts that express the mechanism of attachment in all its forms: fixation, merger, incorporation, identification, interjection, and internalization, to name several. They are all phenomena that describe our need to link with another, to use Bion's phase, in the quest for drive satisfaction. Since the work of Mahler, the concept of an innate maturational push for separation has been ours to use, but we have studied it less fully, especially in regard to phenomena that require nonattachment: individuation and originality. Psychoanalysis, as Bloom points out, is a theory about love not about creativity.

Since a major concern of ours has been the development of creative thought in psychoanalytic science, we were struck by Bloom's (1978) plaintive note that "it remains one of the worries of both psychoanalysis and literary criticism that as modes of interpretation they continue to be antithetical to one another" (356). Despite the extreme confidence he notices among psychoanalysts when they proceed to analyze a work of art—a confidence very necessary to the healing work, he adds—they have been less than convincing to others in their role as literary critics. The artists have, by and large, resisted the psychoanalysts. Heeding Bloom's call for artists and psychoanalysts to consider one another, his notion of the anxiety of influence became important in relation to an investigation we were making into Otto Rank's theory of creative will.

Bloom tells us that strong (original) poets wage a silent war against their precursors—those who have gone before them, and whose works, they fear, will take priority over their own. For, despite the fact that acts of creativity are acts of unique individuation, Bloom (1982) is correct when he refers to the historicity of literature—that is, literature's "inescapable historical being" (p. ix). He has returned poetry to history and certainly we can see, within psychoanalysis itself, that there has been a history of ideas, even though the time-span has been short compared to poetry and literature. Although not always conscious of it, each theoretician takes his or her place within a continuum of ideas. Within our own realm, strong or original theorists must of course wrestle with Freud, whose primacy still holds sway not because of the relative recency of his influence but because of the astonishing power of his originality. Each of the rebellious sons—Jung, Adler, and Rank—wrestled but could not hold fast within the confines of the movement. Each sacrificed merger with Freud in obedience to their own originality. As Bloom puts it, "Strong poets are infrequent . . . poetic strength comes only from a triumphant wrestling with the greatest of the dead, and from an even more triumphant solipsism" (1975, 6).

However, Freud's dominion, against which we would expect all succeeding theorists to struggle, while not exempt from stimulating the anxiety of influence, is not its only source. Each post-Freudian theorist in turn becomes the precursor for those who come after him in time. Bloom tells us that "each strong reader wishes to find his own original relation to truth" (1975, 3). He was probably not aware that Rank (1929–31/1972b) had almost the identical thought some fifty years earlier in *Truth and Reality*. Rank said, further, that the person of strong creative will cannot accept the collective truth—that such a person must take his inner reality and project it outward as a truth—that is, as an artwork or theory. If his individual truth is then accepted, it in turn becomes part of the collective truth.

One of the ways that the strong poet, the strong reader, the strong theorist, deals with the awful priority of his precursors, Bloom tells us, is to "misread their words in order to clear imaginative space for themselves." This misreading works in the following way in the creation of poetry:

> The ego and the poet-in-his-poem both proceed by a kind of "misconstruction," a defensive process that Lacan calls meconnaissance in psychoanalysis, and that I have called "misprision in the study of poetic influence. . . ." The poet while expressing previously repressed thought, desire or emotion, is able to continue to defend himself against his own created image by disowning it, a defense of un-naming it rather than naming it. (1975, 370)

We will turn to an example of what seems to be this un-naming process as Erich Fromm and Leslie Farber grappled with their precursor, Otto Rank, and tried to evade his influence in the formation of their own work on the will. This specific case will perhaps open the way for a more general consideration of the nature of the anxiety of influence in the creation of theory in our field. We shall also look at the possible relevance of the observation by Gilbert and Gubar (1979) that, insofar as one is engaged in a literary oedipal struggle, "a man can only become a poet by somehow invalidating his poetic father" (47).

THE "MISREADING OF RANK"

Rank's Theory of Will

Otto Rank, who is known as the author of *The Trauma of Birth* (1924/1973), left the psychoanalytic movement not long after the publication of this gift for his beloved "Professor." *The Trauma of Birth* was to locate the actual biological roots of all later anxiety, including castration anxiety, on which Freud had rested the basic paradigm of psychoanalysis. It was clear that until the presentation of this work, Rank was to be Freud's heir. It was intended that Rank assume the presidency of the Vienna Psychoanalytic Society. This is well known to history. What is probably less well known is his subsequent body of work on the creative will, written after his departure from the movement.

Rank's conception of the human will was developed in a series of works, particularly *Will Therapy* (1929–31/1972a), *Truth and Reality* (1929–31/1972b), and most remarkably in *Art and Artist* (1932). Having consciously wrestled with his predecessors, he concluded, in his own originality, that his concept of the will was not the evil will of the pessimistic Schopenhauer, not the glorified romantic (but destructive) will of what he called the megalomanic vision of Nietzsche, nor was it identical to the notion of the "wish" so important to Freud. The will, for Rank, was neither good nor evil, but the central fact of psychological existence. While the wish might be seen as the faint echo of the will, Rank's will was a guiding, purposive, and, importantly for this chapter, constructive force—not a mere longing. It is what enables one to be forward moving despite the determining factors of the past and the clamor of biological drives. It never allows one to be reduced only to those factors, as important as they may be. It is the human capacity to form and go beyond the givens of one's existence.

For Rank, the will is intimately connected to human creativity, which in turn rests on the drive towards individuation, and the unique expression of self. It is fueled, but not caused by, the age-old thirst for immortality. Thus, the products of the will form the content of our history of culture. Individuation, or the separation of self from others, then, is seen by Rank as fundamental to the creating of the self as it is to the creating of the artwork. Indeed, for Rank, the personality is the artwork of the creation of the self, although it might fall short. When it fails, when the will is turned against the self, or remains locked in a willful protest against the necessities of one's realities or one's archaic voices, we have a failure in the highest expression of creative will development and, by definition, Rank's concept of neurosis.

Like his descendent Kohut, who bears a strong if unwilling family resemblance to Rank in matters of narcissism and the self, Rank offered a line of development of the human creative will, which like the line of development of narcissism offered by Kohut, is now conceived of in constructive and positive terms. They gave new meaning to concepts that were once thought of as negative, as in the "infantile" cast given to narcissism in classical theory, and the evil aspect of the will as in the will-to-power and domination of Nietzsche and Adler's concepts. Now, narcissism is also used to describe the cohesive sense of self and well-being, and will describes the highest level of ethical and creative achievement. But Kohut and Rank have strongly wrestled those concepts away from their precursors and put their own stamp on them. Both have had difficulties in remaining related to the mainstream and there is a solipsistic cast, as Bloom might call it, to their resulting originality.

Fromm's and Farber's "Misreading" of Rank

Rank's will is thus a will heroically wrestled away from the negative cast put on it by his predecessors. In the interest of brevity, we will now give a much condensed account of Fromm's and Farber's misreading in which Rank's achievement is negated. The more encompassing is that of Fromm (1939) who reads the underlying philosophy of Rank's will as comparable to that of fascism. Fromm, called a "strong poet" by Arthur Feiner (1979), was a theorist of vast productivity, who was deeply affected by both his exposure to Freud (whom he never wished to abandon) and the consequences of the Nazi evil. His original contributions centered around the attempt to marry Freudian theory to his own great idealism and wish for social reform. It is striking, therefore, that although he believed that "Rank had no intention to do so," he concluded that Rank's view of truth, external reality, and dependency, as is expressed in *Will Therapy* and *Truth and Reality*, bore a close line with fascist philosophy.

Another, less strong reader, might not equate Rank's perspectival view of truth (that is, a view of truth as relative to time rather than belief in an absolute truth) with the fascist bending of the truth for power; nor might another reader equate Rank's profound understanding of subjective reality with a lack of enlightened concern with external reality as does Fromm; nor might another reader find in Rank, who had grave reservations about interminable analyses, and who himself experimented with end-setting for a time, much data to suggest that he would advocate a lifelong dependency on the analyst. Indeed, Rank's person of the highest creative will, who acts in obedience to self-created ideals, is the antithesis of the person who is susceptible to the fascist leader's hold over the powerless.

What Fromm achieves in this misreading is to ascribe back to Rank that Schopenhauerian view of will as evil that Rank had detached himself from in the wench away from the voice of Freud. For it was in Freud's determinism and pessimism that Rank heard the faint echo of Schopenhauer. Rank's human creative will is what Bloom would call a catastrophic negation of the pessimism and evil of Schopenhauer's will and, by extension, that of Freud's. Later, in his own work, Fromm went on to describe his view of the rational man, the biophilic man, the free man, in much the same terms as Rank did his person of strong creative will. The most highly developed person, free of incestuous mother-ties, is Fromm's direct descendent of Rank's separated, individuated, self-ideal obeying individual of creative, ethical willing. Both, in turn, had wrestled with Freud over the primacy of libido and both had shifted from the primacy of the oedipal, with its tie to the father, to the primacy of separation, with its tie to the mother. Fromm was not to acknowledge this in his precursor, Otto Rank.

The issue for Farber (1966) did not involve the struggle with Freud, but an attempt to obey the voice of a more recent paternal claim, that of the great theologian Martin Buber, who told him that our field needed a psychology of the will. Farber first had to grapple with Rank's primacy in that area and he acknowledged that Rank had been the exception to the general neglect of will. But he quickly concluded that Rank's will therapy is primarily concerned with techniques of "willing without guilt." This conclusion was formed despite the extensive attention Rank had paid to the inevitability of the condition of guilt for a human being, who must suffer it if he denies willing or, if the will is obeyed. Farber again ascribed back to Rank that romantic Nietzschean will that Tank had specifically and powerfully negated. Yet later, Farber writes of his own "will of the first realm" that is strikingly like Rank's creative will in its constructive intent. He says:

In the first realm of the will, the will is enjoined to all appropriate human capacities mental and physical, intellectual and emotion, to form a seamless whole . . . that pushes it in a particular direction . . . rather than toward a particular object. (Farber 1966, 8)

And as Rank had said before him:

The will is the united and balancing force between impulses and inhibition: [it is] an autonomous organizing force in the individual which does not represent any particular biological impulse or social drive but constitutes the creative expression of the total personality and distinguishes one individual from another. (1939, 50)

Fromm's and Farber's Anxiety of Influence

What Fromm and Farber have done, in their "misprision" of Rank, is to negate the struggle that he had already won for himself against that part of Freud which obeyed nineteenth-century scientific determinism. As Esther Menaker (1982) tells us in her recent book on Rank, his voice is that of the "approaching period of relativism and indeterminacy" in science. In their misreading, they have incorrectly removed him from his place in the twentieth century in the historicity of psychological ideas and placed him back in the nineteenth century of German Romantic philosophy, from which he indeed came, but from which, very early in his theoretic work, he wrestled and departed, as he was later to depart from Freud in search of a theory of human creativity. It is interesting that both readers missed in Rank the intricate and essential transmutation of willing from a negative force to an ethical necessity.

Therefore, in the service of his own originality, Fromm possibly misprisioned Rank's view of the human will in its constructive aspects because his own important contribution centered on the forces of human evil and destructiveness which had greatly affected him in his own time and against which his own voice of enlightened messianic reform was dedicated. Similarly, Farber may have diminished the importance of Rank's discovery because his own originality and voice were directed elsewhere. Farber's own fine contributions are with will's disabilities—the anxiety of willing that which cannot be willed. Rank, too, had not been unmindful of this aspect of the will, but it was with the will's creativity that he achieved his priority. The invalidation of Rank by Fromm and Farber gave them imaginative space to bring the will back to what may be looked at as their own twentieth century updating of the nineteenth century view of its dark side. Bloom (1973) points out that while negation of another is of no therapeutic value for the individual, it can liberate him into the linguistic freedom of poetry and thought.

CONCLUSION

We had two other brief thoughts in concluding our research on the anxiety of influence in theoretic creativity. The first has to do with the relationship of belatedness to historicity—that is, the relationship of belatedness to the history of ideas in our field. Perhaps one of the differences between literary creativity and creativity in psychoanalytic thought is that belatedness is a tragedy for the poet, while being ahead of one's time turns out to be the tragedy of creativity in our field. For poets, as Bloom (1973) tells us, "own, they are, what they become first in naming" (64). However, to come too early for the strong poet in our field has often meant the necessity of having to split off, or being split off, from the mainstream of thought, with its attendant loss to all. Certainly this seems clear in the case of Rank; and psychoanalysis, largely unaware of his work, still searches for its understanding of the constructive human will, its function in human creativity, and its role in the therapeutic encounter.

Our final comment returns us to Freud and the relationship of the anxiety of influence to his wish to have psychoanalysis rest on a foundation of scientific objectivity. In case we have erred too much on the side of likening our science to an art, we would like to conclude with a look at the nature of the science of our art. The essence of our science, paradoxically enough, is in our subjective knowing. Unlike Stolorow and Atwood (1979), who equate one's subjectivity with pathological causality and thereby devalue this form of knowing, we found compelling the fact that these three original thinkers made similar subjective observations. Although their ultimate creative intent differed, yielding a different amount of attention paid to the phenomena in their body of work as a whole, similar observations were nonetheless made about will and willing. Taken in the light of the anxiety of influence and these thinkers' need to differentiate themselves from, if not invalidate, their precursor, their confluence lends an objective validity to subjectively arrived-at phenomena. Not only does it allow us to consider the human will as more than a "mere projection" of Rank's subjective difficulties in the narcissistic realm (Stolorow and Atwood, 1979), but it supports Freud's vision of psychoanalysis as a science of observation, despite the fact that it is also subject to the vicissitudes of art.

REFERENCES

Bloom, H. (1973). *The anxiety of influence.* New York: Oxford University Press.

———. (1975). *A map of misreading.* New York: Oxford University Press.

———. (1978). Freud and the poetic sublime. *Antareus, 30*(no. 31), 355–379.

———. (1982). *The breaking of the vessels.* Chicago: University of Chicago Press.

Farber, L. (1966). *The ways of the will.* New York: Basic Books.

Feiner, A. (1979). Countertransference and the anxiety of influence. In *Countertransference* (pp. 105–128). New York: Jason Aronson.

Fromm, E. (1939). The social philosophy of will therapy. *Psychiatry, 2,* 229–237.

Gilbert, S., & S. Gubar. (1979). *The madwoman in the attic.* New Haven: Yale University Press.

Menaker, E. (1982). *Otto Rank: A rediscovered legacy.* New York: Columbia University Press.

Rank, O. (1932). *Art and the artist.* New York: Knopf.

———. (1939). *Beyond psychology.* New York: Dover.

———. (1972a). *Will therapy.* In *Will therapy and truth and reality.* New York: Knopf. (Original work published 1929–31.)

———. (1972b). *Truth and reality.* In *Will therapy and truth and reality.* New York: Knopf. (Original work published 1929–31.)

———. (1973). *The trauma of birth.* New York: Harper and Row. (Original English translation published 1924.)

Stolorow, R., & G. Atwood. (1979). *Faces in a cloud: Subjectivity in personality theory.* New York: Jason Aronson.

Chapter 2

The Creative Dilemma: The Influence of Schiller's Aesthetics on the Life and Work of Otto Rank

Claude Barbre

INTRODUCTION

Ralph McInterny once remarked that from the time of Plato, "the study of philosophy was not a cultural adornment, the fifty drachma course that assured success in Athens. *Lebensphilosophie* and philosophy were the same thing" (Basehart 1987, 82). Indeed, the life and work of psychologist Otto Rank reflects this vital symmetry. As Esther Menaker points out, "Otto Rank has sometimes been called a philosophical psychologist, for his theories did not grow initially or primarily out of a concern with therapy, but rather out of a preoccupation with the meaning of life" (Menaker 1995, 17). In this chapter I will explore several themes in the history of philosophy and aesthetics that no doubt impacted on Rank's life view, in particular, the writings of Friedrich Schiller. I will compare and contrast Schiller's major themes—specifically his notions of "the aesthetic impulse," "will," and his concept of *harmonia*—with aspects of Rank's contributions, namely, his notions of creativity and the art of living. I will contend that although Rank has focused on analyzing Schiller's *own* psychology in his early writings, there are strong philosophical similarities with Schiller that are both *implicit and explicit* in Rank's later theory and work, especially after his departure from the psychoanalytic movement. Finally, I will argue that Schiller's aesthetics anticipate Rank's writing on will and self-creation, and demonstrate the philosophical roots of Rank's many theories, especially in light of his "will therapy."

THE INFLUENCE OF SCHILLER'S PHILOSOPHY ON OTTO RANK

First, let us regard some *explicit* examples of Rank's familiarity with Schiller's work. We know that Rank became enamored of Schiller's work as early as age 15. After Rank's older brother, Paul, arranged to get student tickets to the theater, "the first performance they attended was Schiller's *The Maid of Orleans*, which so impressed Otto that he became a steady patron of the performing arts" (Lieberman 1985, 4). Inspired by Schiller, Rank's initial appointments of himself as an artist widened into his first written work, *Der Kunstler* (*The Artist*), which eventually brought him to Freud's attention. Freud recognized in this 21-year-old a creative will that prevailed over the cultural and emotional poverty of his background (Barbre, 1999). Rank saw in Freud a mentoring, positive, and paternal presence and kindred spirit. Yet Rank's explorative mind often seemed to find new material in the increasingly mapped terrain of psychoanalysis. Exemplifying a typical trait of his, Rank sought to bring his readings of psychoanalysis into his own language and idiom when writing *Der Kunstler*, using the new-found theories to explore the creative forces of the artistic personality by employing the word "artist" much as Freud did the word "sexuality" (Kramer 1996, 3). The burgeoning emphasis on the spontaneous growth of the self, and the undetermined potentialities of the psyche, became for Rank the expression of will in theory and in life.

During Rank's deep involvement with the psychoanalytic movement, Schiller's influence is often cited and developed by him. For example, the Vienna Psychoanalytic Society's minutes for March 4, 1908, record Rank's presentation on Schiller's eye infirmities, connecting Adler's general theory of "organ inferiority" to the "roots of his Tell figure," alluding to the "myth of the blind archer and to some characteristic passages in the William Tell drama." The ensuing discussion is critical of Rank's idea, one discussant (who had not read Adler's work) lamenting "an application of the theory where it does not belong." As was customary, Freud had the final word: Rank's interpretation is "a particularly beautiful mythological confirmation of Adler's principle and [is] secure as are few interpretations," adding, "a number of objections can be dismissed" (Nunberg & Federn 1967, 341–343; Stepansky 1983, 91–92). Freud went on to confirm Rank's contribution to the psychology of myths, in particular several paragraphs on the subject of "the family romance" in Rank's second published book, *The Myth of the Birth of the Hero* (1909).

Freud's enthusiasm at that time for Rank's writings on Schiller is not surprising for two prominent reasons. First, as Peter Gay notes, Schiller was one of Freud's favorite poets whom he could "quote by the hour." Freud wrote in 1884, "Hunger and love: that, after all, is the true philosophy, as our Schiller has said." Gay comments, "Years later, Freud would resort to this line more than once to illustrate his theory of the drives: hunger stood for the 'ego drive' which serves the survival of the self, while love, of course, was a polite name for the sexual drives, which serve the survival of the species" (Gay 1988, 46). Second, as our example illustrates, Rank's early writings were "Freudian," in that they predominately focused on the application of Freud's theories to his particular interests. These creative applications pleased the Professor. For instance, Rank collected several essays on Schiller into his 1912 magnum opus, *The Incest Theme in Literature and Legend: Fundamentals of a Psychology of Literary Creation.* Here, the influence of Freud is apparent as he discusses types of incest dramas, including themes of brother hatred and sibling complexes—in short, analyses of what he thought were Schiller's incest fantasies. Peter Rudnytsky remarks that in the case of Schiller as a focus, Rank not only shows some of the "ecumenical spirit that prevailed through 1910 in the discussions of the Vienna Psychoanalytic Society," but it also shows "his Freudian colors," adding that some of this material was deleted from the 1926 edition of *The Incest Theme* when Rank "no longer had reason to cast himself as Freud's disciple" (Rank 1912/1992).

Rank's integration of philosophical wisdoms (most notably, those of Kant, Schiller, Kierkegaard, and Nietzsche) into his theories of psychology eventually led to tensions with Freud and his circle. For instance, intrigued with his realization that willing leads to guilt, Rank began to search for the origins of anxiety, which he thought he found in the experience of birth. An attempt to conform his original thoughts to Freud's biological determinism influenced the work that is usually immediately associated with his name, *The Trauma of Birth* (1924/1973). In it he considered the initial physiological separation from the mother as creating an anxiety-producing experience which becomes the prototype of future anxiety. Rank would later depart from this literal interpretation, suggesting that the birth experience is a metaphor for the struggle for psychological separation and self-discovery. Although Freud was at first pleased with Rank's efforts, the emphasis on the mother-child interaction as primary clashed with Freud's theory of the Oedipus complex and castration anxiety, for "by claiming that the ambivalent pre-Oedipal relationship between mother and child is the heart of transference, he thereby relegated fear and love of the Oedipal father to a secondary place" (Kramer 1996, xiv). Up to this time, psychoanalytic understanding of human psychology had been predominantly patro-centric, and the theory of anxiety focused for the most part on the idea of castration anxiety. Rank's creative act of writing *The Trauma of Birth* was construed as a challenge to the libido theory itself. Eventually, Rank's modification of theory and therapeutic procedure (later developed in *Will Therapy; Truth and Reality; Art and Artist; Psychology and the Soul;* and *Beyond Psychology*) contributed to his break with Freud which came in 1926, and to his dismissal from the American Psychoanalytic Association in 1930. By the time of his death in New York in 1939, Rank had contributed extensively to the study of the role of creativity, the meaning of birth and separation, the fear of mortality and the wish for immortality, and the nature of the will (Menaker, 1982).

After 1924, and *The Trauma of Birth*, Rank further developed his interest in the creative development of art and artist by integrating many themes from Schiller's aesthetics into his constructive and relational psychology. These themes included the human struggle to find freedom from the tyranny of one-sided views of life, the reconciling and separating force of the will, the mediating function of play and illusion, and the obligation to affirm the aesthetic impulse in human existence. Both "philosopher-poets" accentuated the viable force of human potentiality in conjunction with the centrality of imagination. The artist would later symbolize for Rank a clear example of human striving for self-expression, growth, and change. He would reject explanations of the artist and his or her work in terms of causal psychological terms, and instead apply his perception of the operation of the creative process to the understanding of human psychology in general and to life overall. Rank would say explicitly, "Creativeness lies equally at the root of artistic production and of life experience" (Rank 1932, 38).

SCHILLER'S THEORY OF PERSONALITY

Schiller embodies the figure of the creative personality striving for expression. He studied theology, law, and medicine, but with the success of his 1781 drama, *The Robbers*, he shifted his focus to writing. He wrote poetry, plays, philosophy, and major histories. He later abandoned philosophy, having become disillusioned with what he believed to be the excessive claims to certainty and finality of the scientific determinism of his day. This theme will reappear in Rank's writing on truth, especially in his criticism of psychoanalytic moralism. Schiller had at first attempted an objective aesthetic theory in the spirit of rationalist philosophy, but later developed an aesthetic view of life after reading Goethe, Fichte, and Kant. The power of art and creativity became an integral account of life and the indispensable role played in it by what Schiller called "the aesthetic impulse."

Among many of Schiller's strengths are his psychological insights, and his ability to combine practical experience with philosophy. Although Schiller was not a systematic thinker, we can discern several phases of his work which led to the development of his aesthetic theory. These themes, I will argue, permeate Rank's own thoughts on creativity. Schiller's dissertation, entitled *Uber die Philosophie der Physiologie* (1779), and the *Letters* (1794), reveal a strong preoccupation with the psychology of poetic creation, and the profound effect of emotion on the body. Schiller's interest in the theory of personality is already discernible in the two versions of his dissertation in which he discusses the loss of equilibrium caused by ecstatic experience, and how this phenomenon affects the whole physical organism. As Margaret C. Ives notes, "In this early dissertation, Schiller sees the health of the physical organism as depending on certain principles of cooperation and balance between the various parts, and this state of health, where all parts of the organism are in tune with each other, may perhaps be designated as one of physiological harmony" (Ives 1970, 77). Schiller employs a musical metaphor to suggest that the psychological and the physiological are like two or more notes that blend together to form a whole, in the way that the body has various parts that cooperate to form an organic whole (Pugh 1998, 287–366).

Thus, Schiller offers a *theory of personality*, in that he suggests that the state of physiological harmony effects the mental state of the person. The disturbances of the personality, then, can manifest themselves as physical symptoms. Schiller thus suggests an interdependence of the physical organism and the personality of body and soul, and this leads him to offer a theory of psychological harmony, of a psychic as well as physical organism (Ives 1970, 77). We can see here in Schiller's early personality theories clear precursors to psychoanalytic preoccupations—strong indications of why Freud and Rank would frequently discuss his poetry, plays, and philosophy.

Schiller's developing theory of aesthetics also reflects his early medical training: He once treated a young boy's depression by maintaining what he called "the equilibrium of the physical well-being so that the boy's spirits might revive" (Schiller 1779; Fricke & Gopfert, Vol. I, 1984). Schiller wrestled with new terminology to describe this creative dilemma of finding *harmonia*—the search to find a life-balance—with the term *Mittelkraft*, a word describing the substance by which sense-impressions are turned into messages capable of being received through the nerves. Such concepts as *Natur*, *Vernunft*, *Wille*, and *Einbildungskraft* are introduced in connection to creative striving (Fricke & Gopfert, Vol. I, 1984). Thus, Schiller's essays illustrate his abiding interest in the problems of the personality, the methods whereby psychological harmony or equilibrium may be both created and maintained, and the struggle to approach this balance.

THE IMPACT OF SCHILLER'S IDEAS ON RANK

Rank reveals an indebtedness to Schiller, among others, when he remarks that "psychotherapy does not have to be ashamed of its philosophic character, if only it is in a position to give the sufferer the philosophy that he needs, namely, faith in himself" (1945, 96). Rank cites Kant about this vision in *Will Therapy*: "You will learn from me not philosophy but to philosophize, not thoughts to be imitated but to think" (Rank 1945, 1). In addition, Rank states that an epistemological psychology begins where Kant placed the problem, namely, "how can the individual determine himself from himself, or why does he do this with such difficulty?" (Rank 1945, 2). This is the essence of the will-guilt problem, the creative dilemma, that would occupy Rank's writing. Schiller's aesthetic theory is also a reworking of Kant's aesthetics. Schiller wished to move beyond the rational language and method adopted by Kant, to a way of discourse directly appealing to the *imagination*. As E. M. Wilkinson has noted, the difference between Kant and Schiller "is that whereas Kant was trying to make a clear distinction between the several faculties of mind, Schiller was trying to illustrate "the dynamic interplay between the fundamental aspects of human nature: sense and spirit, nature and freedom, finite and infinite" (Wilkinson, in Ives 1970, 37).

Kant's system divides human experience into two distinct domains: the sensuous, understood as our necessary existence in the physical world; and the rational, or moral, in which we find freedom in our self-determining behavior. In his later work, Schiller reconceptualizes this Kantian dualism as a historical progression from necessity to freedom in terms of individual as well as cultural perspectives, and in doing so addresses Kant's account of the role of art. Schiller found Kant's writing on art inadequate, for he believed that Kant's understanding of aesthetics overemphasized the individual *subjective* experience rather than the living presence and purpose inherent in the art object. By underscoring the vital role of art and aesthetics in human lives, Schiller's rethinking of Kant's epistemology opened the door to numerous accounts of art as a creative activity and theories of the imagination. As Hegel acknowledged, "It is Schiller who must be given great credit for breaking through the Kantian subjectivity and abstraction of thinking and for venturing on an attempt to get beyond this by intellectually grasping the unity and reconciliation as the truth and by actualizing them in artistic production" (Pugh 1996, 20). We can already see a similar dialectic in Rank's thinking. Indeed, as Fay Karpf said well, "Dynamic dualism was for Rank a fundamental principle of life, manifest in all sorts of contrasts: male and female, heredity and environment, individual and collective, impulse and inhibition, positive and negative etc.—the formula of thesis and antithesis" (Karpf 1953, 110).

Schiller offers an analysis of human nature as comprising three impulses: the material and formal impulses (*Stofftrieb* and *Formtrieb*), corresponding to Kant's dualism of sense and reason, and a third impulse, the play-urge or aesthetic impulse (*Spieltrieb*) that mediates and reconciles the impulses into an integral unity or harmony. Stephen Kurtz puts it well:

> If the *Ding-an-sich* is inaccessible, Schiller reasoned, then all interpretations of phenomena must have equal weight. Those guided by the form impulse, for example, see the world in terms of structure. Those guided by the *Stofftrieb* (material impulse) are moved especially by content. Believing these positions to represent the truth, their adherents dispute them passionately. But since they are not about the truth, no position ever triumphs. Schiller then offers a third mode of apprehension: the *Spieltrieb* or play impulse. Those guided by it—principally artists—are not persuaded of the reality of their vision. Instead they play with the appearances they themselves construct and in this way free themselves—to a degree unknown by others—of any binding dogma about the real. (Kurtz 1989, 171)

The importance of this third impulse, the play-urge, will anticipate Rank's emphasis on creativity as the way the self grows and develops—in essence, what animates the "true nature" of the self "beyond psychology" (Rank 1941/1958, 16). When our two natures are joined by the play-urge, Schiller writes, "The object of the play drive may therefore be called living form: a concept serving to designate all the aesthetic qualities of phenomena, and, in a word, what in the wildest sense of the term we call beauty" (Fricke & Gopfert, Vol. I, 1984, 577).

Schiller's view that art is the center of human experience echoes Rank's view of the personality as an expression of what may be called the "art-work of the self" (Kainer 1983). Rank would maintain that the urge to create, be it the self directly in personality, or the self in the form of the artwork, is not tied to pathology, but is innate (Rank 1932, 415–431). Likewise, we have emphasized that "Schiller's aesthetic speculations express the belief that there is a means by which we can regain our freedom from division, and that the means is art, taken in a very broad sense" (Adams 1971, 417).

THE AGE OF SCIENCE AND THE ART OF LIVING

Schiller and Rank share a common criticism of the one-sidedness of scientific determinism. For example, Rank (1945) rejected the prominent psychology of his time where the "principle of causality is applied to the psychic," pointing out that such an application "is in fact an attempt to equalize or equate men; this principle was to reduce the infinite variety of men to an ordered, indiscriminate set of causes-and-effects in which differences were effectively ignored or were condemned" (1945, 82). Although Rank tells us that his conception "was *not* that the principle of causality was 'false,' but that it no longer sufficed for our current level of awareness" (1945, 171), he remained uncomfortable with the extent to which value judgments implicit in psychoanalytic theory condemned individual difference or deviation from a so-called social norm. In fact, Rank's trenchant remark in *Beyond Psychology* revivifies Schiller's own discomfort with the reductionistic epistemologies and moral rigorism of his day: "Almost every manifestation of human thought and behavior has been labeled 'pathological' or 'abnormal,' except the psychology itself which is claimed as an unfailing standard" (1941/1958, 288). In short, Rank underscores the fact that Freud did not, for the most part, acknowledge the necessary relativeness and general limitation of his idea of normality.

Rank's discomfort with Freud's positivism mirrors Schiller's point of view in his philosophical poem, *The Artist* (1790). Here, Schiller anticipates Rank's awareness of the tension between science and the art of living. On the one hand, Schiller warns the scientist not to despise the arts as obsolete (*Der Kunstler*, lines 383–392); on the other hand, the arts are given the task of integrating the disseminated and abstract findings of the sciences, and presenting them in concrete and sensuous form to a public that could not appreciate them otherwise. We hear a struggle in Schiller's poem to reconcile a perceived opposition, that we can be led from the mysteries of science into the broad daylight of common knowledge—a view indicative of Schiller's penchant for antinomies and resolution. Although we notice that his suspicion of the scholastic program places him firmly in the humanistic tradition, Schiller's theory of modern art advocates a potential relationship with science—a hard-won mutuality which is a creative goal in itself. As he notes in *The Aesthetic Education of Man* (1794):

> We shall be seeking new conquests for science in the field of experience, searching for laws where chance seems to play and arbitrariness to prevail. In this way we believe we can help to remove the partition that separates, to their mutual disadvantage, the worlds of art and learning, and can introduce well-founded knowledge into social life and cultivation into the sciences. (Pugh 1998, 211)

Subsequently, Schiller says, "If a scientific totality raises itself above an artistic totality, it can only do so by becoming a work of art itself" (Ives 1970, 108). This attitude is clear in Otto Rank's chapter, "On Nature and Spirit," in *Psychology and the Soul*, in which he discusses the relationship between physics and psychology, and the constructive possibilities in creative exchanges between the two.

Rank would insist that a scientific psychology founded on unquestionable ideology resembles a negative morality which undermines the freedom and expression of creative inquiry. As he noted in his later work, "that Freud's psychology did not even permit individuals of the same race and social background to deviate from the accepted type led me beyond these differences in psychologies to a psychology of difference" (1941/1958, 29). Likewise, Schiller conceives of the human personality as living in a changing world of space and time: "If these changes and circumstance are allowed to exert an unrestricted influence upon a person, he is said to be in a state of passivity" (Ives 1970, 163). The adjective that Schiller generally uses to describe such a state is "leidend" (suffering). When the individual seeks to impose his own ideas on the world around him, Schiller calls him "tatig" (active) or "schaffend" (creative). Notice, as in Rank's writing, that will, activity, and creativity are closely linked: The world challenges us with changes, and we cause changes back into the world.

Clearly, Schiller's vision, like Rank's view of the individual in society, is drawn to view the reciprocal relationship between the personality and the outside world. How each of us responds to the existential dilemma of difference contains the unifying possibilities of will. For Schiller, the will of the individual, namely, the order imposed from within each person by their *essential pattern* creates variety and change in the outside world. For the human personality to develop fully, thinks the philosopher-poet, we should try to realize all the different aspects of our personality and simultaneously strive to use all the different aspects of life to help us in this task. This striving is also a hallmark of Rank's notion of the creative will.

Schiller's phrase "beauty is freedom in appearances" suggests that freedom is not in reason alone, as in Kant, nor a "natural phenomenon," as in Goethe, where we lack the mediating force of creative will and are passive recipients of inspiration. Rather, it is a hard-won autonomy that involves both the rational and irrational forces in unity (Pugh 1998, 287–367). We will see that Rank also accepted a certain randomness in the life process which he called "irrational forces." For Rank, the duality between self-realization and self-submergence through identification with social, political, or religious ideology becomes a way in which the individual seeks to ensure immortality (Rank 1941/1958; 1945). This view enabled Rank to see beyond the value of human, rational understanding to its limitations and potential. In comparison, Schiller thinks the will defeats unthinking spontaneity with conscious action.

Since courses of action differentiate between these two polarities of nature and reason, thinks Schiller, there will be conflict in the personality, and harmony (*harmonia*) between the two leads to an integrated wholeness. Schiller offers two ways that conflict may be resolved: (1) the demands of instincts and impulses are suppressed by the power of will, and (2) the demands of instinct and impulses are obeyed. As psychoanalysts will later revisit, Schiller understood that nature suppressed may lead to revenge and self-deception—our psychological constitution undermined. The struggle is to harmonize the demands of nature with those of reason, and this will to harmonize can lead us to do what's best for ourselves and society. According to Schiller, this mediation, the resolution of conflict between the two sides of the personality held in complementarity, is achieved through the mediation of the aesthetic potential in human experience. Rank will show the creative dilemma in the struggle for *harmonia.*

HARMONIA AND CREATIVE WILL

Rank acknowledges the importance of an aesthetic mediation in terms of the "creative impulse." He notes in *Will Therapy* that Schiller's thinking about the two sides of personality connotes the idealistic and optimistic view that humans are not simply determined by nature, but that they are also capable of free personal acts of reason (1945, 143). Adding to Schiller's dualism, Rank states that in contrast to both conceptions, "I have again emphasized the individual factor, which, through the given and through that which has been appropriated by identification, finally makes something of its own, and in truth so much more, the stronger the personality, or whatever forms its nucleus" (Rank 1961, 147). We see here not only Rank's understanding of the paradoxical dilemma of human life, where we exist between necessity and freedom, but also a correspondence to Schiller's notion that a healthy life depends on certain principles of cooperation and balance between the various parts that form the whole of society.

This balance is described in Schiller's famous metaphor of the interdependence of many branches that make up a tree. In short, Schiller emphasized that natural society is organic: all the parts are integrated with the whole, contrasted with modern society which emphasizes abstract speculation and necessity. How can the two be united? The uniting force is art which brings together abstraction and concrete realization in *harmonia*. In comparison, Rank would say psychology strives after the whole person, the striving of the individual after unity. Indeed, Rank's chapter, "Total Ego, and Partial Ego," in *Will Therapy*, echoes this major theme of Schiller's—namely, that human existence struggles in the middle space of separation and unity. As David Pugh suggests in *Dialectic of Love*, Schiller's conception of beauty as synthesis, and the sublime as separation, echoes Artistole's aporia of *chorismos* (separation) and *methexis* (participation)—the thread that leads us through most of Schiller's philosophy (Pugh 1996, 67–70). For both Rank and Schiller, this notion of intermediacy is central.

Like Schiller, Rank would also privilege the will as the building blocks of life. Departing from Freud's structural model, Rank did not think that the child's development depends only upon ego responses torn between instinctual forces and repressive environmental influences. Instead, through the responses and choices a person makes, he or she begins to make use of both the inner and outer forces for personal growth and development. To these organizing, volitional, and choosing processes Rank ascribed the term "will."

Schiller's writing on the tensions between instinct, impulse, and intuition are keenly resonant with Rank's notion of will, framed by the philosopher's characteristic focus on dualism and reconciliation. For Rank, the balancing forces between impulse and inhibition illustrate a life dilemma: both impulse and inhibition are understood by Rank as initially organic, or present from birth as vital elements of the life process. But Rank is clear in arguing that these instinctual needs for gratification exist in more ways than in a physical sense. Rather, they depend on *psychosocial* influences as well—that is, our need for response requires social acceptance, affirmation, and attachment. To reflect the interaction between the self and the social world, between the psychological and social aspects of instinct, Rank used the term "impulse." On the other hand, Rank viewed inhibition as a controlling process that operates to guard the self from the destructive effects of uncontrolled instincts. Thus Rank saw this process of inhibition as derived from inner forces and a response to the external environment. He would view both impulse and inhibition as sources of will—the powerful collective, directing, and organizing force that seeks balance and control. In contrast to psychoanalytic views, Rank maintained that this "dynamic dualism operates as a force of balance and not only as a source of conflict" (Hofstein 1977, 65). Clearly, Schiller's notions of *harmonia* strike a strong resonance to Rank. In the end, Rank rejected Freud's biological, psychological, and social determinism which he felt denied the personality the very qualities which make our life human: autonomy, responsibility and conscience. As we have discerned, these themes overlap with Schiller's lifelong preoccupations.

CONCLUSION

Throughout his writing, Rank stresses that a neurotic individual suffers from an inhibition in the ability to will. This inhibition Rank saw as largely the result of the interaction of original endowment with a primary environment which failed to affirm the will of the growing child. Simply put, the task of therapy is to address this developmental deficit in order to support and affirm the patient's will. The notion of the aesthetic impulse and will within each person and between persons resonates with the agency of the life-force in us, and is, as we have seen, ultimately expressed in the creative experience—in Schiller's vernacular, a movement from necessity to freedom through will and play (*Spieltrieb*). As Menaker says so well: "It is the ability to take experience into oneself, fashion it so that it will nourish the growth of the self and then to project an expression of the self in a way that may be helpful or enjoyable to others, that Rank called creative. It is this opportunity that is given us in the therapeutic situation" (Menaker 1996, 10). It is also an opportunity, as both Schiller and Rank remind us, that expresses the art of living.

REFERENCES

Adams, H. (1971). *Critical theory since Plato.* New York: Harcourt Brace Jovanovich.

Applebaum-Graham, C. (1970). The structure of the personality in Schiller's tragic poetry. In M. C. Ives, *The Analogue of Harmony.*

Barbre, Claude. (1999). Reversing the crease: Nietzsche's influence on Otto Rank's concept of creative will and the birth of individuality. In J. Golomb, R. Lerner, and W. Santaniello, *Nietzsche and Depth Psychology.* Albany: State University of New York Press.

Basehart, M. (1987). Edith Stein's philosophy of person. *Carmalite Studies, 4.*

Fricke, G., and G. Herbert Gopfert. (1984). *Samtliche Werke* [*Collected Works*] (5 vols.). Darmstadt: Wissenschaftliche Buchgesellschaft.

Gay, P. (1988). *A life for our time.* New York: W.W. Norton.

Golomb, J., R. Lerner, and W. Santaniello. (1999). *Nietzsche and depth psychology.* Albany: State University of New York Press.

Hesse, H. (1974). *My belief: Essays on life and art.* T. Ziolkowski, ed. New York: Farrar, Straus, and Giroux.

Hofstein, S. (1977). Will, choice, and fate perspectives in Rankian thought. *The Journal of the Otto Rank Association, 12*(Summer), 65.

Ives, M. C. (1970). *The analogue of harmony: Some reflections on Schiller's philosophical essays.* Pittsburgh: Duquesne University Press.

Kainer, R. G. K., and S. Gourevitch. (1983). On the distinction between narcissism and will. *Psychoanalytic Review, 70*:535–552.

Karpf, F. B. (1953). *The psychology and psychotherapy of Otto Rank.* Westport: Greenwood Press.

Kaufmann, W. (1974). *Nietzsche: philosopher, psychologist, antichrist.* Princeton: Princeton University Press.

Kramer, R. (1996). *A psychology of difference: The American lectures of Otto Rank.* Princeton: Princeton University Press.

Kurtz, S. (1989). *The art of unknowing.* Northvale, NJ: Jason Aronson.

Lieberman, J. (1985). *Acts of will: The life and work of Otto Rank.* Amherst: University of Massachusetts Press.

Menaker, E. (1982). *Otto Rank: A rediscovered legacy.* New York: Columbia University Press.

———. (1995). *The freedom to inquire.* Northvale, NJ: Jason Aronson.

———. (1996). Some thoughts on Rank's view of creativity. Unpublished paper.

Nunberg, H., and E. Federn, eds. 1967. *Minutes of the Vienna psychoanalytic society, 1908–1910.* New York: International Universities Press.

Pugh, D. (1996). *Dialectic of love: Platonism in Schiller's aesthetics.* Montreal: McGill-Queens University Press.

Rank, O. (1909). *Der Mythus der Geburt des Helden.* F. Robbins and Smith Ely Jaliffe, trans. *Nervous and Mental Disease Monograph Series, 18,* 1914.

———. (1924). *Das Trauma der Geburt und Seine Bedeutung für die Psychoanalyse. Internationale Psycholanalytische Bibliotek, 14,* 1924. Harper & Row, 1973.

———. (1932). *Art and artist.* New York: Knopf.

———. (1945). *Will therapy and truth and reality.* New York: Knopf.

———. (1958). *Beyond psychology.* New York: Dover. (Original work published 1941.)

———. (1961). *Psychology and the soul.* New York: A.S. Barnes, Perpetua Edition. Also James Lieberman, ed. Johns Hopkins University Press, 1998.

———. (1964). *The myth of the birth of the hero.* New York: Vintage.

———. (1973). *The trauma of birth.* New York: Harper and Row. (Original English translation published 1924.)

———. (1992). *The incest theme in literature and legend: Fundamentals of a psychology of literary creation* G. Richter, Trans. Johns Hopkins Univ. Press, 1991.

Schiller, F. (1779). Dissertations: Uber die Philosphilie der Physiologie. Leipzig and Vienna: Franz Deuticke. (Original work published 1912.)

———. (1790). The Artist.

———. (1794). *Letters.*

Seif, N. (1980). *Otto Rank: On human evil.* Unpublished dissertation, Yeshiva University, New York.

Stepansky, P. E. (1983). *In Freud's shadow: Adler in context.* Hillsdale, NJ, and London: The Analytic Press.

Wilkerson, E. M., and L. A. Willoughby, eds. (1967). *Friedrich Schiller: On the aesthetic education of man.* Oxford: Clarendon.

CHAPTER 3

Why Did Ferenczi and Rank Conclude that Freud Had No More Emotional Intelligence than a Pre-Oedipal Child?

Robert Kramer

In February 1926 Sándor Ferenczi offered to analyze Sigmund Freud, his beloved Professor and mentor. "I find it actually to be tragic that you, who endowed the world with analysis find it so difficult to be—indeed, are not at all—in a position to entrust yourself to anyone," Ferenczi told Freud, who had been tormented for three years by cancer of the jaw and was, in 1926, also suffering from heart pains. "I will come to you for a few months and place myself at your disposal as analyst—naturally: If you don't throw me out" (Falzeder & Brabant 2000, 250). Few human beings understood Freud's emotions more deeply than Ferenczi who, for almost two decades, had immersed himself, with all his heart and soul, in Freud's most intimate thoughts, anxieties, and feelings. "Don't forget," Ferenczi once reminded Freud, "for years I have been occupied with nothing but the products of your intellect, and I have always felt the man behind every sentence of your works and made him my confidant" (Brabant, Falzeder, & Giampieri-Deutsch 1993, 219).

"A MOST THOROUGHGOING SELF-SCRUTINY"

Ferenczi analyzing Freud? In the recent explosion of writings on Ferenczi, I have found no one—not a single analyst, writer, or historian—who has been willing to take Ferenczi's offer seriously. It seems inconceivable, especially to institute-trained analysts, even those favorable to Ferenczi, that Freud could have benefited from therapy with Ferenczi. Did Freud need emotional insight from Ferenczi, of all people? Absurd! It was Ferenczi, the quintessential needy child and lovesick *enfant terrible* of psychoanalysis, who was the patient, not Freud. What emotional insights could Freud, the aging Oedipal father, have possibly experienced in analysis with an ill "wise baby"? The very idea is preposterous, unspeakable, unthinkable—subversively calling into question the integrity of Freud's self-analysis, the foundation stone of all psychoanalytic theory and practice.

According to historians such as Peter Gay, and resolutely maintained to this day by legions of institute-trained analysts and psychoanalytically inclined academics in the arts and humanities, Freud's self-analysis of his infantile emotions in the late 1890s was a brilliant success and established the Oedipus crisis as the nodal point for the attainment of maturity. During the late 1890s, Freud, in correspondence with Fliess, struggled against almost insuperable odds to reach the neurotic harbor of his own Oedipus complex, writes Gay, by "subjecting himself to a most thoroughgoing self-scrutiny, an elaborate, penetrating, and unceasing census of his fragmentary memories, his concealed wishes and emotions" (Gay 1988, 97).

Some recent writers, while sympathetic to Ferenczi, claim that Ferenczi "wished to analyze Freud, his own analyst, so that Freud, in turn, would be enabled to complete Ferenczi's analysis" (Aron & Harris 1993, 4). Who could deny that Ferenczi pleaded, in dozens of letters, year after year, for emotional help from Freud, his revered master and friend? But something is missing, I feel, from such a one-sided—or, may I say, "one body"?—perspective. There are two hearts and two minds, plus a host of internal objects, entangled in every analysis. All analysis is mutual. Ferenczi, a pioneer of "two body" psychology, the most compassionate and empathic of the early clinicians, considered himself a "specialist in peculiarly difficult cases" (Ferenczi 1931/1980b, 128)—the last glimmer of hope for souls who had abandoned all hope.

Unlike those who infantalize Ferenczi by refusing to take him at face value, I believe that by offering to analyze Freud, in addition to wanting to complete his own analysis, Ferenczi was unselfishly and sincerely offering an extraordinary gift to the Professor, his friend and mentor: an opportunity to experience emotionally—*perhaps for the first time*—the genuine possibility of healing in the therapeutic encounter. "I am also [not] that psa. superman whom we have constructed," Freud once admitted to Ferenczi (Brabant et al. 1993, 221). In a slip of the pen, Freud forgot to write the word "not" in this confession of humility. But surely Ferenczi saw at once that Freud's slip was an all-too-human cry for help. And who better than Ferenczi, trusted above all others, to reach out and help Freud in a time of such great need, when the Professor had been diagnosed with an agonizingly painful, and eventually fatal, oral cancer?

"WHENEVER AN EMOTIONAL REACTION IS SUPPRESSED, INTERRUPTED, OR REPRESSED, SOMETHING IS ACTUALLY DESTROYED IN US"

I began to be curious about the intent of Ferenczi's offer to analyze Freud only recently, after spending many years studying the lifework of Otto Rank,

Ferenczi's close friend and collaborator in the early twenties (Kramer 1995, 1996, 1997). Following the trail blazed by Esther Menaker's rediscovery and masterful exposition of Rank's legacy (Menaker 1982, 1995, 1996), I became convinced that Rank, of all the early pioneers of psychoanalysis, was the most brilliant and the least appreciated, although his prescient writings on will and emotional intelligence would later capture the imagination of Carl Rogers, Rollo May, and other founders of humanistic psychotherapy (Kramer 1995). Like Ferenczi, Rank was exceptionally intimate with Freud, but, unlike Ferenczi, Rank ultimately refused to recant the pre-Oedipal "heresies" he had championed (and shared with Ferenczi before publication) in *The Trauma of Birth* (1929). Confronted with Freud's decisive opposition, Rank chose to resign in protest from his positions as vice president of the Vienna Psychoanalytic Society, director of Freud's publishing house, and editor of *Imago* and *Zeitschrift*, the two leading psychoanalytic journals, and move to Paris and, later, America, where he enjoyed great success as a therapist, lecturer, and writer until his death in 1939 (Lieberman 1985).

Although Ferenczi and Rank, the two most creative thinkers of Freud's inner circle, had broken off their relationship by early 1926, I began to wonder about the timing of Ferenczi's offer to analyze Freud in February 1926. Even after Ferenczi publicly attacked Rank in the psychoanalytic journals, it is evident, based on a reading of Ferenczi's recently published *Clinical Diary* (1988), that Ferenczi still harbored all of Rank's pre-Oedipal "heresies." Was it merely coincidence, I thought, that Ferenczi mentioned to Freud "your jaw malady" (Falzeder et al. 2000, 250) in the February 1926 letter in which he offered to analyze the Professor?

"Whenever an emotional reaction is suppressed, interrupted, or repressed, something is actually destroyed in us," says Ferenczi in his *Clinical Diary*. "The annihilated part of the person falls into a state of decay and decomposes" (1988, 88). I can easily imagine that by 1926, after he had "proved" his loyalty to Freud, the keenly sensitive Ferenczi might very well have felt that Freud's oral cancer, the gaping hole in Freud's jaw, was a kind of *teratoma:* a physical expression of the isolated fragments of Freud's arrested infantile experience and feelings—the return, so to speak, of the repressed. "My own analysis," Ferenczi confided to his *Clinical Diary*, "could not be pursued deep enough because my analyst [Freud] . . . could not follow me down into those depths" (1988, 62)—obviously, the same pre-Oedipal depths plumbed so fearlessly by Rank. With respect to how Freud's incomplete self-analysis might have inadvertently harmed his own unfinished analysis with Freud, Ferenczi asked poignantly in 1932: "Is it not possible, or even probable, that a doctor who has not been analyzed well . . . will not cure me but, instead, will act out his own neurosis or psychosis at my expense? (1988, 92–93).

In early 1926 Ferenczi knew that Freud had long been fed up with therapy, seeing it as impossible, and equivalent, as Freud once told Rank, to "the white-washing of the Negro" (Rank 1941/1958, 272). By then, Freud had lost almost all hope for the curative potential of classical analysis, focusing his energies instead on "scientific investigation" of the unconscious and building his increasingly complex psychoanalytic theory. Couldn't Freud, therefore, learn something from Ferenczi's analysis of him? Now that Rank, the only other intellectual peer of Freud, had been catapulted out of the inner circle, whom but the empathetically gifted Ferenczi was left to grasp Freud in the deepest emotional strata of his unconscious?

"THE TEARS OF DOCTOR AND PATIENT"

Let us, for once, take Ferenczi's offer seriously. If we do, the question arises: What would the emotional experience of analysis with Ferenczi have been like for Freud in the role of patient? Unfortunately, we are immediately stymied—no one can possibly know the answer to this question. But what if we tried to consider this offer from Ferenczi's frame of reference? How might Ferenczi, for example, have conducted himself in the role of analyst? Here, I think we can be more confident in our guess. It seems safe to predict that Ferenczi, no matter how awed he was by Freud's genius, would have treated Freud along the lines of the tender encounters he describes, with such poignancy, in his *Clinical Diary:*

> Should it even occur, as it does occasionally to me, that experiencing another's and my own suffering brings a tear to my eye (and one should not conceal this emotion from the patient), then the tears of doctor and patient mingle in a sublimated communion, which perhaps finds its analogy only in the mother-child relationship. (Ferenczi 1988, 65)

The neurosis, Freud once warned Ferenczi, "is the motherland where we first have to secure our mastery against everything and everyone" (Brabant et al. 1993, 247). Psychoanalysis seeks mastery of the *motherland?* Throughout Freud's writings, the mother is a ghostly phantom, invisible and unthinkable, yet always present, between the sheets of his text. "I probably underestimate the power of this [mother] complex," Freud told Ferenczi in 1916, "probably out of personal inexperience" (Falzeder & Brabant 1996, 121). *Did Freud not have personal experiences with mother?* By the early twenties, it had become clear to Ferenczi and Rank that the psychic root of emotional joy and emotional suffering, mental health and mental pathology, lies buried in the "dark continent," as it were, of the earliest mother-child relationship. A new experience in a deeply emotional relationship with an empathic analyst—what Ferenczi and Rank in *The Development of Psychoanalysis* (1924/1956) had called *Erlebnis* (or experiential) therapy—*is* necessary for healing. "This, then, is the New," said Rank, "which the patient has never experienced before" (Rank 1929–31/1977, 65). Mere Oedipal interpretation by a cool, indifferent analyst, Ferenczi and Rank insisted, is more traumatic than helpful. In addition to tactfully analyzing transference and countertransference, and plumbing infantile history to its most painful roots, the analyst needs to relate to the patient, person to person, soul to soul—I to Thou, Thou to I—in the here and now of the analytic situation. According to Rank, all psychic life is grounded in the present. In *Will Therapy*, published in German in 1929–31, Rank uses the term "here and now" for the *first time* in psychotherapeutic literature: "Freud made the repression historical, that is, misplaced it into the childhood of the individual and then wanted to release it from there, while as a matter of fact the same tendency is working here and now (Rank 1929–31/1977, 39). Instead of the word *Verdrängung* (repression), which laid stress on unconscious repression of the past, Rank preferred to use the word *Verleugnung* (denial), which focused instead on the emotional will to remain ill in the present: "The neurotic lives too much in the past [and] to that extent he actually does not live. He suffers . . . because he clings to [the past], wants to cling to it, in order to protect himself from experience [*Erlebnis*], the emotional surrender to the present" (Rank 1929–31/1977, 27).

So how was "here and now" experiential therapy to be effected if the patient were Sigmund Freud? Says Ferenczi in his *Clinical Diary:* "A contrast to the environment surrounding the traumatic situation—that is, sympathy, trust—mutual trust—must first be created before a new footing can be established" (1988, 169–170). Surely Ferenczi would not have practiced "classical analysis," which he held in low regard, with Freud. He must, therefore, have intended some form of *Erlebnis* or experiential therapy, along the lines pioneered by him and Rank. But how might Freud benefit from such an experience with Ferenczi? By fully experiencing the deep empathic understanding of Ferenczi, the proud but anguished creator of psychoanalysis might, at long last, become more open to his own emotional *Erlebnis*, more open to experiencing feelings that seemed to him so terrible that he had never been able to recognize their existence in himself. With Ferenczi's loving help, Freud might become more open to working through the pain of his archaic childhood, more open to loosening the chains that tied him to his tormented past, more open to letting go of defenses against threatening aspects of his experience—more open, in short, to warming the frozen sea inside his soul. Freud, under the care of the trusted Ferenczi, might for the first time become acquainted, gently and compassionately, with elements of his buried painful infantile experience, that, in his continuing self-analysis, tragically, he had found too threatening or too damaging to integrate into his adult psyche.

Offering to analyze Freud must have taken enormous courage, great fortitude, for Ferenczi, who was keenly aware of his own tendency toward infantile dependence on, and ambivalence toward, Freud—a gigantic intellect, to be sure, but also a frail, sympathetic, suffering human being, a small boy trapped in the craw of an adult, who needed love and acceptance just as any other living person did. No matter how "ill" Ferenczi felt, he was convinced, I believe, that only the tender care of a "wounded healer" could help another "wounded healer" to find the courage to face the deepest and darkest truths, conquer the demons of his unconscious, and recover, finally, the will to heal himself.

"HOW SHOULD I MAKE FRIENDS WITH ONE THAT IS HARMFUL FOR MY LOVED ONES!"

Now let us turn to how Freud responded to Ferenczi's offer. Curiously, the usually suspicious Freud did not question Ferenczi's motive in offering to analyze him; rather he thanked him warmly for the "moving proposal [*rührenden Vorschlag*]" and conceded that there might, indeed, be a "psychical root [*psychische Wurzel*]" to his dangerous physical condition (Falzeder et al. 2000, 252). Just three years earlier, in 1923, Freud had been diagnosed with oral cancer. Until he died in 1939, Freud would suffer through 33 operations on his mouth and be forced to wear a series of painful prosthetic devices, severely limiting his hearing and speech—the very means, ironically, by which psychoanalysis, the talking cure, relieved neurosis. None ever fit properly. "I am constantly tortured by something," Freud complained to Max Eitingon, a member of the Secret Committee (Romm 1983, 71). For the rest of his life, Freud called his prosthesis and oral cancer a "monster" (Jones 1957, 99), "an uninvited, unwelcome intruder whom one should not mind more than necessary" (Romm 1983, 33). Yet, unaccountably, Freud never seemed interested in analyzing the emotional origins of his demonic oral suffering, although he once told Thornton Wilder, the American writer, that someday it might be revealed that cancer is related to "the presence of hate" (S. Freud 1992, 297–298) in the unconscious. Who or what did Freud "hate" in his unconscious?

In his February 1926 response to Ferenczi, Freud was kindly but made clear that he was *deliberately* choosing not to let Ferenczi analyze him, giving his age—he was then approaching 70—as the major reason. But, almost in passing, he added another, more puzzling, reason: "how should I make friends with one that is harmful for my loved ones! (Falzeder et al. 2000, 252). Ferenczi, Freud's most intimate and devoted friend, *"harmful for my loved ones"*? Let us pause here for a moment. Freud's cryptic response bears study and raises a number of questions, which no one has yet answered satisfactorily. Why, exactly, did Freud fear and resist analysis by Ferenczi? Take his first reason. Could it really be age? It was well known by Ferenczi and everyone else in Freud's inner circle that "Freud never ceased to analyze himself, devoting the last half hour of his day to that purpose" (Jones 1953, 327). Age and closeness to death never affected Freud's daily self-analysis, although, in truth, he held little hope for analysis of older patients. The puzzle remains: What kind of "harm" did Freud fear that Ferenczi's analysis would do to Freud's "loved ones"? Who, exactly, were the "loved ones" that Freud felt were threatened? And what was the nature of this threat?

In his March 1926 reply, Ferenczi brushed aside Freud's argument concerning his age or his fear of "harm" to "loved ones." Instead, Ferenczi suggested, with remarkable candor, that overcoming resistance to emotional insight was possible even for the creator of psychoanalysis: "Please keep in mind that as soon as your disinclination (should I say resistance) has been half-way overcome, I can come to Vienna immediately" (Falzeder et al. 2000, 253). No one in psychoanalysis believed in the transforming power of insight more than Freud. Psychoanalytic treatment, Freud had insisted from the beginning of his self-analysis, is "founded on truthfulness" (*S.E.*, Vol. 12, 164), ripping away all veils, facing the darkest truths of the soul, fearlessly filling in all the gaps of memory. The treatment "may be said to have filled in this gap and to have abolished man's infantile amnesia" (*S.E.*, Vol. 13, 183). The repressed must "gain a hearing," declared Freud tirelessly (*S.E.*, Vol. 21, 53). Even more than hearing, no metaphor was as beloved to Freud as vision—that is, psychoanalytic "insight" or seeing within: "Turn your eyes inward," he demanded of his patients no less than of himself, "look into your own depths, learn first to know yourself! Then you will understand why you were bound to fall ill" (*S.E.*, Vol. 17, 143). Analytic insight is all.

"NO MORE INSIGHT THAN A SMALL BOY"

Six years after offering to heal Freud and being turned away, Ferenczi wrote his *Clinical Diary*, musing about Freud with a mixture of love, sadness, bitterness, and anger. Throughout the diary Ferenczi repeatedly expresses profound disillusionment with Freud's capacity for self-insight—with, what orthodox historians like Gay (1988) continue to call, Freud's "most thoroughgoing self-scrutiny" (97). On many pages, Ferenczi shows unequivocally, in the words of Judith Dupont, that "Freud could not renounce defending himself" (in Ferenczi 1988, xii). A few days before his last meeting with Freud in 1932, Ferenczi went so far as to tell A. A. Brill that "he couldn't credit Freud with any more insight than a small boy," using, Jones (1957) adds, the "exact phrase" that Rank did when he left Freud (172). What can it mean, I wondered, that the two men closest to Freud, in their final assessment of Freud's capacity for self-insight, are in perfect agreement? I have no doubt that this shocking judgment—*Freud has no more insight than a small boy!*—was purposefully quoted by Jones, a bitter enemy of both Ferenczi and Rank, to support his claim that the two men had fallen into psychosis: both, charges Jones, "developed psychotic manifestations that revealed themselves in, among other ways, a turning away from Freud and his doctrines" (Jones 1957, 45). But we know now, as Dupont says, that the *Clinical Diary* "provides substantial proof, if any were needed, of Ferenczi's sound mental health" (in Ferenczi 1988, xi) in 1932. Likewise, my own research shows that the reason for Rank's departure from the inner circle was not psychosis but Freud's refusal to accept the pre-Oedipal theory of object relations that Rank had constructed by the early twenties (Kramer 1996). As Menaker (1982) long ago demonstrated, Rank was the first to propose a comprehensive psychoanalytic theory of ego psychology and object relations. Following Menaker's pioneering research, I documented that it was also Rank who first used the term "pre-Oedipal" in a public psychoanalytic forum (Kramer 1996, 43). (In the next edition of the *Oxford English Dictionary*, Rank will be credited with coining this term.) Rank's pre-Oedipal theories, he once wrote to a friend, were "already in the *Trauma* . . . before anyone else dared to conceive them" (Kramer 1996, 43).

Rejecting Jones's animus, we would be better served to understand Rank and Ferenczi's sad, final analysis of Freud as having "no more insight than a small boy" in a deeper, more psychoanalytic way—in the poignant terms, for example, in which Ferenczi spoke about patients who suffer from infantile trauma:

> The greater part of the personality becomes, as it were, a *teratoma*, the task of adaptation to reality being shouldered by the fragment of personality which has been spared. Such persons have actually remained entirely at the child level, and for them the usual methods of analytical therapy are not enough. (Ferenczi 1929/1980a, 121)

By describing Freud in 1930 as having "no more insight than a small boy" could Ferenczi have meant, I wonder, that the creator of psychoanalysis, tragically and ironically, was unable for a lifetime to reach the maturity of the Oedipus complex, remaining forever chained in his unconscious, like a small boy, to the loved and hated maternal object? Could it be that this is why Rank, when he left the inner circle in 1926, used "the exact phrase" that Ferenczi did (Jones 1957, 172)?

As an outcome of the castration complex, Ferenczi and Rank had maintained in *The Development of Psychoanalysis* (1924/1956), the small boy's anxious introjection of the powerful and loved mother serves the purpose of *avoiding* the Oedipus role (Kramer 1996, 18). Was Freud blinded by a small boy's paralyzing need to protect the internalized image of his beloved mother and, therefore, unwilling to analyze his conflicted attachment to the first "good" and "bad" object? In his 1926 American lectures, Rank points out that Freud refused to "see" behind the Oedipus situation to the primal, ambivalent pre-Oedipal object relationship, denying the role of the powerful mother in the infant's development and splitting off his hatred onto women in general:

> [Freud] sees in the mother merely the coveted sex object, for the possession of which the child battles with the father. The "bad mother" he has never seen, but only the later displacement of her to the father, who therefore plays such an omnipotent part in his theory. The image of the bad mother, however, is present in Freud's estimation of woman, who is merely a passive and inferior object for him: in other words, "castrated." (Rank 1996, 101)

"†MOTHER DIED 8 A.M."

None of Freud's closest colleagues, many of whom paid courtesy calls on Amalia Freud, the *Ur-Mutter* of psychoanalysis, ever wondered aloud about Freud's relationship with his mother (Roazen 1993, 35). Who, exactly, was she? Even today, after an avalanche of books and articles on every aspect of Freud's life and work, almost nothing is known about his emotional relationship to his mother except for a few scattered reminiscences (Kobler 1962). "She was charming and smiling when strangers were about, but I," writes Judith Bernays Heller, the maternal granddaughter of Amalia, "at least always felt that with familiars she was a tyrant, and a selfish one. Quite definitely, she had a strong personality and knew what she wanted (Heller 1973, 338). "I really feared [her]," says Heller (1973, 338).

Freud's son, Martin, describes his grandmother Amalia as "certainly not what we would call a 'lady,' [she] had a lively temper and was impatient, self-willed, sharp-witted, and highly intelligent" (Gay 1988, 504). Even when ill or recovering from his dozens of operations for oral cancer, "Professor Freud always found time on Sunday mornings to pay his mother a visit and give her the pleasure of petting and making a fuss over him" (Heller 1973, 339).

Amalia Freud died on August 12, 1930, three years before Ferenczi. "Up to the last four months she continued to make her will felt," according to Heller. "With her going, the strong and vivid bond that held the family together was broken" (Heller 1973, 340). Freud's entry in his *Kurzeste Chronik* or "short diary" for August 12, 1930 reads, in English translation: "†Mother died 8 A.M." (S. Freud 1992, 6). The cross is the regular mark Freud used in his laconic diary to symbolize death. There are many places in Freud's correspondence where he uses this symbol. For example:

On November 5, 1899, to Fliess: " . . . I do not have the slightest idea what to do with the ††† female aspect, and that makes me distrust the whole [Oedipal sexual theory] (Masson 1985, 382).

On January 1, 1907, to Jung: " . . . I am referring to ††† sexuality" (McGuire 1974, 19).

On June 5, 1910, to Pfister: "The transference is indeed a cross" (Meng and Freud 1963, 39).

On April 23, 1926, to Ferenczi, after Rank took his final leave of Freud: " . . . we can make the sign of the cross over him" (Falzeder et al. 2000, 257).

On April 18, 1932, to Eitingon: "Isn't Ferenczi a cross to bear?" (Gay 1988, 582).

"HE RECOILS FROM THE TASK OF HAVING A SEXUALLY DEMANDING MOTHER AND HAVING TO SATISFY HER"

What, exactly, was the nature of the "cross" that Freud bore so heavily throughout his life? No one can possibly know for sure. But traces of Freud's unconscious are scattered everywhere in the body of his writings, and they often leak out, like an open wound, through the cracks in his text. Freud chose not to attend his mother's funeral in 1930, even though it was held in Vienna, sending Anna in his place. "I feel only two things," he tells Jones after his mother's death: an "increase in personal freedom" and "the satisfaction that she obtained at last the deliverance" that she richly deserved (Paskauskas 1993, 677). He added that he did not share the grief or sorrow "displayed so painfully" by his brother, Alexander (Paskauskas 1993, 677). But these one-sided remarks devoid of emotion are belied by a more ambivalent feeling that Freud seems to have had toward his mother, hinted at in a letter to Eitingon, a few months earlier: "Since, as you know, one must pay and atone some time for every unasked thing that one has received and enjoyed, the love of a mother as well . . ." (E. Freud 1960, 278). In March 1926, a few weeks before Rank left Freud for good, Freud wrote to Ferenczi: "Everything must be paid and atoned for, that is my new insight [*Einsicht*] even when no civil guilt is present" (Falzeder et al. 2000, 253). But what "unasked"-for love did Freud receive and enjoy from his mother? And how, exactly, did Freud "pay and atone" for this gift of maternal love?

In his *Clinical Diary*, Ferenczi (like Rank in his 1926 American lectures) wondered about "the ease with which Fr[eud] sacrifices the interests of women in favor of male patients." Although unable to engage in an authentic "two-body" psychoanalysis with Freud, Ferenczi hypothesizes, without offering specific evidence:

> [Freud] may have a personal aversion to the spontaneous female-oriented sexuality: idealization of the mother. He recoils from the task of having a sexually demanding mother, and having to satisfy her. At some point his mother's passionate nature may have presented him with such a task. (The primal scene may have rendered him impotent). *Castration of the father, the potent one, as a reaction to the humiliation he experienced, led to the construction of a theory in which the father castrates the son* and, moreover, is then revered by the son as a god. In his conduct Fr[eud] plays only the role of the castrating god, he wants to ignore the traumatic moment of his own castration in childhood; he is the only who does not have to be analyzed. (Ferenczi 1988, 87–89)

"I HAVE TO BLIND MYSELF ARTIFICIALLY"

Could Ferenczi, the most compassionate of clinicians and a "specialist in peculiarly difficult cases" (Ferenczi 1931/1980b, 128), have helped relieve the agonizing pain of his beloved Professor and provided emotional support? We will never know. "I have to blind myself artificially in order to focus all the light on one dark spot," the tortured Freud once told Lou Andreas-Salomé. "[F]or my eyes, adapted as they are to the dark, probably can't stand strong light or an extensive range of vision" (E. Freud 1960, 312). Like Moses, with whom Freud also identified, was the Promised Land of Oedipal maturity always just over the horizon, tantalizingly out of reach for the anguished discoverer of psychoanalysis, whose "insight [*Einsicht*] that the difficulties in treatment are due to the fact that in the end one is laying bare the patient's evil inclinations, his will to remain ill, is becoming stronger and clearer" (Masson 1985, 268–269)? After a lifetime of daily self-analysis, did Freud ever conquer his own "*will to remain ill*"? In a 1926 American lecture, at the same time that Ferenczi was offering to go to Vienna to analyze Freud, Rank suggested that the small boy "must, so to speak, make his father bad, in order to keep his picture of the good mother clear" (Rank 1996, 142–143). Freud, concluded Rank in almost the same terms as Ferenczi, was tragically "blinded by the castration theory" (Rank 1996, 119).

What are we to make of the final, sad assessment by Rank and Ferenczi of Freud as, secretly, an *enfant terrible*—a great intellect with the emotional intelligence of a small boy who seems to have lived, almost willfully, a life tormented by infantile love and infantile hate, trusting no one? Did Freud, as Rank hinted, live too much in the infantile past and, to that extent, not live in the present? Was Freud's refusal to be analyzed by Ferenczi due to a small boy's fierce will to cling to the pre-Oedipal past "in order to protect himself from experience [*Erlebnis*], the emotional surrender to the present" (Rank 1929–31/1977, 270)? "I find it actually tragic that you, who endowed the world with analysis, find it so difficult to be—indeed, are not in at all—in a position to entrust yourself to anyone," Ferenczi told his beloved Professor in February 1926 (Falzeder et al. 2000, 250). Were Ferenczi and Rank, the two men closest emotionally to Freud and most supportive of the cause during its formative years, "psychotic" for the heresy of "turning away from Freud and his doctrines" (Jones 1957, 45) and fostering emotional intelligence by pioneering object-relational, pre-Oedipal, experiential, client-centered, interpersonal and existential psychotherapies?

REFERENCES

Aron, L., and A. Harris. (1993). Sándor Ferenczi: Discovery and rediscovery. In L. Aron and A. Harris, *The legacy of Sándor Ferenczi*, 1–35. Hillsdale, NJ: The Analytic Press.

Brabant, E., E. Falzeder, and P. Giampieri-Deutsch, eds. (1993). *The correspondence of Sigmund Freud and Sándor Ferenczi: Vol. 1. 1908–1914*. Cambridge: Harvard University Press.

Falzeder, E., and E. Brabant, eds. (1996). *The correspondence of Sigmund Freud and Sándor Ferenczi: Vol. 2. 1914–1919*. Cambridge: Harvard University Press.

———. (2000). *The correspondence of Sigmund Freud and Sándor Ferenczi: Vol. 3. 1920–1933*. Cambridge: Harvard University Press.

Ferenczi, S. (1980a). The principle of relaxation and neocatharsis. In M. Balint, ed. *Final contributions to the problems and methods of psycho-analysis*, 108–125. London: Karnac Books. (Original work published 1929)

———. (1980b). Child analysis in the analysis of adults. In M. Balint, ed. *Final contributions to the problems and methods of psycho-analysis*, 126–142. London: Karnac Books. (Original work published 1931)

———. (1988). *The Clinical Diary of Sándor Ferenczi*. J. Dupont, ed. Cambridge: Harvard University Press.

Ferenczi, S. and O. Rank. (1956). *The development of psychoanalysis*. New York: Dover. (Original work published 1924)

Freud, E., ed. (1960). *Selected letters of Sigmund Freud*. New York: Basic Books.

Freud, S. (1992). *The diary of Sigmund Freud, 1929–1939: A record of the final decade*. M. Molnar, ed. New York: Charles Scribner's Sons.

Gay, P. (1988). *Freud: A life for our times*. New York: W.W. Norton.

Heller, J. (1973). Freud's father and mother. In H. Ruitenbeek, ed., *Freud as we knew him*, 334–40. Detroit: Wayne State University Press.

Jones, E. (1953). *The life and work of Sigmund Freud: Vol. 1*. New York: Basic Books.

———. (1957). *The life and work of Sigmund Freud: Vol. 3*. New York: Basic Books.

Kobler, F. (1962). Die Mutter Sigmund Freuds. *Bulletin des Leo Baeck Instituts 5:* 149–171.

Kramer, R. (1995). The birth of client-centered therapy: Otto Rank, Carl Rogers and "the beyond." *Journal of Humanistic Psychology 35:* 54–110.

———. (1996). Insight and blindness: Visions of Rank. In R. Kramer, ed., *O. Rank, a psychology of difference: The American lectures*, 3–47. Princeton: Princeton University Press.

———. (1997). Otto Rank and the cause. In T. Dufresne, ed., *Freud under analysis: Essays in honor of Paul Roazen*, 221–247. Northvale, NJ: Jason Aronson.

Lieberman, E. J. (1985). *Acts of will: The life and work of Otto Rank*. New York: Free Press.

Masson, J., ed. (1985). *The complete letters of Sigmund Freud to Wilhelm Fliess 1887–1904*. Cambridge: Harvard University Press.

McGuire, W., ed. (1974). *The Freud/Jung letters: The correspondence between Sigmund Freud and C.G. Jung*. Princeton: Princeton University Press.

Menaker, E. (1982). *Otto Rank: A rediscovered legacy*. New York: Columbia University Press.

———. (1995). *The freedom to inquire: Self psychological perspectives on women's issues, masochism, and the therapeutic relationship*. Northvale, NJ: Jason Aronson.

———. (1996). *Separation, will, and creativity: The wisdom of Otto Rank*. Claude Barbre, ed. New York: Jason Aronson.

Meng, H., and E. Freud, eds. (1963). *Psychoanalysis and faith: The letters of Sigmund Freud and Oscar Pfister*. New York: Basic Books.

Paskauskas, R., ed. (1993). *The complete correspondence of Sigmund Freud and Ernest Jones, 1908–1939*. Cambridge: Harvard University Press.

Rank, O. (1929). *The trauma of birth*. London: Routledge & Kegan Paul.

———. (1958). *Beyond psychology*. New York: Dover Books. (Original work published 1941)

———. (1977). *Will therapy*. (J. Taft, Trans.). New York: Norton. (Original work published 1929–31)

———. (1996). *A psychology of difference: The American lectures.* R. Kramer, ed. Princeton: Princeton University Press.

Roazen, P. (1993). *Meeting Freud's family.* Amherst: University of Massachusetts Press.

Romm, S. (1983). *The unwelcome intruder: Freud's struggle with cancer.* New York: Praeger.

CHAPTER 4

The Evolution of Psychotherapy since Freud

E. James Lieberman

In 1906, Sigmund Freud (1856–1939), neurologist and first psychoanalyst, hired a young locksmith, Otto Rank (1884–1939), as secretary of the Wednesday Psychological Society—the future Vienna Psychoanalytic Society. Freud, then 50, became a second father to the brilliant, self-taught, working-class youth who was alienated from his own father, Simon Rosenfeld, an artisan jeweler hot-tempered and given to alcoholic excess. It was probably Alfred Adler, having read an essay by Rank on the psychology of the artist, who recommended the youth to Freud. Adler, Rank's family physician and a member of Freud's inner circle, recognized the value of Rank's (1907) essay, which used the new psychoanalytic theory to create a "sexual psychology of the artist" (subtitle of essay).

Much impressed, Freud hired Rank and sent him back to complete the Gymnasium so he could go on to University. Thus began a 20-year professional and personal relationship between the two men, closer than those between Freud and his sons or Rank and his father. With Freud's help, Rank finished his education in six years, becoming the first "lay" or nonmedical analyst. When he obtained his Ph.D. at the University of Vienna in 1912, Rank already occupied an important role at Freud's side as specialist in history, philosophy, art, and mythology. Evidence of the esteem in which he was held appears in *Die Traumdeutung* (eds. 4–7), Freud's masterwork, where Rank's name appears on the title page as contributor of two chapters in addition to his work as editor and bibliographer (Rank 2003).

The year 1913 stands out in the history of psychoanalysis. After the departures of Alfred Adler and Carl Jung over theoretical differences, a committee, "The Ring," was founded to guide and control the evolution of the new science. Besides Freud himself the members were: Ernest Jones (1879–1958), British biographer of Freud and longtime president of the International Psychoanalytic Association (IPA); Karl Abraham (1877–1925), head of the Berlin Institute for psychoanalytic training; Sándor Ferenczi (1873–1933), the affable, creative intimate of Freud and Rank, from Budapest; Otto Rank, the only member in Vienna with Freud; and, in Berlin, Max Eitingon and lawyer Hanns Sachs (the only nonphysician besides Rank).

World War I blocked communication among the Committee, but the members began to meet and correspond beginning in 1918. The northern axis of the group, London and Berlin, tended to be conservative. Jones and Abraham interpreted psychoanalytic theory narrowly, at times opposing Freud himself, who was flexible and able to change his views. Supporting certain changes, Rank and Ferenczi, the southern axis, elaborated an "active therapy," which made the analyst less isolated—more a partner in exploration than a surgical authority, masked and removed. Besides listening and interpreting, the therapist would guide, support, and challenge the patient. Thus began relationship or interpersonal therapy, as we know it today.

Freud heartily endorsed Rank and Ferenczi's innovation, proposing a prize for the best paper on active therapy in the next IPA Congress (1922). During the next two years disputes raged among the "brethren" under Freud, as the northern and southern contingents strove for Freud's approval and, ultimately, his mantle. Jones and Abraham saw a departure from the rigorous science begun by Freud who, in 1912, had written that the ideal analyst would conduct himself as a surgeon, with objective expertise, emotional detachment, and authority.

Even Freud, however, did not conduct himself so. In both speaking and writing, he balanced scientific authority with human warmth, charm, and humility. These qualities evidently resonated more in Ferenczi and Rank than in Jones and Abraham. Over the years, observers have remarked that Freud was less orthodox than his most fervent disciples—beginning, I suggest, with the latter two.

An amusing comment on this phenomenon comes from the pioneer analyst Abram Kardiner, who was in Vienna with mainly American and British analysts-in-training in the early 1920s. He reported that there was tension between the two groups, the former mostly Jewish, the latter not (Ernest Jones was the only non-Jew on the Committee). One day the British invited the Americans to tea to discuss the different experiences of the two nationalities in working with Freud. The British analysands were perplexed in finding Freud almost totally silent. They had heard that he talked quite freely with at least some of the Americans. Was it true?

Yes. Often Freud would discuss books, theoretical points, and even art and politics in the analytic hours.

Apparently, the British, not to feel chagrined, concluded that Freud conducted a more serious analysis with them than with their casual, rather motley American counterparts. Kardiner, an immigrant from Europe, heard complaints over the years about long, silent, ineffectual analyses by members of the British school during which "the analyst says nothing except 'good morning' and 'good day'" (unpublished oral history tapes, Columbia University).

He added, significantly, that Freud had not conversed with a New Yorker in the Vienna group who was held in lower esteem. Evidently Freud, despite his remark about the surgical attitude, did not hide behind the blank screen of analytic expressionlessness. Those who pleased Freud made him more active. The phenomenon of forthcoming responsiveness is now being taken more seriously by the analytic profession—for instance, in discussions of mirroring and in renewed interest in the Ferenczi-Rank monograph of 1924, *The Development of Psychoanalysis.*

The Committee was shaken badly when, at age 67, Freud was afflicted with cancer of the palate. The next year, 1924, fraternal rivalry intensified for heir apparent. Freud never attended another IPA Congress, presumably because of embarrassment or discomfort in speaking and eating due to a prosthesis. But he lived another 16 years, to age 83, enduring repeated operations. He continued to analyze and write, even radically changing his theory about anxiety (*Inhibition, Symptom and Anxiety* 1926), partly in rebuttal to Rank's *The Trauma of Birth* (1924).

The leadership of the IPA was not elected by the membership but chosen by the Committee from within. Freud never took the presidency but approved the decision. Jones, on account of his power in the expanding English-speaking movement, presided for many years; Ferenczi, because of problems in Hungary, stepped down after brief tenure; Abraham died in 1925; and Rank never served, breaking with the movement in 1926. Freud, always afraid that psychoanalysis would be identified as a Jewish science, acceded to Jones although he did not trust the man. Jones and Rank despised each other cordially, and Jones merely gave lip service to Freud's support of lay analysis. Sachs, Reik, Anna Freud, Melanie Klein, Beata Rank, and others—but especially Otto Rank—proved that medical training was not needed to be a good practitioner, theorist, or teacher of psychoanalysis.

Ferenczi also fought in the losing battle to keep the IPA open to nonmedical professionals. The active, interpersonal, time-limited therapy which he initially championed with Rank came in response to the Freudian furor after World War I. Physicians and others were lining up to be trained in the new profession, patients were lining up to be treated, writers and critics were taking a new approach to literature, sex was discussed in a new way, and no field was immune to psychoanalytic interpretation. Freud's *Introductory Lectures* (1917) had been translated into at least seven languages.

According to Ferenczi and Rank, the practice of psychoanalysis had stagnated due to overly strict devotion to theory, and clinical results were too often unsatisfactory. Freud wanted to work out a general psychology more than a method of treatment, and he did not presume much about the therapeutic effect of his discoveries. A pessimist, he said that successful psychoanalysis could only transform neurotic misery into ordinary unhappiness.

Nevertheless the idea of real help became popular; Ferenczi and Rank firmly held this view and tried to understand and teach its basis.

They criticized the practice of the time for its emphasis on the past; need to uncover—in order to interpret—a basic oedipal complex in every analysand; excessive use of the concept of transference, which concerns the appearance in the analytic situation of a constellation of emotions in the patient toward the therapist, representing unconscious emotions attached to important [parental] figures from the past.

Theoretically, the process of analysis postulates an inevitable transference neurosis which can be analyzed through profound knowledge of the history, fantasies, dreams, and free associations of the patient. But according to the new critique, too many practitioners strove to follow an exact—but nonexistent—Freudian formula. Like Freud, they valued research above helping; at times they imposed inappropriate interpretations about a hidden oedipal complex, and analyzed any resistance until the patient yielded to the truth.

Dr. Clara Thompson, an American psychiatrist whose own analyst was Ferenczi and who analyzed Harry Stack Sullivan, once wrote vividly about the new attitude. She disliked the tendency to analyze everything in relation to parents and the past because, as Rank taught, this diverts attention from the actual relationship.

"Rank was the first to point out that in doing this the patient was led away from the living present, at the area of real feeling. As he put it, it is always easier to talk about the past because it is not present. He and Ferenczi stressed, for the first time, that not every attitude toward the analyst is transferred from the past, that there is some reaction to the analyst in his own right, and that it is actually anxiety-relieving and, therefore, stops the progress of analysis, to point out to the patient, for instance, "You do not really feel this way about me but about your father." Thus, if the patient finally gets the courage to tell the analyst he looks like a pig, the whole issue may be conveniently buried by referring it to the past, saying, "That must be what you thought of your father." Two things may happen as a result: The analyst does not have to face the fact that he does look like a pig; and the patient thinks, "I got safely out of that one," but does not feel more secure thereby because he knows he really meant the analyst and not his father. From that day on he is likely to assume that the analysts' feelings have to be protected. Realizing this, Rank and Ferenczi discovered the importance of the picture of the analyst in his own right—thus transference became more precisely defined as only the irrational attitudes felt and expressed toward the analyst" (Clara Thompson, 1964, 234).

Soon Jones and Abraham attacked Ferenczi and Rank. Besides that book, Rank added fuel to the fire with his birth trauma theory, which established the nurturing (pre-oedipal) mother-child relationship as primary in psychological development. At first enthusiastic, Freud gradually aligned himself with the northern axis against the innovators.

In 1924, at age 40, Rank sailed to New York for the summer to analyze and teach. Received warmly as Freud's emissary and then in his own right, his accolades included honorary membership in the American Psychoanalytic Association. Increasingly bitter about the attacks and Freud's withdrawal of support, Rank finally emigrated to Paris in 1926, visiting the United States almost every year until his permanent move there in 1934. He died a month after Freud in 1939, at age 55.

Among those who knew Rank and acknowledge his influence are Frederick Allen, pioneer child psychiatrist; Carl Rogers and Jessie Taft, psychologists; and Virginia Robinson, social worker—the last two associated with the Pennsylvania School of Social Work. Many others hid their indebtedness to Rank, since acknowledging him could only hurt them when Freudian psychoanalysis dominated American psychiatry, psychology, and social work. In the twenties Rank was one of the most sought-after analysts. After 1930, his former analysands were required to undergo reanalysis with a certified Freudian to qualify for IPA membership.

Ferenczi died in 1933, having broken first with Rank and then, in the end, with Freud and the movement. Jones, who completed his massive Freud biography just before his death in 1958, attributed the defections of Rank and Ferenczi to mental illness. This calumny continues to crop up in histories of psychoanalysis, but gradually the writings of these creative pioneers are coming back into the mainstream with the help of interpreters like Leo Stone, John Gedo, Esther Menaker, Robert Kramer, and Arnold Rachman.

Sigmund Freud attempted to secure a scientific basis for knowledge of the psyche belonging previously to poets and philosophers. Regardless of the validity of his theory, he invented a new form of human interaction, the analytic situation. His followers used and modified this invention to its present status, chiefly in psychotherapy, 100 years after its beginning.

With a schematic representation of contrasting emphases, we can look at differences in viewpoint, ideology, and practice which characterize the Freudian and divergent (Rankian) psychodynamic systems which now include the interpersonal, existential, client-centered, time-limited, and humanistic.

1. Freudian/classical: Science—objective general

   Rankian/modern: Art—subjective unique

Freud admired artists but considered himself a scientist who worked to validate objectively the intuitions of poets and philosophers. He tried to avoid the appearance of speculative thinking, even denying the influence of Nietzsche. Otto Rank willingly embraced philosophical and artistic sources, and once offered this paradoxical principle: "For each patient I need a different theory" (Lieberman, 1985, 360).

2. F: Analysis, exploration
   R: Therapy, helping

Freud borrowed the word analysis (Greek: "separation") from the vocabulary of chemistry. Therapy, on the other hand, derives from the Greek and Latin with meanings of serving, care, and healing. Otto Rank, after leaving Freud, used the word "psychotherapy" to describe his work, even alluding to himself as a philosopher of helping. Other pioneers who found a similar path from analysis to helping include Franz Alexander, Karen Horney, Erich Fromm, Frieda Fromm-Reichmann, Harry Stack Sullivan, Sandor Rado, Michael Balint, Erik Erikson, and John Bowlby.

3. F. The past, memories, childhood
   R: The present, here and now

Clara Thompson's statement illustrates this point.

4. F: The unconscious, repression, suppression by the ego
   R: The conscious, expression of the ego

If Freud devoted the analytic hour to free that of which one is not aware, Rank used the occasion to confront that which the patient knows but fails to express in words or action.

5. F: Wish, instinct
   R: Will, creativity

In psychoanalysis, conscious will has virtually no place; Freud dismissed the will as found in nineteenth-century psychology. Rank put it back as a central factor, the essence of human identity. Will expresses both ego and instinctual energy. His approach was called "will therapy." This signifies not willfulness but the ability to combine strong goal-directedness with self-discipline and free, spontaneous improvisation.

6. F: Understanding, intellect
   R: Experience, emotion

Rank believed that the neurotic suffers precisely because of too much self-analysis, while lacking the courage, on account of guilt and life-fear, to engage in appropriate experience and action. If for Freud (as with Socrates) the unexamined life is not worth living, then with Rank we can say that the uncreative life is not worth living, and the unlived life is not worth examining.

7. F: Transference, interpretation
   R: Actual relationship, intimacy

Rankian actuality and existentialism de-emphasize childhood projection, the kernel of the transference neurosis. Instead, Rank postulates real relationship as the core of therapy, one which (somewhat paradoxically) has a professional kind of intimacy and openness, in contrast with Freud's method in which the analyst remains removed and unknown.

8. F: Biology
   R: Psychology

Freud used the Oedipus myth as a deterministic model of human family dynamics. He argued that every boy unconsciously wishes to kill his father and marry his mother. But Oedipus, an adoptee, loved his psychological parents; of course, he did not know his biological ones because they abandoned him as an infant. Oedipus pursued literal truth over the edge, into tragedy. Knowing who he is biologically and historically superseded prudent warnings and Jocasta's petition that he abandon the quest and pursue life. Emotional truth is often not congruent with the factual kind; having relations can mean being related biologically or being intimate. With Jocasta, Rank favored psychological over biological relationship, and he gave philosophical primacy to self-creation over predetermination.

9. F: Death fear
   R: Life fear

According to Freud, the patricidal son controls himself for fear of paternal punishment—castration-fear, which symbolizes death. In contrast, Rank sees the problem as one of individuation after involuntary birth. Can we, starting as unwilling newborn creatures, attain a stage in which we embrace our lives, affirming creative will and human responsibility without paralyzing guilt and fear? If so, this signifies a psychological rebirth, the transformation of creature to creator.

10. F: Normality
    R: Individuality

According to Rank, the challenge to us in the post-Freudian world is to create an individual personality. In this respect, one who positively engages his or her own will becomes a successful artist—not by painting or composing, but by living according to one's own genius, spirit, and limitations. Life is a loan, death the repayment. The creative type invests or spends it; the neurotic, also strong-willed but paralyzed by fear, is a failed artist who (neurotically) tries to deny death: "It can't be all over, I haven't begun to live yet. . . ."

This schematization oversimplifies categories but may be useful in viewing the whole. It should be clear that Rank, if not the originating source of everything attributed to him, is a major forerunner—largely unacknowledged—of what is now accepted psychotherapeutic theory and practice.

REFERENCES

Ferenczi, Sandor, and Otto Rank. *The development of psychoanalysis* (Vienna: Internationale Psychoanalytischer Verlag, 1924).

Kardiner, Abram. Oral history interview with Abram Kardiner, unpublished, Columbia University, 1954. Rare Books and Manuscript Library, pp. 114–120.

Lieberman, E. James. *Acts of Will: The life and work of Otto Rank* (New York: Free Press, 1963).

Rank, Otto. *Der Künstler* (The Artist). Vienna: Heller, 1907, subtitle.

———. Dreams and poetry. Dream and myths. In *Dreaming by the book,* eds. Lydia Maurinelli and Andreas Mayer. (New York: Other Press, 2003), pp. 191–221, 221–237.

Thompson, Clara. *Interpersonal psychoanalysis.* (New York: Basic Books, 1964), 234.

CHAPTER 5

What Is a Fact? Eva Rosenfeld and Historiography

Paul Roazen

The problem of evidence has to be of central concern for each kind of historian. In order to investigate the problem of facts, I would like to turn to the specific historiographical problems associated with the life of Eva Rosenfeld (1892–1977) and how it might be possible to use a series of different perspectives, from an unusual variety of sources, in order to follow her career. One recent book, written by two distinguished British intellectuals, goes so far as to maintain: "Among the Vienna-based women who moved in Freud's and Anna's orbit, Eva Rosenfeld was, next to Ruth Mack Brunswick, Freud's undoubted favorite."[1] Such a position, put forward by Lisa Appignanesi and John Forrester, might be capable of being sustained, although since we know so little about Ruth Brunswick it can seem secondary to be moving on to Eva Rosenfeld. Helene Deutsch was far more productive than either of the other two women, but she was independent enough to try to steer at a relative distance from Freud's most immediate circle and, unlike Eva and Ruth, Helene never received the gift of a signet ring from Freud. Eva was a remarkable woman, and I found her to be especially frank and outspoken in the course of interviews, so it should be important to keep straight, as best we can, what her standing was vis-à-vis Freud.

Let me begin by quoting from a letter Freud sent Eva when she had written him about the possibility of her having a further analysis, following ones under Freud (and Felix Boehm), with Melanie Klein. Eva's son dates the letter from 1937,[2] but Appignanesi and Forrester place it in 1936. Eva was a practicing analyst living in London by then, having moved from Berlin in 1936; Klein was in those days much sought after as a clinician, supervisor, and theoretical guide. For years, however, Klein had been involved in a heated controversy with Anna Freud over the practices and theories of child analysis, and Freud was convinced that Klein's work represented a disguised assault on himself. Because by now Kleinianism has become a central part of British analysis, it is not easy for most analysts there, and the academic community friendly to them, to want to acknowledge just how heretical Freud found Klein to have been.

It had been through the intercession of her intimate friend Anna Freud that Eva had first been analyzed in 1929 (and off and on a bit later). Evidently, Eva was considering either a four-week analysis back with Freud or one with Klein. Appignanesi and Forrester, writing with my own information silently in mind, observed: "although certain commentators have implied that Freud resentfully cut her off when she decided on Klein, his letter to her reads rather more like an attempt to allow her to think that matter through clearly for herself and points her in the direction of Klein, a direction, he suggests, she has already decided on. It is a telling reminder of Freud's impartiality, at least towards some of his friends and former patients."[3] Because I think this conclusion, as well as the chain of reasoning, is all wrong, I will first quote the letter of Freud's that is in question, and then explain why I disagree that it means anything like how it has been interpreted.

> There are other aspects of that matter to consider, one that could prove disagreeable to you, another that could proved disagreeable for me. You know what my attitude toward Melanie Klein's work is. I, too, think that she has found something new, but I don't know if it means quite so much as she believes, and I am certain that she has no right to use it to place theory and technique on a new basis. Our four weeks would naturally attempt critically to unravel what you have found in yourself to confirm the Kleinian theories. It is possible that I might bring you to another judgement of these things. Then you would go back to London and find yourself in opposition to the circle and direction of work when you would manifestly prefer to stay in tune with both. On the other hand, it wouldn't be possible for you to hide from the English group the influence that you have experienced through me, and that would kindle an antagonism I have gone out of my way up until now to avoid.
>
> The other possibility, that in four weeks you would convince me of the fundamental significance and correctness of Kleinian findings, I do not really think is a probable outcome. I think then that the piece of inner work that is now thrust upon you, the resolution of your intellectual allegiance as well as of your father and mother influence, is something that you will have to sort out without help, at least without mine. Because as always I take a lively interest in your destiny, I am naturally unhappy that such a problem should have posed itself, particularly for you.[4]

Freud, in turning aside Eva's request that she once again come into analysis with him over a holiday, was replying with patience and tact. He assumes she already knows that he would try his best to undermine the bases for her interest in Klein's "findings." He allowed himself so many words, in refusing Eva, that it can be possible to miss his central thrust in the midst of his

Viennese manners. Freud could at times, when he wanted to, be brutal in turning a supplicant aside; he rejected the entreaties of seeing someone like Herbert Silberer,[5] or analyzing Victor Tausk,[6] and both men, for different reasons of their own, ended up as suicides. Eva was not of the intellectual rank to match Silberer or Tausk, but she was an unhappy and troubled former patient of his and, above all, an old friend of his daughter, Anna. Freud was trying to let Eva down carefully, and one has to read between the lines to discover his real meaning. Others may disagree with my reasoning, but I want to present it in contrast to Appignanesi and Forrester who do not seem willing or able to acknowledge just how much Freud "loathed" (to quote from one of my interviews with Eva) Klein and what she stood for.

At the same time, Freud was politic enough not to want to risk alienating the British supporters analysis had attracted. When Freud broke with Jung, it had meant the loss of almost the whole of analysis in Switzerland. British analysis was under the leadership of Ernest Jones, a long-standing ideological ally of Freud's who happened to be most sympathetic to Klein's point of view. From Eva's perspective, she had reason to share Freud's desire for peace; to cross him (or Anna) would absolutely threaten her professional practice. Jung complained he had been clinically ruined by Freud for years.

Freud was, at length to be sure, saying no to Eva; he did not want to analyze her again, and he was putting that in a handwritten note as opposed to dictating a letter to be typed up by Anna, who had long been acting as his secretary. It was widely known how during the past years Klein had been making Anna Freud's life unpleasant, both in print and at conferences. Freud turned 80 years old in 1936 and was weakened by a 13-year-old struggle with his cancer of the jaw. By then he was more dependent than ever on Anna's care and attention. He was as closely identified with her standing as she with his. Freud felt protective of Anna, wanting to ensure her future within analysis after his death; yet he did not want to encourage any open polemics with Klein, since he felt too feeble for ideological battling like he had once engaged in. Both Adler and Jung, for instance, had turned—in his view—against himself; Freud's personal affection for Rank was such that Freud rarely answered him by name. Freud had learned not to enhance anyone's reputation by denouncing them. In Klein's case it was possible for Freud to evade an outright confrontation with her.

Freud was making of Eva's interest in Klein a question of "allegiance"; he was also finding an emotional, psychoanalytic matter when he contrasted the "father and mother influence." In his view, her interest in Klein was psychologically motivated by her problem with men, which he had attributed to her bad relationship with her father. He was making an ad hominem point about her attraction to Klein's theories being based on unresolved inner conflicts. Freud's silence about what Eva's turning to Klein had to mean to Anna herself is in itself notable, although reasoning from the absence of evidence can be notoriously misleading. One wonders what Anna's response might have been if Eva had been writing to her instead for a second analysis. Appignanesi and Forrester, in their account of Freud's rejection of Eva's request, are in my opinion unsound. They observe: "If Freud seems altogether sanguine here, and more concerned about Eva than about psychoanalytic politics, then it is more than possible that Anna, on the other hand, took her decision to begin a Kleinian analysis as a sign of betrayal."[7] How do these scholars think that it can be possible to drive such an interpretive wedge between what Anna felt and how Freud reacted? These two people had developed an almost symbiotic tie, and it is far-fetched to think that if Anna considered herself betrayed, Freud did not respond in her behalf similarly.

Not long after Freud's death, the so-called Controversial Discussions broke out within the British Psychoanalytic Society, and Klein's enemies thought that with the support of the Viennese analysts who had emigrated to London it might be possible to curb her power, and the influence she was threatening to exert on future analytic training.[8] Eva did stay back, as Appignanesi and Forrester note, from the worst of the quarrelling. But if the Viennese Willi Hoffer could ever, in a passage they do not document, have gotten into "an attack of fury" against whatever Eva had been saying, he, as an ally of Anna's, must have felt the presence of Eva's Kleinianism. (In 1962 Eva published the official obituary of Hoffer's wife.) That Klein herself did not accept Eva as an apostle of her own only means that Eva's moderation had not succeeded in appeasing Klein's need for strict adherents.

These early analysts, following Freud's lead, were engaging in theologically tinged differences. It is, I think, no disrespect to any of these analysts to contend that they were battling over rival conceptions of how the good life ought to be lived. Just as Adler represented one moral approach, and Jung another ethical perspective, so did both Rank and Wilhelm Reich. In the case of Klein, one needs to plow through the pages of the Controversial Discussions to see just how rare were the clinical examples that were ever brought up. Klein had an almost messianic fervor that she was being more royal than the king following in Freud's principles more strictly than the founder himself. Reich, in his own work, shared a similar belief, although he was going in the direction of sexual emancipation and family reform. It is a telling aspect to the way the history of analysis has been written about that Peter Gay, in his loyalist Freud biography, entirely censors the existence of Reich out of the story.[9] It is impossible to describe the Vienna Psychoanalytic Society without mentioning Reich's technical contributions and the dispute that arose in connection with them.

I do not want to give too central a place to that one letter of Freud's to Eva, but an understanding of it does pave the way to the different sorts of pieces of evidence that have accumulated. A volume of Anna Freud's letters to Eva has been published, and that correspondence bears directly on the problems I have been discussing. It makes sense when the editor tells us that in their later years, 1946–1977, the letters on the part of Anna were confined "to brief and/or business like communications, while Eva continues on a largely unrequited quest for their former intimacy."[10]

Eva's son could openly write how the "one great gash, deliberately—some would say provocatively—inflicted by my mother was her ripening friendship with Melanie Klein." In 1929 Anna had been capable of writing to Eva: "you are I and I am you and any part of me you can use, you must always take, because you have a right to it." In 1947 Eva wrote to Anna in an allusion to her going to Klein; Eva referred to "how much I hurt you in 1938."[11]

Still another source of information, in addition to Freud's own letter and the correspondence between Anna and Eva, has to be the hundreds of pages of an unpublished autobiography that Eva undertook. Scholars have grown used to treating such explicit self-disclosures with caution, whereas we are tempted, I think, to believe that letters are a private form of communication that rank ahead of formal publications. As Freud's various correspondences come out, it will be increasingly tempting to think of them as at least as authoritative as what he put into print during his lifetime.

Eva's autobiography communicates a lot of information about her background and conflicts, but she only glancingly touches on the sensitive matter of her having turned to Klein for analysis. "I inflicted on myself a horrible wound—I felt that my interest in Melanie Klein's teaching estranged me from Freud in the eyes of the analytic world, and I felt an outcast." Eva went on diplomatically: "It is due to Anna's dignified and humane attitude to me that I never was made to feel that I lost her friendship." I find it hard to believe, knowing the story up to now and how relatively distant Anna held herself from Eva, that we should not take these words of Eva with the proverbial grain of salt. Eva concluded what little she had to say about this incident by admitting: "But I lost a position and that is the lot of many independent persons."[12]

Eva added autobiographically that before she had started analytically with Klein, Eva had written "about my problem to Professor Freud. He wisely thought, since I would not convince him in Mrs. Klein's favor, I had better solve this problem myself. I did in the course of many painful years." Eva tried to limit the scope of her defection, and she quoted Klein as having said to her once: "You have sacrificed your analysis to the friendship with Anna Freud. . . .[13]

Still a further source of evidence consists of my series of interviews with Eva, which took place in the mid-1960s, at the same time that I was seeing people like Edith Jackson and Anna Freud. (Eva told me she had seen Kurt Eissler for the Freud Archives, and that he had been interested in finding out Freud's views of Klein; this material remains sealed until the year 2008.) It is quite difficult to pin down exactly what one learns from any such interviewing experience aside, of course, from getting to know the person. I read to Eva, late in our contact, a then-unpublished letter of Freud's to Lou Andreas-Salomé following Tausk's death. The letter was new to me and still seems startling in its lack of compassion: Eva chimed in that Freud had once been through with her too, meaning as a result of her going to Klein.

Freud's real feelings may have been muffled in the generous-sounding way that he wrote to Eva, yet she was in no doubt what she had lost. She had continued to see him on occasion after he moved to London in 1938, but the former intimacy was affected. Freud even saw Melanie Klein, all the while telling someone like Edward Glover that it was the first time a so-called deviant had been able to be held within the analytic movement. Within a short time Glover, who had once been influenced by some of Klein's ideas, had joined with Anna Freud in doing battle against Kleinianism within the British Psychoanalytic Society. To repeat a point made earlier, today's British analysts are apt to feel uncomfortable acknowledging just how standoffish Freud was about Klein's work. He might have cited her, but those who knew him were aware how he really felt about what he regarded as a psychoanalytic heresy. But here I have to rely on my own interviewing of Glover, which once again cannot be made demonstrable. As I hope to have shown, the written word has its own ways of being misleading.

I feel confident that Eva's letters to me tell a different aspect of the story I have sought to communicate. After my book *Freud: Political and Social Thought* came out in 1968, I sent Eva a copy, and she responded in accordance with her enthusiastic nature. She was pleased that I had quoted her at one point; her technical papers—the few she published—would, of course, make another source for biographical evidence. It is worth noting that she had told me in interviews that when she had shown Jones what she had written about Freud, quoting him from her analysis when she was living with him in the same house on a holiday, Jones had insisted that she take out the fact of her residence with the family. Jones also did not approve of Eva's interpretation of Freud's childhood nanny, and how it might bear on Freud's later anti-religious beliefs, since Jones was the kind of atheist who did not find anything lacking in Freud's own approach to religion.

In 1956, Eva had given a talk about Freud, on the occasion of the centenary of his birth, for the British Broadcasting Corporation. I could find nothing that Anna might have objected to in what she said, when I read a copy of the transcript years later at the Library of Congress, but then it is impossible to predict the subtle sensitivities of family members. Eva's son, fully loyal to Anna, realized that his mother, "talkative and indiscreet," was "a threat" to Anna. "And she had intimate knowledge of family matters quite apart from the letters. In a broadcast talk Eva gave for the BBC, she reminisced harmlessly about the Freuds. Anna's wrath was quite disproportionate to the offense and suggests deeper apprehensions: if anecdotes today, why not letters tomorrow?"[14]

Based on my own knowledge of what Eva was like, I would guess that Anna knew how frank (and disloyal) Eva could be. Eva's going to Klein for that analysis must have been the culmination of years of frustration; Dorothy Burlingham had displaced Eva as Anna's most intimate friend, and Eva's treason-seeming act (likely not the first) was one that Anna could never forgive. Eva might outwardly maintain her links with Anna, and she was on excellent terms with Anna's older sister Mathilda. But in the course of what Eva told me about Anna, she was uninhibited and strikingly irreverent.

Eva was nonetheless shocked by the 1969 appearance of my book *Brother Animal: The Story of Freud and Tausk.* She wrote me at length about it in 1970.

> It is excellently written and very well argued, but why did you write it while the family of Freud's is still alive? It is both embarrassing and misleading to those who read it today, and feel glad to put their knife into the old man. For myself I must say that if you intended such a book when we had our confidential talks, I would not have provided you with the material I did.

In reality, I had broken off the story of Tausk while engaged on the writing of my book *Freud and His Followers*, which only appeared in 1975. If I had not separated the Tausk tale it would have threatened to assume too large a dimension over my larger study of Freud's circle.

Eva claimed to have specific grounds for objecting to *Brother Animal:*

> Not because there is anything wrong in a great man having his faults and angers, but because it amounts now to just a scandal story which only unpleasant people will relish. You must forgive me for being so frank with you; I consider you a friend and I would blame myself if I did not tell you the echo that this book will have. A book about Tausk would have been interesting, even though you could not have known him and also his family are still alive, but the title as a story of Freud and Tausk is really most unpleasant.

Today's readers should remember that that book had come out before the wave of revisionist Freud scholarship that followed in the next decades, and prior to the appearance of Henri Ellenberger's *The Discovery of the Unconscious* in 1970. *Brother Animal* could be read at one long sitting, while Ellenberger's encyclopedic text changed people's minds in a different and slower way. I had been hoping that *Brother Animal* would be understood as an expression of my interest in historiography, as I had been trying to put Tausk back into the history books. To Eva, however, who doubtless by then knew Anna Freud's own horror at the book, I had failed completely.

Eva could not restrain herself from psychoanalytic inquiry:

> One must ask oneself: what was really your purpose, we are all much too well-informed about the storms of a person's life as to need to be told it once again in the shape of a man who disliked quick intuition and intelligence because he found it ruinous to scientific progress. In a sense that was his greatness. I did not admire his personality, but you had to admire his work and there is time enough to criticize him when all those who knew him will not read your book any more. I suppose you will get many

angry letters. I hope also admiring ones, because your penetration into the subject is, of course, admirable.

Eva welcomed me to come see her once again "so to make sure we are still friends." I replied to Eva not as to someone who had been of historical importance, but as to a human being who had helped my research yet seemed blinded by Freud idolatry. I wrote to her, from a passage later quoted in the book of Anna Freud's correspondence with her, that "a great many is all of a piece, the good with the bad, one cannot have the one without the other."[15]

Eva replied, pursuing her understanding of the problem with my book:

Yes, the title is misleading. [I had taken "brother-animal" from an eloquent passage about Tausk in Lou Andreas-Salomé's diary of her stay in Freud's Vienna.] In German the word *Brudertier* means something close and almost tender. The translation in English transforms it into a nasty word, meaning "we are no better than animals." I would have called the book "Tausk, the . . ." and then some important word giving him his due. But the two names and the pictures shown together like in a correspondence (see Freud-Zweig) are journalistic and whets the appetites of gossipmongers.

Eva was obviously having second thoughts about what she had written me at first.

I regret that I wrote to you: "I did not admire etc. etc." What I meant was, there is never a complete identity between a man and his genius, that is why we need not admire his person whilst having the greatest admiration for what he gave and will give to the world. Had you delved into the tragedy of more of Freud's loneliness and Tausk's torment, then you would have written a history of unavoidable struggle of a genius manqué, i.e. Tausk the psychotic (?) and Freud the inexorable, and we would have learned once again what we have known all through history (See Beethoven, Dürer etc. etc.) that those are not loved who follow their internal tyrant.

Brother Animal described what then seemed to me an unusual form of human enmeshment, as Freud had rejected Tausk for an analysis but sent him instead to a newcomer, Helene Deutsch, who was herself in analysis with Freud. It was a few months after Freud gave Helene, one of my prime sources, the choice between ending her own treatment or dismissing Tausk, that Tausk committed suicide. Eva, as an analyst, tried to put her own professional understanding to work:

Have you—may I ask—experienced analysis from the inside? If so, you will know—and if not you cannot know what final destruction an analysis with Freud would have brought to Tausk. The only hope was for someone else to undertake the task, and H. Deutsch was probably as good as anybody. It is more true to say that Freud must have felt that he still keeps an eye on this promising but demonic fellow.

My argument was that the Tausk-Deutsch-Freud setup had helped worsen Tausk's considerable problems even if it provided Freud a measure of control.[16]

Eva was obviously stung by other aspects of *Brother Animal:*

> Whether Freud analyzed his daughter or whether I lived in their house in Grundlsee is not relevant to the story of Tausk; it is only incomprehensible to the young generation who has not our stamina, cannot imagine how free we were in spite of vicinity and that of course rules are made for the masses, not for individuals.

Eva was arguing that Freud's special technical licenses, at odds with his written therapeutic recommendations, ought to be tolerated; in the context of those years then I thought it important that these exceptions had never been publicly revealed before *Brother Animal.*

Tausk's death bothered Eva, as it did others, but she somehow spared the founder of psychoanalysis from any share in the tragedy:

> Tausk's suicide was only insofar concerned with Freud as he probably murdered Freud within himself, but to come home from the War penniless, engaged to be married, yet tied to wife and children is plenty of reason in reality. In my eyes it was a very clever solution!

Eva was not the only analyst to want Tausk to vanish. The problem for orthodox Freudians was that if Tausk had been psychotic, Freud and Helene Deutsch should not have treated him that way, but if he was only neurotic he should not have killed himself.

At the time I wrote the book I had worried that Helene Deutsch would react badly to the paragraphs in which I described her own unwitting involvement in Tausk's undoing, but she responded, as Eva did too, with concern over how I might have damaged Freud's reputation. Eva continued:

> Freud was a simple and shy human being. He did not surround himself with the aura of greatness, admiration embarrassed him, the aura of his lonely simplicity was often mistaken for the opposite.
>
> I knew him well. I observed him closely when he was old. He fought for analysis, but he did not grant us the pleasure of admiring "a great man."
>
> And now, good-bye and good luck. Please don't quote me as saying "I did not admire. . . ." He did not wish any admiration.

(That sensitive passage from her letter to me appeared first in the 1992 edition of Anna's letters to Eva.)

By June, Eva was intrigued to know more about what my research had come upon. I must have alluded to Ruth Brunswick in a letter:

Do you mean to say that Ruth committed suicide? I never heard that. Was she your first analyst? I only heard that she had a fall, an accident in her bathroom. I never questioned this. It happened the night before the Princess Bonaparte was due in New York. Do please tell me what is rumor and what fact!

Despite how Eva had reacted to *Brother Animal*, her own appetite for information had been aroused. And however much she disapproved of the way that the book had presented its material, she still trusted me enough to ask about the circumstances surrounding Ruth Brunswick's early death (at a time, incidentally, when I was a young boy).

In September, Eva was thinking about writing about Frederick the Great and his France-loving son: "to write about dead people is so rewarding. They can't tell us that we are wrong; it is as if we put them under an anaesthetic and then we can cut about and they don't feel anything." Eva thought that Voltaire's late book on Frederick the Great, "his erstwhile friend," was "a little bit like" my *Brother Animal:* "One cannot help regretting that he wrote it. So there you get scolded again," as she closed with "cordial greetings." I had evidently asked how others had responded to *Brother Animal*, and Eva replied:

You asked me whether nobody liked the book *Brother Animal.* I must sincerely answer that nobody did. Now I wonder very much what the next one is about, but I shall not take up your time by asking you to give me advance information. I shall wait patiently until it appears and I only hope that my name has vanished in case it is a book about Freud. You cannot well imagine what an unimportant little speck of dust I am in that circle.

Whatever Eva and the oldest group of analysts in London might have thought, some of my reviews in England were excellent.

Kurt Eissler had published in 1971 the first of two books criticizing *Brother Animal*, and I sent Eva a 1972 reply[17] that I finally found a journal brave enough to be willing to publish it. She wrote:

Your article is of course very well thought out and I hope you understand that there must be zealous people like Kurt Eissler, there must be non-belligerent souls like me, but I think, I still think that the role you took upon yourself in writing *Brother Animal* was to your disadvantage as well as that it gave us "dismay." It is not unusual that an unhappy man will commit suicide, but nobody needs to get the blame for it explicitly.

That was not wise of you to imply, because it means that you expect somewhere "perfection." I don't and never have.

"As a punishment" for my "misdeeds" she talked about sending me her autobiographical memoirs, but she specified that they were about herself, not Freud.

In 1973, when I was finishing my book *Freud and his Followers*, I needed help in identifying some of the people in the group photograph of analysts taken at the 1929 Oxford congress. Eva agreed to help me, although she was not able to "guarantee" to be right about who was who. "In any case do not use my name, the Freud ladies would be very angry with me." Eva was alluding to Anna and Mathilda. Eva could not help wondering whether I might be up to "some mischief." I suspect that Eva must have written something nice about me to Anna, who at the time was throwing up road-blocks in the form of the Freud copyrights to prevent me from getting the right to reprint photographs—unless I were willing to show them the manuscript prior to publication. It was, I think, in this context that Anna wrote Eva in 1974: "All I can say is that Roazen is a menace whatever he writes."[18]

The contact that I had with Eva (and Anna's 1974 letter) is a source of some pride to me, and I am happy that Eva gave me enough material about her analysis with Freud to include her in a chapter of my 1995 book, *How Freud Worked: First-Hand Accounts of Patients.*[19] If I had succeeded with Eva, in spite of how she reacted to *Brother Animal,* I would like to think that my own respect for her, combined with her own qualities as a peacemaker, led to a happy outcome. I always thought that my own natural deference to these elderly analysts was a help in overcoming reticences they might have about being interviewed.

It was Eva who first taught me that Freud had had in mind that psychoanalysis be "a moral medal," and she was convinced that he harbored ethical purposes alongside scientific ones. I was in part attracted to psychoanalysis because of its great bearing on the age-old questions concerned with how we ought to live. Eva herself was sensitive to the legitimacy of religious questions: One of her few papers was on the problem of Moses, and she returned to the theme of Freud as a Jew in a 1956 essay.[20] I suspect that Eva knew that this was a side to the creator of psychoanalysis that Anna would not have appreciated being explored. Klein had a religious dimension to her thinking, communicated by her concept of the "depressive position," that had helped attract Eva in the first place. According to the early view, psychoanalysis was a neutral body of knowledge detached from cultural influences. And if Freud's Jewishness was a problem for some of his first disciples, more recently Jacques Lacan's Catholicism has been a troubling issue for the French psychoanalytic community.[21]

The historian, then, has an awesome task; like Flaubert's conception of the artist, who was supposed to be like God, present everywhere yet visible nowhere, historians aim for the greatest possible degree of detachment. In my own case, having been so involved in research with the help of people like Eva, it would be phony to try and pretend to be exempt from inevitable personal bias. Yet, at the same time, I did try, I hope, to be as objective as humanly possible. I remain committed to the importance of the ideal of impartiality, no matter how difficult it may be to succeed.

Goethe is supposed to have maintained that "every fact is a passion," and people do perceive reality in the light of special expectations and values. As a result, history gets written in a way that is bound to become capricious. Yet at the same time there has to be a line differentiating partisanship from the pursuit of truth. One should be obliged to explain the different kinds of sources one has relied on, and something about one's own relationship to the way in which material has been accumulated. Even if omniscience may be humanly impossible, at the same time the ideal of objectivity remains a worthwhile quest.

I have tried to suggest how one goes about ordering the different set of sources about Eva. It is hardly a scientific process by which one weighs every bit of historical factuality as part of the competing possibilities of interpretation. I hope to have helped establish that publications can be at least as misleading as oral testimony at its most unreliable. I have reasons to suspect that Eva may have been even more upset with *Brother Animal* than she wrote me. But I am presenting this collection of material in order to show how it is inevitable that contrasting evidence does not fit together without requiring judgments to make sense of the past.

Betrayal and desertion have to be understood in the special light of the conflicts in the history of psychoanalysis. By my supplying various perspectives in connection with Eva Rosenfeld, I am trying to make it possible for future researchers to be able to make use of my own work for achieving different results, while at the same time I am struggling to say something about the nature of historiography itself.

NOTES

1. Lisa Appignanesi and John Forrester, *Freud's Women* (New York: Basic Books, 1992), 380.
2. Peter Heller, *Anna Freud's Letters to Eva Rosenfeld*, trans. Mary Weigand (Madison, CT: International Universities Press, 1992), 45.
3. Appignanesi and Forrester, 383.
4. Ibid.
5. Paul Roazen, *Freud and His Followers* (New York: Da Capo, 1992), 338–41.
6. See Paul Roazen, *Brother Animal: The Story of Freud and Tausk* (New Brunswick, NJ: Transaction, 1990), 41.
7. Appignanesi and Forrester, 383.
8. See Paul Roazen, *Oedipus in Britain: Edwin Glover and the Struggle over Klein* (New York: Other Press, 2000).
9. Paul Roazen, *The Historiography of Psychoanalysis* (New Brunswick, NJ: Transaction, 2001), 245–47.
10. Heller, ix.
11. Ibid., 44, 116, 182.
12. Eva Rosenfeld, *Recollected in Tranquility* (unpublished), Ch. 24.
13. Ibid.
14. Heller, 16.
15. Ibid., 71. See also Peter Heller, "Trois lettres d'Anna Freud à Eva Rosenfeld," *Revue Internationale d'Histoire de la Psychoanalyse*, 6 (1993): 490.

16. Paul Roazen, "Presence de Victor Tausk dans la correspondence Freud-Ferenczi," *Études freudiennes* (September 1993).

17. Paul Roazen, "Reflections on Ethos and Authenticity in Psychoanalysis," *The Human Context* (Autumn 1972); Paul Roazen, *Encountering Freud: The Politics and Histories of Psychoanalysis* (New Brunswick, NJ: Transaction, 1990), 95–108.

18. Paul Roazen, *Meeting Freud's Family* (Amherst: University of Massachusetts Press, 1993), 201.

19. Paul Roazen, *How Freud Worked: First-Hand Accounts of Patients* (Northvale, NJ: Jason Aronson, 1995), Ch. 8.

20. Eva Rosenfeld, "The Pan-Headed Moses," *International Journal of Psychoanalysis* 32 (1951): 83–93; Eva Rosenfeld, "Dream and Vision," *International Journal of Psychoanalysis* 37 (1956), 97–105.

21. Paul Roazen, "Lacan's First Disciple: An Interview with Lacan's Brother," *Journal of Religion and Health* 35 (Winter 1996).

CHAPTER 6

Freud's Analysis of His Daughter Anna: A Confusion of Tongues

Arnold Wm. Rachman

A FATHER'S MISGUIDED LOVE

I believe a scholarly examination of Freud's unusual clinical behavior with his daughter, Anna, is long overdue and will help to lift the taboo that has existed in our field ever since the analysis occurred in the early 1920s. Such an examination is in the tradition of the dissidence that Esther Menaker pioneered in her questioning of Freudian tradition (Menaker 1995). What is more, Esther has been willing to enter into a dialogue on this topic even though it involves her own analyst. She was a significant contributor to Freud's analysis of Anna (along with Paul Roazen, the dissident historian of psychoanalysis who first mentioned in print Freud's actual analysis of his daughter [Roazen 1969]), whose contributions I organized to begin a scholarly discussion of the issue within the psychoanalytic community (Rachman 1996b). Esther fully endorsed the idea that Freud's analysis of his daughter Anna needs full examination and has implications for theory and technique.

The desire to enter into an extraparental relationship with one's child has occurred in science before and after Freud's analysis of his daughter, Anna:

> There have also been the innovators' investigations of their own children—cf. Darwin's studies of his first son; Piaget's observations of his children's cognitive development. It is possible that Roentgen conducted experiments on his children, etc. (Tolpin 1992, 11, fn. 4)

I therefore make a distinction between Freud's desire to analyze his daughter Anna, and his actually performing the analysis. It can be an act of love to entertain the fantasy to help your child by offering your expertise. It is not an act of love to actually analyze your child, no matter how well intentioned you are. I believe Freud's analysis of his daughter, although well intentioned, was born of a desire to fulfill narcissistic needs.

TODSCHWEIGEN (DEATH BY SILENCE) AND ANALYTIC TRADITION

The origin of psychoanalysis is based on the discovery that neurosis was caused by childhood incest. Freud's original discovery was a monumental one, worthy of a Nobel prize, since it could have sparked a professional revolution in the treatment of neurosis and a wider variety of psychological disorders. The emphasis on the oedipal theory of neurosis which was heralded as an intellectual tour-de-force by the analytic community, could have joined the seduction theory as having equal significance for psychoanalytic theory and technique. Not only was the seduction hypothesis fundamentally discarded as having little or no significance, but subsequent attempts to revise its usefulness as an explanatory device (Ferenczi, 1933/1980b), and the development of a new technology (Ferenczi 1930/1980a, 1931, 1932/1988) were suppressed, censored, or ignored (Rachman 1989, 1991, 1994, 1997a, 1997b, 2002).

These attempts at revision were given the silent treatment by the traditionalists. The silent treatment, or *Todschweigen* (Rachman 1998; Rachman and Menaker, personal communication, January 1996), is a very important mechanism in the analytic community to deal effectively with dissident voices. In essence, it involves totally ignoring the dissident voice so that its message and potency are rendered lifeless. In essence, *Todschweigen* is "death by silence." The practice of *Todschweigen* was originally developed to silence dissidents, such as Jung (Roazen 1975), Ferenczi (Rachman 1997a, 1997b) and Rank (Menaker 1982). *Todschweigen* took an interesting turn when the silent treatment was successfully used to keep secret that Sigmund Freud analyzed his daughter, Anna.

Freud seemed blinded to the possibility that in analyzing his daughter he was involved in a form of emotional seduction that had decided sexual overtones (Klein and Tribich 1982). This analysis occurred even though there were other very qualified psychoanalysts who could perform the clinical task.

FREUD AND CHILDHOOD SEDUCTION

There are many issues to examine in the analytic experience between Sigmund and Anna Freud. The one that has fascinated me is the debate about the abandonment of the seduction theory. More specifically, was Freud's willingness to analyze his daughter an indication of an emotional blindness to the issue of seduction in theory and method? Was Freud's vehement and mean-spirited objections to Ferenczi's courageous attempts to reformulate the seduction theory, especially in Ferenczi's "Confusion of Tongues" paper (Ferenczi 1933/1980b) and his *Clinical Diary* (Ferenczi 1932/1988), also partially fueled by his emotional blindness to the issue of seduction? In fact, was Freud's campaign to suppress and censor Ferenczi's "Confusion of Tongues" paper, one of psychoanalysis' dirty little secrets (as was the secret of Anna's real analyst)? In a series of letters and telegrams, it is clear that Freud—along with Jones, Eitigon, Rivère, and others—prevented Ferenczi's "Confusion of Tongues" paper from being published (Rachman 1997a, 1997b), through the practice of *Todschweigen* (Rachman 1998).

Freud, in an amazing statement, suggested that the analyst cannot traumatize, corrupt, or seduce a child by introducing sexual material into their discussion (Rachman and Mattick 2002). Consequently, he freely introduced sexual interpretations into the analysis of Dora (S. Freud 1905), because the presence of her "hysterical" symptom *meant the child (Dora) had sexual thoughts*. The symptom is the expression of a sexual wish. A hysteric is like a repressed pervert: They have sexual feelings and ideas they don't sublimate, but they repress and turn the desire into symptoms. Freud, therefore, felt fully justified to say sexual things to Dora—such as that she had the fantasy of wanting to have oral sex with her father—when there is no evidence to support this approach (Rachman and Mattick 2002); or to analyze his own daughter without concern of emotionally seducing her. Freud's statement about seduction in the analytic situation, as he stated in the case of Dora, was as follows:

> There is never any danger of corrupting an inexperienced girl. For where there is no knowledge of sexual processes even in the unconscious, no hysterical symptom will arise; and where hysteria is found there can no longer be any question of "innocence of mind" in the sense in which parents and educators use the phrase. With children of ten, or twelve, or of fourteen, with boys and girls alike, I have satisfied myself that the truth of this statement can invariably be relied upon. (S. Freud 1905, 42)

THE CONFUSION OF TONGUES THEORY OF CHILDHOOD SEDUCTION

The issue of child seduction returned to psychoanalytic attention in the form of Ferenczi's "Confusion of Tongues" paper (Ferenczi 1933/1980b).

Ironically, Ferenczi presented new evidence that encouraged him to reconsider Freud's original seduction hypothesis: "Even children of very respectable, sincerely puritanical families fall victim to real violence or rape much more often than one had dared to suppose" (Ferenczi 1933/1980b, 161).

These words were almost the identical ones used by Freud in 1897 when he reported, "it then turned out that her otherwise noble and respected father regularly took her to bed" (S. Freud 1887–1902/1954, 238).

What is more, Ferenczi challenged the traditional notion, found both in Freudian psychoanalysis and in the lay public, that the report of sexual abuse is the fantasy of the child and, therefore, unreliable: "The immediate explanation that these are only sexual fantasies of the child, a kind of hysterical lying—is unfortunately made invalid by the number of such confessions, e.g., of assaults upon children, committed by parents actually in analysis (Ferenczi 1933/1980b, 161).

The Confusion of Tongues theory is basically a description of a relational psychology of child–parent interaction. It is an elaboration of the interpersonal, relational dimension of the family drama based on the real experiences between parents and children, not solely on the child's intrapsychic developmentally driven fantasy life. As such it was a reinterpretation of the oedipal tragedy. This version of the oedipal drama encourages the clinician to examine the nature of the object relations between family members, acknowledge actual trauma, help individuals to differentiate their pathologies from those of their caretakers, and develop strategies to help individuals recover from the personal and interpersonal damage of abusive relationships (Rachman 1994, 2000, 2002).

The parent, usually the father, misinterprets the natural need for affection and relatedness by his child, usually the daughter, as lust, which is his own projection onto the child. This does not mean the child doesn't have sexual feelings. There is a phase-appropriate element of sexuality and sensuality embedded within the overall, total parent–child interaction. But the overtly sexual interaction must be kept at the level of fantasy. When the parent, under the pressure of his or her own unhealthy narcissistic and inappropriate needs, distorts the total motivation of the child, reducing it to a predominately sexual, erotic one, the stage is set for pathological incestuous acting-out with the child.

The parent confuses the natural phase-appropriate longings for tenderness, sensuality, affection, and attachment-oriented play by the child for erotic sexuality, thereby reducing the complexity of normal attachment, striving for merely one of its components. The parent initiates a part-object relationship and uses the child as a discharge object rather than as a whole object, in which the capacity for sublimination and concern predominates.

The child's sense of reality can be seriously altered in such an interaction, where the adult exercises status, power, and control over the child. Ferenczi first emphasized sexual seduction of the child but also mentioned parental unresponsiveness to the child's needs (Ferenczi 1980b/1933, 1988/1932). Balint extended Ferenczi's ideas of trauma, elaborating the nature of trauma in non-sexual experiences (Balint 1968). What is more, the parent is emotionally unavailable to help the child understand what has happened. This is especially true when the adult denies the reality of the seduction experience or the unresponsiveness, attempting to convince the child that a different experience has taken place. In the case of sexual seduction, the parent attempts to convince the child that a loving experience has occurred. In the case of emotional unresponsiveness, neglect, or abuse, the child also feels abandoned and at the mercy of his or her own feelings without parental acknowledgment that a disturbing experience has occurred. This insidiously invalidates the child's perception of reality.

The parental seducer can seriously influence the child's sense of reality, because the child's reality testing is still in the process of developing. A child's sense of reality can easily be destabilized when trauma and associated reactive fantasies intrude. Fantasies that occur as a reaction to real trauma are distinguished from the traditional (Freudian) notion that there are innate sexual fantasies caused by innate drives.

The child is developmentally inclined to believe the parent's presentation of reality because acceptance of parental authority is associated with love, protection, and object attachment. Seduction fosters a profound sense of betrayal, not in just the perception of the parent, but in the capacity to perceive reality accurately. This, then, engenders a serious difficulty in trusting one's perceptions and feelings.

The child becomes confused about the reality of the experience. What is more, a child can actually deny his or her subjective experience while adapting to the parent's distorted reality. The child is then left in a confused state which, once dissociated, remains essentially the same. Because the sexual experience is traumatic, the child splits off the traumatic experience, including the image of himself or herself at the time as a victimized, helpless, overwhelmed, frightened, angry, and confused individual (Bollas 1991; Modell 1990; Searles 1986; Stierlin 1959). Once repressed, this dissociated state fails to change (it remains unconsciously timeless), becomes semi-autonomous, and continues to influence the adult personality, unconsciously. It thereby exerts an ego-weakening, disruptive effect on healthy adult functioning, especially in the area of mature object relations.

Beside the alteration of reality, parental authority also prevents the child from talking about his or her sense of confusion. The child is confused, realizing at some level that the experience is derived from the parents, but the child cannot give voice to this difference, because it is associated with the danger of loss of parental love, retaliation, and abandonment. In essence, the child becomes tonguetied, both literally and figuratively. This is further compounded by the fact that the child actually needs the parent's help to understand and verbalize what has happened to her or him. This requires truthful explanations given in the context of emotional support, something which the abusive parent is quite unable to do (Ferenczi 1933, 1933/1980b; Rachman 1991, 1993, 2000, 2002). Emotional support cannot come from a parent who is narcissistically intruding his or her needs onto a child and is hence insensitive to the child's needs. Because the child is not helped to understand and verbalize the effects of the seduction, a pathological split-off nucleus (of traumatic affect, self-image, and relational interaction) develops and becomes the basis for later psychopathology by arresting and distorting moral development. This effects all subsequent developmental stages and tasks, including the ego functions of drive regulation, reality testing, self and affect regulation, and object relations during each stage.

The major defenses that Ferenczi described that enable the child to cope with the actual sexual seduction are: splitting, dissociation, denial, detachment, blunted affect, confusion, and identification with aggressor (Ferenczi 1932/1988, 1933/1980b).

Identification with the aggressor (IWA), a mechanism first mentioned by Ferenczi in 1933 in his "Confusion of Tongues" paper (162), was incorrectly attributed to Anna Freud (Masson 1984; Rachman 1997a). Anna, as secretary of the IPA, did hear Ferenczi's presentation. In presenting the "Confusion of Tongues" paper, was Ferenczi trying to send a message to Freud and Freud's daughter about parent–child seduction? Was Ferenczi trying to communicate to Anna about the Confusion of Tongues experience in her relationship with her father? What is very interesting about Ferenczi's message to the analytic community that day was that Anna presumably heard, retained, and integrated a particular portion of the Confusion of Tongues theory. Anna, without acknowledging it directly, was captivated by the notion of IWA. She unconsciously adapted the IWA concept, making it an integral part of her theory of ego functioning and the manner of dealing with anxiety. So, one could speculate that Ferenczi was successful in reaching Freud's daughter in a way he could not influence the father (Ferenczi discussed his Confusion of Tongues theory with Freud in his *Clinical Diary* [Ferenczi 1932/1988]).

THE ATTEMPT TO SUPPRESS AND CENSOR THE CONFUSION OF TONGUES

Freud's intensely negative and judgmental reaction to the "Confusion of Tongues" paper bears examination. I would speculate that his condemnation of Ferenczi's ideas may have constituted a personal reaction based on a suppression of the emotional seduction of his daughter Anna. The reaction to the Wiesbaden presentation was uniformly negative by Freud and the traditional analytic community for some other very important reasons as well: (1) Ferenczi suggested that middle- and upper-class families were guilty of incest; (2) he verified that parents in respectable families were regularly molesting their children; (3) by implication, the audience who heard Ferenczi's paper, who were upper-middle-class males, were akin to those fathers in his clinical studies who molested their daughters; (4) Ferenczi's clinical findings on sexual trauma could also be applied to the few women analysts who attended the Confusion of Tongues presentation—by implication, were these the daughters who were molested by their fathers?; (5) Ferenczi's notion of retraumatization in the psychoanalytic situation due to coldness, detachment, unresponsiveness, and clinical hypocrisy must have been perceived as an attack on Freud and the classical method, rather than as a step toward the evolution of a two-person psychology and the empathic method; (6) did Anna and the audience of male analysts hear Ferenczi indite not only themselves but, what was worse, Sigmund Freud?; (7) did Ferenczi's frank and compassionate plea for the understanding of the dilemma of the molested child stimulate an unconscious chord in the analytic gathering?; and (8) did they reject his ideas so that they could protect their denial system regarding their professional and personal issues regarding seduction?

Freud's decision to suppress Ferenczi's theory was a complicated and overdetermined reaction. Among the plausible explanations for censorship are: (1) Freud's desire to protect his oedipal explanation of neurosis as the cornerstone for psychoanalytic theory (Masson 1984); (2) Freud's *mistaken conclusion* that Ferenczi's "relaxation therapy" and Confusion of Tongues theory were regressive measures fueled by psychopathology rather than creativity (Rachman 1997a); (3) Freud's anxiety that Ferenczi's dissidence signaled his desire to reject him and leave mainstream psychoanalysis as Jung and Rank had done (Gay 1988); (4) Freud's denial that sexual seduction was a relevant clinical variable in his own life (Krüll 1986); (5) Freud's disdain for the more disturbed patients who needed empathic rather than interpretative interaction (Kohut 1984; Mitchell, 1988; Rachman 1997a, 2002); (6) Freud's clinical practice and philosophy of therapy sufficiently differed from Ferenczi (Roazen 1975). Freud, during the period of the "Confusion of Tongues" paper, was involved in many training analyses, while Ferenczi was analyzing incest survivors. Freud, although he was more clinically flexible than is generally known (Roazen 1975), did believe in psychoanalysis as a treatment for neurosis. Ferenczi, on the other hand, was extending the boundaries of treatment to include pregenital disorders (narcissistic, borderline, and psychotic disorders).

Freud's abandonment of the seduction theory and the development of the oedipal theory served some very important functions: (1) It shifted the focus of a sexual act to a sexual wish or fantasy; (2) it described the experience as an intrapsychic event, not an interpersonal occurrence; (3) at issue was the child's sexuality, not the parent's sexuality; (4) it removed any idea that the sexuality was occurring in a disturbed object relationship where parents were mistreating (abusing) their children; (5) this not only served a theoretical function but, perhaps, a personal one—Freud could maintain the denial that childhood seduction had played in his own life (Krüll 1986); and (6) the issue of parent-child sexuality became a developmentally appropriate phase in personality development—there was no need to search for parental responsibility.

THE CONFUSION OF TONGUES BETWEEN ANNA AND SIGMUND FREUD

I don't know if Ferenczi knew of Freud's analysis of Anna. But I can imagine his thinking of it as an example of the Confusion of Tongues. Freud's analysis of his daughter inherently created an emotionally seductive experience based on the following reasoning using my understanding of the Confusion of

Tongues theory (Rachman 1989, 1994, 1997a, 2002; Rachman and Mattick 2002). Anna wanted tenderness, affection, and love from her father in submitting herself to being analyzed by him. Did she approach him for an analysis or did Freud volunteer? Did either of them question the wisdom of their decision?

The issues of seduction, intrusion, and betrayal must be considered as factors in the analysis of one's child. In Freud's analysis of his daughter, Anna, the issue of emotional seduction must be raised. Freud's oedipal theory clearly suggests that the child's need to fantasize about sexuality must be protected. A child, according to the Oedipal theory, needs to have the opportunity to desire the parent sexually, in the privacy of his or her own mind. This oedipal fantasy needs to be protected from parental intrusion in order to be maintained at the level of fantasy. Any discussion of it with the *actual parent* contaminates the experience as a wish and could initiate the idea of acting upon it. The parent, in pointing out the sexual desire of the child for him, sexualizes the interaction. He creates the situation that sex is the central topic, but then disavows that he has an interest in being in such an interaction. This creates a classical Confusion of Tongues. He takes a situation, *which is not explicitly defined as sexual* and defines it as a sexual one. But he does not admit he is so defining the situation. It is his daughter's wish to seduce him. *The seducer, became the seduced.* The technique of the seducer is to ascribe the technique of seduction to the other person. The child experiences some negative interaction with the parent, which is denied and projected onto the child. Confusion as to what has transpired in the relationship ensues. The child does not trust his or her own sense of reality and begins to accept the parental version of the drama. This is where Identification with the Aggressor becomes a significant mechanism.

In agreeing to analyze Anna, Sigmund created an expectation that he would be able to be a full transferential figure. He led her to believe he would be a container for all her feelings, whether sexual, dependent, or aggressive. In essence, he would contain all of her psychopathology. What father could hear his daughter's masochistic fantasies—for example, her beating fantasies—as Freud did, and maintain a neutral, objective, therapeutic stance? It seems so easy to be overconcerned, to want to intervene so as to soothe her hurt before one heard out and explored the full extent and meaning of the subjective experience of wanting to be beaten as a stimulus to masturbation. Was Freud the exceptional father-scientist, that he could hear Anna's masochistic fantasies and treat her like a female stranger who needed his detached objectivity? If he plays the scientist, is he being a good father by not soothing his daughter? If he soothes his daughter, however, he is not being the scientist and following his method. But can one's own child experience the father in the role of objective analyst as warm, caring, responsive, and affectionate? Anna is placed in an emotional compromise. She must not ask for soothing, to be the good analysand. So to be a good daughter, she must not disappoint him and be an inadequate analysand. She can't, therefore, require him to be a good father. If Anna wanted a nonanalytic response, then Freud would be obligated to give a transference interpretation. ("Both Freud and his daughter located the origin of post-oedipal beating fantasies in repression of the 'love fantasy' a child has for his or her father" [Young-Bruehl 1988, 109]).

Anna would be obligated to accept this interpretation. The result of this interaction would have been that Freud had encouraged his daughter to say she had sexual feelings for him. Imagine the emotional impact this could have on a daughter: If she accepts this interpretation, she is responsible for her sexual feelings toward him. Then he is not responsible for creating any sexual stimulation in their interaction. He is only uncovering the truth. As in the Dora case, Freud is not responsible for the sexualized interaction.

As we can see from Ferenczi's work during the period when Anna was undergoing her analysis, roughly 1918–1924, some analysands reacted negatively to the interpretative analyst, feeling they were being retraumatized by the cold, distant, detached observer who exerted his power, control, and status over them with sexual interpretations (Ferenczi 1932/1988). Balint (1968), Winnicott (1965), and Kohut (1984) were to confirm these findings as they brought Ferenczi's original observations into psychoanalysis' modern era. Needing warmth, affection, and responsiveness, Anna settled for interpretation. What kind of interpretation did Freud offer to his daughter when she told him of her beating fantasies? The connection between Sigmund Freud's paper, "A Child Is Being Beaten" (S. Freud 1919), with Anna's paper, "Beating Fantasies and Daydreams" (A. Freud 1966–1980, p. 155), has been made:

> This fifth patient sounds very much like Anna Freud . . . But the sixth patient is not directly described at all, and this may signal that Freud protected his daughter's privacy with silence. Beating Fantasies and Daydreams [A. Freud's paper] was modeled—in general, if not in complete detail—on her own case, and her essay's descriptive framework is identical with the one that applies to two of the female cases in Freud's essay. (Young-Bruehl, 1990, 104)

Interpretation, if Freud was true to his method, was his gift to his daughter. Is interpretation sufficient to encourage the child to feel loved and attended to in an analysis? To be a good girl—to be "daddy's good girl," accepting interpretations—was her duty. As Young-Bruehl (1990) has indicated, "he [S. Freud] certainly knew the degree to which her fantasy life was susceptible to regression and her intellectual energies to inhibition" (108). Could Anna Freud reject an interpretation by her father? Could one imagine her saying to the founder of psychoanalysis, "That is an interesting interpretation you have offered me, but I don't think it applies to my case?" Could Anna have followed Dora in not only rejecting the sexual interpretations but by also terminating her analysis? How, then, did the necessary phenomenon of resistance emerge and develop in this analysis? Resistance, although conceptualized as the enemy of change, was nevertheless the necessary impetus for growth, and the emergence of the self striving to metabolize the insights of the doctor who was the enemy of neurosis. Was Sigmund able to challenge an analysand to express her negative transferential feelings directly to him, as was his pupil Sándor Ferenczi? Ferenczi complained of his analysis with Freud, which occurred before Anna's, in that his analyst would not enter into a dialogue about their relationship (Ferenczi 1932/1988). Freud remained aloof, as he had done earlier with Jung, refusing to relinquish his position of authority by making associations to a dream he had told Ferenczi and Jung on their joint crossing of the Atlantic on the way to the Clark lectures (Rosensweig 1992). Had Freud changed this behavior by the 1920s? Did he behave differently with his daughter?

IMPLICATIONS FOR THE ABANDONMENT OF THE SEDUCTION THEORY

The Freudian formulation of child abuse was very different from the Ferenczian Confusion of Tongues dynamic. Recently, there have been attempts to examine the Zeitgeist in Europe, and in Vienna in particular, which can shed light on the issue of childhood abuse during Freud's training as a physician and during his formative years of clinical practice. Masson has chronicled the incidence of child abuse and child murder to which Freud was exposed during his period of training with Charcot (Masson 1984). In fact, Freud participated in autopsies of child abuse victims. Recent meticulous research in German archives has shown that Freud was a pediatrician for a 10-year period, from 1886 to 1896, during which he was responsible for the department for nervous diseases at the Public Institute for Children's Diseases in Vienna, directed by Max Kassowitz (Bonomi 1994). For this 10-year period, he worked with hysterical children three days a week.

In a fascinating study, a historian has researched the incidence of reported child abuse at the fin-de-siècle in Freud's Vienna (Wolf 1988). Child abuse was very prevalent in Freud's Vienna, and chronicled in the daily newspaper. There were four sensational cases of child battering and murder at the turn of the century in Vienna that dominated the newspapers and caused dramatics in the courtroom trials. These child abuse sensations of 1899 were not commented on by Freud, whose great intellectual spirit dominated the landscape of fin-de-siècle Vienna. Of particular importance, in my opinion, was that the child abuse cases of 1899 did not seem to have any influence on his first case study, the analysis of Dora, undertaken about 1902, two years later (S. Freud 1905). In Dora we have an adolescent, the victim of an attempted molestation by Herr K., an adult old enough to be her father.

In a letter to Wilhelm Fleiss dated October 14, 1900, Freud announced he had found the ideal case (the Dora case) to demonstrate the efficacy of his oedipal theory: ". . . I have a new patient, girl of eighteen; the case has opened smoothly to my collection of picklocks" (S. Freud 1887–1902/1954, 325).

Paul Mattick and I have reanalyzed the Dora case from the vantage point of the Confusion of Tongues theory (Rachman and Mattick 2002). We have found several passages that indicate that material relevant to child molestation was overlooked, deemed irrelevant, or interpreted as infant sexuality:

1. Dora's relationship with her mother was very disturbed, but no analysis of the significant object relationship was included, nor was any investigation made of possible parental abuse.
2. The negative feelings for the mother were treated as oedipal jealousy, and no thought was given to any real trauma in their object relationship.
3. Freud's presentation of the case ignored an attempt at molestation by Herr K. In fact, this incident is used to demonstrate Dora's sexual difficulty.
4. In a classic example of a Confusion of Tongues dilemma, Freud interpreted Dora's negative reaction to Herr K's attempt at seduction as her aversion to her oedipal longings for her father. Eventually, Freud interpreted Dora's symptomatology as manifestation of her unresolved oedipal wishes for her father, Herr K., and her analyst.
5. At no point in the Dora essay is any investigation or comment made about the imprudent assault by Herr K. as being an example of sexual seduction or abuse. Freud actually thought Dora should have been grateful that Herr K. was interested in her.
6. Ten years after analyzing Dora, Freud's Schreber case was another dramatic example of ignoring or denying child abuse as a causal factor in psychological disorder (Lothane 1992).

Freud coined a term, *affectionate abuse*, which indicated at the very least his ambivalence about actual abuse (Wolf 1988).

Freud's abandonment of the seduction theory has had a profound effect on the evolution of psychoanalysis (Rachman 1991, 1997b). The suppression of Ferenczi's work, ideas, and technical innovations was so successful that the study of his work was virtually stopped for over 50 years. In particular, the disappearance of Ferenczi's work also meant that the study of the incest trauma virtually disappeared from psychoanalysis.

Analysts' coming to terms with the issue of seduction involves understanding its appearances and disappearances within the history of psychoanalysis. In regard to the issue of seduction and to its treatment by the analytic community, Freud's analysis of his daughter is an important case. Its discussion has, I hope, only begun.

REFERENCES

Balint, M. (1968). *The basic fault: Therapeutic aspects of regression.* London: Tavistock.

Bollas, C. (1991). The trauma of incest. In *Forces of destiny: Psychoanalysis and human idiom.* London: Free Association Books.

Bonomi, C. (1994). Why have we ignored Freud the "Pediatrician"? The relevance of Freud's pediatric training for the origins of psychoanalysis. In A. Haynal and E. Falzeder, eds., *100 years of psychoanalysis*, 55–99. London: Karnac.
Ferenczi, S. (1931). Child analysis in the analysis of adults. In *Final contributions*, 126–142.
———. (1980a). The principle of relaxation and neo-catharsis. In M. Balint, ed., *Final contributions to the problems and methods of psychoanalysis: Vol. III*, 108–125. New York: Brunner/Mazel. (Original work published 1930)
———. (1980b). The confusion of tongues between adults and children: The language of tenderness and passion. In *Final contributions*, 156–167. New York: Brunner/Mazel. (Original work published 1933)
———. (1988). The clinical diary of Sándor Ferenczi. J. Dupont, ed. (M. Balint and N. Z. Jackson, trs.) Cambridge: Harvard University Press. (Original work published 1932)
Freud, A. (1966–1980). *The writings of Anna Freud: Vol. I–VII.* New York: International Universities Press.
Freud, S. (1905). *Dora: An analysis of a case of hysteria.* New York: Collier Books.
———. (1919). "A child is being beaten:" A contribution to the study of the origin of sexual perversions. In *The standard edition* (Vol. 17, 175–195), London: Hogarth Press.
———. (1954). *The origins of psychoanalysis: Letters to Wilhelm Fleiss, drafts and notes: 1887–1902.* New York: Basic Books.
Gay, P. (1988). *Freud: A life for our time.* New York: Norton.
Klein, M. L. and P. Tribich. (1982). Blame the child: Freud's blindness to the damaging influence of parents' personalities. *New York Academy of Sciences 22*(8), 14–20.
Kohut, H. (1984). *How does analysis cure?* A. Goldberg and P. E. Stepansky, eds. Chicago: University of Chicago Press.
Krüll, M. (1986). *Freud and his father.* New York: Norton.
Lothane, Z. (1992). *In defense of Schreber: Soul murder and psychiatry.* Hillsdale, NJ: The Analytic Press.
Masson, J. M. (1984). *The assault on truth: Freud's suppression of the seduction theory.* New York: Farrar, Straus & Giroux.
Menaker, E. (1982). *Otto Rank: A rediscovered legacy.* New York: Columbia University Press.
———. (1995). My analysis with Anna Freud. In *The freedom to inquire*, 27–241. Northvale, NJ: Jason Aronson.
Mitchell, S. A. (1988). *Relational concepts in psychoanalysis: An integration.* Cambridge: Harvard University Press.
Rachman, A.W. (1989). Confusion of tongues: The Ferenczian metaphor for childhood seduction and emotional trauma. *Journal of The American Academy of Psychoanalysis 17*(2), 182–205.
———. (1991, December). *Psychoanalysis, sexual seduction and the contemporary analysis of incest.* Presentation at the American Academy of Psychoanalysis, New York.
———. (1993, December). *The evil of childhood seduction.* Presentation at the American Academy of Psychoanalysis, New York.
———. (1994). The Confusion of Tongues theory: Ferenczi's legacy of psychoanalysis. In A. Haynal and E. Falzeder, eds., *100 years of psychoanalysis*, 235–255. London: Karnac.

———. (1996, February). *Self expression: Analysand and analyst.* Symposium conducted at the eighth biennial conference of the New York University Psychoanalytic Society.
———. (1997a). *Sándor Ferenczi: The psycho-therapist of tenderness and passion.* Northvale, NJ: Jason Aronson.
———. (1997b). The suppression and censorship of Ferenczi's "confusion of tongues" paper. *Psychoanalytic Inquiry 17,* (4, August).
———. (1998). The issue of Todschweigen (death by silence) in the traditional treatment of dissidents in the history of psychoanalysis. In R. Prince, ed., *Is psychoanalysis dead? Murder, suicide or rumor greatly exaggerated.* Northvale, NJ: Jason Aronson.
———. (2000). Ferenczi's "confusion of tongues" theory and the analysis of the incest trauma. *Psychoanalytic Social Work* 7,(1), 27–53.
———. (2002). *Psychotherapy of "difficult" cases: Flexibility and responsiveness in contemporary clinical practice.* Madison, CT: Psychosocial Press.
Rachman, A.W., and P. Mattick. (2002). *Freud's "confusion of tongues:" Issues of power, control and status in the analysis of Dora.* Unpublished manuscript.
Roazen, P. (1969). *Brother animal: The story of Freud and Tausk.* New York: New York University Press.
———. (1975). *Freud and his followers.* New York: Knopf.
Rosenzweig, S. (1992). *Freud, Jung, and Hall the king-maker: The historic expedition to America (1909).* Seattle: Hogrefe and Haber.
Searles, H. F. (1986). *My work with borderline patients.* Northvale, N. J.: Jason Aronson.
Stierlin, H. (1959). The adaptation to the stronger person's reality. *Psychiatry 22:* 143–152.
Tolpin, M. (1992). *Self-esteem, beating fantasies and a life-saving twinship resolution: a study of Anna Freud.* Presentation at the American Psychoanalytic Association Seminar for Clinicians, New York and Chicago, December and May.
Winnicott, D.W. (1965). *The maturational process and the facilitating environment.* New York: International Universities Press.
Wolf, L. (1988). *Post cards from the end of the world: An investigation into the mind of fin-de-siècle Vienna.* London: Collins.
Young-Bruehl, E. (1990). *Anna Freud: A biography.* New York: Summit Books.

Part II

The Psychoanalytic Process

CHAPTER 7

The Psychoanalyst and Freedom

Jeffrey B. Rubin

With its *simultaneous* sensitivity to determinism—the circumscribed nature of human freedom—and the potential for self-transformation, Freud's "deterministic psychology of freedom" (Gay 1990, 89), offers the *possibility* of a unique perspective on freedom. Freud manages to neglect neither the determinism pervading human life nor the possibility of rationality, choice, and self-transformation.

But the radical potential of the psychoanalytic conception of freedom—and the liberation it might engender—often remains unrealized because of an unresolved tension in psychoanalysis between its liberating and constricting tendencies. These are embodied in its emancipatory interrogation of, *and* enslaving conformity to, its own theories and practices. Too often, the capacity of psychoanalysts to self-correctively expand analytic concepts in light of what they learn from patients, and thus promote self-transformation and expansion, is subverted by their tendency to fit the analysands (and themselves) into established psychoanalytic theories and procedures, which can foster self-imprisonment.

The Freudian theory of dream practice illustrates the constricting and liberating dimensions of psychoanalytic practice. It also sheds light on what obstructs and facilitates freedom in the analyst and has important implications for the psychoanalyst's relation to his or her own theories and practices. Recognizing the tension between these two facets of dream practice elucidates how the emancipatory possibilities within Freudian practice might be tapped so that the conservative and constricting tendencies within Freudian theory do not enslave us.[1]

THE FREUDIAN THEORY OF DREAM PRACTICE

Dream interpretation is the process by which the latent meaning of dreams is illuminated. According to Freud (1900/1953), previous investigators adopted one of two typical approaches to dream interpretation: They assumed that there was a singular symbolic meaning to a dream as a whole or utilized a fixed key for decoding the meaning of a dream (1900/1953, 96–97). In the latter view, the decoding method, dreams are treated as "a kind of cryptography in which each sign can be translated into another sign having a known meaning, in accordance with a fixed key" (1900/1953, 97).

Freud challenges the legitimacy of this approach because it does not realize that "the same piece of content may conceal a different meaning when it occurs in various people or various contexts" (1900/1953, 105) and "every element in a dream can, for purposes of interpretation, stand for its opposite just as easily as for itself (1900/1953, 471).

The meaning of a dream, according to Freud, is arrived at not by translating dream material into the a priori meaning and "fixed-key" of a "dream-book" (1900/1953, 96–97) but by eliciting the dreamer's unique associations. Freud's method "imposes the task of interpreting upon the dreamer himself [or herself]. It is not concerned with what occurs to the interpreter in connection with a particular element of the dream, but with what occurs to the dreamer" (1900/1953, 98, fn.1).

An important exception to this occurs when the analyst determines that the dream contains what Freud terms *symbols*, by which he means certain elements of the dream which indirectly represent latent dream thoughts, which are not derived from the day residue, are not revealed by free association, and must be decoded by the *analyst*. "As contrasted with other dream-elements, a fixed meaning may be attributed to them [symbols] . . . since we know how to translate these symbols and the dreamer does not . . . it may happen that the sense of a dream may at once become clear to us as we have heard the text of the dream, even before we have made any effort at interpreting it, while it still remains an enigma to the dreamer himself" (1933, 12–13). "The concept of a symbol," Freud (1916–17/1958b) admits, "cannot at present be sharply delimited; it shades off into such notions as those of replacement or representation, and even approaches that of an illusion . . . You see, then, that a symbolic relation is a comparison of a quite special kind, of which we do not as yet clearly grasp the basis, though perhaps we may later arrive at some indication of it" (152, fn).

Freud recommends a "combined technique" when dealing with "those elements of the dream-content which must be recognized as symbolic" (1900/1953, 353). The "combined technique" on one hand "rests on the dreamer's associations and on the other hand fills the gap from the interpreter's knowledge of symbols" (1900/1953, 353).

Freud does not specify *how* the analyst knows that a given portion of the dream is a *symbol*, rather than something that needs to be examined anew using the associative method (Lansky 1992a, 13). That this can open the door to interpretive confusion is suggested by his acknowledgment that "the presence of symbols in dreams not only facilitates their interpretation but also makes it more difficult" (1900/1953, 352, fn). One important difficulty, to use Freud's image in a different but compatible context, is that the analyst "interprets *into*" the analysand's utterances what cannot be "interpreted *from*" them and thus assimilates the uniqueness of the dream material into the "fixed meaning" of his or her generalized lexicon.

The Freudian theory of dream practice—with its clashing conceptions of the associational and symbolic approach to the ideographic dream material—both illustrates and provides resources for transforming the tension between the constricting and liberating dimensions of psychoanalysis. The presumption that the analyst can ascertain that particular material in a dream is *symbolic*, and can be interpreted without the dreamer's associations, funnels the radically novel content of the dream into the preexisting categories of the *analyst's* dream meanings—the "fixed key" of his or her personal "dream book"—and thus prevents the uniqueness of the analysand's subjectivity from fully emerging. It also reinstitutes the very lexical method of dream interpretation that Freud elsewhere eschews (e.g., Lansky 1992a, 13) and thus paves the way for an authoritarian analytic ambience in which the analyst possesses The Truth, to be dispensed to the passive patient. This sort of approach usually promotes a narcissistic and imprisoning investment in one's own theories; when we believe we possess The Truth we tend to aggrandize and excessively identify with our own beliefs and to discount the potential value of alternative ways of thinking.

Freud (1931/1960) claimed that the patient's free-associating (as well as its complement, the analyst's evenly hovering attention) is "the methodological key" (402–3) to psychoanalysis. In recommending that the analyst listen afresh to the dreamer's associations, the associational approach facilitates the emergence of the unique meanings of the analysand's dream material and opens up the possibility of experiencing previously hidden aspects of the patient's subjectivity. But if free association and evenly hovering attention can encourage the expression of disavowed and neglected thoughts, feelings, and fantasies and can challenge our familiar and narrow narratives about ourselves and thereby open up unforeseen possibilities in living, then why do our ideological preferences seem to be left intact so much of the time? Why, in other words, do Lacanians tend to usually discover self-alienation, not interpersonal reenactments? Why do self psychologists tend to find self-defects or why do missing self object functions not compromise formations? The fact that the ideological preferences analysts start with are so tenacious and self-revision is so difficult suggests that it might be prudent to reexamine whether free association or evenly hovering attention offer an infallible, unmediated contact with ourselves or others.

Let us consider the treatment of a woman I shall call Arlene, a kind, highly intelligent, depressed, lonely single woman in her early fifties, who experienced profound emptiness and meaninglessness in her life. She likened her self to an "empty space" and "void" and indicated that she did not feel that she had a life that was her own. Her life was permeated by compliance and submission to the needs of others. What *she* wanted lacked significance for her and those she often became involved with. She felt deeply unfulfilled and adrift, damaged and inherently unfixable. Arlene not only did not have a life; in fact she did not even feel entitled to having one.

This was not surprising given what we knew about her family background and childhood. Her family was a parent-centered home in which she felt invisible. Arlene was a twin who felt that she had no independent emotional life of her own. She experienced a "twinship" with her mother as well as her sister. In her relationship with her competent, highly self-absorbed, and unintrospective mother she felt a mandate to be the sort of person her mother wanted her to be. Arlene felt that with her mother everything but her came first and that she was not important or special in her mother's eyes. The price of connectedness to her mother was to lose herself. To not conform to what her mother wanted was to jeopardize the relationship.

Her father was a highly competent, stern, and inaccessible executive who was much more interested in work than in his family. Arlene experienced her father as a self-absorbed presence who was rude and abrasive to others—including his daughter, whom he saw as inferior. He constantly criticized and rebuked Arlene and did not affirm her own identity in any way.

Arlene put her parents on a pedestal (which also entailed devaluing herself) so as to retain an emotional tie to them. One salient form that this took was the unquestioned belief that her parents' way of living—denying feelings and treating others as a means rather than an end—was natural and correct. "If my parents' way of living didn't work for me," Arlene assumed, "then something must be wrong with *me*." One of the mystifying aspects of her relationship with her parents was the notion they inculcated in her, and which she uncritically accepted, that things come naturally to people: that one just accomplishes tasks, has relationships, and masters avocational pursuits without the need for learning, experimentation, failure, risk, and effort. Her experience of not being able to do things—have relationships, learn new hobbies, and so forth—was doubly difficult for her because her parents (1) did not teach her how to think about these things *and* (2) taught her that it all comes naturally.

Arlene experienced herself as a force driven by habit out of control. Her life oscillated between self-neglecting and depriving connections with others and painful social isolation, both of which left her feeling invisible, self-doubting, and directionless. Her relationships were usually stamped by a self-abnegating attention to the needs of the other. Adopting a negative identity of being nonjudgmental and nondiscriminating—so as to not be critical and elitist like her father—led to her flowing with the needs and demands of others rather than considering and respecting what she felt and needed. She habitually got involved with self-centered men who seemed uninterested in her emotional needs. She was left feeling neglected and deprived.

Her unsplendid isolation was what she termed a "survival mechanism" which was designed to protect her against interpersonal exploitation, self-loss, disappointment, and deprivation. Isolation and hyper-independence enabled her to deny her needs and ensure that she would not be connected to others and nullified. It also resulted in a life of pervasive inhibition, minimal risk, lacunae in experience and skills, and a painful sense of emptiness.

Arlene saw life as one of two deadly options: relatedness to others, which resulted in self-loss, *or* disconnection from others which generated profound deprivation. Socially withdrawn, emotionally and spiritually unfulfilled, she felt a pervasive hopelessness about ever having a meaningful and fulfilling life. In fact, such a life for her seemed like an impossibility.

Towards the end of a session in which Arlene had begun to realize that neglecting her own needs contributed to her sense of pessimism about having a meaningful life, she expressed appreciation for the changes she had recently experienced in treatment. She indicated that she was definitely learning to listen to and trust her own feelings instead of simply reacting to the needs of others. This gave her more of a sense of choice. But she felt slightly self-indulgent coming to treatment. After all, she continued in a tone we had come to associate with her father, what good is it to talk about the further changes that she wishes to make—reacting less to the demands of others and developing more of a direction in her life? She just needs to do it; to *act*. She values treatment, but what of value, she wondered, had really happened in today's session?

Arlene had said this sort of thing several times in the year or so that we had been working together, especially after she had undergone some important growth or there had been a disruption in the treatment because of either a vacation or some misunderstanding on my part. I had taken different tacks at different times depending on a range of factors including the state of the transference-countertransference and what seemed to have greatest motivational saliency at a particular clinical moment. We had generated various possible meanings and purposes through free-association and evenly hovering attention. At certain times, unconscious themes and conflicts regarding fear of psychic growth and individuation seemed most germane. At other times, her pessimism seemed to embody pre- and postlinguistic *moods* of sadness and hopelessness. We had wondered whether she was treating herself the way her father had treated her or unconsciously recreating frustrating and depriving relations with her parents. Sometimes she seemed to be maintaining a link with her depriving past so as to keep alive the faint hope that she might eventually gain acceptance and love from her distant and self-involved parents. And finally, it sometimes appeared as if I was cast in the role of her father and she was turning the tables on me by maintaining the status quo. Even though we had generated a good deal of insight about the possible sources and function of her pessimism, it had not really impacted on either her pessimism or the possibilities for a meaningful and fulfilling life.

I was intrigued by Arlene's assessment of the session because from my perspective, something very important *had* happened on an emotional level in the session although I was aware that she still felt trapped in a life that felt empty. As I reflected on Arlene's remarks about the insignificance of the session, I asked myself what function it might serve her to experience the session in a pessimistic way. I then said to her: "Since it feels impossible to imagine a world in which you are central and your needs are valued by you and those close to you, does it seem that it is irrelevant to even talk about your pessimism let alone work on it?" "I feel, she replied," that it will never happen. I am just now realizing that I have an investment in my pessimism; in keeping it alive. This is something that I have never thought about."

It was something that neither of us had thought about until I had the freedom to imagine—and then share with Arlene—an image of a mode of being that she may never have known, namely non–self-annihilating connectedness, which opened up another way of being-in-the-world. In non–self-annihilating connectedness, which was different from the two deadly life-denying options that had structured and delimited her life and our work together up until this moment, one is neither related and nullified nor socially isolated and deprived. Rather, one is connected and enriched.

Arlene began the next session with a dream: "I was suddenly pregnant in the hospital having a baby. My sister was also delivering. I was sad that my baby was not alive. My sister's baby was okay—actually she had twins, a girl and a boy."

After recounting the dream Arlene began talking again about pessimism. "Pessimism allows me to maintain my lifestyle which I'm attached to. It allows me to say: 'I'm a hermit/recluse.'" I eventually asked about her associations to pregnancy. "Being pregnant," she indicated, "is giving birth to optimism—it means giving up pessimism. I don't remember any *dead* baby in the dream—they said 'it didn't work out.' I never saw a trace of any dead baby." I asked her if she had experienced a lifelong sense from those close to her—such as her parents (the 'they' in her associations to the dream who told her 'it didn't work out?')—that things didn't work out for her; were not and could not be generative. Arlene added a pregnant alternative: "*Or,* I *could* be pregnant but not with something of *mine.*" I asked her if she experienced the options for her life as being either no pregnancy/generativity or a self-alienating pregnancy: giving birth to something that was not of or for her. "Yes . . . I had dreams that I have never talked about in which I was trying to scream/communicate but I couldn't. Pessimism is acceptance: This is the ways things are and they won't change. No highs and lows but everything is manageable. This will hold me together. I don't get too low but I self-medicate [food, Valium]."

I asked if pessimism could be a kind of *mental* self-medication. She got sad and pensive. "I can remember when I looked forward to doing social things; when I felt bad if I was not included. There was a point in my life when I felt more human. It [social isolation] is a way of not rendering myself vulnerable. My parents were strong and dominant. They had no appreciation of differences; how I was different from them. Not to have any one see you as a child. That is so sad. I never realized that I was so deprived. I thought everyone had these feelings. I remember in grade school every night crying myself to bed. There was no outlet for it or talking about it. To fit in with my family you had to destroy it [negative feelings]. Like they are not there. Through talking with you I have come to see the importance of this. I was like a girl in a washing machine with a lot of starch. A starched girl."

She began the next session by describing an encounter with a friend from out of town who told Arlene that she had never been listened to so well. "It came after our session where I felt deeply listened to by you. I was never aware that I felt I was never seen or heard by my parents. I just felt deprivation. A large part of that was that I was not seen for who I am by them but for who they wanted me to be." Arlene ended the session by speaking about her growing recognition of her reclusiveness and the way it protects against losing herself which often happens when she is with others.

In the next session she spoke about seeking out and talking with an interesting women she met at a party and engaging in a long and satisfying conversation that felt authentic and interesting. She felt inspired by the women's commitment to social justice and also felt a sense of optimism that she might eventually meet other like-spirited people. They exchanged phone numbers and agreed to keep in touch. It felt to Arlene like the dawn of a new era.

"Every metapsychology," notes Levenson (1992), "contains the seeds of an incipient counter-transference" (464). Exploring the roots and meanings of Arlene's pessimism through the methods of free-association and evenly hovering attention made it possible for us to understand various meanings and purposes of her hopelessness including, for example, the way it gave her a stable identity, normalized her depriving past, and linked her to her parents while keeping alive the hope of finally gaining their acceptance and love. But the void and emptiness that permeated her life still remained. She still had glaring deficits in self-confidence, self-assertion, and relational skills and was unconsciously committed to perpetuating limited modes of being and relating derived from the past.

The problem with the tendency to valorize free association (or evenly hovering attention) as a royal (even if not exclusive) road to the patient's or analyst's unconscious as I and others (e.g., Barratt 1994) have done, is that it assumes what certain contemporary hermeneutically-sympathetic analysts (Atwood and Stolorow 1984; Goldberg 1990) and psychoanalytic social constructivists (Hoffman 1991), among many others, have taught us to be suspicious of: namely, immaculate perception. Observation and theorizing always occur in specific historical, sociocultural, linguistic, and psychological contexts which shape and delimit the methodology that is utilized, the questions that are asked (and not asked), and the conclusions that are drawn. There is thus no impartial or totalizing perspective from which to speak or listen, observe or theorize.

Indelibly influenced by the analyst's personality and theories, the analyst's evenly hovering attention is not an infallible road to the patient's unconscious experience. If theory is what we *already* know about human experience, then it can actually filter the analyst's evenly hovering attention, and convert the potentially pluralistic universe of the patient into a psychic territory that has already been mapped. The analyst's evenly hovering attention *shapes* rather than simply records the patient's subjectivity.

Evenly hovering attention and free-associating are therefore *necessary* but insufficient aspects of psychoanalytic method. They have the capacity to resist closure and constriction, interminably question the foundation of one's thought and practices, and reveal the unmanifest, even as the theory-laden nature of listening and theorizing draws us toward the past—what we *already* know—and thus preempts the future.

With its notion of *nonattachment*, or commitment with the capacity for continual disidentification and self-transformation, Eastern meditative disciplines offer a less egocentric way of relating to our theories (e.g., Rubin 1996). There are intimations of this stance toward practices and theories in psychoanalysis at its self-reflexive best (e.g., Ferenczi 1955; Winnicott 1971; Kohut 1984, 202–3; Phillips 1993, 1994).

A nonattached relation to our own formulations would foster recognition of the necessity *and* the inevitable contingency and partiality of our theories and practices. We can neither afford to overidentify with them and thereby imprison our capacity for self-modification and transformation, nor eschew them in a quixotic dream of a theory-free contact with our patients, ourselves, or the world.

This stance promotes a fluid awareness, what I would term a *freedom-within-structure*, which helps the analyst de-center from the frameworks of understanding he or she habitually utilizes. Freedom, in this perspective, always occurs within a context of constraint. When we have a nongrasping commitment to, and a nonpossessive and nondefensive delight in, the concepts and methods that we value, a nonauthoritarian, non-narcissistic, and unfettered relationship to one's own theories may develop.

A sense of freedom-within-structure can facilitate for the analyst the neglected and liberatory logic of psychoanalysis—and that, in turn, can be freeing for both the analyst and the patient. When the analyst is liberated from the constraint of a suffocating relationship to her theories and practices, the patient is able to participate in the analysis in a freer way—as a partner engaged in a process of searching and self-creating. Such a therapeutic environment can encourage the analysand to be more self-trusting and playful; indeed, it can be empowering.

But the analytic relationship is of course never so free. It is all too often constrained by the analyst's narcissistic relationship to his or her own theories.

As I became less attached to free association and evenly hovering attention as privileged methodological principles and tools in my own work with Arlene, I recognized that my own freedom of thought and responsiveness as an analyst had been constrained by the very methodology that had initially facilitated freedom. Something a martial artist and teacher once said to me then became clearer: Systems of thought and practice and the methods they utilize are designed to solve particular problems (Inosanto, personal communication, January 1997). They may be quite useful in solving a particular problem—for example, how to reveal buried experience in a culture that encourages inhibition—but when they are treated as idols (as I may have done with free association and evenly hovering attention), and their validity is universalized, then their value is compromised. Treating a method that has applicability in a local, or particular, therapeutic context as a kind of Procrustean bed into which all experience is fitted—even a heuristic method such as free association—fosters closed, congealed systems of thought and practice.

The idea of *open* and fluid systems of practice and thought—while perhaps enticing—seems like a psychoanalytic oxymoron. We have trouble conceiving of—let alone creating—systems that recognize their own essential contestability and contain the possibility of error-detection and self-modification. Such models recognize that the methods that one utilizes—no matter how cherished—are provisional and need to be open to, and deeply value, the potentially enriching facets of alternative, foreign practices. This spirit can help us recognize what is idiosyncratic and partial about our own preferred notions (e.g., Bernstein 1992, 328), which encourages continuous reexamination and modification of the methods we employ. When we treat our favored theories and methods as provisional we are less locked in to any theory or practice. We are then freer to creatively transform our training and our theoretical preferences. We might then practice a psychoanalytic art that is "open to all ways [yet] . . . bound by none" (Lee 1986).

Psychoanalysis has identified two crucial kinds of self-pathology—an insufficiently structuralized self and a pathologically structuralized self (e.g., Atwood and Stolorow 1984). For Freud, pathological structures such as hysteria were a recurrent problem. Because of its focus on pathological structures, psychoanalysis has often neglected and insufficiently elaborated the building of self-structure and the development of an identity. Recognizing that one has lived an inauthentic or empty life does not automatically foster a life of authenticity or meaning. In fact, a great deal of therapeutic work—such as learning new modes of self-care; experiencing new ways of relating to others; developing new skills, capacities, and views of oneself, and so forth—may be necessary before such a person feels alive or vital.

Because Arlene did not have a sense of self and felt empty and directionless, she needed to construct an identity—not simply discover a buried self or resume aborted development. The method of free association and evenly hovering attention—which seems better suited to working with a pathologically structured self rather than an insufficiently structured self—provided necessary but insufficient tools for addressing her difficulties in living. Empathizing with or interpreting the self-defects would not build a new or missing self-structure. Something else was needed, namely, the analyst's *imagination.* If it is true that methods are designed to solve particular problems—and I suspect that it is—then the question becomes: "What problems need to be solved in a particular therapeutic context and what is the best tool for the job at hand?"

The analyst's own freedom, according to Bollas (1989), is central to successful psychoanalytic treatment. It is one of the multiple functions he or she plays. As I lived with Arlene's hopelessness about a life that she could call her own, it was clear to me that engaging her life differently—which was crucial if she was to construct a personally meaningful identity—depended in part on my own freedom of being. The constraining grip of Arlene's self-annulling past and present was loosened, and the treatment opened up in new and productive ways as I was freer to utilize my imagination in my work with her.[2]

"There are some things," notes Aristotle, "about which it is not possible to pronounce rightly in general terms." A comprehensive discussion of the complex topic of the analyst's use of his or her imagination is beyond the scope of this chapter. Because questions about how analysts might draw on their imagination, or when facets of the analyst's imaginative life—images, daydreams, fantasies, dreams, and so forth—might be shared, are context-dependent and therefore do not suit themselves to a standardized answer, it would perhaps clash with the spirit of this chapter to offer any generalized recommendations. Instead, let me offer some brief reflections. (For a fuller examination of this topic, see a previous work [Rubin 1998].)

Analysts working within every school of thought have undoubtedly made therapeutically disciplined and creative use of their own subjectivity. Heimann, Little, Searles, Loewald, Bollas, Ogden, and Mitchell, among others, seem to have felt most comfortable drawing on the potential resources of their own imaginative life.

With imagination, like one's relation to one's preferred theories, what may get us the most therapeutic yield is attending to our experience while not being attached to it; sailing an ever-changing course between fearing or overvaluing our experience; and being neither phobic nor narcissistic about what we imagine, think, fantasize, or feel.

Judicious and selective use of one's imagination—based on an understanding of the transference-countertransference matrix shaping the treatment—is crucial, as is the analyst's motivation for doing so. Other considerations might include the patient's readiness to utilize and freedom to play with the material that is shared. There may be some patients for whom one could never usefully express one's subjective life (e.g., Bollas 1987, 211). In situations where this is not the case and it may be generative for the analyst to share what he or she has imagined, then the analyst needs to present it in a provisional as opposed to authoritative way (e.g., Winnicott 1971; Bollas 1987). The patient needs to feel free to utilize or reject whatever is suggested by the analyst.

When I began writing this chapter, I hoped to illuminate something that I felt psychoanalysis had to offer about freedom, particularly its deterministic psychology of freedom and its ability to foster the expression of the patient's unique subjectivity. I end this chapter months later with the sneaking suspicion—that may not be unrelated to the topic—that I have moved in an unexpected direction away from the territory that I started from and was familiar with. The analyst's fluid, evolving, non-narcissistic relationship to his or her own guiding framework (even a heuristic one such as free-association and evenly hovering attention) *and* his or her capacity for imagination is crucial to the topic of psychoanalysis and freedom.

Because what is imaginative in the present may be imprisoning in the future, the possibilities for freedom that Arlene and I generate in the present will probably need to be overcome in the future in order to preserve our freedom. Arlene and I may need to imagine what is currently unimaginable for us in order to keep alive her fragile hope for a life that might feel like her own.[3]

NOTES

1. Not all conservative tendencies within psychoanalysis in general or Freudian theory in particular are constricting. Tradition can either enable or constrain or both.

2. This section was enriched by the suggestive reflections of Phillips (1993, 1994).

3. My highlighting of the importance of the analyst's imagination is not meant to deny or minimize the importance of the analyst's understanding, insight, interpretations, capacity for mirroring, availability as a source of identification or idealization, challenger of rigid and punitive conscience, delineator of self and others, metabolizer of affects and so forth. I just mean to stress a key, neglected dimension of the multiplex therapeutic action of psychoanalysis. In my own pluralistic view of the therapeutic process, a multitude of factors including the analytic ambience, the analytic relationship, the analyst's provision of a variety of functions, and the analysand's capacity for self-reflection and change are crucial at different times and in different ways.

It might be argued that drawing on the analyst's imagination contaminates the treatment and violates neutrality. Frank (1993) has thoughtfully explored the place of action and (non-neutral) directedness in psychoanalysis. From my perspective, neutrality is illusory and not even itself neutral. It is an artifact of psychoanalysis' attempt to be scientific and has a particular impact that is no less formative for often being neglected. For a patient I recently heard about in supervision, for example, a man with a cold and self-preoccupied mother and a highly detached father, the analyst's neutrality repeated the glaringly unresponsive familial milieu that had characterized his childhood and left him feeling neglected, lost, and directionless. We would get the most therapeutic mileage, in my view, not in laboring under an anxiety about our therapeutic influence which results in our trying to eliminate our impact by creating an antiseptic analytic environment, but in illuminating the analyst's inevitable shaping presence—in this case the impact on the patient of the analyst's use of his or her imagination.

REFERENCES

Atwood, G., and R. Stolorow. (1984). *Structures of subjectivity: Explorations in psychoanalytic phenomenology.* Hillsdale, NJ: Analytic Press.

Barratt, B. (1994). The psychoanalyst's theorizing. *Journal of the American Psychoanalytic Association, 42,* 697–723.

Bernstein, R. (1992). *The new constellation: The ethical-political horizons of modernity/postmodernity.* Cambridge, MA: MIT Press.

Bollas, C. (1987). *The shadow of the object: Psychoanalysis of the unknown thought.* New York: Columbia University Press.

———. (1989). *Forces of destiny: Psychoanalysis and self experience.* New York: Hill and Wang.

Ferenczi, S. (1955). *Final contributions to the problems and methods of psycho-analysis.* New York: Brunner/Mazel.

Frank, K. (1993). Action, insight and working through: Outline of an integrative approach. *Psychoanalitic Dialogues, 3*(4), 535–77.

Freud, S. (1964). New introductory lectures on psycho-analysis. *Standard Edition,* vol. 22, 3–182. London: Hogarth Press. (Original work published 1933)

———. (1953). Interpretation of dreams. *Standard Edition,* vols. 4 and 5, xxiii–627. London: Hogarth Press. (Original work published 1900)

———. (1958). Introductory lectures on psycho-analysis. *Standard Edition,* vol. 16, 243–63. London: Hogarth Press. (Original work published 1916–17)

———. (1960). Letter # 258, February 7, 1931 to Stefan Zweig. In *The letters of Sigmund Freud,* ed. Ernest Freud, 402–403. New York: Basic Books. (Original work published 1931)

Gay, P. (1990). Freud and freedom. In *Reading Freud: Explorations and entertainments.* New Haven: Yale University Press.

Goldberg, A. (1990). *The prison-house of psychoanalysis.* Hillsdale, NJ: Analytic Press.

Hoffman, I. (1991). Discussion: Towards a social-constructivist view of the psychoanalytic situation. *Psychoanalytic Dialogues, 1,* 74–105.

Kohut, H. (1984). *How does analysis cure?* Chicago: University of Chicago Press.

Lansky, M. (1992). *Essential papers on dreams.* New York: New York University Press.

———. (1992a). The legacy on the interpretation of dreams. In *Essential papers on dreams,* ed. Melvin Lansky, 3–31. New York: New York University Press.

Lee, B. (1986). Liberate yourself from classical karate. In *The legendary Bruce Lee,* eds. Jack Vaughn and Mike Lee, 62–29. Burbank: Ohara Publications.

Levenson, E. (1992). Harry Stack Sullivan: from interpersonal psychiatry to interpersonal psychoanalysis. *Contemporary Psychoanalysis, 28(3),* 450–66.

Phillips, A. (1993). *On kissing, tickling, and being bored: Psychoanalytic essays on the unexamined life.* Cambridge, MA: Harvard University Press.

———. (1994). *On flirtation: Psychoanalytic essays on the uncommitted life.* Cambridge, MA: Harvard University Press.

Rubin, J. B. (1996). *Psychotherapy and Buddhism: Toward an integration.* New York: Plenum Press.
———. (1998). *A psychoanalysis for our time: Exploring the blindness of the seeing I.* New York: New York University Press.
Winnicott, D.W. (1971). *Playing and reality.* London: Tavistock.

CHAPTER 8

Changing Clinical Orientation, Humor, and the Transitional Space

Peter L. Giovacchini

The relationship between therapist and patient has radically changed during the last several decades. Psychoanalysis was submerged in an aura of seriousness, and the interaction between student and mentor was often formal and stilted. Around forty years ago I noted, when attending professional meetings, that the atmosphere was funereal. Bearded psychoanalysts smoking huge cigars would make profound judgments with such solemnity that it appeared that the future of civilization was at stake. Arguments could become acrimonious, and heaven help the heretic who threatened the supremacy of Freud's pronouncements.

Regarding our mentors and training, a subgroup of eminent psychoanalysts lacked a sense of humor, which may have been reflected in a lack of imagination and forceful dogmatic assertions, usually punctuated with a foreign accent. Somehow, many of my generation mistook some of these peculiarities for greatness, which, in many instances, concealed a sadistic orientation.

The psychoanalytic community was, in essence, a cult; and the training program and hierarchy were ritualistic, competitive, and mysterious. Often it was also confusing.

One of my teachers had a reputation for being brilliant and intuitive, although he never presented or published a paper. He was known as a very serious person totally dedicated to his clinical work. He did not believe anyone should do anything outside of psychoanalysis, because that would mean that that person was ambivalent about being a practicing psychoanalyst. This even involved teaching.

I remember being interviewed when I was applying for matriculation at the Chicago Institute for Psychoanalysis by this seemingly dedicated but humorless analyst. He asked me to sit down, and for about a minute we sat in silence. My anxiety built up as I sat in the dark, depressing room with a small window. Finally, he spoke and asked me a question. He asked me to tell him my name. I thought this was strange, because he had my application blank in front of him, but then I conjectured that maybe he wanted to hear how I pronounced it, because it is often mispronounced. I poised myself for the next question, which came after another moment of silence. A minute under those circumstances seemed as if it were an eternity. He asked where I lived. I answered his question but, again, if he wanted to know the answer, all he had to do was look at my application on his desk. I did not know how to elaborate on his questions or free-associate to them. I reasoned that maybe he was building up to something, that this was part of some byzantine strategy. After several minutes, he stood up, shook my hand, and dismissed me.

My peers were, of course, anxious to hear about my interview. When I told them, they were puzzled but concluded that this analyst was subtle and shrewd and had made me submit to some type of stress interview. I agreed about the stress, but I could not, in any way, understand the purpose of this silent inquisition without the exchange of any relevant information.

I felt that I had absorbed some of the humorless, depressed atmosphere of that office and carried it with me for about two weeks. My spirits were lightened, however, when I received a letter announcing that I had been accepted for matriculation. I was still puzzled, not knowing what had happened, but I was willing to forget about the whole episode because the outcome was good.

About two years later, I had to face another administrative hurdle that once again required being interviewed. As the fates would have it, this analyst was once again assigned to interview me. I did not feel a great amount of trepidation, because at this advanced level of my training, no one, so far as I knew, had ever been rejected. I also expected that his being closer to being my colleague might make him more sociable and pleasant, and perhaps even talkative.

I was partially correct. He was a little more talkative in that he added a sentence to our discourse that he had not included in our first interview. Otherwise, the interview was an exact replica of the first. This time I was even more puzzled when he asked my name, since I had been at several parties that he had attended and had introduced him to my wife and, on one occasion, someone had introduced me to him. In this second interview, before dismissing me, he enigmatically said, "Psychoanalysis is a serious business." To this day, I do not know whether this was a rebuke. I certainly had not felt frivolous in his dour presence. Or perhaps he was sharing a bit of wisdom with me. In any case, as I had anticipated, I was again accepted.

I give these examples because I believe that psychoanalysts are particularly prone to the "emperor's new clothes" phenomenon, a situation in which one attributes significance and importance to some event or phrase when there is in fact nothing there. My interviewer made me feel as if I was a masochist and, in spite of his reputation, I could not see anything profound in his conundrum, "Psychoanalysis is a serious business." I could only perceive a humorless, depressed man who was substituting a misguided allegiance to psychoanalysis for living.

Many analysts have narcissistic problems that lead to unconscious but profound feelings of inadequacy. There may be accompanying problems in their capacity to understand and assimilate subtle and difficult theoretical issues. To compensate for their shortcomings and to bolster their narcissism, they construct theories in a ponderous, pedantic but serious fashion to cover up their lack of substance. I am not referring to any particular system, but I suggest that the reader pick up a prestigious psychoanalytic journal, open it at random, and pick out a sentence. Chances are that after the sentence is parsed and then put in simpler words, it will make no sense.

The older generation of analysts were different in that many of them wrote in a lucid, elegant style. Still many of their writings were restating or extending Freud's doctrines. As emphasized, they did not tolerate deviations and, for a while, this stifled the creation of new ideas or paradigms. In the United States we have lagged decades behind Great Britain in that we are just beginning to recognize the importance of Melanie Klein and D. W. Winnicott. The eastern establishment, in particular, has clung to the classical position.

As has been noted, many of these older generation psychoanalysts were depressed, and among them were an unusually large number of suicides. These were driven, humorless men. Many of them would have considered a light-hearted approach to psychoanalytic concepts blasphemous, and anything that deviated from Freud would be labeled as capricious and irresponsible.

It is interesting, however, that Freud, although he frequently demonstrated that he was depressed, especially in his letters to Fliess (Bonaparte, Freud, and Kris, 1954), nevertheless had a keen sense of humor. He enjoyed jokes and was capable of turning witty phrases. He gathered a depressed group of followers around him, and many did not have his sense of humor, as was true of my interviewer who had been in Freud's group as a young analyst.

HUMOR AND THE TRANSITIONAL SPACE

Without attempting a precise definition, humor can be viewed as a human attribute that involves a mode of perceiving, and an attitude and outlook about relations between the internal world of the psyche and the external milieu. It contains both primary and secondary process elements as does creativity (Giovacchini 1960, 1974, 1993), and it is related to creativity. Certainly wit, as Freud (1905) refers to it, is a creative accomplishment, and a good joke is recognized by its appreciative audience, a quality that Kris (1952) found to be indispensable for creative activity.

Play is associated with humor, humor always having a playful quality. Winnicott (1953) conceptualized a transitional space as an area in which play and illusion develops. I have conceptualized the creation of this transitional space as a developmental stage (Giovacchini 1996).

This transitional stage represents a watershed in which the child moves into the external world and simultaneously moves it into himself. Perceptions and judgments about inner and outer reality stem from inner stimuli, impulses, and needs rather than from external sources and impingements. According to Winnicott, this is the area of illusion and omnipotence as well as creativity.

When the child has progressed to this stage, he has made considerable progress on the road to establishing object relationships and the recognition of an external world separate from the self.

Winnicott believed that because of optimal mothering the child believes he is the source of his own nurture. The baby feels hungry and then is fed. *It is as if a need creates its own gratification* and there is no recognition of the mother as mother. Winnicott referred to this belief of self-sufficiency as omnipotence, but it is doubtful that infants could sustain such a complex phenomenon as omnipotence. Rather, they feel secure in that their needs will be met, and, at such a young age (around six months), there is not much of a concept about the source of nurture.

Because of maturational forces, infants begin to make more discrete and accurate discriminations between inside and outside. Finally, the illusion of being the source of their own nurture, most likely a *primal illusion*, gives way to the recognition of the mother as the fount of gratification. However, under optimal circumstances, the illusion is not shattered. Instead, the child plays with it. These children can relinquish it, but they can bring it back by playing with it. Instead of omnipotence, as Winnicott postulated, they develop the capacity to play and can maintain equilibrium and mastery through play, as well as the deliberate creation of gratifying fantasies.

Play later in life is an extension of the primal illusion of self-sufficiency and complete autonomy. Within the context of play these beliefs are maintained, but at the same time dependent feelings and vulnerability co-exist. It is the pretended denial of such feelings or their satirical or caricatured exaggeration that constitutes humor.

HUMOR AND CLINICAL PERSPECTIVES

The child, during the transitional phase, is simultaneously living in two worlds through the use of humor. Humor is the product that permits harmony between reality and illusion as it introduces a viewpoint that can make potentially grave situations appear not only nonthreatening but also amusing. I have often stated that *the task of psychoanalytic treatment is to convert grim reality into playful fantasy*, and this occurs in the transitional zone. Often this conversion is accompanied by humor, a by-product of this transformation. Putting this process in the form of a sequential progression, grim reality changes into playful fantasy, and this produces humor.

In structural terms, the act of entering or creating the transitional zone also generates humor, which, in a positive feedback fashion, contributes to detoxifying reality as it is replaced by playful fantasies. This introduces an observational perspective in which patient and analyst examine the patient-analyst relationship and if, on occasion, there is some lighthearted banter in their dialogues, it is in the interest of therapeutic resolution.

Humor is a developmental achievement and involved in the establishment of object relationships. It is both a mode of relating and an adaptive technique. Freud (1905) distinguished between wit and humor; the former being a type of manipulation in which hostile feelings are mitigated. It is concerned with feelings of vulnerability and their mastery and is the outcome of transitional relatedness.

The transitional space is a structural entity that represents a developmental achievement. It contracts and expands as it moves back and forth from the inner world of the psyche and external reality. The intermingling of fairly primitive interior psychic processes with secondary process perceptions and judgments of external reality occurs in the production of both humor and creativity. As the psyche focuses on primitive layers, this might be considered to be a regression, but this would be a regression in the service of the ego as Kris (1952) described some time ago. He was describing the operations of the ego during creative activity, but I believe something similar occurs with the production of humor, which, as stated, is similar to creativity.

At a clinical level, humorless patients are usually hard to work with and tedious. I find myself whenever possible giving them early morning sessions so I am still fresh and energetic and can look forward to the rest of the day, because they can be difficult to deal with and exhausting. In part, this is due to the fact that they are not particularly psychologically minded. Their thinking tends to be concrete and mechanistic and this makes it difficult to construct an observational platform on which the patient and therapist can stand. For the most part such patients are schizoid and narcissistically constricted. They have a paucity of object relationships, lack the capacity for symbolization, and are devoid of imagination.

Their prognoses often depend on their capacity to develop humor and to advance to a state of object relatedness that is compatible with the formation of humor. With some patients, even severely disturbed patients, there are occasional episodes when they, in spite of their misery and suffering, can poke fun at themselves or simultaneously view and evaluate a catastrophe in the external world as horrible but also as having a funny or ironic twist. Sometimes, this type of humor is black or Gothic.

Besides being a positive ingredient for the establishment of a therapeutic relationship, humor can also be a barometer that indicates the degree of ego-integration. As with other psychic processes, it can lead to developmental advances or it can regressively degrade as the outcome of psychic disintegration.

For example, a usually good-humored middle-aged salesman suffered a tragic loss when his wife was killed in an automobile collision while he was driving. He suffered considerable grief, but in a clumsy attempt to console himself he said, "It could have been worse; at least I had collision insurance." His therapist did not find this remark funny. In fact, he was offended by the crudeness of the statement, a failed attempt to make the best out of a bad situation.

It is interesting how the analytic attitude can dispel untoward reactions to a totally misfired humor. When this analyst told a colleague about this interchange, the colleague, who had some emotional distance from the situation, responded that he felt compassion for the patient. He sensed the underlying misery that the patient felt and which he was covering up with such a crass comment. What had the semblance of humor had misfired because the patient was overcome by his loss, something that he wanted to make light of. The pent-up hostility that was precipitated by the accident burst through to the surface; his attempt to contain it with a humorous twist failed. Some hostile narcissists might have found something funny in what was essentially sadistic, but the analyst's colleague's reaction was concerned with the patient's decompensation that was manifested in a weak defensive response that did not succeed in comforting him. The analyst's colleague was trying to explain the patient's misguided humor in psychodynamic terms.

Humor or lack of humor are characterological traits that, as mentioned, determine how people adapt to the external world as well as how, as patients, they will progress in a therapeutic context. There seems to be a direct correlation between the degree of psychopathology and the lack of humor. I believe this generalization, though there are notable exceptions, is more valid than the equation that states that the more severe the psychopathology, the less capacity to effectively function. Some very disturbed patients, from a characterological viewpoint, can be eminently successful, at least financially.

COUNTERTRANSFERENCE AND PLAYFUL ANALYTIC EXPLORATION

Therapists have discovered that the analysis of the countertransference has become as important as the analysis of the transference. The treatment process has become more of an active interaction than previously, emphasizing that therapy as well as emotional development has to take place within an object relation context.

No longer do clinicians adhere to the model of the neutral nonparticipating analyst who keeps himself emotionally isolated in a sterile field as Freud (1912) recommended. The interplay of the patient's and analyst's feelings and the interactions of their unconscious processes leads to insight and reenactments of infantile constellations as dictated by the repetition compulsion. This is a far cry from the adversarial unilateral relationship that characterized the psychoanalytic relationship years ago. The analyst is much more than a receiver who unscrambles the patient's messages.

Ogden (1994) believes that an analytic "third" is an important element in an analytic relationship. He defines the analytic third as "the experience of being simultaneously within and outside of the intersubjectivity of the analyst-analysand which I will refer to as 'the analytic third.' This third subjectivity, the intersubjective analytic third . . . is a product of a unique dialectic generated by/between the separate subjectivities of analyst and analysand within the analytic setting" (64). Ogden is emphasizing that an interaction creates meanings which become essential ingredients of the therapeutic process, but it would have been helpful if he had defined some of his terms such as subjectivity, intersubjectivity, and dialectic. This analytic third can also be examined in terms of Sterba's (1934) self-observing function.

I also believe these concepts can be discussed in terms of countertransference which, as I have repeatedly emphasized, has become a crucial element in any analytic interaction. Focusing on the transference-countertransference axis makes conceptualizations about the treatment process relatively simple and clinically relevant. This does not mean that all feelings between patient and therapist are exclusively based on transference and countertransference, but as every thought and feeling can be viewed in terms of a hierarchy between the unconscious and conscious, there is always some degree of transference and countertransference. It may not, however, be clinically useful.

Ogden (1994) would qualify these statements about countertransference as relating to everything the analyst thinks and feels because it "obscures the simultaneity of the dialect of oneness and twoness, of individual subjectivity, that is the foundation of the psychoanalytic relationship" (74). Again, it would be helpful if he defined his terms, but I believe that if psychic processes are viewed in terms of a hierarchy based on a balance of primary and secondary processes, it is more clinically useful to think in terms of transference-countertransference interactions than the philosophical concept of dialectic, which even in philosophy has different meanings. I believe Ogden may be somewhat in agreement about countertransference when he states, "Neither of these 'poles' of the dialectic exists in pure form and our task is to make increasingly full statements about the specific nature of the relationship between the experience of subject and object, between countertransference and transference at any given moment" (74).

As Freud (1910) discussed, countertransference can be a hindrance and disruptive of the treatment process especially when it is operating at an unconscious level. When understood, however, it can become a valuable ally in the quest for progress and therapeutic resolution. This happens through the understanding the therapist gains and perhaps the enactment and resolution of the repetition compulsion. This does not mean, however, that analysts must disclose everything they feel to their patients. As Ogden would state, there are different levels of intersubjectivity which would determine whether analysts should reveal their countertransference feelings to their patients or if they should keep such feelings to themselves in order not to burden them. Such determinations should be made after carefully exploring different levels of patient-analyst interactions.

I recall a professional man in his thirties who constantly berated me for practicing psychoanalysis when I should be following the tenets of Gestalt psychology. I felt somewhat annoyed because I was being constantly criticized, although I knew he had a need to put me down. However, I did not know exactly why.

During a session, the patient accused me of having been gruff and discourteous the previous session. I had no recollection of such behavior but I was curious as to what had happened, so with a spirit of inquiry we started exploring what might have happened the previous session. Through the patient's associations and the fantasies he provoked in me, I learned that he made me feel that I did not exist. I had been suffering from existential anxiety that I covered up with reactive anger. Then I remembered that I had become edgy and tart in my tone. The patient had succeeded in projecting a depreciated father imago onto me that had also become part of his self-representation.

His mother had treated her husband as if he did not exist because, being a social climber, she was ashamed of his coarse Eastern European accent and what she considered to be his peasant manners. Nevertheless, he was able to support her extravagant lifestyle and to pay his son's tuition for graduate school as well as for his analysis.

The son had internalized the mother's picture of his father and succeeded in projecting it onto me. I, in turn, reacted to his projections without being aware of what was happening. He was always depreciating me, as mentioned, but for the most part, I recognized that this was a transference phenomenon, and I was able to tolerate what he was openly verbalizing. During the session I have been discussing, he let me make what I thought was a significant interpretation and then went on with his associations as if I had said nothing. I was not aware of this interplay, but during the following session I had several childhood memories in which I believed I had made an exciting observation which was ignored, and then I was placed in a perilous situation.

During childhood I had not seen the connection between creative jubilance and the following peril. Later I was able to see, at least, a sequential link. As in childhood, with the patient I was also not able to see such a sequence, but I, nevertheless, reacted as evidenced by my anger, a reaction similar to that of the patient when he compensated for the internalization of the depreciated father by angrily attacking me.

The two of us were looking at the interreactions of the previous session as if we were on an observational platform discussing what was going on between us in a collaborative session. He acknowledged the shutting out of my interpretation and conjectured that I was having reverse oedipal feelings, the older man being threatened by the younger man's vigor. I admitted that was possible but that it did not feel right. Together, we were able to acknowledge that I felt something much deeper than oedipal rivalry; that I had, in fact, experienced an existential crisis.

I had no impulse to tell him about my childhood memories that would have been irrelevant to his treatment and not at all connected to his infantile environment. I would have been bringing parts of my personality into the treatment that would have been similar to introducing a foreign body into a setting in which it did not belong, and it would have had no therapeutic purpose. It would have been tantamount to dumping on the patient.

The patient and I worked together on a problem that commanded our attention. When we both climbed on the observational platform, his anger was mitigated and replaced by investigative curiosity. I was enthusiastic about our pursuit, and the atmosphere we created was now imbued with good feelings rather than anger, discomfort, and guilt. Our observational platform was located in a transitional space in which we could playfully explore complicated transference-countertransference reactions and I could objectively tease out of the data that was made available those elements that I believed would be therapeutically useful. From being subjectively involved, I could step backward and view what had transpired from an objective and perhaps neutral fashion. It had been necessary, in this instance, to relinquish neutrality in order to gain objectivity.

SUMMARY AND CONCLUSIONS

For years, I have stressed that treatment is not a unilateral process. Two persons are involved, and it is the fit between the two that determines whether the patient is treatable by that particular therapist, not the patient's psychopathology alone, as Freud frequently insisted.

On the other hand, I also believe that provided the therapist remains in an analytic frame of reference, at least in his thinking if not in his behavior, he will be able to understand various structural configurations and react eventually in a proper therapeutic fashion. He need not have a particular psychic configuration that may be more in resonance with the patient's needs. This means that no special skills or forms of psychopathology are required to work with severely disturbed patients and schizophrenics.

As always, this brings the clinician back to countertransference. In all therapeutic situations, countertransference is as inevitable as transference. The therapeutic task is to maintain a similar analytic attitude toward the countertransference as toward the transference, but there are, nevertheless, certain qualities analysts will find useful to make it easier to establish such an analytic viewpoint. I am referring to the ability to view feelings and events in terms of humorous tolerance, including idiosyncrasies and foibles that may be part of many therapists' personality makeup.

As long as such foibles are not too intense, they may lead to analytic progress, although they may temporarily upset the balance of the treatment process. When analysts display such attitudes, they are, undoubtedly, reacting to their own narcissistic needs and grandiosity. Rather than feeling guilty or defensively denying having such reactions, they should maintain a viewpoint of self-observation. This means that analysts are looking at countertransference feelings with benevolent tolerance in the same nonjudgmental fashion in which they view transference (see Searles 1959, 1961, 1986; Schulze and Kilgalen 1969). To condemn or to be rigid about the self is just as poor an analytic attitude as if they harbored similar feelings toward patients.

Being nonjudgmental toward the self also requires a sense of humor. Human foibles are neither objects of derision nor should they be subjected to superego condemnation or ego-ideal humiliation. Humor enables the analyst to look at himself as an object of interest which allows him not to take himself too seriously. As stated, this is also an optimal therapeutic perspective as it is directed toward the patient, although therapists take their patients seriously.

Still, analysts do not look at their patients as tragic victims who have been crushed beyond repair. Many patients may have been treated with inhuman cruelty leading to profound feelings of hopelessness and despair. Therapists can feel deeply about their patients' plight, but, to be effective clinicians, they must have hope, not to be overwhelmed by despair, and maintain cautious optimism. This is a serious but not grim attitude, and its purpose is eventually to construct a transitional space in which humor can play an increasingly significant role.

I conjecture that many analysts have narcissistic and grandiose configurations. What is important for therapeutic purposes is how the analyst reacts to such feelings—how he acknowledges them and otherwise responds. Narcissism and grandiosity are still, for the most part, considered in a pejorative fashion, although much has been written about healthy narcissism.

I imagine that Archimedes may have chuckled when he boasted that if given a spot to stand on he could move the world. Einstein and Bohr playfully related to each other in a competitive childish fashion as they constructed brilliant hypothetical experiments in which Einstein tried to undermine some of the fundamental principles of quantum mechanics. String theory, which deals with bubbles and sheets, is impossibly abstract, vastly grandiose in scope going way beyond the fourth dimension and, yet, it seems to be the result of a playful and quirky imagination. Feynman (1989a, 1989b) could be deadly serious as well as devastatingly playful, as he illustrated by safecracking and playing bongo drums (Gleich 1992).

Grandiose theories are formulated by grandiose persons. Sometimes, grandiosity goes astray and becomes offensive and disruptive, especially in a therapeutic setting. However, if it is kept in a humorous context, it is not necessarily an overcompensatory stance for damaged self-esteem, but simply a state of feeling good about the self; then, it can lead to creative accomplishments and analytic progress.

Humor and creativity are essential ingredients of the analytic interaction.

REFERENCES

Bonaparte, M., A. Freud, and E. Kris. (1954). *The origins of psycho-analysis: Letters to Wilhelm Fliess, drafts and notes.* New York: Basic Books.

Feynman, R. (1989a). *What do you care what other people think?* New York: Norton.

———. (1989b). *Surely you must be joking Mr. Feynman. Adventures of a curious character.* New York: Bantam.

Freud, S. (1905). Jokes and their relation to the unconscious. *Standard Edition*, vol. 8. London: Hogarth Press.

———. (1910). The future prospects of psycho-analytic therapy. *International Journal of Psychoanalysis, 11*, 139–153.

———. (1912). Recommendations to physicians practicing psycho-analysis. *Standard Edition*, vol. 12, 109–121.

Giovacchini, P. L. (1960). On scientific creativity. *Journal of the American Psychoanalytic Association, 8*, 407–426.

———. (1974). Characterological factors and the creative personality. *Journal of the American Psychoanalytic Association, 19*, 524–542.

———. (1993). The ego-ideal of a creative scientist. In *Treating character disorders.* Northvale, NJ: Jason Aronson.

———. (1996). *Schizophrenia and primitive mental states: Structural collapse and creativity.* Northvale, NJ: Jason Aronson.

Gleich, J. (1992). *Genius: The life and science of Richard Feynman.* New York: Vintage Books.

Kris, E. (1952). *Psychoanalytic explorations in art.* New York: Basic Books.

Ogden, T. (1994). *Subjects of analysis.* Northvale, NJ: Jason Aronson.

Schulze, R. and B. Kilgalen. (1969). *Case studies in schizophrenia.* New York: Basic Books.

Searles, H. F. (1959). The effort to drive the other person crazy. In *Collected papers on schizophrenia and related subjects*, 521–555. New York: International Universities Press.

———. (1961). Phases of patient-therapist interaction in the psychotherapy of chronic schizophrenics. In *Collected papers on schizophrenia and other subjects*, 521–559. New York: International Universities Press.

———. (1986). *My work with borderline patients.* Northvale, NJ: Jason Aronson.

Sterba, R. (1934). The fate of the ego in psycho-analytic therapy. *International Journal of Psychoanalysis, 15*, 117–126.

Winnicott, D. W. (1953). Transitional objects and transitional phenomena. In *Playing and reality*, 1–26. London: Tavistock.

Chapter 9

In Praise of Small Talk

Julie Joslyn Brown

> Psychotherapy has to do with two people playing together.
> —D. W. Winnicott

> You're not crazy if you can find one sane person who you can talk to.
> —Anne Sexton

As I sat in the waiting room with my Crazy Eddie's shopping bag I eagerly looked forward to the moment when my analyst would open the door, smile kindly, and ask, "Oh, you've bought some records?" Session after session he listened, with delight in his eyes, to my detailed recounting of what music had captivated me that particular day, which rare single I had tracked down, or how one particular genre or group related historically to another genre, group, or artist. This went on year after year without interpretation. Was I wasting my time and money? Was this psychoanalysis?

Apparently Helena Deutsch did not believe it was. In her account of psychoanalysis in 1930s Vienna, Esther Menaker (1989) describes her husband's traumatic analytic encounters:

> I'm sure Bill began his analysis bravely enough, but apparently he failed to produce the analytic "material" that was routinely expected by his therapist. Dr. Deutsch accused him of not "associating freely," of filling his sessions with Cafe Haus Gesprech (coffeehouse chatter), in other words, with trivia. As if it were a matter of his intentionally sabotaging the analysis, she was critical of his every attempt to produce what she wanted. Of course the situation deteriorated. (57)

Many analysts and analytic candidates feel anxious or guilty about engaging in small talk with patients and fear they are violating the basic tenets of psychoanalysis. I believe, however, that small talk is an essential aspect of the analytic process. It is pivotal in establishing a context of shared experience, a unique subjective world, created jointly by analyst and patient, within which the therapy lives. An example from my experience supervising analytic candidates demonstrates this dilemma. A candidate came into her supervision session worried about the treatment she was providing. She went on to describe her patient, a 75-year-old man who had been quite depressed for some time. He was barely living life and was surviving almost solely on cans of Ensure, a nutritional supplement drink. His diet seemed emblematic of his lack of joy and his emptiness—taste and texture were missing from his world. The candidate's "problem" was that this patient had begun to stop on his way to her office at Zabar's, a wonderful carnival of a store stocked with every food imaginable and filled with heady smells and delicious treats. All he wanted to do each session was talk about his most recent shopping trip with its bountiful array of sumptuous foods. In particular there was a very special and wonderful cheesecake that he loved. The candidate felt shame and guilt about letting this go on, feeling she was not in fact "doing analysis" and certainly was not earning her money. The analysis could only move forward when she came to realize how crucial it was for her to listen to his detailed accounts and experience along with him the joy of Zabar's. It was also important for her to share with him the tantalizing tastes and smells of the foods she loved as well. The special cheesecake ultimately replaced the cans of Ensure, the patient came alive, and his eyes began to twinkle anew.

As we saw in Helena Deutsch's disparaging accusations, it is a common misconception that small talk in sessions deflects the analytic process from the "real issues" or the "real material." On the contrary, small talk, like every other aspect of the analytic experience, may have a variety of meanings and functions at any given moment. It is not necessarily an expression of resistance, nor is it inferior, subordinate, or peripheral to what we come to view as analytic material. In fact, at times small talk may be at the heart of the treatment and may open a window to the essence of our patients. It is how we best come to experience their world. It serves to establish what I like to think of as the "themes of our lives." In his discussion of authenticity and the use of humor, Bader (1995) speaks of a "naturally occurring private language that usually comes to exist within an analytic couple" (293). Small talk is often an expression of this private language.

We can turn to music theory for a particularly illustrative metaphor. The pedal tone that we hear in a Bach chorale or in nineteenth-century instrumental music is a sustained or reiterated chord or tone over which the chord changes take place. It effectively sets off the melodic material evolving above it but does not necessarily always belong to the chordal material. It usually begins and ends as a consonant chord member but then deviates from this tonality (Jones 1974). Despite this dissonance, the pedal tone serves as a kind of reference point to which we return over and over as it enriches the melodic movement of the piece.

So, too, does small talk effectively function in our work: it is not necessarily a part of the material or so-called meat of the analysis but serves as a thematic home base to which we can return over and over. Whether it is talk of how the Knicks are doing, new recipes, films or concerts we've seen, or the latest episode of a favorite TV show, one can find with each patient a place where our real life experiences and interests converge, creating a pedal tone to which we can safely return.

While the recognition of the importance of the intersubjective context in the analytic situation (Atwood and Stolorow 1984) has gained wider acceptance within psychoanalytic circles, the relevance of the role of small talk in establishing such a context remains underappreciated. Its therapeutic validity has found much greater acceptance in the fields of social work, social psychology, and particularly in the work with adolescents and juvenile offenders. In Beinstein's (1975) study, "Small Talk as Social Gesture," she examined conversations held by barbers, beauticians, and pharmacists in local public places throughout Philadelphia and discovered that more diverse and less cohesive communities relied on small talk to a greater extent than more homogeneous communities. Small talk was used to control disagreements, prevent potential conflicts, and to bridge existing socioeconomic and racial gaps. It also served to "protect personal space" and to facilitate "confident entrance into novel encounters" (147). In other words, small talk was used to create a safe environment within which various relationships could subsequently develop.

In his work with juvenile offenders, Whiskin (1975) recognizes how critical small talk can be in establishing contact with extremely disconnected adolescents. He describes how he spent many hours talking about transoceanic radios, 10-speed racing bikes, TV shows, or the latest dance craze. He also addresses the problem of the analyst's need for analytic material:

> Yes, we all want to get to the "pay-dirt," the "material" or whatever one wants to call the significant verbal productions of the patient, but, particularly with the frightened, very much threatened juvenile, we must bide our time and talk about the "trivia," which really are not trivial since they are the only bridge to a relationship which, once established, can later be brought out (35).

Schmideberg (1976), who also worked extensively with this same population, feels it is essential for the therapist to spontaneously allow his or her real personality into the therapeutic relationship and to create a shared normalized reality. Much of this is established through small talk:

> So often the art of therapy, especially in the beginning, consists in navigating between the devil of triteness and the deep blue sea of touching on "loaded topics" too early or too clumsily. It matters when, in what context and how a question is put or an issue

broached. Even ten minutes small talk that puts the patient at ease and enables him to gain an impression of the personality of the therapist, may allow the latter to bring up matters safely, the mention of which a few moments earlier would have been disastrous. Talking for the sake of talking, even for a number of sessions need not be a waste of time, if it helps rapport (11).

What appears "trivia" to the pathology-oriented psychiatrist may be an important normal interest to a teenager. A patient listens not only to what is being said, but still more to the voicc and manner. "Chit-chat" gives both partners in therapy time to assess each other . . . But even after a fairly friendly relationship has been established, and "loaded topics" been touched upon, I find it important to return again and again to ordinary things and discuss everyday reality (12).

It seems obvious in working with this hard-to-reach population that creating a context of shared subjectivity is essential. Though it may be subtler, I believe the same task, the same struggle to find common ground, is crucial to the success of our psychoanalytic work as well.

For one patient, an idle comment about scones at the beginning of a session opened a world of shared experience that came to have a great deal of meaning. As we both mourned the disappearance from the neighborhood of our favorite scones, we came to realize that not only did we both know each and every shop and what types of scones they stocked, but we also discovered that we loved the same kind. We both had searched frantically for our beloved scones after their sudden disappearance from one of the nearby cafes. We rejoiced together when they subsequently reappeared at yet another neighborhood market. Throughout the treatment, scones functioned as a kind of pedal tone to which we could always return. The patient described it as "absolutely emblematic of our work together—there is a snapshot in the scone!" The joy and ebullience in the discovery of a shared reality is unparalleled. The certainty that one's experience is truly understood forms the scaffolding upon which the analysis is built.

Interestingly, our shared experience of scones was simultaneously created and discovered by my patient and myself, just as Winnicott's (1971) baby both creates and discovers the transitional object. Small talk resides in the potential space between therapist and patient and it embodies the most vital aspects of play at its best. Small talk as a transitional phenomenon evolves from both the patient's and the analyst's subjective worlds to create something new that then exists and thrives both outside, inside, and in between patient and analyst. It is not quite our inner world, not quite our external reality. It takes on a life of its own. Winnicott (1971) describes this beautifully:

And on the basis of playing is built the whole of man's experiential existence. . . . We experience life in the area of transitional phenomena, in the exciting interweave of subjectivity and objective observation, and in an area that is intermediate between the inner reality of the individual and the shared reality of the world that is external to individuals. (64)

Pizer (1996) builds on Winnicott's elegant and groundbreaking theories in his discussion of the necessity of play and the preservation of potential space in the psychoanalytic setting: "Indeed the establishment, enlargement, and playful negotiation of potential space lies at the heart of therapeutic action in any analysis"(693).

Analytic play, in its range from hilarity to high seriousness, entails an intersubjective exchange of "squiggles" that mark, or re-mark on, the personal world of the patient and the shared world of analytic space (692).

Transformations born out of the experience of analytic play often go—and in fact should remain—uninterpreted. Interpretation has the power to seriously violate the potential space between analyst and patient and may be experienced by the patient at these moments as extremely destructive. The experience of a shared reality created by small talk and analytic play must be allowed to live in an arena that exists in actuality or in real life as analyst and patient create anew their shared subjective world. This new world has its own veracity—its own reality. Winnicott (1971), in his discussion of transitional phenomena, recognizes how critical this "realness" is to the creation of transitional objects when he states, ". . . the object, if it is to be used, must necessarily be real in the sense of being part of shared reality, not a bundle of projections" (88). To reiterate: The shared reality created by small talk in analysis must remain just that—a real thing between patient and analyst. Like Winnicott's transitional object, if it is interpreted or analyzed as a "bundle of projections" or even more generally as "symbolic," it is in effect destroyed. Anyone who has had this experience can probably recognize the feeling—it is palpable and dramatic. Like the sudden deflation of a soaring balloon, the vitality and joy in the session seems suddenly to evaporate, and the patient is left flattened.

Lachmann and Beebe (1995) present an instructive case. In their discussion of a patient who for two years spent her analytic sessions discussing the intricacies of soap operas, they make the point that this endless discussion of soap operas was not a resistance but, instead, a crucial opportunity in the treatment. In this case it was an opportunity to reverse a "representational configuration derived from a repetitive experience in her family and with her father" (379). Whereas she had been silenced by her awe of her truly idealizable father, she found her voice in her analysis as her therapist listened to these details with amazement and joy. This is small talk at work at its most effective. Had the analyst analyzed these soap opera tales as a form of resistance or in any way attempted to steer the patient toward "important material," she would have been retraumatized and the treatment imperiled. Even if she survived the assault, I believe the heart of the treatment would have been sacrificed. Indeed, Lachman and Beebe discuss how the analyst was in fact challenged by his colleagues who questioned his enjoyment of his patient's stories and suggested this was a denial of his aggression toward the patient. He was obviously negligent in his refusal to analyze the resistance! It is clear from this vignette that interpretation in this case would have destroyed a rare opportunity for this patient to reexperience herself in a new way.

When the analyst engages in small talk, the question of the analyst's authenticity naturally arises. Starting with Greenson's (1967) concept of the real relationship and culminating in recent discussion of authenticity, analytic choice, anonymity, and self-revelation, analysts have engaged in heated debate about where to draw the line and how to understand the inclusion of the analyst's subjectivity in the analytic situation (Aron 1997; Atwood and Stolorow 1984; Bader 1995; Crastnopol 1997; Frank 1997; Gerson 1996a, 1996b).

Aron (1997) and Crastnopol (1997) both address the essentially paradoxical nature in the patient-analyst relationship: We are always simultaneously known and unknown, revealing and concealing aspects of ourselves and our subjectivity. Frank (1997) takes a strong stand in favor of the analyst's authenticity as opposed to analytic anonymity and believes an "attitude of willingness to be known by the patient" (309) is essential. Bader (1995), on the other hand, defines the analyst's authenticity as his or her genuine interest in enhancing the healing process of the analysis, whatever that might be (including at times a stance favoring anonymity). He does not imply any attitude toward the analyst's degree of spontaneity or self-revelation. In other words, authenticity relates solely to the genuine efforts on the part of the analyst and patient in their joint project of the analysis.

Frank (1997) makes another point that directly pertains to concerns about the potentially self-revealing nature as well as the relevance of small talk. His view (with which I certainly agree) is that all aspects of the analyst and the analytic climate have meaning and communicate some degree of self-revelation. Doesn't the silent classical analyst communicate as much about him- or herself vis-à-vis his analytic stance as the analyst who chats with a patient about a favorite book or film? Crastnopol (1997) puts it succinctly: "In short, nothing is 'off the record' in a psychoanalytically informed treatment—there are only parts of the record whose contents aren't read aloud" (335). In other words, when considering the analytic nature of small talk we can conclude that small talk is no different from any other communication. We can reassure those who fear that small talk is outside the bounds of the analysis proper, that everything within the analytic scene has meaning and is part of the analysis. Small talk is as much an expression of our subjectivity as anything else that occurs within the analysis. It is neither more nor less self-revealing than any other communication or gesture.

In discussing the importance of small talk one may easily get the erroneous impression that "anything goes" and that small talk embodies some sort of ideal of authenticity. Believing in the important role that small talk plays in psychoanalysis does not give us the license to blather on in sessions without a clear understanding of what is going on. Nor does it guarantee authenticity or rapport. As with all aspects of our analytic work, it is our utmost responsibility to be as aware as possible of the meaning, moment to moment, of each and every nuance within the analytic arena.

Inevitably, the concept of neutrality must be addressed in our discussion of small talk. Engaging in small talk with patients may seem to violate conventional notions of neutrality. However, due to a new appreciation of the critical importance of the analyst's subjectivity in the analytic process, many analysts would agree that a reconception of such concepts as self-disclosure and neutrality is needed. Gerson (1996a, 1996b) postulates a new definition of neutrality that is particularly relevant to our discussion of small talk. He describes a process by which "neutral moments" are created within the analysis:

> Yet, in each moment of neutrality a degree of mutual recognition and trust is established and becomes an available haven, one that may be found again in the midst of a repetitive engagement in a transference-countertransference scenario. The analysis proceeds through the gradual and arduous accumulation of such neutral moments, and the safety they contain, into an ever-widening arena of clarity and potential space for both patient and analyst. (Gerson 1996a, 631)

One might go so far as to say that through small talk we are actually not relinquishing our neutrality but, rather, may be creating these neutral zones within which the analysis evolves.

Turning now to a case in which small talk played a pivotal role throughout more than ten years of treatment allows us to appreciate the complex meaning and function of small talk within the psychoanalytic experience. Patrick, a man in his thirties, spent a portion of every session speaking of cooking, comics, films, and sports. Of particular importance were his love of boxing and his lifelong involvement with Superman. Patrick was a true intellectual and was in the process of completing a Ph.D. degree. He also had a great love of comic books that continued into his adult life. A central theme in the treatment was his shame and humiliation and his ongoing attempt to "pass" in social and intellectual circles. A "working class kid" from Brooklyn, he operated successfully in the esoteric world of academia and abstract ideas but nevertheless always felt he was falling short—"a loser." His shame and reluctance in speaking with me, particularly because I was a female analyst, about his love of Superman was apparent. But when I reacted with enthusiasm, interest, and knowledge about the subject, he felt able to go into greater detail. In fact, Superman served as a "pedal tone" throughout the treatment and provided a rich image that we could count on to understand his inner experience. Various dimensions of Superman—the "Fortress of Solitude," his DC Comics death in 1993, his powers and vulnerabilities—served us well in the analysis.

Another topic that came up repeatedly was boxing, which I coincidentally became even more interested in during the course of his treatment. Boxing was something special Patrick shared with his father. They would watch the fights together and Patrick derived a strong sense of maleness in this connection with him. A powerful and idealizable figure, his father was also shaming and humiliating, calling his son a "sissy" for crying on his first day of school. In general he was unable to tolerate any degree of emotionality or sensitivity on the part of my patient as a young boy. In our sessions Patrick and I would discuss the latest Mike Tyson fight, and I occasionally lent him videos of Tyson or old footage of Muhammad Ali. He experienced himself as vital and alive in connection with me and my obvious delight in discussing these events. In this context I was able to join him in the macho world of boxing and be a "guy" with him, while also appreciating the depth of his emotional life. I was neither shaming nor humiliating. In addition to the fear of humiliation, the other major dread in the transference was that I might be weak, clingy, and needy like his mother. Enjoying boxing with Patrick reassured him that even though I was a woman like his mother, I was strong, powerful, and aggressive.

Cooking and food were other favorite topics, and he eagerly shared the details of the newest recipes he had created as well as the most recent microbrewery, restaurant, cooking utensil, or special ingredient he had discovered. When he described the meals he had cooked, I could almost taste them! We also discussed films we recently had seen and videos we had rented the previous weekend and made recommendations to each other.

Perhaps the most pivotal interaction and example of the power of small talk took place very early in the treatment. On this particular day, Patrick entered my office describing how he had taken the bus past the pornographic movie houses on Forty-second Street. He recounted with great amusement some of the outrageous and hilarious titles of the XXX-rated films. I responded spontaneously and playfully with "My favorite one is 'Yank My Doodle, It's a Dandy!'" Years later he revealed that this was a critical moment in the treatment: It proved to him that I was the "right therapist for him." This experience enabled him to truly trust me and to know that I could see and appreciate all aspects of who he was—that I would not be moralistic and squeamish and that, most importantly, I had a good sense of humor and I could play.

What is so illustrative about the function of small talk in this case is how many dimensions of the analysis it touches. Small talk helped us establish a world of shared experience and subjectivity—a context for our life together. In addition, my patient's rich, almost visceral, description of food, films, comics, and boxing gave me a greater understanding of who he was. It conveyed with detailed texture and imagery an experience of his inner world. Another important dimension was his inclusion in the analysis of various recurring symbolic figures: Superman, Mike Tyson, and Muhammad Ali. They were variously idealizable heroes as well as fallen angels. Play, as described by Winnicott (1971) and Pizer (1996), was crucial as we talked about boxing and playfully joked about the XXX-rated film titles. Lastly, small talk allowed various aspects of the transference to emerge at different times. My patient could merge with me as his powerful, idealizable, very male father without the accompanying shame and humiliation. He could face the dread in the transference of this humiliation as well as my potential to fail him like his weak, clingy mother. Mirroring aspects of the transference were in the foreground as I listened with delight to his descriptions of his newest culinary creations and innovative recipes. Twinship was affirmed as we critiqued films, excitedly discussed the Tyson fight round by round, or reveled in Ali's greatness and grace.

Through the vehicle of small talk my patient was able to reexperience himself in a new and multidimensional way in my presence, thus allowing for the building of a new self structure. He was both sissy and jock, street kid and brainy intellectual, playful adolescent and responsible adult, strong sexy man and needy child.

The transference opportunities provided by small talk are evident as well in Lachmann and Beebe's (1995) previously discussed case of the woman who spoke about soap operas for two years of her analysis. Mitchell (1993) also describes a case where a patient's "environmental monologues" (his ongoing discussion of the environment, pollution, the authorities' greed and lack of concern for protecting future generations, etc.) fit so perfectly with the therapist's beliefs and concerns that it clearly established a shared subjectivity. In addition, the therapist's delight in and rapt attention to the monologues served an important transference function. While Mitchell poses many explanations for why this worked for the patient and the analysis, he concludes, "I would give considerable weight to the way in which the fit between us enabled me to stay with him and enjoy him while he was not doing what he was 'supposed' to be doing" (189).

Another function of small talk not previously addressed is its potential for preserving the organization of one's subjective world. Interestingly, my patient Patrick literally described it as such. He said that if he didn't talk about all these (small talk) things "I wouldn't be able to organize myself. If I just allow myself to talk about all these things I begin to feel a sense of order. It's like a skeleton or coat rack that I can hang everything on." Atwood and Stolorow (1984) speak of objects and enactments as having the power to organize one's subjective world in much the same way: "The basic psychological process that mediates the relationship between experience and action is concretization—the encapsulation of structures of subjectivity by concrete, sensorimotor symbols. . . . [T]he use of concrete symbolization serves to crystallize and preserve the organization of the subjective world" (116).

Until now we have mostly been discussing ways in which small talk enhances and is a manifestation of intersubjective conjunction (Atwood and Stolorow 1984). Disjunction is always a risk, however, and we may inadvertently cause a derailment in the transference. An innocent comment about the weather, with the assumption that our patient agrees with us, can be disastrous. A comment with implicit displeasure such as, "Oh my god, isn't it cold out!" can be countered by our patient's "I love the cold weather! I grew up in Vermont." Suddenly, thinking we have reached out to establish a shared experience, we have instead "blown it." At times this may be extremely elusive and subtle in nature. With small talk, as with all other aspects of our analytic work, we cannot make any assumptions about our patient's experience nor impose on them our own subjectivity. A patient for whom any reference to oneself replays the dreaded narcissistic parent will be retraumatized and the treatment may be threatened if we insist on engaging in small talk. We may feel we are reaching out to establish common ground when all the while we are actually enacting a deadly transference-countertransference scenario. Indeed, I once had a patient for whom this was so extreme that she literally forbade me to use the pronoun "I." She even panicked when I would with reassurance say, "I know how you feel." Obviously, engaging in small talk was out of the question at this point in the treatment. Particular caution needs to be taken with patients when there is an archaic mirror transference—any reference to oneself, no matter how minor, can be seriously disruptive.

Perhaps the most poignant aspect of the function of small talk in psychoanalysis is twinship and the experience of essential alikeness. Through small talk we derive what Kohut (1984) describes as the young child's "vague but intense and pervasive sense of security as he feels himself to be human among humans" (200). Related to this feeling of being "human among humans" is the importance of experiencing oneself as healthy—as normal. Matefy (1972) describes how small talk was utilized to "normalize" a hospitalized schizophrenic patient. After five years of psychoanalytic therapy with this patient, the hospital staff implemented a behaviorist approach along with continued psychotherapy in an attempt to diminish the patient's continuing psychotic behavior, which included choking herself and urinating on the floor. More importantly, the plan involved the rewarding of "non sick" behavior, thus helping the patient and those in her environment to experience her as other than "sick." In addition to not responding to psychotic behavior, an early component of this program involved providing her with one half hour a day of small talk during which time no reference to the patient's sickness would be made. The creation through the use of small talk of a "normal" space within which one can reexperience the self can be as crucial to the psychoanalytic patient as it is to the wildly psychotic one.

Similarly, Schmideberg (1976) and Whiskin (1975) discuss their work with juvenile offenders. Schmideberg (1976) describes a case of a boy who attempted to kill his father; despite the fact that he "must have many strange thoughts that rightly worry him," she understands the "need for him to find normalcy." To reassure himself about his rationality he clings to the interests that he has in common with other boys, and he can make contact only with a therapist who is ready to appreciate this side of him (12). "[T]here is more to a person than his problems or offenses. By discussing matters of 'normal' interest we take note of the patient's positive personality and allow him to display his knowledge and judgment"(11). Whiskin (1975) describes a poignant example of a teenage girl who had been totally unrelated and uncommunicative, who had never been able to even say goodbye upon leaving the therapy session. A turning point came during a session when she began to talk about all the latest teenage dances. She talked animatedly about the "Watusi" to her attentive and interested therapist. As a direct result of this session of small talk "the patient realizes that she is not so bad that she can't 'be.' And when this happens, she in turn, can acknowledge that the therapist also 'is' (exists) making it possible for her to say her first goodbye" (34).

Small talk reassures us that we "are"—that we exist in a real world with other real people sharing real things. The shared experience we establish within our analytic life together allows us to know that we are, in fact, "human among humans." We are not so alone when we find another who speaks our language. As the poet Anne Sexton once wrote to a young woman who would one day be sitting in her analyst's office with a Crazy Eddie's shopping bag:

> I thought of wiring you three daffodils but I write you on yellow-sun paper instead. The sun will come back, I promise. . . . I really did think of sending you those flowers . . . Could you find any? I think if you would try to look at one—not even three to begin with—just one, it might help. I have a feeling I could hand you one and you'd look at it. . . . I used to say to my doctor "You're not crazy if you can find one sane person who you can talk to." (Personal communication, June 1968)

REFERENCES

Aron, L. (1997). Self-disclosure and the interactive matrix. *Psychoanalytic Dialogues* 7: 314–318.

Atwood, G., and R. Stolorow (1984). *Structures of subjectivity.* Hillsdale, NJ: The Analytic Press.

Bader, M. J. (1995). Authenticity and the psychology of choice in the analyst. *Psychoanalytic Quarterly* 64: 282–305.

Beinstein, J. (1975). Small talk as social gesture. *Journal of Communication* 25, no. 4: 147–154.

Crastnopol, M. (1997). Anonymity, desire, and authenticity in the analytic relationship. *Psychoanalytic Dialogues* 7: 327–335.

Frank, K. A. (1997). The role of the analyst's inadvertent self-revelations. *Psychoanalytic Dialogues* 7: 281–314.

Gerson, S. (1996a). Neutrality, resistance, and self-disclosure in an intersubjective psychoanalysis. *Psychoanalytic Dialogues* 6: 623–645.

Gerson, S. (1996b). Is self-disclosure a personal proclivity or a principal of technique? Reply to commentary. *Psychoanalytic Dialogues* 6: 671–674.

Greenson, R. R. (1967). *The technique and practice of psychoanalysis, Vol. 1.* New York: International Universities Press.

Jones, G. T. (1974). *Music theory.* New York: Harper Collins.
Kohut, H. (1984). *How does analysis cure?* Chicago: University of Chicago Press.
Lachmann, F. M., and B. Beebe (1995). Self psychology: Today. *Psychoanalytic Dialogues* 5: 375–384.
Matefy, R. E. (1972). Operant conditioning procedure to modify schizophrenic behavior: A case report. *Psychotherapy: Theory, research and practice* 9, no. 3: 226–230.
Menaker, E. (1989). *Appointment in Vienna.* New York: St. Martin's Press.
Mitchell, S. A. (1993). *Hope and dread in psychoanalysis.* New York: Basic Books.
Pizer, S. A. (1996). Negotiating potential space: Illusion, play, metaphor, and the subjunctive. *Psychoanalytic Dialogues* 6: 689–712.
Schmideberg, M. (1976). Relationship therapy: Making contact. *International Journal of Offender Therapy and Comparative Criminology* 20, no. 1: 9–17.
Whiskin, F. E. (1975). Juvenile offender therapy: Clinical vignettes. *International Journal of Offender Therapy and Comparative Criminology* 19, no. 1: 33–41.
Winnicott, D. W. (1971). *Playing and reality.* New York: Basic Books.

Chapter 10

Imagining Ithaca: The Impact of the Analyst's Worldview

Spyros D. Orfanos

> And if the soul is to know itself it must look into a soul.
>
> —Socrates

In our postclassical psychoanalytic culture we have come to understand that all of the great conceptual contributions to psychoanalysis have a very personal origin in the life experiences of the contributors. In their 1983 landmark book, *Object Relations in Psychoanalytic Theory*, Greenberg and Mitchell claimed that only by an analysis of an analyst's vision of human experience can his theoretical position be accurately assessed. I believe that if they were writing their book today they might also add that only by an analysis of the analyst's vision of human experience could his or her *clinical* position be accurately assessed. For purposes of this paper, I equate vision of human experience with worldview—what in German is called *Weltanschauung*. Freud held that any worldview, any *Weltanschauung*, is subject to secondary revision by defensive processes. Of course, the genius of Freud is that this stance also helps us question Freud's contributions.

Although we believe in the critical importance of the analyst's personality, most clinical case examples tend to appropriately focus on the analysand's background and context, but very, very little on the analyst's. Clearly, the problems with presenting life history material about the analyst are complex: self-disclosure, charges of narcissism, hubris, and so forth. But, if the patient and the analyst are both simultaneously subject and object (Aron 1991), and if we believe that the transference-countertransference matrix has no delineated start, then how can we justify just providing information on the background of the patient and not that of the therapist? I do not have much of an answer to this other than to try an experiment in this chapter. (This experimental attitude was given much support and encouragement by my first psychoanalytic supervisor, Esther Menaker.)

There are three main parts to this chapter. The first part will focus on a facet of my clinical work with a patient I call Tom. A clinical case is composed of a myriad of important facets and dimensions, but one cannot usually write about all such dimensions in a single chapter—or book for that matter. I will attempt to demonstrate one facet of my interaction with Tom in the hope that this will begin to illustrate my point. The second part of this chapter will engage in self-disclosure on my part regarding my personal background, worldview, and choice of psychoanalytic theory. My reason for this will become self-evident. Third, I return to the clinical material that Tom and I continued creating. I do not intend anything I say as prescriptive, that is, I do not believe any other clinician should necessarily follow my lead and methods. Further, what I write may seem linear, but it lived more like nonlinear phenomena. Life is not so well ordered.

A word about the term *worldview.* It is a difficult one to define. It could entail anything from the personal to the philosophical. By personal, it could mean whether you see the world and the people that populate it as good or bad—whether this is a safe or unsafe world to live in. The philosophical entails a view of the human condition in a Judeo-Christian, scientific, existential, or other mode.

I tend to think of worldview as multidimensional, including the personal and the philosophical, the emotional and the cognitive, the individual and the social. However, I cannot write about all these things at the same time. In this chapter, I wish to deal with one aspect of worldview: the stance I hold concerning the tragic. I use the words tragic and tragedy in their more modern versions to mean an unhappy or fatal event or series of events in real life; a dreadful calamity or disaster.

A MUTUAL CONSTRUCTION

> Creativity lies equally at the root of artistic production and of life experience.
>
> —Otto Rank

Tom was referred to me in 1991 by one of my former patients, a woman he works with. He arrives for the initial consultation and enters my office carrying a large shopping bag from an upscale store. He tells me that he only works with gay professionals but is consulting with me because of his colleague's trust in me. Tom is 27 years old and an immigrant from northwest Canada on a student visa. Despite the student visa, he works as a department store window dresser. He is a handsome, tall, and blond man with the stereotypic hand and voice gestures that communicate he is gay. I was struck by how "other" he felt to me—his ethnicity, his sexuality, and his muted emotional language.

The presenting problem is that he is breaking up with his boyfriend, Seth, after a two-year relationship. The boyfriend is 15 years his senior. According to Tom, Seth is a hip and highly experienced New York City gay man. Tom is devastated over the breakup. He feels lonely, betrayed, and exhausted. He volunteers that in the shopping bag he is carrying a gift for his ex-boyfriend's birthday. "I don't know why I'm doing this. I'm so confused," he exclaims.

We discuss his expectations of psychotherapy, a process he has never experienced before, and while I indicate that I would like to work with him, I also state that perhaps he might also consult with other therapists so that he can feel he's made a choice. He does not want to consult with a woman but agrees to have an initial session with another therapist, a gay man. The therapist I referred him to, a highly experienced, senior clinician, telephones me after their consultation to thank me. We briefly discuss a few clinical matters pertaining to Tom, and at the end of the conversation he jokingly adds, "I'll never forgive you if he decides to work with you because you're more handsome then me."

Having decided on which therapist he would like to work with, Tom sets up an appointment with me. He tells me he does not know why he chose to work with me. He liked the other therapist, felt comfortable with him, and felt that he was insightful, but decided to go on his gut feeling and work with me. We begin on a once-a-week psychotherapy. Over the year, I learn that Tom grew up in a provincial small city in a very cold and dark part of northern Canada. His family consisted of his parents and two older sisters. His father was an insurance executive who once represented Canada in the Olympics. His mother was a homemaker who always longed to be a fashion designer. At the time, my assessment of the mother's personality was that she was a cross between Blanche Dubois and Sharon Stone. My assessment of the father's personality was that he was a potted plant. The oldest sister was very athletic. She interacted little with Tom. The second sister was extremely maternal and doted on Tom. He was often her doll.

Tom grew up very interested in art and encouraged by his mother to develop his talents—although she related to him and his talents in a dominating and narcissistic way. The family emotional climate was cold. Tom had a dog named Wilson. He told of often huddling in a closet with Wilson when his mother was angry with him. He and Wilson would stay in the closet for what seemed like hours. When Tom was about 12 years old, Wilson became very sick. There were many visits to the vet. One day, his dad carried a very sick Wilson to the car to go to the vet. He returned without Wilson and not a single word was said by anyone about Wilson being put to death. This was Tom's first major experience with loss. He told this story with little affect. I remember shedding a few tears when he shared this experience with me. He looked perplexed at my response.

Two years into treatment and after the resolution of his feelings over Seth, we move to twice-a-week therapy, and by the third year three-times-a-week therapy (1994–1996). In recent years, we alternated twice-a-week and once-a-week due to scheduling issues, and last year we completed our work together. The reason for the increased therapy despite the resolution of the initial presenting problem was Tom's interest in a deeper understanding of his feelings of being "stuck" at work and his relationship to his family. More importantly—and at the beginning of this phase of the treatment this went unsaid—Tom's circle of close gay friends was beginning to feel the effects of AIDS. His friendships were a great source of love and security and support for Tom. In my view, the friendships Tom made in New York City were rare for their depth and affirmation. The losses were devastating.

The impact of AIDS on Tom's life becomes a major focus. Tom is safe and HIV negative, but his best friends are dying. At one point, he drew up a list, and after the number reached 23, he stopped counting. Mourning and bereavement became the true focus of the therapy. He was a repeat survivor. The clinical work with Tom, the AIDS survivor, was especially difficult because the trauma was ongoing. We could not set aside the past and make a new beginning. He had devastating survivor guilt. It was during this period that I learned that the gay therapist I had originally referred Tom to had died of illness related to AIDS. I wondered if Tom chose to enter treatment with me because of an unconscious sense that I was more likely to stay alive.

For close to two years Tom cries a river, and I am often moved and cry with him. I become his witness and attempt to help him address the anxiety-laden future. Death anxiety is omnipresent. He has difficulty having sex, because it reminds him of death. He develops irritable bowel syndrome. Despite early promise, his career as a window dresser is going nowhere. His experience of nasty office politics and the peccadillos of the department store industry leave him feeling empty. We are working at the edge of some final boundary. Tom thinks about committing suicide. I get extremely anxious when he makes preliminary plans. He gets through this but there are still no exits.

When Tom immigrated to New York City at the age of 25, he believed that he would "find himself." By this, he meant that he would make the shift from being in unsatisfying intimate relationships with women to satisfying intimate relationships with men. He wanted meaningful love. Now he was dealing with death. Tom often lamented how unfair all this was. How could this be? What kind of destiny was this? How terribly unfair his destiny: to be a closet homosexual for 25 years and then, when he came out, to suffer the agony of such losses.

During one particular session, as he is talking about the recent death of a friend from illness due to AIDS (we both know the routine—anguish, crying, memories, the odors of rotting flesh), my mind wanders off. It wanders to a Greek poet named Odysseus Elytis, also known as the poet of light and the Aegean. Elytis, who won the Nobel Prize in literature in 1979, witnessed the death of countless men during the Albanian campaign at the time of World War II. Specifically, I thought of his observation that, "During the years of Buchenwald and Auschwitz, Matisse painted the most juicy and unripe, the most charming flowers or fruits which were ever made. . . ." I stayed with this thought and these words in my head, and the feelings they evoked, as if there were something comforting and reassuring about them.

"What are you thinking?" Tom asked.

"I was thinking about a remark by a poet. It is in Greek, but the idea behind the words is, I guess . . . Let me consider this for a moment . . . My thoughts went to, I believe the need to go beyond events, horrible events and to counterbalance them. That's what I was thinking."

After a long pause, Tom said, "I don't know if I understand that."

"I recognize the idea. I have to consider this," I responded and after a short while added, "Do you have any thoughts about why I came up with this now?"

"Well, maybe the obvious. The need for balance. But that would be too simple," he responded.

"Simple is not always so bad. Say more about the need for balance," I said.

A discussion followed related to the macabre and tragic events that he was experiencing. Perhaps he and I both thought it was time to "counterbalance" the events.

"How would you do that?" I asked.

"With beauty," he said with wisdom.

"An old idea," I commented.

Following that session and many more that dealt with the matter of how he was to counterbalance the horrors and psychic wounds experienced over the catastrophic losses, Tom went on to a profound creative resolution. He began to paint. He shared his art with me and, as if driven by an internal muse, steadily developed from having a talent to becoming a creator. The crying reduced. In part, no doubt, because the AIDS plague had already devastated Tom's entire community. He grieved, mourned, and let go of the dead. The dead were dead, but not forgotten. It was as if they had become a part of him and a part of his beautiful and stark paintings, and hence immortalized. By day, he dressed mannequins, and by night, he painted people and objects that were once removed from the horrors of the AIDS plague. He once painted a split screen in which on one side were magnificent red roses and on the other dirty, used syringe needles. It is a very striking painting.

In our sessions, Tom began to struggle with the choice of whether to leave his secure but boring job and pursue an uncertain but fulfilling career as a painter. However, was that really the option? Often we talked about it in terms of choosing a life-affirming activity over a deadly one. When it came to leaving his lover, Seth, the choice was a healthy one. He was not in danger of enacting a pattern of flight from intimacy and commitment. Seth was not a good enough "object choice" for Tom. That was a relatively easy decision. In the case of Tom's conflict over choosing a secure, steady job or taking a serious risk and becoming an artist, we talked about it in at least two ways. First, that to throw himself into painting would be an expression of individual will (Menaker 1982) in relation to a long-overdue attempt to defy his mother's expectation that he would fail at art without her guidance. Second, that to paint was to mourn and immortalize his friends—a creative expression of courage (May 1975). I was not neutral in this struggle. I believe I leaned towards the light of the Aegean, toward the paintings by Matisse. I did, however, encourage Tom to be aware of my personal biases.

Perhaps the interactions between us also involved unconscious communications. Nevertheless, the communications were not simple ones. It was not: become an artist versus stay at your job. That would be a dichotomous approach to understanding the analytic process, to understanding the transference-countertransference matrix, and perhaps to life in general. I believe that in the clinical moments I presented above, there is an irreducible ambiguity, that the situation is open to multiple interpretive constructions (Hoffman 1998). I believe that what took place in the analytic space between us were conscious and unconscious processes that involved constructed choice. We constructed a mourning process that situated his depression in the context of meaning and emergent creativity. Tom's gains in analysis did not emerge in a vacuum. I was very much a contributor. I was not some kind of neutral, therapeutic tool. Tom and I were engaged in a mutual construction. Further, we collaboratively chose to consider my participation and my subjectivity. We had a real, personal relationship, and we paid attention to it. It may have been one of the reasons he did not move into a fatal depression.

Tom was letting go and holding on to his dead friends simultaneously; thus creating continuity and a balance that allowed him to move forward in life. Tom is able to creatively balance two opposites, life and death, in a deeply profound way. This is his creativity in everyday life. Often he integrates these two states with his art. This is his artistic creativity. Otto Rank claims that the first creative decision an artist makes is to decide to become an artist. By the way, Tom is now a highly successful artist in continental Europe.

IMAGINING ITHACA

I was born into a family that migrated to New York City from a very tiny Greek island called Ereikousa. Ereikousa is located right were the Adriatic and Ionian Seas meet. It is so small that it is not even on the Greek map. The island had no electricity or running water. My mother's defining experiences before the trauma of emigrating revolved around the German occupation of the island during World War II. The occupation was brutal and sometimes deadly. My mother hid a Jewish family from the mainland who came to hide in the hills of the island.

Some of my first memories as a child are of being huddled in a corner of the kitchen, in a cold walkup in Chelsea, listening to my mother tell stories about how the Germans disrupted the idyllic island and how the islanders lost their innocence about the world. My mother told her stories with great affect and sorrow. She would go on and on about these losses and, in a peculiar way, I was her witness.

When it was time for me to go to Greek school, her separation difficulties were pronounced, and I desperately needed to get away from her. Besides, the world was a most exciting place and I loved exploring it. When in Greek school I learned my first lessons via the stories of Homer, I knew that there was no returning to my mother. The Iliad and the Odyssey inspired me. It was also a way to be in contact with my distant and depressed father. He enjoyed my intellectual achievements especially if they involved the Greeks. I believe this is the only thing he ever accepted me for. As an aside, I believe that you can live with the fact that your mother and father do not accept you, but you cannot live in a world that does not make sense to you. The Iliad and the Odyssey helped me make sense of the world. Of course, they are just one narrative of the world. Nevertheless, its significance for me lies in the fact that it was one of my early narratives and thus quite influential. Once, when I was eight and on a freighter boat with my father traveling on the Ionian Sea, the boat docked on Ithaca to deposit some cargo. Passengers were not allowed to get off. I pleaded with my father to let me go onto the island to find the castle of Odysseus, but he would not permit it. It was the closest I have ever gotten to Ithaca.

In childhood, I was greatly taken by the 12 gods of the Ancient Greeks. Later when I was introduced to the Greek Orthodox God, I was a little confused. How could all those complex assignments that each of the 12 gods has be encompassed in one God? A God that unlike the Olympic gods was not subject to human qualities, such as libidinal desires and drives for power. Nevertheless, I obeyed and did not question much of this until much later.

In adolescence, I was not rebellious but I did have a safe, secret self. I grew disillusioned with my parents and the Judeo-Christian ethos—the poet Wallace Stevens once wrote that the death of one God is the death of all gods. Greece is a place where creativity, history, and tragedy mix naturally, and during this period of my life, I became enthralled with the music and cause of a Greek composer named Mikis Theodorakis who was an artist and an activist with pacifist and Marxist views. Theodorakis had often been jailed, banished to concentration camps, and tortured for his political views. Theodorakis's uniqueness was in being able to write sublime melodies; to wed the melodies to Greek, European, African, and South American poetry; and to have all economic and social classes in Greece singing the same songs (Orfanos 1997). My mother, who has a second-grade education, and my father, who has a sixth-grade education, sing Noble Prize-winning poetry because of Theodorakis. His themes were and continue to be about Eros and Thanatos, about war, loss, mourning, and the affirmation of life. His response to the tragic was to act responsibly and to oppose with dignity. He acted in spite of despair. He was interested in fighting fascism, all kinds of oppression, and champions what he calls "internal liberation," that is, a clarity of individual and social purpose. His music became my ethical guide.

So I entered young adulthood with a personal view of the world as harboring all kinds of external dangers and that sometimes I had to be able to sit with the tragic and just be there and survive. Further, that sometimes I had to act to oppose the tragic. I learned that the individual is always in relation to the other. I learned that there was great beauty in the world. I learned that life is not fair, it just is.

Young adulthood was both an anxiety-provoking and exciting time for me: I was thrown out of college, matured, went back to college, discovered Sophia (I do not mean *sophia* as in the Greek word for wisdom, but Sophia, the woman of my dreams). We had a child, a beautiful and graceful girl, named Lina, with a sublime singing voice. A few years later, I became a psychologist. I was not, however, particularly interested in psychoanalysis. My own analyst was very interesting to me, and I was interesting to him, but most of those I knew who were analysts seemed depressed or obsessional to me. When I finally realized that psychoanalysis was a powerful therapy and I felt that in clinical work my personal presence and participation would be welcomed, my desire to become an analyst blossomed. I was attracted to theories that were pluralistic and left doors open. Reductionism was never of interest to me. Neither was the emphasis on rationalism and objectivism. I liked the shift in emphasis to subjectivism and personal meaning.

I always felt uncomfortable with the idea of a single, underlying truth. The Freudian notion of a deep self as being a seething cauldron of drives seemed to me to be just one truth. The Sullivanian need for security operations was another truth. The Kleinian notion of the self as the container of childhood terrors was another truth. The Winnicottian true self another, and the repressed chains of signifiers of Lacan again another truth. I also knew that reduction, as Peter Gay says, is an accident of psychoanalytic history, not its core (1988). I think it was Marx who said that all revolutions are taken over by clerks. Edgar Levenson talks about how each theory gets the disciples it deserves. I needed a psychoanalytic theory that allowed for 12 gods and, despite Sullivan's notions of the therapist as expert, I found interpersonal theory less dogmatic. It is open and ultimately leads to the current integrative and elegant views of some of the progressive relational positions on the transference-countertransference matrix (Mitchell and Aron, 1999).

More specifically, the dialectical-constructivist approach is quite appealing to me. It holds that there is dialectic between understanding and action in the psychoanalytic process. It abhors dichotomous thinking. When we say this comes from the patient and this comes from the analyst, we are thinking dichotomously. When we say that psychoanalytic experience is often ambiguous but not amorphous we are thinking dialectically (Hoffman 1998). Often a constructivist approach is misunderstood to mean that the analyst cannot feel sure of anything. That is not so. It is rather, as Merton Gill (1994) says, that the analyst should not function with the idea, for example, that he is dealing with unquestionable facts as to what human nature universally is. The analyst may work with confidence, but he or she never abandons the perspective that he or she may be mistaken. How can you be the final arbiter of the patient's subjective state? This holds especially true for unconscious states.

THE WRONG ORACLE

Tom claims to have gotten a great deal from his analysis. He credits his creative success to our work together. However, I also got a great deal from the collaboration. In fact by 1994, I was beginning to become greatly intrigued by the psychology of creativity. I began to study and read about it voraciously. It was so gratifying to be thinking about creativity and not pathology. I read Freud, Rank, Jung, and the creativity researchers. My sense of psychoanalysis as a creative process evolved and, not surprisingly, I found myself wanting to interview my hero, Theodorakis. It was not easy to decide to take time off from work and go to Greece. I had a full-time independent practice, I engaged in many professionals activities, and Lina, age 14, was having some peculiar and perplexing medical problem.

Theodorakis was 70 in 1995 when I traveled to Greece in the second week of January. We sat and talked for hours in his study. The study had a full and breathtaking view of the Parthenon. It was one of the peak experiences of my life. Here I was sitting with the man whom I adored and considered a genius, and I was asking him questions about his creative muses and his battles with irrational authority. I felt I was on Mt. Olympus. I would call home every day and talk to my wife and daughter about the experiences I was having. I cannot begin to describe my elation. On the last day of my visit to Athens, I could not get a hold of my wife and daughter to tell them what I had bought for them. When the plane landed at JFK airport Friday, I was surprised to be greeted by my best friend, Sam. I could not understand why he was there. As we waited for the bus to get to the parking lot, he told me that my daughter was in the hospital, that she was hospitalized under emergency conditions, and that she was complaining of brutal headaches and was vomiting. She had been subjected to CAT scans and MRIs. She was diagnosed with a brain tumor. I was in shock. It was as if I had been abruptly pushed off Mt. Olympus and was plunging into Hades. Surely, this was the wrong oracle.

Lina had her surgery on Monday morning. She had a total of three brain surgeries in nine days. Despite repeated insults and assaults, Lina survived. Our friends provided heroic support. After three weeks away from my practice, I returned to work. My first workday was a Friday. No doubt, I thought that I could have the weekend to return to my daughter and to recover from whatever the clinical fallout might be. My first patient was Tom.

Before my first appointment, I had considered what I would tell my patients. I know that some espouse a "tell all" attitude and some a "tell nothing" attitude. I decided on a middle course. I would try to track, through careful listening, what my patients' reactions were and what my reactions were. I would try to determine how much they wished to know and how much I could in fact say. Tom walked into my consulting room. He began by asking me what had happened.

"How much do you want to know?" I asked.

"Whatever you feel comfortable telling me," he responded.

For the next 45 minutes, I described what had happened to my daughter. I told him I was upset and scared. I felt his deep caring and compassion. He knew how to listen to the tragic story I was narrating and living. Towards the end of the session, I tried to regain some semblance of the role of analyst and I asked him how he felt about hearing all this from me. He said he knew this was unusual for me to tell him so much about what was going on for me, but that I was a very important person in his life and that I had helped him over the years and that he cared about what I was going through. I felt his love.

In the sessions that followed, we talked some more about my daughter, and over the last few years that talk became less frequent. I would tell him that Lina was getting stronger and that her recovery was going well. I would also tell him she continued her vocal studies. We both understood the importance of her singing. You cannot be depressed and sing at the same time, even if you are singing sad songs.

During the winter of 1995, Tom told me in casual passing about a flower show that was coming to New York City. It was enormous and would have some of the most beautiful flowers ever shown in the city. A few weeks later, I took Lina out for her first trip after the surgery. With a bandage to cover her shaved head and walking slowly and tentatively, we went to the flower show. For a short hour, we roamed the huge exhibit hall on the West Side piers. She wanted to buy red roses. Of course, I bought them for her. The roses reminded me of those in Tom's painting. We did not see the whole show (Lina was too tired), but the fact that we were there and that Lina was enjoying beauty was a great gift to me. I never analyzed Tom's mentioning of the flower show, but I did tell him that Lina and I had gone there and that we found it life affirming and a counterbalance to the terrors we were experiencing. I told him it was healing.

CODA

I do not wish to leave the reader with the impression that my disclosures were in the deliberate service of the analytic process. I agree with the countless of contemporary psychoanalytic writers who feel that one must disclose with caution and judiciousness. I believe that it facilitates a level of analytic engagement and a level of analytic exploration. Nevertheless, I was not sharing my family crisis in order to deepen the analysis. It was about being a real person. However, this did interact and work dialectically with the more interpretive moments of our work together. Like a number of contemporary psychoanalytic authors (Gerson 1996; Hoffman 1998; Pizer 1992; Searles 1975; Singer 1971), I believe it is helpful to the patient to help the analyst, although I do not think this can be planned; the analyst has to be ready for it but cannot plan it.

Irwin Hoffman, in his 1998 book, *Ritual and Spontaneity in the Psychoanalytic Process*, writes that, "We are not all, to be sure, adult survivors of childhood sexual, physical or psychological abuse; but we are all adult endurers of the ongoing abuse of the human condition. Yet, we feel, most of us, emphatically, that it is worth it. Although the whole challenge of living might be described as the challenge of making the best of poor substitutes, 'the best,' after all, can be something quite wonderful, inspiring, and miraculous, even if also quite terrible" (14). This expression of value reminds me of how the poet Odysseus Elytis put it 40 years ago. Starting with a well-known phrase from a Greek Orthodox religious hymn, "Worthy it is," he added the existential twist, "Worthy is the price paid."

In conclusion, I have traced two tragic events, some clinical moments of mutual emotional impact, and aspects of my worldview. I have done so not in the name of truth but in the name of beauty. Beauty, however, is not a product. In order for it to be meaningful and creative it must be, in my view, a process. So, let me end with an excerpted poem that speaks to the analytic process. It was written in 1911 in Alexandria, Egypt, by a gay Greek man named Cavafy. The poem is titled *Ithaca* (Cavafy 1975).

As you set out for Ithaca
Hope your road is a long one,
Full of adventure, full of discovery . . .
Laistrygonians, Cyclops,
Wild Poseidon-you won't encounter them
Unless you bring them along inside your soul,
Unless your soul sets them up in front of you . . .

Hope your road is a long one.
May there be many summer mornings when,
With what pleasure, what joy,
You enter harbors you're seeing for the first time . . .

Keep Ithaca always in your mind.
Arriving there is what you're destined for.
But don't hurry the journey at all.
Better it lasts for years,
So you're old by the time you reach the island,
Wealthy with all you've gained on the way,
Not expecting Ithaca to make you rich.

Ithaca gave you the marvelous journey.
Without her you wouldn't have set out.
She has nothing left to give you now.

And if you find her poor, Ithaca won't have fooled you,
Wise as you have become, so full of experience,
You'll have understood by then what these Ithacas mean.

REFERENCES

Aron, L. (1991). The patient's experience of the analyst's subjectivity. *Psychoanalytic Dialogues* 1: 29–51.

Cavafy, C. P. (1975). *Collected Poems.* (E. Keeley and P. Sherrard, Trans.) Princeton, NJ: Princeton University Press.

Gay, P. (1988). *Freud: A life for our times.* New York: W.W. Norton.

Gerson, B., ed. (1996). *The therapist as a person.* Hillsdale, NJ: Analytic Press.

Gill, M. M. (1994). *Psychoanalysis in transition: A personal view.* Hillsdale, NJ: Analytic Press.

Greenberg, J. R., and S. Mitchell (1983). *Object relations in psychoanalytic theory.* Cambridge, MA: Harvard University Press.

Hoffman, I. Z. (1998). *Ritual and spontaneity in the psychoanalytic process.* Hillsdale, NJ: Analytic Press.

May, R. (1975). *The courage to create.* New York: Norton.

Menaker, E. (1982). *Otto Rank: a rediscovered legacy.* New York: Columbia University Press.

Mitchell, S. A., and A. Aron. (1999). *Relational psychoanalysis: The emergence of a tradition.* Hillsdale, NJ: Analytic Press.

Orfanos, S. D. (1997). Mikis Theodorakis: Music, culture and the creative process. *Journal of Modern Hellenism* 14: 17–38.

Pizer, B. (1992). When the analyst is ill: Dimensions of self-disclosure. *Psychoanalytic Quarterly* 66: 450–469.

Searles, H. F. (1975). The patient as therapist to his analyst. In P. L. Giovacchini, ed., *Tactics and techniques in psychoanalytic therapy: Vol. 2: Countertransference*, 95–151. Northvale, NJ: Jason Aronson.

Singer, E. (1971). The patient aids the analyst: Some clinical and theoretical observations. In B. Landis and E. S. Tauber, eds., *In the name of life: Essays in honor of Erich Fromm*, 56–68. New York: Holt, Rhinehart and Winston.

CHAPTER 11

Beastly Memories Live in Beastly Memory Land

Judith L. Alpert

Something terrible has happened. I have been a witness to it from a distance. I am committed to the telling. I convey the story in a psychoanalytically informed voice of passion and outrage. I warn you at the outset. This material is an emotional challenge. It is the story of 21 children, 9 girls and 12 boys, who were sexually abused from one to three years by a bus driver of an after-school program.[1]

THE IMPOSSIBLE: CHILDHOODS DRIVEN WRONG

Here are the facts. The children were from a lower-middle-class community in the suburbs in the state of Washington. They attended a five-day-a-week after-school program. They were picked up from school by one driver daily and taken to the after-school program which was a 25-minute ride. The same driver drove the children home after the two-hour program ended. The 21 children included four sibling pairs. All the children were victims. Some abuse took place almost every day over several years in the back of the bus by the driver. It took place on the bus when it was parked on the grounds of the after-school program and in parking lots. Sometimes it took place in the back of the bus while the bus was in motion and the bus driver's cousin or friend drove. The children ranged in age from 5 to 10 years old at the time of the abuse. I evaluated them for forensic purposes five years later, when they were 10 to 15 years old. I met with family members as well.[2]

The abuse involved fondling, oral sex, and sodomy. While every child may not have been involved in all of these acts, every child was involved in some way and every child was a witness to sexual abuse from one to three years.

Many of the children returned from the after-school program with rectal bleeding, and they reported pain when urinating and defecating. Parents found bruises, abrasions, and imprints on the children's thighs and buttocks. They found blood stains on the children's underwear. Despite such physical evidence, dramatic psychological symptoms, and disguised communications, many children were exploited over several years.

Approaches common to perpetrators of extrafamilial child sexual abuse were used. The bus driver gained the children's confidence by befriending their parents, giving the children gifts and candy, and promising them prized meetings with their athletic heroes—playing nonsexual games initially, turning nonsexual games into sexual games, and eventually ensuring secrecy by means of threats. Houses would be burned. Parents would be killed. Siblings would be kidnapped. Violence was not necessary to keep the children in a constant state of fear.

The case initiated by the families of these 21 children was brought against the after-school program. The case never went to trial. Rather, it was settled out of court. At the time of settlement, the driver was already serving a 30- to 60-year prison term for the rape, sodomy, and sexual abuse of 30 other children.

THE IMPOSSIBLE: HOW COULD IT HAPPEN?

How could it happen, you may wonder. How could 21 children be sexually abused on a bus while traveling from school to an after-school program? How could this occur not once but many times over several years? You reason that the children have to be picked up at a certain time. They have to arrive at the program at a certain time. And the ride home from the after-school program also holds its time limitations.

The adults were witness to many signals that something was awry. They did not listen to those signals in that split second of decision making that takes place in the subterranean region. They could think of no one who could be abusing the children. Jim, the driver, was friendly. He had grandkids about the ages of their children. Many parents knew his family. He did not seem like someone who would offend. In fact, the parents could not identify any possible offenders. There was a minor war within each parent that occupied little attention.

On the other hand, the adults thought, Jim is too friendly. The kids seem upset when they get off the bus. The bus is often late. Something is not right with my child. These observations, however, were offset by what adults thought could possibly happen to their children as well as their typecast of a villain. And there was a stalwart desire for nothing bad to have happened. The abuse was nonsensical. It seemed impossible. Given the debauchery of the event, the colossal activity of intervention, the excruciatingly painful quality of the evil, they opted, in the underground region, to not know. Most people embody the capability to delete ghastly messages. Denial is very powerful.

The sexual abuse on the bus was to be denied. Some of the children attempted to tell about the ongoing abuse. Eve, for example, always remembered what was done to her. She tried to tell the adults as best she could. The adults did not hear. The need to not know about the wickedness—the force to know no evil, hear no evil, speak no evil—transcended any desire to take charge of the situation and *really* know. Once the experience was told and not heard, any further longing to tell of the ongoing abuse encountered rebellion from the knowledge that there would be no hearing. When Eve told me what she had told adults, I thought: "This makes no sense. Either someone is not listening or someone is not telling the truth." How could Eve have told in the way that she did without anyone authoritatively pursuing the truth? But Eve was utilizing a vocabulary based on her level of development as well as her shame, and the adults were operating out of disbelief and ignorance about sexual abuse, a desire not to know about evil, and a primitive understanding about child trauma talk. The adult need to not know left the children defenseless in their vulnerability and with a void in both memory and feeling.

THEIR MEMORIES: BEASTLY MEMORIES AND MEMORY BLACK-OUT

What appears to be forgotten may simply be unacknowledged. Or it may be remembered and then forgotten and then remembered again and again. The traumatized may be unable to lose memory. I work with adults in my psychoanalytic practice. However, while the false-memory debate concerns the memory of adults and the authenticity of their memories for abominations presently unknown to them, the wickedness was perpetrated on them while they were children. Thus, while the focus is on adult memory, *the polemic is really about childhood memory*. It concerns whether children can truly forget atrocities that continue to control, consume, and torment them. In order to understand adult memories of trauma, the spotlight needs to be on childhood memory.

Once the abuse on the bus was known, 17 of the 21 children acknowledged that they were sexually abused. Seven of the 21 children reported their sexual abuse when the abuse story erupted and then reported it again to me five years after the initial telling. Their reporting was explicit, specific, and vivid. For example, after the abuse became known, Hank, age 10, described in great detail the famous people that the driver said he knew, listed the names of the children who sat on the bus, indicated who usually sat where, and then described the "games" the driver played with all the kids. He then elucidated acts perpetrated on him. He continued, "Most of the stuff he did was on Mondays. . . . On a lot of Mondays Jim would have a man named Juan on the bus and Juan would drive the bus too. Sometimes he would be hiding on the bus in the back. Jim said Juan was his cousin and he even showed us some credit cards with Juan's name on it. Juan and Jim would sometimes talk to each other in something like French, another language. Juan had two blue earrings in his nose. Sometimes he wore a black ring. Juan had brown eyes, dark brown hair, regular, and he had some freckle marks, just a few around his cheeks on each side. Sometimes a man named Tim would come too. Tim was fat."

There is a second group of children who acknowledged the abuse initially when the molestations became known. Five years later, however, these 10 children retracted their abuse report. When there are multiple traumas or repeated abuse, children may take refuge in the defenses of denial, dissociation, and splitting. They bolster themselves for further abuse. As a consequence, ongoing horror and terror and accompanying pain may be met with psychic numbing. It is as if the child's senses and thinking apparatus are deadened. While such bracing enables them to momentarily survive the abuse, it interferes with the formation of memories as well as the storage and retrieval of memories. The result: Verbal memories may be hazy, fragmentary, or nonexistent. Amnesia may even result.

Consider Nick. At age five, he was a passenger on Jim's bus. During that year, his parents reported that he changed. He became a worrier. Personal safety was his major interest. He had nightmares, somatic complaints, and had become aggressive, angry, and reclusive. His sleeping was disturbed. He was preoccupied with death. He would cry a lot, particularly after he got off the bus.

After the abuse on the bus became known, Nick delineated the acts of abuse that had been perpetrated on him. His description was detailed and graphic, and many of the specifics were consistent with those told by other children. The threats involving fire, the acts of abuse, and the wicked games were some of the particulars that many children reported. There were also some facts that were unique to his story. Nick said that Jim threw a knife at one of the children and that it went out the window. He said that the bus was very noisy and that Jim did not allow windows to be open. He reported that he got very hot. He reported lying on the floor and looking out the back window of the emergency exit when Jim yelled at him. How can his unique observations be understood? They may be his accurate observations. They may be variants of the true trauma. They may represent appended mental representations of earlier or later events into the trauma. They may be condensations of several traumatic or emotionally significant events.

Nick has no memory of some particulars reported by other children. He does not recall the bus stopping in the back lot of Baskin Robbins, the Shell station, or the Gap store, for example. Others identified these locations as places Jim would stop and abuse. He does not recall Juan or Tim or any person besides Jim who drove the bus. He does not recall crying on the bus. He does not recall Jim's "tooshie game" which several children reported that Nick was made to play. And so on. It seems that he erased some of the more dark and wrenching parts. Is this his effort to white out shame?

There were some errors in his story. Although Nick said that Jason was on the bus, Jason walked to the after-school program and walked home from the after-school program that year. Nick is merging two years. Distorted time sense adds inaccuracies to memory. At the time that he reported the abuse, not only were there some inconsistencies within his story, but he was also inconsistent in reporting the abuse itself. He told his male therapist that nothing happened on the bus. Sometimes he denied sexual abuse to his father. Other times he spontaneously told his father his sexual abuse story. While he consistently told the abuse story to his mother, sometimes he reported that it happened but not to him. How does one understand so much inconsistency?

Five years later Nick has rewritten his story. It is now short and consistent. Although he had told me the same story he had told everyone at the time, his five-year-later story was: *It never happened.*

Nick said that all he could remember was "what would happen on a normal bus." He indicated that Jim stopped the bus and yelled at kids who were out of their seats. He insisted that Jim didn't do anything to him, "probably because he thought I was too cool and I would tell." Several times he indicated that "the Jim thing" was not going to make much difference in his life. He told me that it was over, and that he is "pretty tired of going through this."

When the abuse became known, Nick, age 5, dictated his statement to the detectives. His innocent language sharply contrasted with his story of oral sex and sodomy. It ended with a childish signature. After rereading his testimony in my presence, he looked beaten and battle-weary. He announced that he had a stomachache. He had to lie down. He had trouble breathing. Finally, he shouted, "It never happened. Someone must have forged my signature."

Was he abused? Signs point to violation. Nick's parents wondered what was going on. Why did the driver give Nick boxes of candy? Why was Nick so terrified when his mom told him to pull his pants down? She was only going to take his temperature rectally, something she had done often before. Why, when he returned home, were some of his clothes missing and his appearance so disheveled? Why did he have black and blue marks on his legs and his knees? Also, that year and that year only, Nick hurt when he wiped his anus. Why? Noticing that his anus was extraordinarily red, Nick's father questioned him. Finally, his father explained away the redness, as he had done the other signs. He speculated that perhaps Nick had not adequately cleaned himself at school. There was eyewitness validation that Nick was abused. Other children reported that they saw Jim abuse Nick. The perpetrator's perverse character and opportunity to abuse has been established. Perverse character? Yes, Jim was convicted by a jury for rape, sodomy, and sexual abuse. And Nick hated him. Opportunity to abuse? Yes, the bus was often late on Nick's return from his after-school program.

Five years post-abuse, Nick continues to be terrified of buses. He won't travel on buses. He closes his eyes and covers his face when one passes. He avoids other stimuli that suggest the trauma. Many of his initial symptoms continue. His preoccupation with death could be called an obsession. He simply announced the result of his calculation: "One-eighth of my life is over." His overwhelming anxiety has skyrocketed. He knows that bad things happen. He warns his brother about bad people. He sleeps in his parents' room some nights. His chilling nightmares overwhelm. He hates his body. And a new symptom surfaced: incessant sex talk.

I knew I would be witness to the children's abuse stories. In fact, I was witness to that and more. I was also witness to the course of recollection itself, the passages and convergences of the contradictions, concealment, disclosures, turmoil, pain, and blurring of time. Their stories did not hang together. Aware of this, they question themselves and are reluctant to believe their own stories. How can they believe themselves, they wonder, when they are engulfed by the alternating currents of knowing and not knowing and telling and not telling. These children work hard to not know.

David, age 11, explains: "When I worry about something, I forget about it." Cindy, age 15, who neither denies nor acknowledges the sexual abuse trauma, states: "I don't want to talk about it. Whether I don't remember it on purpose or can't remember, I don't know." She continues, "I wish a doctor could make me remember things if they're bothering me inside."

Some of the children locked their diabolical bus experiences in a safe deposit box. One child (Alan, age 13) thinks he will remember at a later time. He said: "By the time I remember, I will be grown up and it will be easier to deal with."

Some of the children describe what happened. They say one thing at one moment and something that totally contradicts that statement the next. These contradictions are, for the most part, specific to the children who no longer acknowledged the abuse.

The children speak:

"Jim never told me not to tell. Even if he did, I never saw anything anyway . . . I never saw anything. I just saw him sitting with kids . . . He messed around with kids on the bus . . . I wish I had told someone something weird is going on." (Ed, age 15)

"I don't remember." And later, "He touched a lot of people's privates." (Arnold, age 11)

"Yes . . . wait a minute . . . do I remember? . . . I think I do . . . I'm not sure . . . I can't remember." (Cindy, age 15)

Consider Mike, age seven. He said that Jim parked the bus in front of his house, got up out of his seat, went over to Mike's seat, pulled his (Jim's) pants down and walked towards him. Mike can't remember what happened after that. Mike said that he "blacked out" when Jim came up to him. To Mike, "blacking out" means fainting. The next thing that Mike remembers is that he was sitting in his seat "in a normal way" and the bus was still in front of his house. Jim was back in his seat. Mike's body didn't feel different and he doesn't remember any pain. When he finally "came to," Mike ran into his house and asked his mother if he could go to his parent's funeral. Although Mike remembers asking, he isn't sure why he asked. Mike isn't even sure whether Jim ever touched him on that day or any day. However, Mike remembers that on that particular day he bled when he went to the bathroom. His mother, in fact, thought he had fissures.

Some children in the second group (those who initially acknowledged and then, five years later, denied) begin to tell how they or others were not abused. However, the story they tell is that of abuse. The madness of these stories and the awareness of the madness moves us to the fringe of realization. Sometimes they report that the abuse occurred but that *they* were not abused. Some children related that the abuse happened. However, they adamantly proclaimed that they were not abused. They told stories of being too smart to be abused or of having a way of avoiding abuse. One boy related that he avoided abuse simply by looking out the window. Despite their proclamations, all signs indicate that these children had not avoided abuse.

A trauma story may be told from childhood play and from adulthood work. However, the stories do not tell exactly what happened. Rather, they tell us that there was trauma. They tell us that there is a need to rework and to understand. They tell us that the narrator feels culpable. And they tell us much more. They are stories of what they think may have happened. They are the stories they don't want to know. They are both stories and obsessions.

There is a developing body of research (see Brown, Scheflin, & Hammond, 1998) that supports that some people who are traumatized forget the trauma and may remember it decades later. Ross Cheit's listing of corroborated cases of recovered memory reports 45 such cases. The reason for nonreporting may be explained by such dissimilar processes as forgetting, repression, dissociation, or reluctance to disclose. The end product, however, is the same: no acknowledgment of prior abuse. Williams's study (1994) is exemplary. She interviewed 129 women who had been treated for child sexual abuse in a city hospital 17 years previously. She found that 38% of the women did not report the abuse which was known to have occurred. Since many of the women reported horrific details of other aspects of their lives, a reasonable conclusion is that these women did not recall the abuse rather than they withheld the information.

The third and final group of children on the school bus is composed of four girls who *never* verbally acknowledged the abuse. They never acknowledged it to their parents. They never acknowledged it to the detectives who questioned them. They never acknowledged it to either the psychologist who interviewed them immediately after the abuse became known or to me, when I interviewed them five years later. According to the children who were on the bus with them, these four girls who never acknowledged abuse were "his pets." They were abused the most. They are also the most damaged.

These children have a difficult time keeping the abuse knowledge hidden. The abuse story appears with a strong although not always explicit voice. Alice was nine years old at the time of her molestation. She never verbally acknowledged the abuse. However, memory cannot be made mute. She told the detectives *her* way. During the initial investigation, she lied in a fetal position on the floor. She would not talk. Five years later, when Alice heard that she was to meet with me, she said, "I wish I knew a week ago because then I would have a chance to run away." According to her parents, she was afraid she would be kidnapped if she "told anything." What that "*anything*" is has never been articulated.

Alice is preoccupied about being kidnapped. If she is alone in the house, she will call a neighbor to stay with her. She thinks the kidnapper would be Jim, should he escape from jail, or Jim's friends or relatives. While she is afraid to sleep in her own house, she embraces sleepovers. The reason: She thinks the kidnapper will not know where she is. Since the abuse, she sleeps on the floor of her parents' room and keeps the windows closed. Before going to bed, she turns on lights. She will not close windows; someone else must do it for her. She is afraid someone might grab her from outside. Although her fears speak to us, she will not tell about the threats that placed her in a perpetual borough of terror. For Alice, *not telling* is an active process. It necessitates motivation, effort, and strain.

Several children who no longer acknowledge or who never acknowledged abuse talked about pushing away internal feelings and thoughts related to the trauma. It appears that forgetting, like remembering and not telling, is an active process. They want to be known. And, at the same time, they do not want to be found.

The children who consistently reported that nothing happened seem the most miserable of all. Time has not lessened their misery. The rumination and plaguing continues despite what may be amnesia, repression, dissociation, or, just simply, refusal to acknowledge. Their relationships with the past are mysterious and marked with anguish. They are crushed and bloody and left with little urge to restart. They want to tell. Yet, they cannot. It's an intricate adventure of hide-and-seek. There is a coexistence: a desperate need to divulge and a still more desperate need not to. The silence is conspicuous. It is not simply not communicating. It is not like an idle or passive circumstance. Rather, it is an alert, occupied, reactive state.

They shut themselves out, down, and off. They disregard opportunity that they believe they are unworthy of and isolate themselves from others whom they perceives as honorable, unlike them. They do not take in. Consequently, learning is affected. Energy is utilized in an effort to keep information out. They cannot know what they do indeed know. It is too awful. Since it is difficult to select what comes in and what doesn't, everything—or, at the least, a lot—may be rejected rather than risk allowing in the abuse material. A simple task like setting the table or learning to use a microwave may not be learned. Schooling, careers, and life shoulder the consequence. There is a physiological explanation as well which relates to excessive stimulation of the central nervous system when the trauma occurs (van der Kolk, 1995). Permanent neuronal changes that have a negative effect on learning, habituation, and stimulus discrimination may result. And many abuse victims seem to be shut off. Chronic problems with modulating affect are evident. We witness extremes: hyperactivity and psychic numbing. As adults, they often do not know how they feel. They may think they do not feel. They may think they have many personalities. And, in fact, they may. While the trauma was ongoing, they removed themselves psychologically from the full impact of the trauma. They dissociated. This served them well at trauma time. They survived. But did they?

A perplexing question remains: Why do some children always remember and others do not? When there is shame, guilt, humiliation, and degradation, there is an inclination to remain silent. While some of us may think that the material is unavailable and others that it is unacknowledged, from the perspective of the victimized, it may simply be off-limits. Although they are not responsible for the debauchery, they are nevertheless, overwhelmed with guilt. Victimized children think little about the forces that caused their situation or the significance of their present troubles. Rather they focus on what they could have done or should have done. In part, this may explain why they do not tell. Their anger and anguish is channeled against themselves.

It is not just the children who never acknowledged who see themselves as defective, culpable, damned, and disgraced. Rather than perceiving the perpetrator as bad and themselves as victim, they see themselves as both the cause of depravity and the ones in need of punishment. So, while we may not hold the victim responsible, they do.

Everything is ruined by trauma and, yet, everything may look surface-right to the observer. The children continue to go to school, parties, and baseball games. They still wear the current styles, listen to the popular music, and attempt to follow the current fads. But their following the current rage when their internal rage is bubbling simply represents a disguise of sorts. While the victimized may look like the others, they are different. They act different and they feel differently and, in fact, some experience feeling nothing at all. Their memories follow different rules.

The children who told initially were miserable. The children who told and then denied were miserable also. The children who never told were the most miserable of all. Silence or the not-telling does not ameliorate either as memory cannot be made mute. Integration appears impossible because the victimized may not have been truly present during the traumatic event. And, if they were present, they will work hard to expunge the memory. *The children work as ferociously to forget as the adults do to remember.*

The material that I have presented indicates that "forgetting" begins early and that some children try hard to forget. Many, in part, succeed. Many forget and then remember. They do this simultaneously or consecutively, and they may do this consecutively decades apart. Retention of verbal memories may be hazy, fragmentary, or nonexistent. Amnesia may even result.

Even when there is verbal memory, it does not follow that the traumatic memory for repeated abuse is fully accurate or the abusive events are completely known. It is much more complicated than that. When the fragments are embroidered into a story, there may be some discrepancies. Forgetting and technical inaccuracies may begin in childhood and may have resulted from efforts to not know, efforts to protect, and honest errors in perception. There is a danger: the discounting of whole stories based on a technical inaccuracy. And while all of the abuse details may not be accurate, they are all telling. The story of abuse is a rather simple story. It is a story of betrayal, fear, misuse of power, and evil—and the dark and wrenching story almost always ends with fury, confusion, and psychic deadening on the part of the victims.

CONCLUSION

What can be concluded from this intricate and chilling rendering of traumatic memory? First, loss of traumatic material begins early. The children work as ferociously to forget as adults do to remember. Wanting to not know persists like a viral infection. Because an analysand said it did not happen does not mean that it did not happen. Alternatively, if an analysand said that it did happen, it doesn't mean that it did. We must believe. We must doubt. We must live with paradox. We must believe that they are telling us the truth as they know and can tell it. We must doubt that it is the full story.

Second, trauma cannot be made mute. Trauma lives forever.

Third, I have described the nature of memory and errors of memory. This material enables us to break out of the polarization of the false-memory controversy. The controversy is, simply stated, brainless. Memory demands a more complicated outlook than a simple true-false dichotomy. Usually the essential components of recovered memories are true. Others are omitted, committed, scrambled, confabulated, condensed, and erased. Distorted time sense adds inaccuracy to memory and contributes to variations of the truth. When dissociated traumas return, they are not necessarily more accurate than traumas that were always remembered. They just tend to be more fragmented. Wholes in memory are predictable.

Fourth, there may be inconsistency in trauma communication. When this occurs within the legal arena, the teller is discounted as an unreliable witness. As psychoanalysts, we understand inconsistency in a different way. The real past as it existed outside the patient is what I have elsewhere called "happening truth" (Alpert, 1997). It may be impossible to know. The raw data of psychoanalysis is psychic reality, the patient's present understanding of the experienced and real past. This is what I call "story-truth" (Alpert, 1997). Analysis emphasizes psychic reality and interpretation and focuses on the conscious and unconscious personal meanings analysands assign to past and present events. A dialogue is demanded between the incongruities that emerge in the patient's developing narrative. Harmony and the masking of discrepancy is not the target. Rather, ambiguity is accepted, challenges are acknowledged, and the discourse and integration continues.

Fifth, I have described a whole web of defense mechanisms. While there is a tendency to consider dissociation as the only defense mechanism, the material presented here indicates more complexity.

Child victims as well as adults who were victimized as children may be silent and voiceless. They may feel alone and unknown. Sometimes they need space to be silent. Other times they need space to tell. They will go back and forth from language to silence. They appear to be one person but they are, in fact, many. There is a battle as to what, if anything, is spoken. Rather than privileging one over the other, analysands need to know that they can access language or silence. They need to choose when and what. The telling can only restore when it is time.

NOTES

1. This is a fictionalized story of a true account. Names and some information were altered and some parallel phenomena created. In some cases, several individuals were merged into one. These alterations should not diminish understanding about traumatic memories.

2. Some say that the man whom I call the "perpetrator" was falsely accused by overzealous public officials. While the man I call the "perpetrator" has a story to tell, I do not tell his story here.

REFERENCES

Alpert, J. L. (1997). Story-Truth and Happening-Truth. In R. Gartner, *Memories of Sexual Betrayal. Truth, Fantasy, Repression, and Dissociation.* Northvale, NJ: Aronson.

Brown, D., Scheflin, A. W., & Hammond, D. C. (1998). *Memory, Trauma Treatment, and the Law.* New York: W.W. Norton.

Cheit, R. (nd). Recovered Memory Project is an internet-based research project directed by Professor Ross E. Cheit of the Taubman Center for Public Policy and American Institutions at Brown University. www.RecoveredMemory.org.

van der Kolk, B. (1995). The Body, Memory, and the Psychobiology of Trauma. In J. L. Alpert (Ed.) *Treating Trauma in the Era of the Recovered Memory Debate,* 29–60. NY: Aronson.

Williams, L. M. (1994). Recall of childhood trauma: A prospective study of women's memories of child sexual abuse. *Journal of Consulting and Clinical Psychology, 62* (6), 1167–1176.

CHAPTER 12

Cinderella's Gender Trouble: Sadomasochism as the Intersubjective Regulation of Uncertainty

Doris Brothers

Dressed in rags and forced to toil in sooty shadows by her heartless stepmother and cruelly rivalrous stepsisters, Cinderella, at the outset of the famous fairy tale, seems to be a veritable poster child for child abuse. Yet, she manages to live happily ever after by pulling off the ultimate female coup: marriage to a prince. No wonder Ann and Barry Ulanov (1983) have used *Cinderella* as a vehicle for the psychological and theological exploration of envy.

Envy, however, is just one of the many facets of human experience that have been studied by means of this richly evocative tale. It has served as a sort of Rorschach test for countless writers who have interpreted its meaning according to their personal preoccupations and theoretical inclinations. Traditional analysts, for example, have tended to view it mainly in terms of oedipal guilt and sibling rivarly (e.g., Bettelheim, 1976) or as illustrating "a simple form of masochism" (Berliner, 1947). Unconvinced that these explanations do full justice to *Cinderella*'s enduring appeal, I attempt in this chapter to offer my own slant on the fairy tale in light of recent discoveries about sadomasochism, trauma, and gender. I contend that sadomasochism, when viewed from an intersubjective perspective, may be understood as efforts to regulate uncertainty about psychological survival in the aftermath of trauma.

Cinderella's antiquity has been well documented. According to Bettelheim (1976), the story was known even before it was first written down in China during the ninth century A.D. Mentioned in sixteenth-century German literature and popularized by Perrault (1697), countless versions have been recorded. To my mind, the secret of *Cinderella*'s long-running success lies in its engaging explication of a pervasive aspect of self-experience: the bifurcation of gender into masculine and feminine. Building on the fresh understanding of masochism advanced by Kohut (1977) and Menaker (1995), and the recent revolution in theories of gender, I hope to demonstrate that *Cinderella* vividly portrays the predicament of women in societies in which masculinity and femininity are differentiated as distinct biologically-determined categories.

I first describe the concept of intersubjective uncertainty regulation. Next I contrast Freud's theory of masochism with an intersubjective perspective. I then attempt to demonstrate that thoughts, feelings, and behaviors traditionally construed as sadomasochistic may reflect uncertainty-regulating efforts in the aftermath of trauma, especially traumas associated with the imposition of gender. After I apply this understanding to the story of Cinderella, I present a clinical example illustrating gender trauma.

THE INTERSUBJECTIVE REGULATION OF UNCERTAINTY

Self psychologists, intersubjectivists, and relational analysts tend to agree that a sense of vital and cohesive selfhood emerges and is maintained in the context of relational experiences (self psychologists call these *selfobject experiences*) throughout the life span. However, we can only trust in the availability of such experiences; Our birth certificates come with no guarantee that they will be forthcoming. Thus, as I see it, uncertainty about psychological survival is a fundamental aspect of the human condition.

Relational experiences with caretakers during formative years convince some people that their psychological needs will always be provided for in a trustworthy way. Such fortunate individuals are not likely to experience debilitating uncertainty about their psychological survival. Indeed they may regard confrontations with the unknown as greatly pleasurable and find a wondrous challenge in the realization that we are born, live our lives, and die amid untold mysteries. They are apt to delight in engaging in creative or risky activities that heighten their sense of uncertainty. In contrast, people for whom relational experiences were inadequate, insufficient, inconsistently available, or traumatically disrupted, are likely to find uncertainty about psychological survival a matter of urgent and ongoing concern.

It is probably apparent that even with optimally responsive caretakers, children are bound, at times, to feel uncertain that their relational needs will be met. The experience of such uncertainty seems, from earliest infancy on, to lead to attempts at its regulation. My reading of the literature on infant research has persuaded me that much of the self and interactive regulatory activity of infants and their caretakers involves the regulation of uncertainty. Even very young infants, this research suggests, show intense interest in contingent relations and are powerfully affected by the confirmation and violation of expectancies. As Sander (1977) notes, infants are intrinsically motivated to order information, detect regularity, and generate and act on expectancies. Moreover, he asserted that all of their activities must be coordinated with that of their caretakers. I view the coordination of gaze, vocalization, and affective expression observed to occur between infants and their caretakers as early modes of intersubjective uncertainty regulation insofar as such coordination provides means by which both members of the dyad feel assured that their relational needs will be met. I also believe that an important aspect of adult interaction, inside and out of the consulting room, also involves the intersubjective regulation of uncertainty. Moreover, I believe that such regulatory processes assume particular prominence in the context of trauma.

THE RELATIONSHIP BETWEEN TRAUMA AND SADOMASOCHISM

In a 1921 revision of *Beyond the Pleasure Principle* (Freud, 1920/1955) Freud hinted that the function of recurrent traumatic nightmares relates to "the mysterious masochistic trends of the ego." In this and in subsequent writings, Freud explained the essence of masochistic phenomena in terms reminiscent of his explanation of the repetition compulsion in that both were manifestations of the death instinct (e.g., Freud, 1937/1964). However, as Freud developed his understanding of masochism, he increasingly downplayed its roots in trauma and emphasized instead its relationship to the psychological development of women (Freud, 1919/1957, 1924/1961a, 1925/1961b). In subsequent writings, Freud (1919/1957) made it clear that masochism is always "feminine" regardless of whether it occurs in men or in women.

Beginning with Horney (1933/1967) and Adler (1927), many analysts through the years have taken strong exception to Freud's theory of masochism. A number of contemporary analysts have reestablished the connection between sadomasochism and trauma and have commented on its self-restitutive functions. Despite differences in theoretical language, Menaker and Kohut understand the relationship between narcissistic decompensation and sadomasochism in similar ways. In 1953, for example, Menaker suggested that masochistic self-hatred, self-devaluation, and feelings of worthlessness are the outcome of traumatic deprivation and serve self-preservation insofar as they are "a means of perpetuating whatever bond there is to the mother" (p. 224). Thus she appears to have anticipated Kohut's (1977) view that narcissistic decompensation as it relates to sadomasochism results from traumatic disappointment in those experienced as selfobjects[1] and the consequent need for self-restitution. Both theorists greatly furthered the understanding of sadomasochism as an intersubjective phenomenon.

Inspired by the pioneering perspectives of Menaker and Kohut, my understanding also emphasizes the roots of what has come to be known as sadomasochism in the traumatic disruption of self-experience. Although my understanding of trauma has undergone considerable transformation over the years (Ulman and Brothers, 1988; Brothers, 1995, 2000, 2001) what has remained constant is my conviction that trauma disrupts a sense of vital, cohesive selfhood. In 1995 I proposed that what lies at the heart of many traumas is an experience of betrayal of one's trust in oneself and/or in others needed to provide the experiences on which selfhood depends. I have since come to understand that a traumatically betrayed person may experience an intolerable sense of uncertainty that relationships with others will sustain his or her sense of cohesive selfhood. (I believe this is what Kohut [1971] meant by his expression "disintegration anxiety.") Restorative efforts in the aftermath of traumatizing betrayals often involve strenuous and, at times, drastic efforts to regulate this sort of uncertainty (Brothers, 2000, 2001, 2002).

In relational contexts in which the threat of retraumatization is strong, survivors may attempt to regulate uncertainty about the fulfillment of their relational needs by acting in ways that seem to recreate trauma as it originally occurred (Freud's repetition compulsion), ways that have been typically construed as masochistic or sadistic.

SADOMASOCHISM AS THE INTERSUBJECTIVE REGULATION OF UNCERTAINTY

In response to traumatizing betrayals of trust, certain trauma survivors relate to their betrayers, and others who resemble them, in ways that seem to invite further trauma. By engaging with such people as if the betrayal had not occurred—that is, in a way that is trusting and vulnerable—their behavior might appear to an outside observer as deserving of the term *masochistic*. However, when this sort of engagement, which sometimes involves a dissociative response to trauma, is regarded as inseparable from the relational contexts in which it arises, it may be understood as a desperate attempt to regain a sense of certainty about the availability of self-sustaining experiences. Consider, for example, a traumatizing betrayal that is inflicted by someone on whom the survivor is dependent for psychological survival, such as a parent or other caretaker. Urgently needing to regain a trusting connection, the survivor may act as trustingly as he or she did in the past. It is as if the survivor were insisting, despite all evidence to the contrary, "This time my vulnerability to betrayal will not be exploited; my trust will be confirmed. I will again feel certain of surviving."

Other survivors attempt to regulate uncertainty following a traumatizing betrayal in a very different way. Instead of experiencing themselves as vulnerable to betrayal, they attempt to experience themselves as invulnerable. Feeling invulnerable, for some of these survivors, means feeling as different as possible from those betrayed. Since no one seems less vulnerable than a betrayer, they may experience themselves as betrayers and behave in ways that are commonly regarded as *sadistic*. Feeling themselves to be powerful instead of helpless, hurtful instead of wounded, they hope to regain a lost sense of certainty about their ability to survive.

People who experience themselves as betrayed and as betrayers often seem irresistibly drawn to one another. Let me suggest one possible reason for these so-called sadomasochistic bondings. Those needing to feel vulnerable to betrayal may disavow incompatible aspects of themselves such as their boldness, anger, or aggressiveness. Similarly, survivors who experience themselves as betrayers frequently disavow their vulnerability, compassion, and fearfulness. They may find the disavowed aspects of themselves embodied in the others. By clinging together, both may feel certain of experiencing a sense of wholeness and safety that they are unable to feel alone.[2] This intersubjective configuration may have led to Stekel's (1953) assertion, "There is no sadism without masochism, and no masochism without sadism" (p. 138). Let us now consider how the intersubjective regulation of uncertainty pertains to gender.

THE IMPOSITION OF DICHOTOMOUS GENDER

As several writers have recently suggested (e.g., Lang, 1984; Lothstein, 1988; Pangerl, 1996), gender appears to be a fundamental organizer of subjectivity. Our experience of ourselves as gendered arises and is maintained intersubjectively. Many contemporary theorists such as Aron (1995), Benjamin (1988), Burch (1993), Butler (1989), Crawford (1996), Dimen (1991), Goldner (1991), and Harris (1991) reject the traditional view of gender as a naturally occuring binary system in which masculininity and femininity are established once and for all in early life. Some (e.g., Goldner, 1991) even suggest that pathological processes are activated in the development of gender as rigidly masculine or feminine—such as the disavowal of "gender incongruent" aspects of self-experience. Building upon this work, I view the disavowal of aspects of gendered experience in terms of uncertainty regulation.

Many people learn, very early in life, that qualities of self are deemed masculine or feminine according to strict cultural rules, and that relational experiences on which they depend for psychological survival are, to varying degrees, contingent on their adherence to these rules. Differential treatment, beginning moments after birth, shapes self-experience by instructing boys and girls as to which of their qualities and behaviors are likely to gain them needed relational experiences and which are not (Lang, 1984). In other words, the imposition of dichotomous gender may create a sense of comforting certainty about psychological survival, provided conformity to gender stereotypes is maintained. However, for some children this certainty takes a great toll. They may experience traumatizing betrayals when caretakers condemn aspects of themselves as inappropriate to their sex and threaten to withdraw needed relational experiences unless they are repudiated (Brothers, 1998).

Regulatory efforts in the aftermath of these betrayals often lead to the disavowal of gender-incongruent aspects of self-experience. Contact with others who embody these qualities (usually, but not always, members of the opposite sex) may restore a sense of self-cohesiveness and a sense of certainty that relational needs will be met. However, relationships based on such contacts appear to result in rigidly maintained gender dichotomies that impose innumerable restrictions on self-experience.

To the extent that dichotomous gender organizes self-experience it may itself be regarded as a means of uncertainty regulation. In other words, by conforming to stereotypic images of masculinity and femininity, men and women regulate their uncertainty about the fulfillment of relational needs.

CINDERELLA'S TRIUMPH

A popular contemporary version of *Cinderella* begins with the death of the child's mother. After her father's remarriage to a cruel woman with three ugly, lazy daughters, Cinderella is forced by these women to live among the cinders and to act as the household drudge. A fairy godmother enables Cinderella to go to the prince's ball by transforming her rags into a gorgeous ballgown, a pumpkin into a coach, and field mice into horses. She warns Cinderella that she must leave the ball at the stroke of midnight at which time everything will return to its original form. The prince, who falls in love with Cinderella, rediscovers her by means of a glass slipper she has dropped and that will fit no foot but her own.

It is possible to understand the reversal of fortune Cinderella suffers in the beginning of the story—she is forced to occupy a place of dishonor in a dark corner beside the hearth (the woman's domain)—as signifying the blow little girls receive when they become aware of themselves as female in a society that favors and privileges males. Her fate is at once understood by children who have already learned that caretakers cannot be trusted to provide needed relational experiences if they dare to exhibit those facets of self-experience associated with the opposite sex. The death of Cinderella's mother may symbolize the sense of loss little girls experience when they discover the extent to which their mothers are devalued in the world. That Cinderella's father disappears from the story and does nothing to protect her from mistreatment at her stepmother's hand may signify the betrayals inflicted by fathers who fail to guarantee their daughters' equality.

Cinderella's stepmother is anything but stereotypically feminine. Ugly, authoritarian, and sadistically exploitative, she is the ultimate caricature of the masculine woman. Yet it is she who won the prize of Cinderella's father. A cautionary figure, she seems to embody the "paradoxical injunction" (Goldner, 1991) on which so many little girls in our society are weaned: You must disavow your masculine-ascribed qualities and embrace stereotypic femininity or risk losing all selfobject provision; but if you do so, you must be prepared to give up all the entitlements of masculinity. Should you, like Cinderella's stepmother, exhibit masculine-ascribed qualites, you will be reviled as a witch or hag.

To my mind the story's enormous popularity attests to its success in solving the little girl's seemingly hopeless dilemma. Having found themselves, much like Cinderella, reduced in status after renouncing their prized masculine qualities, girls may search for ways to regulate uncertainty following this humiliating trauma. Cinderella shows them the way by obediently accepting her role as the exploited serving girl, the prototypical embodiment of the betrayed.

The remainder of the story may be interpreted as a handbook for uncertainty regulation. With her supernatural transformative powers, the fairy godmother appears to give form to a young child's longing for a connection to an omnipotent and eminently trustworthy maternal figure. Who could better instill a sense of certainty about psychological survival than a female figure endowed with such undeniable strength? And what better guarantee of future happiness than to have won the prince's heart?

The glass slipper is an ingenious symbol. Contrary to her stepsisters who aggresively try to force their big (masculine) feet into the tiny slipper, Cinderella's little (feminine) foot slips easily into it. Bettelheim notes, "Since the prince cherishes her slipper, this tells her in symbolic form that he loves her femininity." At the same time, by inserting her own foot into the slipper, Cinderella asserts that she, too, will be active in their sexual relationship. She never was lacking in anything: She has everything that fits, as her foot snugly fits into the slipper. Thus Cinderella offers little children hope that their efforts to regulate uncertainty in the face of traumas associated with the imposition of dichotomous gender will be successful.

Unfortunately, as the clinical example below demonstrates, such efforts rarely succeed in real life.

CINDY

My purpose in describing the initial phase of my therapeutic relationship with Cindy,[3] an obese single woman who entered treatment with me when she was in her late forties, is to illustrate a woman's unsuccessful attempts to regulate uncertainty related to gender both within and outside of treatment. As our therapeutic relationship gradually evolved, I came to think of Cindy's life as a Cinderella story minus the happy ending.

Dr. C., the last of three male therapists Cindy had seen during the previous 15 years, had referred Cindy to me when she relocated to my city for business reasons. Praising Dr. C. for his valiant efforts on her behalf, Cindy blamed herself for failing to lose weight despite having undertaken numerous diet and exercise programs with his support and encouragement. Seemingly intent on convincing me that her obesity was a physical manifestation of her worthlessness, Cindy asserted that her weight had rendered her ineligible for marriage and all of the rewards our society bestows on slim, beautiful women. She minimized her considerable success as a businesswoman and insisted that she was incapable of establishing lasting relationships with men or women.

Cindy needed little prompting to acquaint me with her painful history.

When she was only two years old, her mother died soon after giving birth to a healthy son. Her father placed the boy in the care of his parents for several years and, with the help of a housekeeper, devoted himself to raising Cindy. To Cindy's great distress, he remarried when she was seven years old. Despite her awareness, even as a young child, that her stepmother was kindly and well-intentioned, if not very knowledgeable or sophisticated, Cindy compared her unfavorably to her own mother at every opportunity. Although she had no memory of her mother, Cindy insisted that she had been the personification of virtue, intelligence, and caring. Feeling betrayed by her father and consumed with rage and jealousy that she dared not express, Cindy withdrew in silent despair. She recalled, with obvious pain, being chastized by her stepmother and her father for neglecting her grooming and flaunting her intellectual accomplishments. "I just never measured up to their ideals of feminine modesty and charm," she said.

Much of the problem, according to Cindy, was her appearance. Short, chubby (even as a seven-year-old), and brunette, with a rather prominent nose like her Jewish mother's, her appearance contrasted strikingly with the tall, blond members of her WASP stepfamily. Plastic surgery in adolescence that gave her a snubbed nose much like her stepsiblings' did little to alter Cindy's dim view of herself. Nor did she feel she achieved acceptability by repudiating her Jewish heritage and worshipping at a Protestant church. To make matters worse, Cindy's biological brother, who was restored to his father's care when he was five, was tall and sandy-haired like their father. Cindy envied his sunny disposition and the seemingly effortless way in which he accomodated to life with his new stepfamily.

Because, from an early age, Cindy chose female friends with pronounced psychological or physical disorders, these relationships often ended abruptly and traumatically in painful loss. The few men she dated, several of whom were married, invariably left her for other women. At the time she entered therapy with me, Cindy was convinced she was destined to live out her life in lonely isolation. In our early sesssions, she seemed wary and distant. Any time the flow of dialogue halted, she would complain that things were not going well between us. "I'm wasting your time and mine," she would sigh. Since Dr. C., a man of considerable renown (as Cindy often reminded me), had not helped her to lose weight, she thought it highly unlikely that I could. Although she never denigrated me as female openly, implicit in the doubts she voiced about my competence vis-à-vis Dr. C. was the fact that I am a woman. In fact, Cindy seemed preoccupied with my femininity. She frequently commented on my appearance (she saw me as slim and pretty), my soft voice, and the fact that I am married (I wear a wedding band). Admiring a dress of mine as "graceful" and "feminine," she remarked wryly, "I stopped looking like a woman a hundred and fifty pounds ago,"

In spite of her complaints about me, I enjoyed Cindy's incisive mind and her considerable wit. I also felt engaged by her and moved by her painful situation. Believing that she had begun to feel more trusting of me, I was startled and dismayed when, after approximately three months of weekly sessions, Cindy suddenly announced that she was considering leaving therapy. "You're Jewish, aren't you?" she said confrontingly. When I acknowledged that I was, she said, "Dr. C. didn't tell me you were Jewish when he referred me to you. I don't want to be reminded of all the pain I felt on account of my religion."

Suspecting that her concerns about my Jewishness reflected even more meaningful treatment issues, I urged her to explore this possibility with me before she left. In answer to my questions, Cindy admitted that she had suspected that I was Jewish from the outset. Asked why she had chosen this point in our relationship to confront the issue, she confessed that she had begun to feel anxious about feeling connected to me. When I suggested that my being Jewish might have reminded her of her mother, and that it would be understandable if she dreaded the repetition of some painful loss as the result of our connection, she became tearful. She thanked me for understanding how much she suffered on account of her mother's death. "Most people think I don't feel anything because I can't even remember being with her," she said. "It makes sense to me," I said gently, "that you might want to leave me to make sure that you won't get badly hurt again by a woman you want to take care of you." With some hesitation, Cindy agreed to continue therapy.

On returning after a brief visit to her stepmother, Cindy seemed quite depressed, and even more self-contemptuous than before. Several weeks passed before she finally described the events of her trip home. Her stepmother, she recounted, had casually commented on her mother's risking her life to give birth to Cindy's brother. She explained that doctors had warned her mother early in her pregnancy that she had a cancerous growth in her uterus and might die if she carried to term. However, believing that she would give birth to a boy, Cindy's mother had decided it was worth the risk. "If I had really made her happy," Cindy wept, "she might still be alive today. I guess having me, a girl, just wasn't enough for her." Her stepmother had expressed surprise that this information was news to Cindy since it was common knowledge in the family. "Could I have really known all this before and forgotten it?" Cindy wondered.

In the months that followed this disclosure, Cindy and I slowly came to understand the devastating meanings associated with her mother's death. There is little doubt that Cindy experienced her mother's choice to risk death in order to have a son as a massive betrayal. Not only was her trust in her mother shaken, but her trust in herself was shaken as well. Her failure to keep her mother alive represented an extreme self-betrayal. Only by dissociating her awareness of the circumstances of her mother's death was she able to maintain her idealization of her mother.

Cindy appears to have attempted to regulate her uncertainty in the face of this traumatizing betrayal by experiencing herself as vulnerable to betrayal.

For example, by involving herself with frail, sickly women who resembled her mother, Cindy apparently hoped for a different outcome. If a woman miraculously overcame her illness and maintained her connection to Cindy, her trust would be justified. Unfortunately, her regulatory efforts appear to have been doomed to retraumatizing failure as these relationships invariably ended in loss.

We also discovered that Cindy's obesity both concretized her mother's betrayal and played a major role in her uncertainty-regulating efforts. As a very young child, Cindy may have been able to recapture some experience of being connected to her pregnant mother by adding mass to her own little body. As she got older and came to believe that her mother valued maleness, and despised femaleness, Cindy appears to have repudiated her femaleness. However, growing up in a family that stressed conformity with stereotypic femininity, Cindy found herself faced with an insoluable dilemma. In order to win the esteem of her family members she needed to embrace all the qualities that society deems feminine. However, to do so meant that she would have been forced to repudiate her one basis for maintaining a trusting connection to her dead mother: the qualities she associated with being male. Being overweight thus provided a means, albeit a very problematic one, of maintaining her connection to her mother while appearing to accept the values of her stepfamily. As long as evidence of her gender was hidden with a padding of flesh, she could maintain the illusion that no betrayal had occurred.

In treatment with her male therapists, none of whom was Jewish, Cindy was able to find embodied in them the idealized attributes associated with masculinity and WASP entitlement she disavowed in herself. Unfortunately, instead of helping Cindy to integrate the dissociated aspects of her self-experience that were associated with both femininity and masculinity, these therapists seemed to endorse the ideals of dichotomous gender that shaped her childhood; they seemed bent on helping her to conform to the ideals of femininity (which necessitated her being thin) as an indication of psychological well-being.

In contrast to her male therapists, I appeared to have embodied all the qualities Cindy associated with her own disavowed femininity and Jewishness. Terrified that closeness with me would subject her to a retraumatizing betrayal, her uncertainty-regulating efforts involved experiences of herself as the betrayer and the betrayed. By criticizing me, comparing me unfavorably to her male therapist, and expressing her wish to end treatment, Cindy appears to have experienced herself as a betrayer. Not only was she critical and rejecting, but she hoped to make certain that she would not be retraumatized by leaving before she could be left. However, her choice to remain in treatment made her feel as if she had once again left herself vulnerable to retraumatizing betrayal.

By acknowledging the threat of retraumatization I posed to her, I not only bore witness to her suffering, but I helped her to believe that trusting and being trusted are not always preludes to pain and loss. Feeling more certain of my continuing availability, she was able to reclaim her knowledge of the circumstances of her mother's death, a first step toward integrating the dissociated gender-linked aspects of her self-experience. Without recourse to magic wands and glass slippers, much less to the appearance of a Prince Charming, Cindy and I have no illusion that our therapeutic relationship will unfold with fairy-tale ease and certainty. Yet, we are increasingly committed to traversing the twists and turns of our own emerging story together.

SUMMARY

The delightful fairy tale, *Cinderella*, can be understood as an allegorical account of uncertainty regulation related to the imposition of dichotomous gender. This reading provides an alternative to the traditional understanding of sadomasochism. Despite the happy outcome of Cinderella's regulatory efforts which involved her stance of vulnerability to betrayal, the prototypical masochistic posture, attempts by most real women to respond to gender traumas in this way rarely succeed. The case of Cindy, who experienced traumatizing betrayals related to gender with her mother's death when she was two, illustrates how such regulatory efforts can lead to enormous suffering. It also suggests how the concept of intersubjective uncertainty regulation may enhance the effectiveness of a therapeutic relationship.

NOTES

1. Selfobject experiences are those interactions among people that are perceived as facilitating the development, maintenance, and restoration of a sense of cohesive selfhood.
2. In earlier publications I refer to alter-ego selfobject experiences (Brothers, 1993, 1994, 1995)
3. I have changed my patient's name and disguised her identity in many ways.

REFERENCES

Adler, A. (1927). *Understanding human nature*, New York: Permabooks.
Aron, L. (1995). The internalized primal scene. *Psychoanalytic Dialogues*, *5*(2): 195–238.
Benjamin, J. (1988). *The Bonds of Love*. New York: Pantheon.
Berliner, B. (1947). On some psychodynamics of masochism. *Psychoanalytic Quarterly*, 16: 459–470.
Bettelheim, B. (1976). *The Uses of Enchantment: The Meaning and Importance of Fairy Tales*. New York: Knopf.
Brothers, D. (1995). *Falling Backwards: An Exploration of Trust and Self-Experience*. New York: Norton.
——— (1998). Exploring the "bi" ways of self-experience: Dissociation, alter ego selfobject experience, and gender. In: *Progress in Self Psychology*, Vol. 14, ed. A. Goldberg. Hillsdale, NJ: Analytic Press, pp. 233–252.

———. (2000). Faith and passion in self psychology, or, swimming against the post-modern tide of uncertainty. Presented at the 23rd International Conference on the Psychology of the Self. Chicago, November 11.

———. (2001). Ghosts of the silver screen and other self psychological reflections on the acceptance of death. Presented at the 24th International Conference on the Psychology of the Self. San Francisco, November 10.

———. (2002). After the towers fell: Terror, uncertainty, and intersubjective regulation. *Journal for the Psychoanalysis of Culture and Society* *8*(1): 68–76.

Brothers, D., & Lewinberg, E. (1998, October). *Contemplating the Death of Oedipus: Survival Tips for Self Psychologists.* Paper presented at the 21st Annual International Conference on the Psychology of the Self. San Diego.

Burch, B. (1993). Gender identities, lesbianism, and potential space. *Psychoanalytic Psychology, 10*(3): 359–376.

Butler, J. (1989). *Gender Trouble.* New York: Routledge.

Crawford, J. (1996). The severed self: Gender as trauma. In: *Progress in Self Psychology,* Vol. 12, ed. A. Goldberg. Hillsdale, NJ: Analytic Press, pp. 269–284.

Dimen, M. (1991). Deconstructing differences: Gender, splitting, and transitional space. *Psychoanalytic Dialogues, 1*(3): 335–352.

Freud, S. (1955). Beyond the pleasure principle. In: *Standard Edition,* Vol. 18, ed. and trans. J. Strachey. New York: Norton, pp. 3–64. (Original work published 1920)

———. (1957). A child is being beaten. In: *Standard Edition,* Vol. 17, ed. and trans. J. Strachey. New York: Norton, pp. 175–204. (Original work published 1919)

———. (1961a). The economic problem of masochism. In: *Standard Edition,* Vol. 19, ed. and trans. J. Strachey. New York: Norton, pp. 153–170. (Original work published 1924)

———. (1961b). Some psychical consequences of the anatomical distinction between the sexes. In: *Standard Edition,* Vol. 19, ed. and trans. J. Strachey. New York: Norton, pp. 243–258. (Original work published 1925)

———. (1964). Analysis terminable and interminable. In: *Standard Edition,* Vol. 23, ed. and trans. J. Strachey. New York: Norton, pp. 216–253. (Original work published 1937)

Goldner, V. (1991). Toward a critical relational theory of gender. *Psychoanalytic Dialogues, 1*(2): 249–272.

Harris, A. (1991). Gender as contradiction. *Psychoanalytic Dialogues, 1*(2): 197–224.

Horney, K. (1967). The problem of feminine masochism. In *Feminine Psychology,* ed. H. Kelman. New York: Norton, pp. 214–233. (Original work published 1933)

Kohut, H. (1971). *Analysis of the self.* New York: International Universities Press.

———. (1977). *The restoration of the self.* New York: International Universities Press.

Lang, J. A. (1984). Notes toward a psychology of the feminine self. In: *Kohut's Legacy: Contributions to Self Psychology,* eds. P. E. Stepansky & A. Goldberg. Hillsdale, NJ: Analytic Press.

Lothstein, L. (1988). Selfobject failure and gender identity. In: *Progress in Self Psychology,* Vol. 3, ed. A. Goldberg. Hillsdale, NJ: Analytic Press, pp. 213–235.

Menaker, E. (1953). Masochism as a defense reaction of the ego. *Psychoanalytic Quarterly,* 27: 205–220.

———. (1995). The Freedom to Inquire: Self Psychological Perspectives on Women's Issues, Masochism, and the Therapeutic Relationship. Northvale, NJ: Jason Aronson.

Pangerl, S. (1996). Self psychology: A feminist re-visiting. In: *Progress in Self Psychology*, Vol. 12, ed. A. Goldberg. Hillsdale, NJ: Analytic Press, pp. 285–298.

Sander, L. W. (1977). The regulation of exchange in infant-caregiver systems and some aspects of the context-contrast relationsip. In *Interaction, conversation, and the development of language*, ed. M. Lewis & L. A. Rosenblum. New York: Wiley pp. 133–155.

Stekel, W. (1953). *Sadism and masochism: The psychology of hatred and cruelty*, Vol. 1, trans. E. Cuthell. New York: Liveright. (Original work published 1929)

Stoller, R. J. (1975). *Perversion.* New York: Pantheon.

———. (1979). *Sexual excitement.* New York: Pantheon.

Ulanov, A., & Ulanov, B. (1983). *Cinderella and Her Sisters: The Envied and the Envying.* Philadelphia: Westminster Press

Ulman, R. B., & Brothers, D. (1988). *The shattered self: A psychoanalytic study of trauma.* Hillsdale, NJ: Analytic Press.

PART III

Psychoanalysis and Culture

CHAPTER 13

Ego in Evolution Revisited: The Menakers' Contribution to a New Psychoanalytic Psychology of Culture

Ludwig Janus and Brigitte Janus-Stanek

INTRODUCTION

As a result of the breadth of its theoretical perspectives and the openness with which it combined biological and psychological insights and allowed each to draw on the other, *Ego in Evolution* (William and Esther Menaker) made a great impression when it appeared in German in 1971. A creative synthesis of biological and psychological knowledge had taken place. Insofar as our knowledge about human behavior had been fundamentally extended by the insights of Lorenz and Tinbergen, compared to the knowledge available to Freud, the book's aim of incorporating this new knowledge was basically a convincing one. However, the Menakers went beyond this by using this basic biological knowledge to show the role and function of the ego in the process of human evolution in a new light. As they understood it, the ego was not merely a product of evolution—it also shaped evolution. This gave human responsibility in the process of life a new meaning.

The Menakers started out from clear clinical assumptions for their far-reaching theoretical considerations. In their psychotherapeutic sessions, they were constantly impressed by the strength with which patients strive for higher levels of integration and articulateness. This corresponded exactly to our observations of the natural vigor with which patients attempt to find a constructive solution to the inconsistencies of their family and social background in the way they choose to lead their own lives. If we take this view as our starting point, psychotherapeutic activity assumes a new focus. It is no longer merely concerned with resolving repression and symptoms, but becomes a form of support for the patient in his or her personal development in the context of the development of society and the age as a whole.

The aim and the basic philosophy of *Ego in Evolution* still seem just as modern as they did three decades ago. However, the preconditions for reaching a wider audience are now more favorable than they were when the book appeared in 1965, when the way in which psychoanalytical groups saw themselves was still very much determined by certain schools, traditions, and loyalties, and related disciplines were rarely incorporated. In this chapter, we will refamiliarize ourselves with some of the important aspects of the book and discuss several expansions on them that have become possible as a result of further developments in ethology and psychohistory.

THE EVOLUTIONARY UNDERSTANDING OF THE EGO

As the Menakers saw it, the ego is both the product and the driving force behind the process of human evolution and is a species-specific entity. It is the ability to synthesize and combine inner strength and the forces of the external environment in a reflective manner. An important instrument in this process is language, which dramatically increases our scope for insight and action. Perception of the self and the formation of symbolic concepts are specific to the human ego and move the capacity for reasonable behavior onto a new plane. In the Menakers' view, one of the important reasons for the development of this specifically human capacity for integration by the ego is the particular helplessness of human infants, with the capacity for inner guidance developing through the symbiosis between mother and child. The mother-child relationship is the social matrix in which the ego develops.

These assumptions are based on our knowledge of developmental psychology, which has vastly increased since Freud's time. In biological terms, this assumption is supported by the research by Portmann on human "prematurity," a summary of which did not appear until after the publication of the Menakers' book (Portmann 1969). Compared with our closest relatives in the animal kingdom, humans are born prematurely in physiological terms and spend the majority of the first year of life in the transitional period of babyhood. Gould (1992) therefore spoke of *human babies as embryos* in order to characterize this peculiarity of developmental biology, which accounts for what the Menakers describe as the "incompleteness of nervous organization" in terms of developmental biology. Thus, in humans, the early relationship between mother and child acquires a very particular significance in terms of developmental psychology as a social matrix, and this significance can be traced back to the prenatal period (Janus 1997a).

Processes involving learning and empathy compensate to some extent for the deficit of prematurity in terms of developmental biology. The Menakers describe in great detail how active learning and orientation processes in the child interact with the mother's understanding behavior derived from her "highly organized consciousness" to supplement the instinctive elements of the mother-child relationship in a constructive way. The "integrative processes of the ego" are communicated in the early interaction between mother and child. Empathic identification is of central importance in this context and provides a stimulus for the continuous development of the child's ego. The inner image that the mother has of her child is of primary importance here. From our current standpoint, the decisive factor is that the mother perceives her child's own specific feelings and desires right from the very beginning and is able to deal with them in a constructive way.

Unconsciously and even before the acquisition of language, the mother's behavior is internalized as a whole, forming the core of identification processes. The mother as a being is thus the first model for the child's ego in its further development. This early interaction between mother and child and between father and child contains great potential for intergenerational learning (Janus 1997b). In this context, new ways of seeing ourselves and our relationships in society can rapidly take on definite form and be implemented in the relationships of the next generation. This might be one explanation for the remarkable developmental dynamics of the human ego, as shown by cultural history.

The fact that the ego is influenced by the age is something that can also be seen directly in the development of the way in which psychoanalysis has regarded the ego. In accordance with the spirit of education in the nineteenth century, Freud's ego is largely at the mercy of the normative power of the superego and the force of its own instincts and can only reach compromises and adapt with great effort, just as the authoritarian structures of the empires in Central and Eastern Europe allowed only very limited scope for development. The Menakers' view of the ego as an integrative, constructive entity with its own creative options reflects the greater personal self-confidence in the developing modern democracies against the background of the democratic tradition founded in the United States. In this context, we can directly observe sociocultural development through the "improvement of autonomous functions of the ego" and the further development of "ego ideals." Social context and the development of the ego go hand in hand.

THE PSYCHOLOGICAL EVOLUTION

The peculiarities of early development in humans and their significance in the formation of the human ego form the background for psychological evolution with its interplay of cultural development and a greater structuring of personality. In the United States, as a result of emigration, each generation had to take great evolutionary steps, and this provided a particular opportunity to observe such evolutionary processes. The Menakers provide clear examples of this and describe the new type of patients who make their developmental tasks their own conscious, personal concern. These observations show that human beings have always been part of sociocultural evolution and that the development of humanity can be regarded in this sense as a creative process of group-related self-design. The process of psychological evolution is essentially characterized by an increasing inner structuring of personality and a greater scope for autonomous action.

The high degree of interaction at the beginning of an individual's life is matched by the close association of the developmental processes that the ego undergoes in adolescence with the social group in which the individual lives. The Menakers use the image of a spider in its web to evoke the interaction between civilization and the ego; the spider lives in the web it has created just as humans live in the civilization they have created, a civilization that they experience as something external. As the behaviorist Morris stated, we are the "only species that builds its own zoo"; however, we would like to add that we can therefore also alter it. The Menakers regard historical development as an ever-improving coordination of the structure of the ego and the social matrix, of the ego and society in the sense of a progressive evolutionary process.

In our view, these ideas create a new constructive framework within which the historical development of the ego and cultural evolution can be understood. What in the religious context was the story of Creation and in Hegel's philosophy was the development of the world spirit now acquires a more definite and more accessible frame of reference in connection with psychobiological evolution. We will now look at this frame of reference in detail.

The first attempt at this was made by Rank in 1930 in his description of the history of the way in which humans see themselves in *Psychology and the Soul—A Study of the Origin, Conceptual Evolution, and Nature of the Soul* (Rank 1930/1998). His concept of will is very close in meaning to the Menaker's concept of the ego.

An important contribution to the historical evolution of the ego was made by Lloyd DeMause in his psychohistory (1974, 1982). His *History of Childhood* opens up the way for the investigation of the history of relationships between parents and children over the centuries (Nyssen and Janus 1997). Analysis of the historical findings on relationships between parents and children allows us to make certain statements about the historical course of development. DeMause, too, believes that the capacity for empathy has increased in the relationships between parents and children, as assumed by the Menakers. General civilizational factors play a role in this context. As a result of the communicative processes in the early relationships between parents and children, there appears to have been an increase in the capacity for empathy, something that Frenken (1997) tried to show by analyzing historical autobiographies. Similarly, Shorter (1986) described an improvement in the relationships between parents and children over the past 200 years. All these insights and concrete examples have considerable social significance. However, due to the fragmentation of scientific disciplines, they are only very gradually becoming known.

EVOLUTION AND CONFLICT

The Menakers' evolutionary view of the ego puts the way in which we see fear and guilt—the cause of so many neurotic and psychosomatic disorders—in a new light. Insofar as the ego, as the force behind the evolutionary process, is always developing, fears and guilt form a fundamental part of human life—the former as a result of feelings of insecurity and change, and the latter as a result of autonomous self-determination. We are no longer living according to the rules of instinctive adaptation and purely biological evolution, but rather as human beings according to the rules of creative individuation and sociocultural evolution, with which by necessity fear and guilt are associated. Thus the concept of conflict acquires the positive significance of a force that promotes the progressing dynamic process of evolution. This leads to a new form of responsibility for our own development in the sense of a new form of ethics. The roots of these ethics are to be found in the potential for empathy and responsibility in the very early mother-child relationship, which in the course of the development of humanity has been extended to cover increasingly wide areas of human relationships and our way of dealing with ourselves.

An issue that the Menakers did not address were the traumatic aspects of the development of human culture and of the historical development of a structured ego. The early mother-child relationship was particularly susceptible to trauma, as this relationship was just as likely to be marked by deep suffering on the part of the mother or the parents and by the experience of violence, as by positive basic experiences. The glorious aspects of human individuation and the creation of the ego occurred against a background of great human misery and suffering. The evolution of the ego is also the history of destructive dangers.

CONCLUDING REMARKS

The Menakers dared to associate what seemed to be our so mentally oriented ego with its biological foundations in the evolutionary process and thus created a new framework for the way in which we see ourselves. The peculiarity of the ego with its inherent structure but at the same time its ability to change in the process of human history is the challenge presented by the new concept, the foundations of which the Menakers had laid for psychoanalysis in their book. There are certain parallels to Jung's thoughts on the ego complex, which have recently been comprehensively presented by Eschenbach (1996). Creative stimuli between psychoanalysis and analytic psychology would be possible here. The Menakers' views have acquired significant support since the publication of their book as a result of further developments in the field of behaviorism. In his book, *Die Rückseite des Spiegels* (*The Back of the Mirror*), Lorenz (1973) to some extent provided a broad fundamental explanation of the comments made in *Ego in Evolution* on the phylogenetic roots of the ego. In the view of Lorenz, the development of the ego function moved our capacity for emotion and insight, which is determined by the fact that we are related to the primates, onto a new plane of integration. The cognitive elements of this step in the evolutionary process are described in detail by Lorenz. At the same time as Lorenz, the Viennese biologist Riedl came to the same conclusions and provided a comprehensive presentation of his biological theory of knowledge in his book, *Biologie der Erkenntnis* (*The Biology of Knowledge*) (Riedl 1979).

In his book, *Ursprung und Gegenwart* (*Origin and the Present*), Gebser (1953) made some fundamental comments on the steps involved in the process of the ego's evolution. Gebser described the development of human consciousness from the magical to the mythical and rational way in which humans saw themselves and the world to the current "aperspective" view of the world. He uses the term "aperspective" to refer to the current possibility of adopting different ways of seeing and understanding things at the same time and of combining them. The entire process of the evolutionary development of the ego is characterized by an increase in the flexibility, responsibility, and creative potential of the ego. As Riedl remarks, we are the first generation to experience the evolutionary process ourselves and are thus the first to be able to help shape it in a responsible way. It is here that great possibilities are opened up to us by the evolutionary concept of the ego as developed in *Ego in Evolution*.

REFERENCES

DeMause, L. (1974). *The history of childhood.* New York: Psychohistory Press.

DeMause, L. (1982). *Foundations of psychohistory.* New York: Psychohistory Press.

Eschenbach, K. (1996). *Der Ich-Komplex und sein Arbeitsteam* [Ego and its working structures]. Bonz: Leinfelden.

Frenken, R. (1997). Aspekte der Geschichte der Kindheit anhand historischer Autobiographien [Aspects of the story of childhood through autobiographies]. In F. Nyssen and L. Janus, eds., *Psychogenetische Geschichte der Kindheit* [Psychogenic story of childhood]. Gießen: Psychosozial.

Gebser, J. (1953). *Ursprung und Gegenwart* (Origin and the Present). *The ever-present origin.* Athens: Ohio University Press, 1985.

Gould, S. (1992). Human babies as embryos. In *Ever since Darwin.* New York: Norton.

Janus, L. (1997a). *Enduring effects of prenatal life.* Northvale, NJ: Aronson.

Janus, L. (1997b). Psychobiologische Wurzeln der Geschichte der Kindheit [Psychobiologic roots of the story of childhood]. In F. Nyssen and L. Janus, eds., *Psychogenetische Geschichte der Kindheit* [Psychogenic story of childhood]. Gießen: Psychosozial.

Lorenz, K. (1973). *Die Rückseite des Spiegels—Versuch einer Naturgeschichte menschlichen Erkennens* [The back of the mirror—exploration of the natural story of human understanding]. Munich: Piper.

Menaker, E., and W. Menaker (1971). *Ich-Psychologie und Evolutionsprozess* [Ego in evolution]. Munich: Kohlhammer. (Original work published 1965)

Nyssen, F., and L. Janus, eds. (1997). *Psychogenetische Geschichte der Kindheit* [Psychogenic story of childhood]. Gießen: Psychosozial.

Portmann, A. (1969). *Biologische Fragmente in einer Lehre vom Menschen* [The biological dimension in the lives of people]. Basel: Schwabe.

Rank, O. (1998). *Psychology and the soul.* Baltimore: Johns Hopkins Press. (Original work published 1930)

Riedl, R. (1979). *Biologie der Erkenntnis* [The biology of knowledge]. Berlin: Parey.

Shorter, E. (1986). Die große Umwälzung in den Mutter-Kind-Beziehungen vom 18.–20. Jahrhundert [The big transformation in the mother-child relationship at 18 to 20 years old]. In J. Martin and A. Nitschke, eds., *Zur Sozialgeschichte der Kindheit.* Freiburg: Alber.

CHAPTER 14

The Human Fascination with Violence as a Response to Mortality Awareness

Daniel Liechty

In one of his last essays before his death, "The Moral Equivalent of War," William James (1910) made an enduringly astute observation about the paradoxical human attitude toward war and violence. James was writing at a time when progressive thinkers in many countries were working more or less on the assumption that in the modern world, major armed conflict between nations was a thing of the past. Modern warfare had become exponentially more destructive than warfare of the past. Recent wars such as those of Napoleon in Europe and the Civil War in America proved that the exclusionary lines of armed conflict were forever blurred. Civilian environments would from now on increasingly feel the direct effects of warfare, both as arenas suffering massive collateral damage and as direct targets of military aggression.

Now that the ravages of modern warfare were increasingly clear to all observers, progressive theorists were quite sure that the old equations which justified warfare, namely gaining loot and extending a sphere of influence, were finally broken. Certainly there was no prospect of enough gain to make the suffering of modern warfare an acceptable price to pay. After all, loot and influence aplenty can be gained just as effectively through peaceful trade as through warfare. Therefore, the sputterings of a kaiser or a general here and there notwithstanding, there was a commonly held assurance that all logic and rationality now stood clearly on the side of the peace parties and that warfare was fast on the way to extinction.

In this atmosphere, James's essay raised a cautionary note. For James saw clearly that although human beings all would agree to the maxim War is hell, he also understood that people are drawn to hell, are fascinated with hell. Simply demonstrating the irrationality and horror of warfare and violence does nothing in and of itself to change this fascination. For the horrors are intrinsic to the thrill. The horrors increase the fascination. We are drawn to massively destructive power by a deeply felt yearning we hardly understand.

James suggested that for the militarists, warfare and violence contained a mystical character that was beyond reason and logic. There is something horrible and yet admittedly attractive and awe-inspiring about warfare, which James described as life in extremis. He read and took seriously the militarist literature which was largely ignored by other progressive thinkers as the death rattles of a perishing breed. In these writings James encountered a mystical love and fascination with warfare which was impervious to rational arguments on the level of an economic cost/benefit analysis.

A world without war and preparation for war was not at all a desirable world in this literature. It was a world of soft virtues and malleable spirits. In the writings of these militarists, war is depicted as a sort of religious sacrament of salvation, salvation from a world dominated by pulpy and tranquil clerks and teachers. A world without the risks and daring which warfare produces is a world without adventure and romance. The possibility of sudden and violent death in the pursuit of a goal is the very soul of romance! This is the spice that makes life worth living. Warfare provides the prizes for those daring to risk even life itself. There is an inevitable blood-tax on any kind of pride and honor worthy of the name. Facing down the enemy in a battle to the death inspires that quality of dispassionate or disinterested contempt for life that is the chief characteristic of moral strength.

Military organization requires that common submission to the discipline of the collectivity which is the root of all that is good in being human. Warfare is a gift from God, the very mechanism by which God calls forth and judges nations on the stage of history, weighing the totality of virtues of each nation in the balance. Through warfare a people proves its superiority before the highest court available—the court of history and of the gods.

This is all very mystical and arcane. It is easy to see why progressive people of reason and learning would ignore it. Yet the wisdom of James's cautionary note against simply ignoring it rings all the truer now, reading it as we do on this side of two world wars, of Auschwitz and Hiroshima, Afghanistan and Vietnam, and the endless stream of armed skirmishes, police actions, left- and right-wing terrorist activities, and revolutions which have characterized the final decades of our century. The mystical attraction to warfare and violence has hardly waned since James penned his essay. These and similar doctrines extolling violence are taught daily in pockets of political extremism, from the militias and neo-nazis on one side to the Kymer Rouge and leftist revolutionaries on the other. We hear it as well in the lyrics of some rap artists who give voice to street gangster philosophies and in the screeds of self-styled murderers such as Charles Manson and the Unabomber.

It is almost too tempting for we peaceful and progressive folk today to ignore this material, to pass it off as lunacy or at least as the product of a vicious and turbulent upbringing. In other words, our temptation is to do whatever we can to insist that this sort of love of violence has nothing to do with us. It only has to do with them. We refuse to acknowledge our own fascination with violence, with military virtues and with massive destructive power. We split it off and repress it, keep the lid on it tight. Don't look at me, look at them. And so we continue to insist on and prove our superiority in a different game, but a game with essentially the same rules.

Ernest Becker's restatement of and expansion on the theories of Otto Rank give us at least some handle on this dark human love of violence and fascination with massive destructive power (Becker 1972, 1973, 1975). Becker would not dispute that this dark love of violence and fascination with massive destructive power is irrational. But as William James did 90 years ago, Becker suggests that there is method in this human irrationality and that any attempts to ameliorate the consequences of this human attraction will be possible only if we face as honestly as possible the sources of this irrational attraction.

Becker's entire work was driven by the overriding question: "What makes people act the way they do?" During the course of his intellectual development, Becker examined each of the major psychological and sociological theories concerning human motivation (Liechty 1995, 1998a). He eventually concluded that the root motivation for human behavior is deeper than sexual and aggressive drives, deeper than power and acquisitive drives, and deeper than imitative or conformity drives. Becker convincingly demonstrated that what appears to be a root motivation in each of these psychological and sociological theories can best be understood as a particular mode or strategy for coping with overwhelming death anxiety. With this discovery of the centrality of death anxiety, Becker developed a psychological anthropology that is able to interpret the wide complexity of human psychological, sociological, and spiritual reality; it avoids the materialistic reductionism of scientistic or Marxian influenced views on the one hand and also avoids the ethereal esotericism of the Jungians or the more flighty humanistic theories on the other hand. Becker's psychological anthropology is firmly rooted in biological reality—the universal fact of death.

There is nothing mystical about this theory, nothing which demands a leap of faith in order to understand or accept it. Yet rooted as it is in biological reality, it also incorporates social and cultural reality in a truly integrated manner. That is, social and cultural reality are as much the meat of the theory as is biological reality. It is not simply tacked on at the end.

Beginning with his earliest writings, Becker was working within an evolutionary model. He assumed that human beings are an evolved species on this planet, engaged in an ongoing, puzzling, and, at times, contradictory task of trying to understand the whole of existence from a vantagepoint of being but part of that wider whole. The main characteristic that sets the human species apart from other species is the human ability to use language—or, more specifically, to use language that contains the first person singular (Becker 1972;

Jaynes 1976). Whatever else is involved in the early socialization process, the very key to what it means to be human is learning the proper use of the linguistic first person. It is in learning this linguistic function that self-consciousness is born. Here we have the emergence of an animal that not only exists, but knows that it exists, and knows that it knows it exists. We might say that the most basic definition of human being is a self-conscious animal.

A self-conscious animal. That is very simple, but it takes on an almost frantic dimension when we realize that a self-conscious animal is actually a sort of oxymoron. In everyday language, our whole orientation to other species is summed up in the phrase "dumb animals." When you examine the way in which those people who work most closely with animals use this phrase "dumb animals"—people such as farmers, veterinarians, horse or dog breeders, perhaps zookeepers—you see that it is not used to mean that animals do not feel pain or have no rights. It is not even used to mean that animals have no emotions or feelings. I don't think any of us doubt that at least for the higher primates, animals experience an impressive level of joy in living, of exhilaration and delight, of anger and rage, of vexation and aggravation, of possessiveness and territoriality, of depression and despondency, and even of affection and attachment bordering on love. Some of us would insist that all animal emotions are instinctual responses and somehow of a different order and therefore less important than human emotions. I wouldn't argue that point; I used to hold that view myself and was not convinced otherwise by logical discourse of argument. I left that point of view behind when, on a National Geographic television special, I watched a great ape cry and mourn over the dead body of her mate. Repeatedly she would lift his head and arms and try to animate the corpse, and then collapse again into howls of grief and lament. Watching this display, I was moved to the view that there cannot be any tangible difference between animal emotions and human emotions and that, furthermore, animal emotions are certainly no less significant than human emotions (McCarthy and Masson 1996).

No, the distinctively human does not abide in the area of emotions. It lies in the area of consciousness. Animals are certainly conscious. But as far as we can tell, even the higher primates are not self-conscious. Or to put it differently, human beings are animals, but among all animal species, human beings are not "dumb animals." At its most basic level, the frantic aspect to this evolutionary product we call the human species is this. The evolutionary process has endowed all living things with a large dose of what we might call Eros, or Primary Narcissism: a survival instinct, an absolutely basic and overriding will to continue existing. It is clear why the evolutionary process would instill this force in all successful living creatures, not only animals but even plants, germs, and viruses; for without it, the species would not long survive.

This same evolutionary process has endowed various species with much different strategies for fulfilling this survival instinct. For most species, the strategies for survival are so focused on the survival of the group that they appear to be downright suicidal to the individual. Worker bees thronging directly into a burning hive so as to furiously beat their wings and thus cool the wax comb in which the larvae are housed is one example of this. However, when one thinks of the entire hive as an entity and the individual bees as cells within that entity, then whether in watching those bees continue to beat their wings furiously as orange flames engulf them, or in watching a cancer patient struggle to suck down just one more breath of air, putting unimaginable effort into the fight to continue existing for even just 10 seconds more, one confronts on a very primitive level the power of this basic Eros, this Primary Narcissism, this instinct for survival.

In producing a self-conscious animal, the evolutionary process has endowed human beings with a very complex survival strategy. Human beings are able to freeze time, to experiment and imagine, and to mentally project the self into as-yet-nonexistent environments. To illustrate this, let us use a thought experiment. An early human being might know from random hard experience that warmth is needed for survival, and hence caves are good places to live because they are warmer than the open air. That same random hard experience also informs this early human being that fire creates warmth. This level of knowledge might be shared with all of the higher primates. But self-consciousness allows the human being to make another mental move. By freezing time frames, mentally existing in the past, present, and future simultaneously, the human being imagines a totally not-yet-existing environment, the cave containing a fire. This same early human being then mentally projects him- or herself into that environment and finds that it is good. Hence, this early human being sets out to create this not-yet-existing environment and to inhabit it.

If you just look at the human body and its natural equipment, it is not very impressive. No sharp teeth or claws, no warm fur, pathetically limited powers of vision and hearing; we can't run fast, we have very limited numbers of offspring per litter, and furthermore, we are subject to middle-age spread in the waistline and male-pattern baldness to boot! Yet because of this strategy for survival, the human species has been able to successfully move into an extremely wide variety of physical environments and thrive there. Our species literally covers this planet; we have mentally projected ourselves onto other planets and are now well on the way to figuring out how we can bring into actuality those not-yet-existing environments in outer space.

There is no doubt that we human beings live at a different level of consciousness than other animals, but, as Becker suggested, here again expanding on an insight of Otto Rank, this is both our blessing and our curse. The blessing is that it has made us a very successful species in comparison to our animal siblings. The curse is that the gift of self-consciousness sets us at odds with that most basic natural Eros, that Primary Narcissism, which we share with all living things. For now that I exist, and know that I exist, and know that I know I exist, and can freeze time and can project myself into the future in not-yet-existing environments, I come upon an inevitable and unavoidable fact. That simple fact is that I am mortal, that death happens to me, that do what I will to survive and continue existing, any success is short term and sooner or later, death will win out.

According to this view, this undeniable fact of death is the very root of our problem. In creating a species whose main survival strategy is in direct conflict with evolution's own universal Eros or Primary Narcissism, evolution has created a self-contradictory animal. In terms of our mental abilities, humans are truly divine beings, transcendent and ethereal. In our minds we create new worlds and sit on the far side of the planets. Yet this divine and ethereal self-consciousness is entirely dependent on a weak and vulnerable physical body which hungers, thirsts, defecates, ages, and finally dies. It dies, and knows that it dies, and knows that it knows it dies.

Awareness of mortality is the dark side of self-consciousness, of not being a "dumb animal" (Kauffman 1995). As far as we know, we are the only species which knows and understands the reality of death years before it happens. Some animals never seem to understand death, even as the predator pounces or the butcher's blade is poised for the kill. Others of our animal siblings do seem to experience a kind of terror just prior to the mortal blow—that look of terror on an animal face has haunted each and every one of us! But we are beings who must live with that furious terror within us, now simmering, now boiling, from that time in early childhood until the day the death angel calls. There is a worm of anxiety and terror gnawing at the core of human existence which is not a symptom of neurosis or morbidity, but rather an integral aspect of who we are as living beings.

Mortality awareness confronting the universal Eros we share with all living things creates an incredible level of terror deep within the psyche of every human being. We confront this terror most nakedly in the experience which St. John of the Cross referred to as "the dark night of the soul"—that experience of sheer horror, of nothingness, when you lay there in a cold sweat mentally, emotionally, and spiritually wrestling with the Devil himself.

According to this view, our general psychic movement is constantly one of repressing the massiveness of that terror and then calling it up and confronting this terror in smaller, more manageable doses. As has now been robustly demonstrated by empirical experimental investigation, finding strategies for taming and managing this most basic terror is quite literally the central human task (Solomon, Greenberg, and Pyszczynski 1998). For without some success in taming this terror—in suppressing it from immediate consciousness—a person would be psychotically stunned and unable to maintain forward movement.

The strategies for taming this basic terror are myriad, but they reflect one of two basic pure types. Examples of the pure types are rare in actual human history. Any actually existing strategy is going to be some combination of the pure types. Before we look at these tendencies, it is important to notice two things. The first is that from any objective perspective, any of these strategies is "fictitious," to use Becker's favorite term. That is, while each of these strategies makes the claim to conquer death and offer immortality, we have no reason based on demonstrated evidence to assume that any of these strategies actually removes from us the specter of death and mortality. Therefore, while it is not logically impossible that one of these amongst all others is right in some absolute sense, we cannot know this and therefore must conclude that in overwhelming likelihood, the claim for any of these strategies to actually conquer death and offer immortality is not real. The conviction of such claims for any particular strategy is contained rather in its power to help us to psychologically manage the terror of death and mortality. The second thing to notice is that because any of these strategies is directly employed to help us confront the mysteries of life and death, of mortality and immortality, any strategy is in the broadest sense of the term deeply religious in character. We may speak of a distinction between secular and religious strategies on the social level, but on the psychological level, all strategies are religious. Religious fascination is our response to mortality awareness.

Now let us look at the two pure types of response. The first tendency is to continue the movement of individuation and to try to earn personal immortality even at the expense of others. This strategy allows one an illusory sense of superiority over the "merely human" by attachment to a game in which one obviously stands above the rest. The child's game "King of the Mountain" suggests this strategy. The second strategy is to move in the opposite direction, finding one's own immortality in the eternal survival of the species. The bee furiously beating its wings in the face of personal death is an example of this pure type. I can't think of any children's games offhand that suggest this type, but certainly many team sports contain a strong element of this energy, in which important roles are given for blockers, decoys, and those who assist and set up the play for another member of the team to do the deed and win the glory. At the same time, any competitive game will also contain at its heart a variation of the "King of the Mountain" energy as well.

As this illustrates, any actual historical example of an immortality strategy will show some mixture of these two pure types. What all have in common, however, is a very identifiable mechanism. This mechanism for taming of the terror of mortality awareness is the creation of symbols of immortality with which people identify themselves and through which people vicariously participate in immortality. It is the creation of and participation in what Becker called "immortality projects," both on a personal and social/communal level, which is the very energy and substance of both individual human psychology and of human culture (Becker 1973; Farrell 1998).

According to this view, we all want to endure and prosper and in some sense gain immortality. But because we are mortal, and therefore subject to overwhelming anxiety in the face of our mortality, we must strive to mask the fact of mortality and suppress awareness of it from consciousness through participation in projects of immortality. Each and every person is doing this all the time. Each and every society and culture contains dominant immortality strategies, those shared by the largest number of people. These generally correspond to what Marx called the dominant social ideologies of a given society. There are subdominant immortality strategies at work as well, and any human culture can be analyzed as a complex amalgam of hundreds and thousands of immortality games and strategies which are offered to the people of that culture and by which the people maintain a sense of individual and collective immortality. This view parallels closely the "game" approach to understanding self-esteem maintenance in the context of communication strategies (Becker 1964; Goffman 1959; Greenberg, Pyszczynski, and Solomon 1993)

Because all immortality projects, games, and strategies are ultimately fictitious, we must expect that each one exacts a certain toll on its participants. There is a tax to pay, in other words, for keeping the credibility of the game alive and functioning. For "King of the Mountain"-type games, the toll is clear. There can only be one winner, and the cost exacted for there to be this one winner is a mountain of losers. In other games the cost exacted is perhaps less obvious. Generally speaking, those who are involved in the game believe in it, literally and religiously, for only the maximum of conviction will keep the game in motion as a buffer against mortality anxiety. They will encounter as threatening anything that either questions the game's absolute importance or points toward the fictitious nature of the game itself.

We tend to encounter "outsiders" with suspicion and as potentially threatening not so much, for instance, because we have had repeated experiences of being physically attacked by strangers, but rather because we have an intuitive sense that they are not invested in our games and therefore have the potential of revealing to us the fictitious character of what we are doing. We neutralize this potential threat by converting them (making them participants in our games) or by denigrating them (convincing ourselves that their differing view is not important or worthy of attention).

Those involved in a given immortality game are likely to be blind to the costs it exacts, as it will seem to them as simply a part of the natural order of things. The costs will be seen more clearly by those less involved in that game. I am amazed, for example, that people deeply involved in the immortality project of capitalist accumulation can so easily downplay the environmental costs of this mode of immortality ideology. On the other hand, I remain most of the time blissfully unconscious of the acres of forests and exotic hardwood trees which have been sacrificed for my own rather extensive collections of books and guitars. When I do think about it, it is mostly to shrug my shoulders.

Our immortality projects are our religion, and we hold to them religiously. If you begin to doubt the absolute worth of what you are doing in life, you may well find yourself courting a breakdown of the worst sort. This is true for individuals, but no less true for whole societies. There are limits, of course, to what nature will allow in terms of an immortality ideology. Ideologies that are successful in terms of cultural evolution do not soon force a confrontation with nature. For example, a game which suggests that immortality is offered to those who jump off high cliffs and fly through the air is never likely to become a dominant immortality ideology. Nature simply won't allow it. On the other hand, a game which offers immortality to those who regularly eat a small piece of bread and sip from a small cup of wine, by which they vicariously participate in the immortality of one who has conquered death and the grave, is not going to be disallowed by nature. So long as this game remains convincing to people, it has a strong chance of becoming or remaining a dominant immortality strategy.

In all immortality ideologies we are seeking protection from our own mortality, that is, from that which we perceive in ourselves as ultimate powerlessness. Human beings have always been drawn to people and ideologies that seem to possess power, for power suggests the possibility of victory over our ultimate powerlessness (Ehrenreich 1997). We are drawn to powers of creativity, for creativity suggests that we are indeed worthy of immortality. Unfortunately, the kind of power human beings are able to maintain over the longest periods of time tend toward destructive powers. This is the root cause of our undeniable love of violence. We are fascinated by displays of military hardware, fighting skills, and victorious violence, that is, displays of coercive or threat power. We are fascinated by displays of wealth and hold in high esteem those who seem able to bend others to their will by wielding economic power. We are also fascinated by the skill of the wordsmith, those able to bend others to their will by employing manipulative, persuasive power (Boulding 1989).

One of Becker's most important suggestions is that we might begin to construct a true discipline of comparative politics, religion, and culture if we approached these subjects from the perspective of a discipline of comparative immortality ideologies (Becker 1967, 1975). Such a discipline would investigate cultural, religious, and political systems with a set of very clear and simple questions in mind. What are the dominant immortality strategies within this system? Do the benefits of participation in these dominant immortality ideologies spread wide among the mass of people or do they accumulate mainly at the top? What are the costs—in blood, toil, mental and physical slavery, and environmental destruction—exacted to maintain various immortality ideologies? Are the costs spread evenly among the participants or do some segments of the society pay disproportionately? By analyzing the many systems of politics, religion, and culture in this way, we begin to gain a better grasp of what works better and what works less well. We might then begin to work toward enhancing those systems that work better and allowing to atrophy those systems that work less well.

Every system of immortality ideology, whether religious or political, posits a problem, a drama of history, and then a solution to that drama which is consistent with the way the problem is framed in the first place. If all of humanity found any one of these systems overwhelmingly convincing at the same time, salvation history would be complete. It wouldn't really matter which one we followed. The fact that one ideology brought salvation would then act as absolute empirical verification that the system was correct in the first place. Granted, universal systems which include in the fruits of salvation all ethnic, racial, or religious groups are more amenable to my personal preferences than those which scapegoat and exclude particular groups. On the other hand, if the murder of, say, the X people had in fact brought about world utopia, it would be very difficult even for the most sensitive among us to feel too bad about it, especially if it happened long ago and far away and the moral practices of the excluded group were quite in conflict with our own. We are now told that the very existence of our species is predicated on the fact that our early ancestors wiped out other, competing (and evidently more peaceful and communal) early hominoid species. It is difficult to feel regret for that now. Tribal peoples are being wiped out quite regularly in South American rainforests for a lot less than global utopia, and most of us, myself included, rarely give it much thought.

As an example of how we might go about exploring this method of analysis, we might pose a simple Chi-square structure for various cultural immortality ideologies, based on whether they promote universal or particular immortality, and whether they promote violent power or persuasive power as the privileged means to achieve its ends. Examples of a peaceful/particular immortality ideology might be the Jehovah's Witnesses or the Hutterites. Violent/particular immortality ideologies might be represented by various stripes of nationalism and certainly by Nazism. Violent/universal immortality ideologies might include classical revolutionary Marxism and Imperialistic Liberalism. Peaceful/universal ideologies would include One World and United Nations visions for the human future, as well as a whole spectrum of pacifist political and religious thought. This kind of classification, as well as awareness of how and when, and the conditions under which, an ideology might move from one category to another, might help us at least make some sense of the clashes we see daily in our violent world.

Elsewhere Becker wrote that the ideal/real model for any society of human beings would be that which offers maximum individuality within a context of maximum community—where the strength of individual meaning is upheld within the context of communal meaning. This continuum would further refine the analysis of particular societies and social ideologies. Of course, no type of analysis, no matter how sophisticated, mechanistically frees us from the need for value judgments. Where would you place a system, for example, that offers widespread participation in the dominant immortality ideology, but which does so by creating a small outgroup which is more or less per-

	Universal	Particular
Violent	(Violent/Universal) Imperialism Revolutionary Marxism	(Violent/Particular) Fascism Nationalism
Nonviolent	(Nonviolent/Universal) Pacifist Utopianism United Nations	(Nonviolent/Particular) Pacifist Sects and Cults

manently condemned to the life of beasts of burden? What about a system in which immortality is offered very convincingly to every person, but in which modern education is forbidden to women? Where on our scale would we place a society that offers widespread peace and prosperity, is ecologically viable, allows people large areas of freedom for personal development, and is very convincing to its people in terms of the social immortality project—but for which the very psychological cement for this society, the act which produces and maintains among its participants the maximum level of conviction necessary to keep the game in motion, is the periodic, public sacrifice of one member of the society? Would it be any better were that human sacrifice a convicted criminal rather than an innocent young maiden? Would a convicted criminal every month be considered better or worse than an innocent maiden once a year or once a decade?

I pose these questions not to be facetious. I do so, rather, to emphasize the point that Becker did not offer yet another salvation ideology, in either religious or political garb. In fact, the more immersed one becomes in Becker's writings, the more one begins to wonder if salvation ideologies are not themselves at least one of our major human problems. More real human and planetary misery has been produced in the name of salvation ideologies than by all the good old-fashioned cynical and sinful hedonism of this world put together.

By way of conclusion, I return to William James and his essay. Given a Beckerian reading of this essay, one would conclude that James was on to something very important. He was telling other progressive and pacifist theorists that we must take with utmost seriousness the immortality ideologies of the militarists. For those participating in the immortality games and strategies of militarism, it is more or less useless to point out the costs exacted by those games. The militarists will be no less blind to the costs exacted by their games than the progressives are blind to the costs exacted by their own games. James suggested, and Becker would have wholeheartedly agreed, that if there is a way forward, it will only come as we are able to offer those caught up in massively destructive immortality ideologies convincing new immortality strategies that are less destructive. Radical conversions are not likely and are inherently unstable. But the views of William James, Otto Rank, and Ernest

Becker do give us some direction for the task before us, of working in small steps to ameliorate at least the worst aspects of our increasingly violent world.

REFERENCES

Becker, E. (1964). *The revolution in psychiatry: The new understanding of man.* New York: Free Press.

———. (1967). *Beyond alienation: A philosophy of education for the crisis in democracy.* New York: George Braziller.

———. (1972). *The birth and death of meaning: An interdisciplinary perspective on the problem of man.* New York: Free Press.

———. (1973). *The denial of death.* New York: Free Press.

———. (1975). *Escape from evil.* New York: Free Press.

Boulding, K. (1989). *Three faces of power.* Newberry Park, CA: Sage Publications.

Ehrenreich, B. (1997). *Blood rites: Origins and history of the passions of war.* New York: Metropolitan Books.

Farrell, K. (1998). *Post-traumatic culture: Injury and interpretation in the nineties.* Baltimore: Johns Hopkins University Press.

Goffman, E. (1959). *The presentation of the self in everyday life.* New York: Anchor-Doubleday.

Greenberg, J., T. Pyszczynski, and S. Solomon. (1993). The causes and consequences of the need for self-esteem. In R. F. Baumeister, ed., *Public self and private self,* 189–212. New York: Springer-Verlag.

James, W. (1910). The moral equivalent of war. *McClure's Magazine* 35: 463–468; *Popular Scientific Monthly* 77: 400–412; J. J. McDermott, ed., *The Writings of William James,* 660–671. New York: Random House.

Jaynes, J. (1976). *The origins of consciousness in the breakdown of the bicameral mind.* Boston: Houghton Mifflin.

Kauffman, J., ed. (1995). *Awareness of mortality.* Amityville, NY: Baywood Publishing.

Liechty, D. (1995). *Transference and transcendence: Ernest Becker's contribution to psychotherapy.* Northvale, NJ: Jason Aronson.

———. (1998). Reading Ernest Becker: His contribution to spiritual, pastoral and psychological counseling. *American Journal of Pastoral Counseling* 1, no. 2: 49–69.

McCarthy, S., and J. M. Masson. (1996). *When elephants weep: The emotional lives of animals.* New York: Delta.

Solomon, S., J. Greenberg, and T. Pyszczynski. (1998). *Zygon: Journal of Religion and Science* 33, no. 1: 9–43.

CHAPTER 15

Considering a Multicultural Perspective for Psychoanalysis

RoseMarie Perez Foster

As psychoanalytically trained clinicians, we carry a secret shame. While being members of a field that prizes the value of all human life and people's efforts to realize their fullest potentials, analysts also know that they, in fact, touch a very narrow range of people. As private practitioners, many of us assuage our guilt by reducing our private fees so that we can see the student, the less privileged, or the immigrant patient. Some of us work in clinics and city hospitals where we offer ethnic minority patients a brand of psychodynamic psychotherapy. But this does not address the real problem. Our hidden shame is that psychoanalysis has a very defined view of life and how it should be lived, and it is this perspective that determines who is to be treated, who is analyzable, who has adequate ego strength, who can meaningfully relate to objects, and who is capable of exploring his or her deep inner self. We see those who do not fit into our life program as "simpler people" who have limited or narrower life goals, "poor people" who are too consumed with the reality-based problems of daily survival, or "foreign people" who come from alien cultures or alien neighborhoods and simply do not fit the picture of self-actualization as we define it in our psychoanalytic culture. The bold fact is that for the most part, we work best with those people who are most like us—the middle class and educated who basically think and live the way we do.

When we stand back and assess the health of the psychoanalytic movement in the United States and its efficacy as a clinical approach for the mental conditions of American people at large, we cannot deny our increasing marginalization.

In the last two decades, the American mental health field as a whole has been engaged in a great deal of self-criticism over the effectiveness of therapeutic services for poor and ethnically diverse groups (Abramowitz & Murray, 1983; Atkinson, 1985; Sue, 1988). Criticism has focused on discriminatory practices directed toward the poor, therapists' lack of knowledge and understanding of the cultural contexts of their ethnic patients, and the inaccessibility of services available to the non–middle class. As a result, studies have uncovered therapist prejudice, clinical bias in diagnosis, and premature termination rates among non-middle-class patients (Sue, 1988). Questions have even been raised about the value of using psychodynamically oriented therapies with minority patients who are clinically described in some literature as lacking the ability to explore the meaning of their experiences (Olarte & Lenz, 1984).

Something has clearly gone wrong with the treatment of those people who are not highly educated, middle class, or of European origin. Given this grim state of affairs, it is rather striking that the psychoanalytic community has, for the most part, remained silent. This theoretical community, which has always attempted to describe, understand, and treat the emotional conflicts of the human condition, seems to have fallen woefully behind its own critical self-examination of the crisis at hand. The crisis may very well be that psychoanalysis as it stands today is simply not made for Everyman and Everywoman (Foster, 1993).

Although I would like to address some of these issues in this chapter, I first wish to note that by suggesting an expansion of the psychoanalytic method into the wider multicultural arena, I am not talking about modifications in technique or the use of so-called parameters in treating the poor, less educated, or culturally diverse patient. I intend to suggest no such value-laden or condescending compromise of the real "analytic thing." Instead, I am proposing a basic reconsideration of how we use our metapsychologies, as well as a reemphasis on the coexperiential human action that lies at the base of our clinical technique. The goal is to develop a method of psychic inquiry that would accommodate a much wider spectrum of living activity as viable and workable data for the therapeutic frame. The large number of people judged as nontreatable by our method must push us as humanistically oriented clinicians to question our theoretical and clinical paradigms. The issue here is not the intellectual excitement of new ideas or the thrill of challenging traditional models but rather, simply, the fact that too many people are not being cared for (Foster, 1993). Just as psychoanalysis clinically matured and widened its range of application to the spectrum of treatable psychopathology, so must it now consider impediments to its application in the wider multicultural/multiracial context.

I would like to go about addressing this issue by highlighting two contemporary thrusts in psychoanalytic thinking that have occupied the stage of recent theoretical debate. The first concerns our epistemological approach to clinical data and our use of theoretical metapsychology. The second concerns clinical technique and the new emphasis on the coexperiential and intersubjective action of the therapeutic field (Foster, 1993).

ON THE THEORETICAL METAPSYCHOLOGY

We are told that all across the intellectual landscape, epistemological currents have shifted from the dogmatic emphasis on certainty and theoretical accuracy to the position that mental images are, in fact, the creations of people and thus speak of a constructed reality (Howard, 1991; Spence, 1982). Recently, psychoanalytic theory has been taken to task as perhaps one of the most dogmatic theoretical frameworks in the social sciences today (Lamb, 1991). Pressured by the wave of these intellectual times, psychoanalysis is being asked to reflect upon itself and take note of its own participation in how it goes about understanding psychic operations. As clinicians, we have traditionally used our metapsychological formulations as frameworks to help us understand what makes people do what they do. There is the instinct story, the object relations story, and the self story, to name only a few. We are passionate about and intellectually invested in our stories of choice. They are the templates through which we see our patients and evaluate their strengths, weaknesses, and ability to undergo our method of treatment.

But voices from outside our field have been quite adamant of late in pointing out that our theoretical affinities suffer from considerable shortsightedness. Social anthropologists (Carrithers, Collins, & Lukes, 1985; Kirschner, 1990; McMamee & Gergen, 1992; Shweder & LeVine, 1984) argue that we have been unable to see the powerful relationship between our theoretical metapsychologies and the cultural environments that created them. They point out that the psychological theories that carry the strongest power are those that rationalize and extend a culture's most deeply rooted and dearly held traditions and beliefs. Psychological theories basically elaborate and formalize a culture's implicit views on how to function within it specifically as a desirable and capable human being. Jerome Bruner (1986) does not mince words when he speaks of modern psychological theories as being, in effect, canonized cultural values!

It has been well documented in the literature how the personal, historical, and contextual elements of Freud's immediate world were powerfully interactive elements in the construction of his theory of the mind. Born out of the intellectual momentum of the European Enlightenment, Freud's theory of human behavior also reflected the social mores of nineteenth-century Vienna. He lived in a Victorian world that placed particular emphasis on social class distinction, appropriate behavioral comportment, and affective restraint. His instinct metapsychology reflected this sociocultural story. He saw the control of impulsive life as the primary imperative of the human condition at that moment in time. Herein, he concluded, lay the source of psychic conflict and psychic pathology.

Freud and every theorist after him were the products of their respective cultural surroundings. We know that when psychoanalysis migrated to the United States, it continued to develop, now in the midst of a very different ethnopsychology. Initially, under the influence of American medicine, it attempted a concertedly scientific approach to psychic functioning (Jacoby, 1983). American psychoanalysis branded the analytic movement with its own specific stamp—its own unique view of the human condition. Whether emerging from the more quantifiably oriented American ego psychology, later Sullivanian interpersonal theory, or Kohutian self psychology, the analytic movement in the United States elaborated a view of the individual and his or her functions that essentially described the ideals of the American cultural ethic: self-sufficiency, self-actualization, forward mobility, and conflict-free action in the world. Thusly informed is our psychodynamically oriented work in the United States and thusly defined are the criteria by which we assess our patients. As American psychotherapists, we are part and parcel of the society that views assertion and independent self-direction as the veritable *essence* of good life. And these are the treatment goals that we either explicitly or implicitly establish for our patients.

And let us not forget the force of the current zeitgeist, the object relations movement—a British psychoanalytic psychology adopted by segments of American psychoanalysis for its very syntonicity with the American way. Bred within religious and secular values that hold individual self-responsibility in high regard, this particularly Anglo-American view of humanity prizes autonomy of the self above all human attributes (Kirschner, 1990). This is a self that develops from dependency with another to ultimate individuated autonomy. We measure the pathology of this self by its ability to titrate the wish for merger with the desire to stand alone. So enmeshed are we as American therapists in this view of the human condition that we hardly stop to question whether this definition of the self is applicable to all people. There are some cultures in which to be a separate differentiated self, as we know it, would be anathema. There are other cultures in which the deep inner self, upon maturity, does not separate but finally merges with the cosmos (Roland, 1988). Although this is a deeply spiritual concept that is foreign to us in the West, we have only to analytically treat a patient from an Eastern culture to be struck by the fact that our metapsychological concept of the self in the Anglo-American West is by no means universal, but highly ethnocentric and circumscribed to our own unique view of humanity (see Chapter 19).

Viewed from a historical, epistemological perspective, psychoanalysis would appear to sit squarely in the middle of the postmodern era's intellectual dilemma: We are seeking to establish systematic, meaningful, and comprehensive bodies of thought and action, only to be reminded of the myriad exceptions to the rule. Can psychoanalysis make its way out of such a paradox? Can it maintain a basic system of beliefs as well as meaningfully broaden its clinical method of inquiry into a larger, varied, and more divergent cultural milieu? I believe that it can, and I propose a perspective based on the philosophical traditions of pluralism, which held to the multiplicity of lived experience even before the dawn of social-constructivist sensibilities (James, 1977).

THE PLURALISM OF THE METAPSYCHOLOGIES

Over the course of his writings, Benjamin Wolstein (1967; 1971; 1973; 1990; 1992a; 1992b; 1994) defined some conceptual parameters in psychoanalytic thought that I believe have fundamental bearing on the influence of the sociocultural context. According to Wolstein, psychoanalytic literature describes two sets of operations conducted by the psychoanalytic enterprise. On one side, psychoanalysis operates as a method of empirical psychological inquiry—a clinical approach aimed at solving psychological distress. No matter what their analytic school of thought, all psychodynamically oriented clinicians—be they Freudian, object relational, ego psychological, interpersonal, or self psychological—believe in a few core notions: (1) the existence of unconscious processes, (2) the basis of anxiety symptoms in some kind of psychic conflict, (3) the presence of transference and countertransference as processes that repeatedly occur in the therapeutic situation, and, most important, (4) the unique psychic connection that is created with each patient in the process of the analytic work. These leading terms of observation are coordinated in the overall structure of psychoanalytic inquiry and treatment, their guiding premise being the belief in unconscious psychic experience. Psychoanalysis has selected these leading elements of observation out of the complex totality of the psychic domain because of their observed ability to expand and deepen self-awareness beyond its initial conscious boundaries (Wolstein, 1994).

However, there is the other side of psychoanalysis—the theoretical, interpretive order of inquiry. Therapists and their patients shape and understand the data gathered from their empirical observations in different ways, depending on which metapsychological visions of human nature they find most appealing. Here, theorists, therapists, and patients exercise speculative intelligence and the freedom of creative imagination. They put a deeply private stamp on their enduring choices of myth and metaphor to interpret the clinical narrative. No single choice is intrinsically better than others. Wolstein (1994) has written that within psychoanalysis, "even a cursory review of the wide variety of metapsychologies now in favor would reveal its many and mutually enriching divergences. With therapists uniquely individual no more, or less, than their patients, one central point of convergence for all is still hard to imagine" (p. 495). For some therapists, it is the discharge of the instincts that drives people to action. For others, it is the search for objects that constitutes the driving imperative of human nature. It is this side of psychoanalytic thinking—the interpretive metapsychological side—that is so rooted in the assumptions, beliefs, and expectations of one's personal, environmental, and cultural surroundings. Furthermore, no two therapists, by virtue of their distinct individuality, approach metapsychological interpretation in quite the same way, despite the consistent metaphors directly received from the various traditional schools of psychoanalysis.

Relevant interpretation of the clinical work is ultimately created in the intimate and unique dialectical discourse between the two members of the therapeutic dyad—each of whom is guided by his or her own experiential and theoretical view of life. Thus it would seem that the more disparate the respective worlds of the members of the dyad, the more the work must be undertaken as a joint quest for understanding, with the therapist needing to exercise particular cautions against rushing to apply their own personal assumptions and metapsychology about minds at large.

Consider the following case vignettes—the clinical use of particular interpretive metapsychologies, and their relevance to understanding the inner experiences of each patient.

Willie

Willie R. was an 11-year-old Spanish- and English-speaking boy, a native of the Dominican Republic, who had emigrated to the United States with his parents at age five. He was referred to an outpatient child and adolescent clinic for defecating in his clothing, a symptom that had developed shortly after his move but which had recently worsened. Willie's soiling had now progressed to occasionally relieving himself outdoors in a deserted area on his way to or from school "if I need to go." The boy was ashamed of his habit, feared that he would be seen as "dirty" by his peers, and conscientiously washed himself and changed clothes after soiling himself.

Willie was a handsome, sturdily built boy whose gentle and smiling social manner only momentarily covered a sad and preoccupied face when at rest. He was often tense and had difficulty speaking freely with me, such that we almost entirely interacted through symbolic play. His fantasies described lost people, houses, and animals swept away by destructive forces, and soldiers parading in uniform.

Willie had become a cause célèbre at the clinic, which was part of a large teaching hospital. He was presented at both pediatric and psychiatric grand rounds. Diagnosed with a secondary encopresis of functional etiology, the patient was viewed psychodynamically as a textbook case of an early anal personality. His soiling, accompanied by compulsive cleanliness (he washed after his accidents), militaristic interests (he played with GI Joes), and emotional constriction (Dominican children rarely initiate conversation with authority figures) were supposedly sure signs of his repressed wishes to explode with rage upon the world that has overzealously imposed anal and behavioral controls on him.

After about six months of biweekly treatment in which Willie's only change was an increased sense of comfort in my presence, his mother told me that Willie was not her biological child. She had adopted him from a poor family in the LaRomana province of the Dominican Republic before coming to the United States. The biological parents had willingly given up this child, who was one of 12, in the hopes of enhancing his socioeconomic environment. This is not an uncommon practice in the international culture of poverty. It so happens that I have traveled in the area of Willie's original home. Families in this part of the Dominican Republic are mostly sharecroppers who live at a subsistence level. Illiteracy is high, electrification is primitive, and horses are still a common mode of transportation. Verdant plains are dotted with grazing cattle and shacks. Toddlers amble unclothed in the heat. There is minimal running water, and there are no indoor toilets.

While busy searching for the anal-aggressive data that would substantiate my psychodynamic formulation, I had missed the painful elements of Willie's reality. Adopted by caring people who had unquestionably improved his physical standard of living, Willie had nevertheless been terminally separated from his mother and the world that he knew. As I would later hear from him, Willie's letting go, especially during times of stress, was his way of returning to Mother and his early life, which for him had included the option to relieve himself outdoors at will. Abandonment, feeling like a lost child in a strange world, and the sense that everything he knew around him could suddenly disappear, was the inner psychic reality in which Willie lived. Though I had not been made privy to Willie's early history from the beginning of treatment, in thinking back, I am sure that he had communicated it to me in some symbolic form in session. Unfortunately, however, this information had fallen on ears deafened by fixed theoretical assumptions about latency-age boys who defecate in places other than indoor toilets!

Notwithstanding the reactive anger that surely resided in Willie, the point here is that his own sense of trauma about his life was derived not from the imposed controls around anal issues but the imposed separation and loss of life as he had known it. Although his open defecation may have, indeed, comprised a form of anal autostimulation, as held by the classical view (Freud, 1905), defecating—as Willie himself eventually came to explain—was part of an attempt to reconstruct his early world. "I used to live in a place," he said, "where people let me do this. I want those people and that place back."

Willie's case demonstrates a real clinical pitfall arising from my assumption of a rather positivistic theoretical posture early in his treatment. First, I imposed a metapsychological interpretation onto his life that was taken from Freud's (1905) construct of the classical anal phase of psychosexual development—a psychoanalytic formulation designed for those who by definition engage in modern, Western, European toilet habits. The validity of applying the presumed vicissitudes of this developmental phase and its impact on character formation to a boy from LaRomana is questionable or limited, at best. Second, firmly entrenched in my conviction regarding the truth of my own theory about Willie's life, I had barely left room for any kind of real dialectical discourse—albeit through play—with *him*. In the interest of building what Quine and Ullian (1970) would call a "seamless web of belief," I rushed toward the elements in the patient's narrative that supported *my* story of his life, foreclosing any additional data from the real author—the boy himself.

Aside from the use of a metapsychological interpretation that came to have questionable clinical relevance to Willie's inner life, the main pitfall in this case was my holding fast to an old and admittedly respectable tradition in the execution of the psychoanalytic method: that of placing prime focus on the intellectual interpretive power of metapsychological theory. This tradition by definition relegated the human coexperience of the therapeutic field to secondary status, as if the knowledge garnered from my living action and interaction with Willie in the process of the therapeutic inquiry could not stand on its own in the process of reconstruction and psychic healing (Wolstein, 1992a; Wolstein, 1994). I will return to this matter later in this chapter.

Manash

Consider the questions posed by the next patient, whose case reflects more contemporary metapsychological formulations about the articulation of the structure of the self and its degree of differentiation.

Manash was a 29-year-old man, a political refugee from a Middle Eastern country. He spoke English—his second language—fluently. His homeland had been taken over by a foreign power and was now under oppressive military rule. The patient entered treatment after about one year in this country, feeling severely depressed and stating that all meaning to his life had vanished. In his country, Manash had belonged to a semi-religious social caste dedicated to public and community service. Given the current political situation in his country, he felt that hopes of fulfilling his function were lost. Following the tradition of all men in his family, Manash had been groomed for his life's work since childhood, having been educated in special schools. He believed that his destiny would now not be fulfilled and that he was nothing without the community group that he was meant to live with, educate, and serve. "I feel so empty and worthless within myself as a man; I am shameful to my father and ancestors."

I struggled to understand Manash's inner sense of loss for many months, while also noting that he was a resourceful man who had managed to start a small import business that was affording him an income. I also struggled with personal and theoretical assumptions about what makes people feel stable and whole. Manash appeared resilient and creative. Surely he would soon find other ways of repairing his sense of narcissistic injury. But he didn't.

These were some of my psychoanalytically informed questions: Was I to view this patient along the lines of Western personality development, possibly using some contemporary metapsychological formulations about the self? Should I consider notions of a pathological self structure (Kohut); of early derailments in separation-individuation (Mahler); of pathological differentiation from the primary object (Fairbairn)? Or might I consider that my theories about how people go about the psychic task of becoming able-minded are simply creative descriptions of how to be a functional self in a particular kind of Western Euro-American cultural life? My patient's culture might very well conceive of the self—and, consequently, its value, wholeness, robustness, health, and developmental metamorphosis—quite differently. As Manash eventually came to show me, the ideal of mental health in his world was not the socially autonomous, externally oriented, self-actualized individual, but rather a person centered in spiritual consciousness, the confluence of will and fate, and the emotional bonding of family and group kinship wherein one's sense of self is deeply involved, throughout life, with others.

As an American-trained clinician I found these values difficult to understand, since my own life and metapsychological views of human nature were intrinsically connected with Western individualism and a deep belief in the autonomy and will of the individual. Unlike Manash, who sought his uniqueness within the life of his group, my values were those of current American culture. Individuals in our world, particularly those of the educated middle class with whom psychoanalytic culture is so enmeshed, push to become free from their family of origin and to create their own unique meaning in life through self-sufficiency and separateness (Roland, 1988). Manash's sense of what made a person esteemed and whole proved to be a world away from mine.

ON THE LIVING INTERACTION OF THE THERAPEUTIC FIELD

I would now like to turn to some issues of technique and their impact on the culturally unmatched therapeutic dyad. The cross-racial, cross-cultural, or cross-class therapeutic dyad, despite our often humanistic, or "politically correct" leanings, is never a quiet enterprise. Beginning with the first contact, the obvious chasm of disparity between life experiences can throw both patient and analyst, consciously or unconsciously, into a veritable whirl of potential estrangement, distrust, or basic anxiety born of a sense of being in the presence of a stranger (Basch-Kahre, 1984). Historically, the analytic method has always provided the clinical protocol for the patient to explore these feelings. But what is the fate of the therapist's subjective reactions? And what does the patient do with observations and inferences that he or she may have drawn about the therapist's real attitudes—especially as they relate to the cultural disparity? If necessary, how can patient and therapist begin systematically to deal with the coexperience of their mutual anxiety in each other's presence?

For psychoanalysis, the resistance to this avenue of inquiry is deeply embedded in its history, and the primacy placed on the intellectual interpretive thrust of metapsychology. In brief, Freud's original reduction of the strivings, affects, and cognitive experiences that occurred within the psychic connection of patient and analyst to the instinctual domain, relegated all experience and behavior to conjectured subpsychic origins and speculated derivation from a biological basis. The interpersonal gap or split that this formulation introduced between the two participants was an arbitrary personal limit that was built into the early model of the therapeutic experience. Most relevant to the present discussion, however, was the decision to reduce as much as possible any processes and patterns that might be explored under the conditions of direct therapeutic relatedness. All interactions were seen as based upon the instinctual derivatives of the id (Wolstein, 1992b).

Aside from early experiments conducted by Ferenczi (1921/1969) on the analyst's psychology and its potential impact on the therapeutic work, Freud's seminal tradition of separating the living mutual experience of the analytic field from metapsychological interpretation was followed by later psychoanalytic contributors such as Rank, Klein, Fairbairn, Winnicott, and Kohut, who used their own brands of metapsychological interpretation to define the subpsychic origins of current life experience.

In these contemporary psychoanalytic times, tides seem to be shifting, however, as more reports bring the lived coexperience of the therapeutic field to center stage. We are being told, for example, that the therapist's own subjectivity, and what the patient comes to know of it, is a vital and often unheeded aspect of the therapeutic work (Aron, 1990; Gill, 1982, 1983; Greenberg, 1991; Hoffman, 1983; Racker, 1968; Wolstein, 1988). Contemporary writers speak here not of transference distortions, parapraxes, or endogenously determined fantasies about the therapist, but of solid observations that the patient is able to make over time about the therapist's own character and inner psychology. The fact is that analysts are neither neutral screens nor simple clay for transferential transformation. They are, in fact, formidable characters who often have robust prejudices.

As noted, given the traditional primacy lent to theoretical interpretation, the trend in most analytic work has been to avoid weighted consideration of a patient's views of the therapist, outside of its transferential context. Furthermore, therapists are aware that inquiry into this part of the patient's mental life is anxiety-provoking, potentially embarrassing, and stimulating of their own psychic resistances (Gill, 1982, 1983; Racker, 1968). Aron (1990) and Greenberg (1991) note that this avoidance can drive patients to sidestep and accommodate aspects of the therapist's psychology. Patients can become quite sensitive to their therapist's real vulnerabilities and come unconsciously to fear that what they observe may endanger the therapist's own well-being, as well as the very stability of the work. These real observations might include the clinician's real greed, impatience, competitiveness, envy, as well as cross-cultural anxiety.

In the case of marked cultural or racial differences in the dyad, where the disparities are often such a source of mutual subjective arousal, side-stepping exploration of the patient's observations inevitably leads to severe impasses in the work. The following is a case example:

Norma

Norma is a 30-year-old chemical engineer whom I saw in psychodynamic therapy for four years. She is Panamanian and originally sought treatment with me because of my own Latin-American background. Norma is a particularly striking young woman with light cocoa skin, brown eyes, and very curly, shoulder-length hair. About a year into the work, I noticed that the patient had never brought up the issue of color or race in session. This is surprising as Latin Americans in general are very cognizant of their mixed racial heritage. Indian, Caucasian, and black lineages are all part of a rich genetic pool in which there is much intermarriage.

For a person of Latin-American heritage, I am viewed as light-skinned. I have blue eyes and curly hair. The patient, on one rainy day, commented that my hair looked shorter, as if I "had gotten a haircut." I decided to say, "No, it's just curlier today in the humidity." I asked her more about this. As it turns out, the patient had been an astute observer of my hairstyle over the year, noting that I probably blow-dry my hair to make it less curly. I nervously inquired on. She had also surmised that I probably did not like my hair, because it is the thing that made me look the most Hispanic. Her exploration of the inner me continued: She described the physical characteristics of my parents and grandparents, the percent distribution of the various races in my blood by virtue of my features, the coloring of my husband and children, and how I felt about all of them. Inevitably this exploration finally turned to Norma's own family. She had been the darkest-skinned of all her siblings. Not only had she been mocked for this and accused of not being her fair-skinned father's child, but also, because of her color, she was offered no hope of succeeding in a white-dominated world. Norma had hidden her racial pain, assuming that I would also dislike her for being a dark-skinned girl.

The exploration of Norma's thoughts about what might be my own subjective issues brought powerful personal poignancy and served a strong facilitating function. Surmising that she and I were products of the same variegated racial pools, she railed against my "genetic luck" to have been the more fortunate one to have emerged lighter skinned. This finally opened vital areas about the patient's self-image, her parents' reaction to color, and the emotional distance that they had maintained with her. Norma would often mention the "permission to get into your head" as a nodal point in her treatment. I am convinced that had I not allowed her—to use a Kleinian metaphor—to climb inside my body and explore the objects within me, she would have resigned herself to a somewhat forced suppression of this material. Norma's perception of my own unspoken conflict, and her effort not to threaten my equilibrium, would have truncated open exploration of her own sense of racial inferiority. In other words, she would have come to know my secrets, but at great expense to herself silently permitted me to hide them.

The recognition of the contributing role of the therapist's own psychology in psychodynamically oriented work could not be more vital than in the treatment of patients whose culture, race, or class markedly differs from that of the therapist. We must no longer delude ourselves and assume that the psychotherapeutic frame can cloak the analyst's inner life. I would add that the myriad of subjective reactions that are aroused in the socioethnic unmatched dyad are a general fact of life—they are in the air, a part of the social-environmental fabric in which we all live. Whether the therapist's attitudes fall within the range of despondency, sadness, or guilt over the circumstances of the patient's life, or whether the therapist's reactions run the gamut of puzzlement, fear, ethnic prejudice, or dislike, they will all eventually be discernible to our clients. A client's silent recognition of a therapist's unspoken, forbidden attitudes will, at the very least, create an impasse in the work, foreclosing exploration of particular dynamic areas; at the very worst, it will lead to premature termination (Foster, 1993).

Our psychoanalytic method clearly needs remediation if we are to catapult it into the multicultural arena. We are heartened, however, by these contemporary intellectual times which offer, as it were, therapeutic interventions for both our theory and our practice. First, with regard to our metapsychology, we are reminded that psychoanalysis need no longer carry the unrealistic (and presumptuous) burden of explaining the universal driving imperative of the human condition. Postmodern academic writers note the shifting, mercurial, and context-bound nature of this enterprise as individuals, shamans, philosophers, psychoanalysts, and artists—across cultures, historical eras, and geographic locales—have all attempted thoughtful and inevitably personalized explanations for the meaning of their lives. Psychoanalysis must learn to admit that it knows the people of its own culture well and those of non-European cultures less well. Analysts need to become less positivistic in their assertions about human nature, and more willing to shape psychodynamic meaning through reciprocal interaction with their patients, especially when their worlds are so markedly different.

REFERENCES

Abramowitz, S. I., & Murray, J. (1983). Race effects in psychotherapy. In J. Murray & P. Abramson (Eds.), *Bias in Psychotherapy* (pp. 215–255). New York: Praeger.

Aron, L. (1990). One-person and two-person psychologies and the method of psychoanalysis. *Psychoanalytic Psychology*, 7, 474–485.

Atkinson, D. R. (1985). A meta-review of research on cross-cultural counseling and psychotherapy. *Journal of Multicultural Counseling and Development*, 1, 138–153.

Basch-Kahre, E. (1984). On difficulties arising in transference and countertransference when analyst and analysand have different socio-cultural backgrounds. *International Review of Psychoanalysis*, 11, 61–77.

Bruner, J. S. (1986). Value presuppositions of developmental theory. In L. Cirillo & S. Wapner (Eds.), *Value Presuppositions in Theories of Human Development* (pp. 19–28). Hillsdale, NJ: Lawrence Erlbaum.

Carrithers, M., Collins, S., & Lukes, S. (Eds.). (1985). *The Category of the Person*. Cambridge: Cambridge University Press.

Ferenczi, S. (1969). *Further Contributions to the Theory and Technique of Psychoanalysis* (3rd ed.). London: Hogarth. (Original work published 1921)

Foster, R. P. (1993). The social politics of psychoanalysis. Commentary of Neil Altman's "Psychoanalysis and the Urban Poor." *Psychoanalytic Dialogues*, 3, 69–84.

Freud, S. (1905). Three essays on the theory of sexuality. *Standard Edition*, vol. 7, 125–245. London: Hogarth Press.

Gill, M. (1982). *Analysis of Transference. Vol. I. Theory and Technique*. New York: International Universities Press.

———. (1983). The interpersonal paradigm and the degree of the therapist's involvement. *Contemporary Psychoanalysis*, 19, 200–237.

Greenberg, J. R. (1991). Countertransference and reality. *Psychoanalytic Dialogues*, 1, 52–73.

Hoffman, I. Z. (1983). The patient as interpreter of the analyst's experience. *Contemporary Psychoanalysis*, 19, 389–422.

Howard, G. S. (1991). Culture tales: A narrative approach to thinking, cross-cultural psychology, and psychotherapy. *American Psychology*, 46, 187–197.

Jacoby, R. (1983). *The Repression of Psychoanalysis*. New York: Basic Books.

James, W. (1977). *A Pluralistic Universe*. Cambridge: Harvard University Press.

Kirschner, S. R. (1990). The assenting echo: Anglo-American values in contemporary psychoanalytic developmental psychology. *Social Research*, 57, 822–857.

Lamb, S. (1991). Comment: An objectivist in social constructionist clothing. *American Psychology*, 47, 80.

McMamee, S., & Gergen, K. J. (1992). *Social Construction and the Therapeutic Process*. London: Sage.

Olarte, S. W., & Lenz, R. (1984). Learning to do psychoanalytic therapy with inner-city populations. *Journal of American Academy of Psychoanalysis*, 12, 89–99.

Quine, W. V., & Ullian, J. S. (1970). *The Web of Belief*. New York: Random House.

Racker, H. (1968). *Transference and Countertransference*. New York: International Universities Press.

Roland, A. (1988). *In Search of Self in India and Japan: Toward a Cross-Cultural Psychology*. Princeton, NJ: Princeton University Press.

Shweder, R. A., & LeVine, R. (Eds). (1984). *Culture Theory*. Cambridge: Cambridge University Press.

Spence, D. P. (1982). *Narrative Truth and Historical Truth*. New York: Norton.

Sue, S. (1988). Psychotherapeutic services for ethnic minorities. *American Psychologist*, 43, 301–308.

Wolstein, B. (1967). *Theory of Psychoanalytic Therapy*. New York: Grune & Stratton.

———. (1971). *Human Psyche in Psychoanalysis*. Springfield, IL: Charles C. Thomas.

———. (1973). The new significance of psychic structure. In *Interpersonal Explorations in Psychoanalysis*. New York: Basic Books.

———. (1988). Introduction. In B. Wolstein (Ed.), *Essential Papers on Countertransference* (pp. 1–15). New York: New York University Press.

———. (1990). Five empirical psychoanalytic methods. *Contemporary Psychoanalysis*, 26, 237–256.

———. (1992a). Aspects of contemporary pluralistic psychoanalysis. N. Skolnick & S. C. Warshaw (Eds.), *Relational Perspectives in Psychoanalysis*. Hillsdale, NJ: Analytic Press.

———. (1992b). Resistance interlocked with countertransference. *Contemporary Psychoanalysis*, 28, 172–190.

———. (1994). The evolving newness of interpersonal psychoanalysis. *Contemporary Psychoanalysis*, 30, 473–498.

CHAPTER 16

Race in the Analytic Situation: Reflections of an African American Therapist

Dolores O. Morris

> . . . humans exist only in a culture . . . cultures simultaneously potentiate opportunities and limit possibilities. . . . every culture develops images of the proper way to be human (i.e., the "self") . . . each era's self has its idiosyncratic vulnerabilities, which must be healed by those designated as healers.
>
> (Cushman 1994, 832)

The values, beliefs and practices of the culture in which we live help shape our identities as individuals, as well as our experience as analysts and patients. One important aspect of culture is race. In America the history of race relations makes this factor particularly salient. In this chapter, I would like to present one exploration of this topic. I will use the term race or ethnicity interchangeably. This paper explores the impact of race as it pertains to the analytic process with respect to its effect on two therapeutic dyads where both therapist and patient are women of color. I will attempt to show how my own background emerged in the course of treatment and ultimately facilitated a deeper understanding of myself and the problems of these two patients.

Too often, black women and men in America inevitably feel torn between accepting a deeply conflicted, often devalued sense of self, absorbed from generations of ambivalent relations with white America, and a more valued individual identity which embraces self-acceptance, a celebration of their racial identity, and a pride in their heritage as African Americans.

The influence of race on the unconscious feelings of both therapist and patient have been illustrated in a number of clinical discussions (Schachter and Butts 1968; Ticho 1971; Griffith 1977; Myers 1977; Holmes 1992; Grey

1993; Thompson 1996; Williams 1996; Leary 1997). The participants in the analytic process may be ethnically and racially different (Schachter and Butts 1968; Ticho 1971; Myers 1977; Holmes 1992; Grey 1993; Leary 1997) or may have common or similar ethnic and racial backgrounds (Calnek 1970; Griffith 1977; Holmes 1992; Thompson 1996; Davidson 1987). Each of these combinations may bring its own transferential and countertransferential influences upon the course of treatment.

Where there is a common cultural experience, the therapeutic process may be facilitated; but at the same time it might be hindered by an overinvolvement or overidentification by one or both of the participants. Issues may go unchallenged because the therapist feels knowledgeable about what the patient is saying. She may accept the patient's understanding of the problem without question. When this occurs, core personality problems (Griffith 1977; Davidson 1987), symptoms, and/or resistances of the patient may be overlooked (Ticho 1971). Thus, cultural similarity may create overlapping blind spots and collusion, as illustrated in my work with patient A.

A., a 28-year-old brown-skinned African American Protestant, was referred to me by her close friend, also an African American. She came to treatment depressed; she had become profoundly disillusioned with her parents when she discovered family secrets. She had grown up in a middle-class, African American community in the Midwest and attended prestigious, integrated schools throughout her academic career, including the Ivy League college from which she graduated. Symptoms of her depression included inability to gain satisfaction from her work and from activities that had previously been a source of pleasure. She no longer had an active social life with friends who represented diverse cultural backgrounds. A. was an associate in a well-known law firm; she aspired to become a partner, yet she felt isolated and alienated in what she described as a predominately white male world. One of the senior partners, her mentor, was black and she spoke to him nearly every day. She idealized his skill and wished that things came as easily for her as they seemed to come for him. Very often, she felt that she did not meet his expectations. She believed that her failure to get a bonus or the assignments she desired was related to her race. She successfully sought employment with other firms yet allowed her mentor to convince her to remain with their current firm.

A. expressed feeling a sense of relief and comfort in coming to a black therapist—someone who could understand her situation. I was impressed by her accomplishments. I quickly realized she saw me as her rescuer, which flattered me. I understood that she was using race to avoid revealing profound feelings of inadequacy. As we examined the realities of the work situation, she acknowledged that most other associates did not receive high bonuses either and that race seemed to have little to do with her work problems. We realized that if she changed assignments she would jeopardize her chances to become a partner. Yet, she still evinced a restless need to change jobs. When A. talked about changing to a job situation that would put her more "in touch with my people," that is, the black community, I had assumed that I knew what she meant. It was concordant with my own earlier wish to return to teach in a traditionally black college. In describing her wish to return to the black community, I felt A. was implicitly saying, "You know what I mean." Because of this, I failed to explore A.'s unspoken communication of her underlying hopes and conflicts concerning this wish; I was implicitly agreeing with her. The unrecognized issues became clearer when A. dreamt the following:

> I was pregnant, but I wasn't me. I was a white woman with long blond hair and I was married to my white coworker. I was in labor and in a great deal of pain with no relief from the doctor or my husband. My husband was driving around looking for a parking space. I thought, 'he is taking too long and is purposely delaying arrival at the hospital.' The doctor would not give me a pain reliever because I was having natural childbirth and he told me that it would be risky and dangerous. I felt that they were prolonging my pain, when the dream shifted. I was no longer the white woman with the long blond hair but myself on the 'outside looking in . . . '

We tried to understand more about what seemed to be a birth struggle and renaissance dream. Through her associations to the dream and our interpretations, we considered the possibility that in her current life she felt accepted by neither the white nor the black world. Further work led us to understand that perhaps she was struggling to give up the falseness of trying to be white; she was suffering and struggling to bring forth the true "natural" self. However, giving up the ideal of whiteness meant giving up the advantage represented by the blond—the social, educated, professional self that was full of pain. Escape from this situation, however, left her feeling isolated, cut off from those upon whom she depended for care—"outside looking in." Her associations led to her awareness that her fear of giving up her parents' defensive notion of her being white-identified led to advantages represented by the white blond self.

A. was the first generation in her family to go to college. She had pursued her current profession at the direction and pleasure of her parents. It brought with it the prestige and recognition that they sought. Her parents were high school graduates. They had grown up in the rural segregated South under poor circumstances and had migrated to a large urban midwest city where they built a successful business. They wanted to provide their only child with everything that they had not had in childhood, and more. They placed their daughter in the white world where they believed she would gain entry, acceptance, and recognition. The doctor in her dream may well have been her therapist doctor and the father who did not help but allowed her to suffer in her powerless position. The therapist doctor taking too long and not being helpful was a source of frustration for her. I was not the rescuer she had expected and was a disappointment to her as had been others in her life.

As our work progressed, her sense of suffering and self-alienation became more evident. She had great difficulty sorting out more authentic self-striving from security operations based on accommodating to her parents' idealized wishes. She was both the trapped insider and the outsider looking in. We began to realize that her speaking of a return to the black community and "my people" represented a breaking away from this dilemma to a true self. In reality, she was struggling to be her own person without the obligations that she believed both the white and the black worlds were placing upon her.

In this case, the common racial identity and life experiences that appeared to bond us had actually served to obscure the authentic A. Initially, I had taken her wish to work in the black community as a simple expression of idealized racial identity rather than as the symbol of a struggle for her true self. I had assumed that her motives were altruistic. This assumption had blinded me from inquiring about the motives behind A.'s wish. The childbirth dream allowed us to begin to explore what was "risky and dangerous." A. began to acknowledge the rage she felt toward her parents whom she believed had betrayed her by failing to maintain the moral standards for themselves that they had insisted upon for her. She acknowledged her fear of losing their support. This breakthrough allowed us to open up, explore, and understand her issues around courtship and marriage.

As the direction of the inquiry deepened, I no longer assumed that I knew what she meant without exploration. In the process, I became more aware of my own anxieties related to the realization that my presumptions had been clouded by my own stereotypes and prejudices, as well as my over-identification with A. as an upwardly mobile achievement-oriented African American woman.

This particular case material shows how powerful social forces from our cultural background are transmitted through the values and attitudes of the family. In this instance, the parent's desire for what they thought was best for their daughter was complicated by their distorted perception of the "white culture" and their overemphasis on and bias toward it.

It has been my experience that anxiety creates a discomfort which interferes with effective functioning. Sullivan (1953) states that individuals avoid anxiety through the operation of the self system, which identifies and avoids those interpersonal crises that elicit anxiety. The defensive consequences of anxiety can be selective inattention and dissociation. In selective inattention, individuals maintain a marginal awareness that there is something that one is supposed to know or attend to. In dissociation the unawareness is total. Comas-Diaz and Jacobsen (1991) refer to selective inattention as affective distancing and cultural myopia in the countertransference within the matched dyad. They point out that in both, the therapist employs cultural factors to explain behavior, neglecting and obscuring intrapsychic factors. The most crucial aspect of the therapist's participation revolves around a vigilant analysis of the countertransference reactions and catching those moments of inattention and anxiety (Levenson 1992)

Just as the encounter with the therapist can trigger social meaning for the patient, so can the patient trigger social meaning for the therapist. An aspect of my work with Patient C. illustrates this experience.

When C., a 32-year-old female, called for an appointment, I asked who had referred her—a routine question. She said that her boyfriend, who I discovered later was an African American, had secured the referral from someone. She resisted giving any more information, creating an air of mystery. She went on to say that he had just put her out of his apartment and told her to make an appointment with me. We set the time for the next day. I was uneasy about this telephone conversation; I felt that she was concealing something. To my surprise, she kept the appointment. She was upset and tearful about being rejected by her boyfriend, indicating that it resonated with early life experiences. She wanted to understand the repeated pattern. C. had previously sought treatment with a white male therapist when her former white in-laws had asked her to leave their home. This marriage had ended in divorce. She said that this therapist had not been helpful, but she could not explain how he had failed her. Treatment had been interrupted when she left for a trip to Europe and did not resume with him upon her return. I noted to myself that she mentioned the race of her husband and therapist but decided to explore this with her at a later time, giving myself the excuse that it was more important first to find out how that treatment had not been helpful. When a reasonable answer was not forthcoming, we moved on to other matters in this initial inquiry.

As we talked about her early life, she reminisced that she had grown up in the neighborhood of my office, which is located in a metropolitan Northern community, and this brought back memories of her childhood. Her remarks reminded me that I, too, had lived in this neighborhood as a child. I caught myself responding to her physical appearance, facial features, coloring, haircut and texture, style of dress, and manner of expressing herself—all of which appeared to be similar to mine when I was her age. C. was the youngest of four siblings. Her family lived in a modest building where her Catholic father was a janitor. He demanded adherence to strict rules. When C. was 16 years old, she did not come home one night. C. was unable to recall the circumstance of her overnight stay but volunteered that she did not do "anything wrong." Her father, in a rage, accused her of being "a slut" and forced her to leave home that day. She packed her things and moved in with an older sister. Since that time, she had only returned to her parents' home for occasional family events. When I remarked that this must have been a shocking and hurtful experience for her, she responded by saying she had "unfinished business with her family," sidestepping the remark. A guidance counselor, sympathetic to her circumstances, helped her to attain a scholarship at a preparatory school. As she continued her education, she earned additional scholarships for college and graduate school. In fact, she was the only sibling to go to college. The others went as far as high school and some were substance abusers. She believed that they resented her for her achievements. Her Puerto Rican background only became known near the end of this first session when she answered the question regarding the birthplace of her parents. They came to this area when they were young adults, married, started a family, and remained. Spanish was spoken in the home. For some reason, which I understood later, I asked her if she would prefer working with someone who could speak both English and Spanish. She indicated that she had not spoken Spanish since she entered elementary school and had forgotten much of what she knew. Once again she sidestepped the remark.

I had assumed that C. was African American because of her physical characteristics and realized that there had been nothing in our exchange early in that first session to give a clue that she was Puerto Rican. In the next session, I told her that I had thought she was African American until she told me her parents were born in Puerto Rico. I had wondered whether this had ever happened to her before. She said that it was not unusual for people to think that she was African American and asserted that she made it clear to them, as her tone was making it to me, that she be identified with her African as well as her Puerto Rican heritage. While she attempted to convey that it was "no big deal" to be thought of as an African American, there was a defensiveness in her tone and body language. I realized that as I felt that she was concealing the identity of the referral source from me, so was I concealing my reactions to her interracial relationships; I wanted to know more about them. Instead of remarking about my assumption that she was African American, I could have inquired about how it felt or what it meant to be in the treatment room with an African American, as well as what it meant for us, an African American and a Puerto Rican, to work together.

Perhaps my competitiveness with her white male therapist stopped me from pursuing this line of inquiry. Perhaps I felt I might be revealing my anxieties and vulnerabilities. My feelings were further complicated by her announcement that she would be going on a vacation to South America in a couple of weeks. I made the observation that it was an interesting coincidence that she was going on vacation at the moment that she was beginning treatment. I wondered whether the same pattern of her not returning to therapy would occur, as in her previous treatment. She denied that this would happen because she now had more of an investment in understanding her behavior.

C. returned from her vacation to the fifth session with a great deal of enthusiasm. She indicated that she had discovered that she had indeed "missed her native tongue" and was surprised by how well she functioned in it. She talked about taking Spanish lessons to regain her fluency. She said she also felt more in touch with her African heritage. Her talks centered on her social activities and political meetings with her friends who were interested in Third World issues. She did not follow up on the Spanish lessons and resisted investigation of earlier family experiences or the issues that brought her to treatment. At the tenth session she claimed that she was overwhelmed by cutbacks at her job and terminated treatment.

In the process of attempting to understand what had occurred between C. and me, I realized how deeply disturbing it could be to be seen as someone other than who you actually are. I began to remember my own identity issues as a teenager. When I challenged C.'s reluctance to study Spanish, was it more my wish for her to affirm her identity than it was her wish? Had C. somehow felt that pressure, causing her to respond with a defensive and distancing shrug and thinking, "Don't make me explore any conflicts I have about my color or my Puerto Rican background?" When I refrained from asking about her cultural background in sufficient detail, was I unconsciously colluding with these security operations? What made me sidestep that issue? I neglected to explore with her what she believed her Puerto Rican identity conveyed, what it meant to attend the best "white" schools, what she valued in the past and what she found important in the present. What did it mean to have had a white husband? What was her life like during this period? What did it mean to have an African American boyfriend who was considered one of the spokesmen in Third World causes? I could have explored with her the significance of coming to treatment after the breakup of each of these alliances. Was it by chance that in dealing with her relationship with her white husband she selected a white therapist and in dealing with her black boyfriend she had selected a black therapist?

"Skin color" represents several physical characteristics, including texture of hair, shape of features, and eye color. These are recognizable upon first contact and trigger preconceived values and notions. The value that our society places on a white skin color and the depreciation of dark skin provokes powerful and painful feelings in some African Americans and other people of color. This often affects their sense of identity and self esteem. Williams (1996) notes that confronting and understanding what this conflict means in the context of one's family, community, and larger society can be troubling in both personal and therapeutic relationships. These issues, in varying degrees, extend to the consulting room when the African American participants have noticeable skin color differences or similarities. It raises both transference and countertransference feelings in the participants regarding their respective experiences of skin color (Comas-Diaz and Jacobsen 1991; Thompson 1996).

As therapists, we benefit greatly from exploring the impact of culture, its values and ideals. This exploration helps us to reach a better understanding of our own prejudices and stereotypes. I recognized the conflicts and ambivalence about racial identity and cultural stereotyping from some of my family members, some of who camouflaged their racial selves. There were family secrets related to identity; keeping these secrets was isolating, confusing, and anxiety provoking for me. The feelings generated by such associations and memories can be onerous ones. One can feel anxious that one will be "found out." As Sullivan noted, maintaining a sense of interpersonal security involves holding a false image of self and sacrifices personal integrity.

The fallacy of my assumption that C. was African American, based on her appearance, moved me to react to the difference in ethnicity by raising the question regarding the language of the therapist. I overgeneralized from the psychoanalytic literature on bilingualism that suggests that the second language can function as a defense against early developmental conflicts (Marcos 1976) and indicates that a bilingual therapist would provide an opportunity for the patient to explore and talk in the native language. In this case, Spanish is associated with very early life experiences and the inner life of the patient, whereas the second language, English, is more identified with the outside, acculturation and control (Foster 1992; Marcos 1976). At that moment I perceived C. as a bilingual person and not the unique individual who was suffering. On the contrary, at the time, the feelings associated with her own family would have been a more appropriate focus for the inquiry.

I had to confront my surprise that C. was not African American and also my concern that she would repeat a pattern of terminating her treatment prematurely just as she had in the past. I realized that my question regarding her preference for a Spanish-speaking therapist involved my rejecting her before she rejected me since I spoke no Spanish. Did it jar me that I mistook her for an African American as others have mistaken me for Puerto Rican? Did I want to put her out of my office as others had put her out of their homes?

C. was clearly ambivalent about and afraid to investigate both earlier and contemporary issues. The shame and humiliation associated with her family and the repeated cycle of being expelled from her parents' home, the home of her white in-laws, and finally the home of her African American boyfriend had profound implications regarding her identification with ethnicity and self esteem, and how she had set herself up for such rejection.

As therapists, we may have been taught that intrapsychic forces are more significant than social forces in determining patient's behaviors. We can be, therefore, more often prone to focus on intrapsychic and transference factors in the two-person model. However, just as intrapsychic forces are unconscious, so can the impact of cultural and social forces be unconscious. Our detailed clinical inquiry about past and present social experiences must be designed to learn about the patient's projections onto others, so that the more unconscious conflicts emerge and become available for scrutiny. We must direct the inquiry, as Wolstein says, to ". . . seek explanations of difficulty and distortion in unconscious psychic experience" (1994, 485). In this way, we can better learn about the anxieties that helped shape their security operations. Naturally, what is less common is a more detailed examination of the anxieties and security operations of the therapist, especially those emanating from the therapist's ethnic and social experiences.

In closing, I would like to reiterate that in psychotherapy, anxiety is interpersonal and affects both parties within an interaction. The task of the therapist is to be attuned to the patient's anxiety, as well as his or her own anxiety, in order to avoid the occurrence of collusive selective inattention. When issues of ethnicity and culture are involved, the difficulty becomes compounded. Phinney (1996) writes that ethnicity is more than a simple category; it is a socially determined cognitive construct—a complex of culture, ethnic identity, and minority status. Any one or all of these variables may become the focal point of the treatment when considering ethnic issues. What shaped the ethnic identity of these two women? A. and C. are contemporaries: One grew up with a Protestant ethic and the other as a Catholic; both had similar opportunities provided to them by prep schools and Ivy League colleges. A.'s parents paid her way; C.'s intellect and funds for "disadvantaged youth" paved the way for her. Both came from intact families. A. had the security and comfort of recognition from a middle-class community, including even "coming out" at a debutante ball. C.'s "coming out" was being thrown out of her home for noncompliance with parental rules. C.'s family was less explicitly encompassing in the message they communicated about the outside world, but her father was clear about moral ethics and how she should appear to the world. Her struggle and mission became one of shaping herself through defiance and rejection. On the other hand, A.'s struggle was for liberation and an expanded awareness of self.

REFERENCES

Calnek, M. (1970). Racial factors in the countertransference: The black therapist and the black client. *American Journal of Orthopsychiatry* 40: 39–40.

Comas-Diaz, L., and F. Jacobsen. (1991). Ethnocultural transference and countertransference in the therapeutic dyad. *Journal of the American Orthopsychiatric Association* 61: 392–402.

Cushman, P. (1994). Confronting Sullivan's spider. *Contemporary Psychoanalysis* 30: 800–845.

Davidson, L. (1987). The crosscultural therapeutic dyad. *Contemporary Psychoanalysis* 23: 659–675.

Foster, R. M. P. (1992). Psychoanalysis and the bilingual patient: Some observations on the influence of language choice on the transference. *Psychoanalytic Psychology* 9: 61–75.

Grey, C. (1993). Culture, character, and the analytic engagement: Toward a subversive psychoanalysis. *Contemporary Psychoanalysis* 29: 487–502.

Griffith, M. S. (1977). The influences of race on the psychotherapeutic relationship. *Psychiatry* 40: 27–40.

Holmes, D. E. (1992). Race and transference in psychoanalysis and psychotherapy. *International Journal of Psychoanalysis* 73: 1–11.

Leary, K. (1997). Race, self-disclosure and forbidden talk. *Psychoanalytic Quarterly* 66: 163–189.

Levenson, E. (1992). Harry Stack Sullivan: From interpersonal psychiatry to interpersonal psychoanalysis. *Contemporary Psychoanalysis* 28: 250–466.

Marcos, L. R. (1976). Bilinguals in psychotherapy: Language as an emotional barrier. *American Journal of Psychotherapy* 30: 195–202.

Myers, W. A. (1977). The significance of the colors black and white in the dreams of black and white patients. *Journal of the American Psychoanalytic Association* 16: 163–181.

Phinney, J. S. (1996). When we talk about American ethnic groups, what do we mean? *American Psychologist* 51: 918–927.

Schachter, J. S., and H. F. Butts. (1968). Transference and countertransference interracial analysis. *Journal of the American Psychoanalytic Association* 16: 792–807.

Sullivan, H. S. (1953). *Conceptions of modern psychiatry.* New York: W.W. Norton

Thompson, C. (1996). The African-American patient in psychodynamic treatment. In R. M. P. Foster, M. Moskowitz, and R. A. Javier, eds., *Reaching across boundaries of culture and class: Widening the scope of psychotherapy*, 115–142. Northvale, NJ: Jason Aronson.

Ticho, G. (1971). Cultural aspects of transference and countertransference. *Bulletin of the Menninger Clinic* 35: 313–326.

Williams, A. L. (1996). Skin color in psychotherapy. In R. M. P. Foster, M. Moskowitz, and R. A. Javier, eds., *Reaching across boundaries of culture and class: Widening the scope of psychotherapy*, 211–224. Northvale, NJ: Jason Aronson.

Wolstein, B. (1994). The evolving newness of interpersonal psychoanalysis: From the vantagepoint of immediate experience. *Contemporary Psychoanalysis* 30: 473–499.

CHAPTER 17

Reflections on Culture and Psychoanalysis

Paul Lippmann

Much of psychoanalysis seems little interested in the impact of culture on human affairs. To a large extent, psychoanalysis has found it possible to disconnect from a most significant source of understanding of human life—the impact of social life outside the consulting room on the world of the consulting room and, in related fashion, the impact of social life outside the nursery on the world of the nursery. Despite the self-congratulatory spirit of some contemporary psychoanalysts who believe our field is correcting its former rigidities by opening and broadening its intellectual range, I suggest, in contradiction, that we are in the midst of creating an increasingly narrow and airless worldview in many of our theories and practices. In my opinion, this narrowing is seen as much in the modern relational and two-person models as in the instinct and one-person models (Lippmann, 1998). I propose that we need to open to the enormously complex universe not only of social life on a large scale, but also of the impact of the natural and physical world, as well as of the spiritual dimension on human affairs. Without a contribution to understanding from these three major components—the cultural, the natural-physical and the spiritual—any view of human life seems too narrow.

It is both surprising and disappointing that we still find ourselves in debate over the relative importance of social factors in human personality. Most everyone trained in psychology and in social work—two of the major contributing disciplines to contemporary psychoanalytic practice—is steeped, in their undergraduate and graduate education, in the rich interplay of culture and personality. But when, as psychoanalytic students, they advance into postgraduate psychoanalytic training of one kind or another, many ignore, forget, suppress, or dispense with their earlier and fuller understanding. One is eager to learn the new language and the new concepts that provide membership in the profession that promises a future and a way of earning a living. Thus, in the evolution of a new psychoanalytic identity, many students may find themselves in an unfamiliar realm of discourse in which it is not taken as a matter of course that culture, social history, economics, and zeitgeist, are among the crucial variables in human development, personality, psychopathology and psychotherapy. As inviting as the new language and the new concepts may be, I am suggesting that an impoverishment in thinking may result if the richly layered role of culture is ignored.

For us, to be invited into a person's life, as we are in our daily work, is to be invited into the collective story of the people from which the patient has emerged. Not just the immediate family, but the community, the culture, the geography, the history, the traditions, the victories and tragedies, the music, the dance, the language, and the accumulated beliefs and dreams and customs of a whole people. When we meet a patient, we meet an entire culture and its entire story. Our task, which can afford a high degree of intellectual pleasure, is found in learning and feeling our way into the history and the deepest stories of an entire people. This is especially so in our nation which is made up of most all the cultures of the world. Most everyone we encounter in this culture has been here for but a few generations compared with their prolonged ancient history in older cultures. These older cultures contain much that can inform our understanding of child-rearing practices, gender differences, vocational goals, styles of sex and aggression, methods for relaxation, attitudes toward illness and death, styles of humor, ways of psychological defense, and so on. In much contemporary analytic therapy, we often show little interest in a detailed inquiry into the circumstances of these older cultures, or into the lives of grandparents and great-grandparents, that is, into the collective stories and myths of origins and changes. The patient's cultural background is not the only forgotten area. We often ignore, as well, our own cultural background, in contemplating and describing the overall clinical situation.

Clinical work in the usual two-person situation involves two individuals, both of whom contain and are surrounded by a vast collection of others. These others can be thought of, somewhat fancifully, as ghosts of the past and as seeds of the future—two whole populations of spirits in differing dialects and rhythms listening in on the two who are engaged in their intimate conversation. The past that has produced these two, as well as the future that will emerge from these two, can be thought of as participating in the discussion. These ghosts and seeds that surround both participants can be imagined as cheering them on or expressing displeasure, as wishing them well or voicing intense criticism of the proceedings. They all have a stake in the procedure and the outcome.

What if we were truly to awaken to the lifeblood of our sociometric categories: Who *is* in the room? Who *are* these two people in intimate conversation? What history, what geography, what traditions, what economics has given birth to them? Who are these two whom we call "patient" and "therapist?" Can we let their histories speak to us? Are they, for example, a tall, old, atheist granddaughter of a *Litvak*, mother of six, sitting together with a short, young, gay, religious grandson of a *Galitzianer? Litvak* and *Galitzianer* have had a long and competitive relationship in the Old Country; atheists and religious believers have engaged in centuries of struggle; heterosexuals and homosexuals have viewed each other with suspicion for ages; men and women have behind them eons of misunderstanding and understanding. Just because the descendents of these people are sitting together today in a therapy office in America does not erase from their historical selves the rich threads of centuries of living. The two participants: Are they a poor light-skinned black woman from northeast Africa via rural South Carolina sitting together with a well-to-do dark-skinned black man from southwest Africa via urban Jamaica—both sitting in a therapy room in New York City trying to figure things out? How many unspoken conversations exist between these histories? Erikson (1950) wrote of "identity-fragments" woven into an overall identity. Can we sense the multitude of identity fragments in conversation in the therapy room?

I wonder why it is that we impoverish our work by moving, as though sleepwalking, directly to the mother and the immediate family for ideas about origins and rarely go deeper to the heart of the culture and to the physical and natural world which gives life and shapes meanings for us all? We need to open and take seriously the sociometric categories. Each is an enormously rich universe for clinical understanding.

To begin, we can to try to imagine the two participants—patient and therapist—lined up side by side, in order to see their contrasting and overlapping backgrounds. Economic, religious, and geographic background; and present status, race, size, looks, intelligence, and verbal and physical skill—lined up side by side. Clinical description seems incomplete unless these categories, in some comparative detail, are included. In teaching, I sometimes ask analytic students to imagine their two parents or their four grandparents sitting around a kitchen table in conversation with their patient's two parents or four grandparents. I ask that they consider that the affect and sound of such a conversation, in imagination, underlies some aspects of the analytic interactions with their patients. Simply put, both participants' parents, grandparents, ancestors, and descendents are present in spirit and make their contribution.

However, it is acknowledged that, at times, these categories tell us little about what counts. There are still mysteries about what comes to have meaning in psychotherapy. The unconscious is not easily known. But I believe we can do better than engage in endless repetition about whether or not "mother was empathetically attuned" or whether or not "father was remote and distant," and whether or not the therapist is a Relationalist or a Freudian. To begin to comprehend what is at the heart of any therapeutic relationship, an informed psychoanalytic perspective will look at the two participants in relation to their recent and deep backgrounds, their immediate and distant futures.

Why do we so quickly forget, in psychoanalysis, what we once knew as college and graduate students—that culture and personality are inextricably interwoven? As R. Fox, quoted in Bartlett's (1938) book on Freud wrote: "Psychoanalysis, for all its brilliant and courageous probing into the secret depths of the personality, has never understood that the individual is only a part of the social whole and that the laws of the whole, decomposed and refracted in the apparatus of the individual psyche like rays of light passing through a prism, change and control the nature of each individual."

While the nature of individual psychological life obviously has its own meaningfulness and significance, it is worth exploring—as follows—the evident and long-standing disconnection between the social universe and individual mental life that has resulted, in my opinion, in an impoverishment in psychoanalytic explanatory hypotheses.

(1) The medicalization and Americanization of psychoanalysis, to Freud's prescient chagrin, acted to impoverish the legacy of a rich European appreciation of the relation of personality and culture. While aspects of Freud's developmental libido theory, together with the effect of his split with Adler, served to undermine a more direct linkage between the social and the personal, the entire range of Freud's writing (e.g., Freud, 1900) shows the depth of his European sensibility which included a deep appreciation of the culture's role in human life. Later, in America, in the development from an orthodox (European) to a classical (American) psychoanalysis, well described by Lohser and Newton (1996), we see both an unfortunate tightening in clinical practice and a concomitant disconnection from the nonmedical disciplines (e.g., sociology, history, philosophy, economics, and the humanities). The disruptive flight from Europe, under the dark shadow of the Holocaust, required a certain rigidifying "cleaning up"—a distancing from Marxist and other "un-American" European social theories (Jacobi, 1983) and a less "Jewish" way of thinking, that is, a turning away from *Tikkun Olam*, the mission to heal the world. As part of the all-encompassing, and ultimately constricting, merger of psychiatry and psychoanalysis, economic and political concerns were certainly involved, but at the same time, an intellectual dissociation of psychoanalysis from economic and political thinking took place.

As a breath of fresh air within the more mainstream psychoanalytic tradition, Erik Erikson, more than any other psychoanalyst, explored and made rich use of the intimate relationship between social and life history, between the cultural and the individual. In *Childhood and Society* (1950) and subsequent writings, Erikson wove together the old European sensibility with an American touch, that is, a deep and broad view of life and culture with an increasingly American interest in youth and the issues of identity.

Outside and critical of the mainstream, the Interpersonal tradition, developed in the writings of Fromm, Horney, Sullivan, and others, gave voice to a cogent and impressive critique of the increasing inattention in the Freudian mainstream to the broad (Fromm) and narrow (Sullivan) social forces operating in human life.

(2) In the modern era, we have seen a loss of deep connection between self, nature, social context, and God. The human is seen in isolation, alone in modern existential separateness, independent, autonomous, and self-reliant in the myth of the American tradition. Thus the patient is seen in splendid and wretched isolation, torn from considerations of context. In psychoanalysis, we have turned this tragic aspect of modern life into something of a virtue, perhaps a goal. Hand in hand with our extolling individual independence, we continually narrow our observations and hypotheses to the infant-mother relationship. While there has been something of a necessary (Kleinian) interest in pre-oedipal life and in mother-child relations—to compensate for Freud's patriarchal bias—this necessary opening into the earliest days in the nursery has become an all-encompassing preoccupation. An understanding of the complexity of the human heart cannot stand on such a flimsy and narrow foundation as the theory of the relationship only between infant and mother and its later transposition into ideas about patient and therapist—divorced from the complex natural, physical, social, and spiritual universe that is our fuller home. In this sense, the mother can be thought of more as an early and significant culture-substitute and a nature-substitute, even a God-substitute, rather than the other way around. Simplistic developmental reductionism is the price we pay for our simple-minded notions of what enters into distinctly human experience. Jerome Kagan (1998) engages productively with such reductionism most recently expressed by those advancing attachment theory.

(3) It is occasionally necessary to remind ourselves that science is, in part, a political activity. Certainly our very own quasi-science is heavily influenced by political currents. During the more liberal times of progressivism and the emergence of both democratic and autocratic socialism, ideas about the impact of social forces on human personality were in the ascendance in our field. The interpersonal challenge to traditional psychoanalysis arose partly from this spirit in the 1930s and 1940s. At the same time, the Freudian-Marxists (e.g., Fenichel) were quietly concealing their socialist interests. At present, of course, we are in a much more conservative politics in which American and world capitalism has transformed the social-economic picture. In this climate, psychoanalysis pretends to be apolitical, value-free, uncontaminated by the dominating and powerful world of economics within the inner sanctum of the consulting room, while expressing alarm and narrow self-interest in the discussion of the threat of the HMO takeover. It should be mentioned that an increasing interest in genes and brain chemistry in thinking about psychological experience, together with an enormously burgeoning drug industry for the alleviation of psychological difficulty, goes hand in hand with the materialist and conservative politics of our day. Some political-psychoanalytic theorists (e.g., Castoriadis, 1997) go further in showing how contemporary

relational psychoanalysis may unwittingly serve the purposes of the market economy in reflecting a positive image of multiplicity and flexibility in the modern self which then is open to more purchasing, that is, the market economy requires a multiplicity of changing needs rather than a single, central core of values and ideals.

(4) Currently, within the psychoanalytic world, there is a great deal of self-congratulations about our move from a one-person to a two-person psychology, from an infant-centered to an infant-mother-centered theory, from a patient-centered to a patient-analyst-centered view, and so on. Such heralding of great progress is seen particularly within approaches that are attempting to liberate themselves from some of the less palatable of Freud's views. Thus happy progress radiates from the modern Freudians, from the object-relationalists, from self psychologists, from intersubjectivists, from social constructionists, post-modern deconstructive hermeneuticists, Lacanians, and so on. But this heady atmosphere seems to me to replace one kind of domination (the classical Freudian) with another (the Relational). While both often claim a certain undeserved knowingness, both most often ignore the broader perspective emphasized in Erich Fromm's interpersonal views (Burston, 1991), in Erik Erikson's ego-psychology (1950), and in James Hillman's neo-Jungian approach (1983). I am suggesting that the apparently more "social" two-person view of the contemporary relational approach engages no more deeply with the impact of cultural forces on personality and psychotherapy than did the earlier instinctivist one-person view of the Freudians. The social perspective of the former seems entirely narrowed, indeed, to two persons rather than one. Not a large shift. Perhaps not a shift at all.

In passing, there is probably a positive side to some aspects of the turn away from a consideration of the broadly cultural-political macrocosmic forces at work in human life. In clinical work, we often need to be more occupied with the relatively up-close, so-called experience-near microcosmic phenomena of baby-mother life and of moment-to-moment psychological experience, especially in the world of the intimate, minute, transference-filled psychotherapeutic exchange. But despite any advantages accruing to this narrower focus, we limit ourselves unnecessarily in ignoring the broad cultural-political realm.

There are occasionally successful efforts to wed these microcosmic and macrocosmic views. (See, for example, Dolores O. Morris's and Robert Prince's chapters in this collection.) Bridging powerful social forces to intimate inner experience and seeing how these two realms interact in psychotherapy is a complex task, not made any easier, in my opinion, by the current fad of diversity training and multicultural studies. These popular and quick fixes to the symptom of intellectual disconnection between personal life and social forces, seen in much psychotherapy writing, lead more to political correctness along with the mistaken idea that in so-called diversity education, one is genuinely engaging with serious social problems. Dividing the world into race, gender, and sexual orientation and punishing or "re-educating" those with "incorrect" views has more in common with the failed Soviet system than with the hard work of genuine solutions to complex social problems. A recent example of the burgeoning field of diversity training shows one aspect of its appeal: A brochure describing an educational opportunity for clinicians advertises that at a cost of $129, one can attend a meeting, receive 5 CEUs, and listen to an "expert" in the field lecture on "how understanding culture, class, race, and gender differences can benefit your clinical practice."

Related to what is in my opinion the mistaken optimism of diversity training is the persistent idea that one needs to be one to know one. That is, a psychotherapist who is gay or black or once sexually abused is the most able in treating a patient who is respectively gay or black or sexually abused. This popular and simple-minded view, which includes the idea that a same-race, same-sex person is the correct role model for a growing child, is simply wrong and too narrow, in my opinion. For example, among the important heroes and models in my own young working-class Jewish life were Paul Robeson, Mother Bloor, Joe DiMaggio, Gershwin and Puccini, Sinatra and Billie Holiday, Emma Lazarus, Langston Hughes, the fictional Lone Ranger and Jean-Christophe—a mix. The virtues of a mix in role models for children is badly understated, as are the virtues of a mix in therapist-patient pairs.

Similarities in background in the two participants in psychotherapy, can, of course, lead to enhanced understanding, but they can also lead to blindness. Sometimes I miss the point with a patient who is a Yiddish-speaking (as am I), 60-plus-year-old (as am I) whose parents were born in Poland (as were mine). Sometimes I can get the point better or deeper with a patient, for example, who is an upper-class lesbian and whose parents were from a German-Protestant background with hidden Nazi connections. But again, in addition to an active engagement with the sociopolitical-economic background of the other, one needs to keep in mind that the psyche and the unconscious are full of surprises. Jung's shadow concept is helpful here. "The Nazi lesbian," as she calls herself, and I—she calls me a "marginally straight Jew Commie"—may share some important world *under the surface*, while my Yiddish-speaking patient and I may inhabit different planets *under the surface*. I notice this over and over in my practice with persons like and dissimilar to myself on the surface. These observations lead to the conclusion that we are often prone to gross oversimplification in bridging the personal and the social.

Yet it is understandable that persons who believe they speak for culturally marginal or disadvantaged populations wish to influence psychotherapy to be more responsive. Psychotherapy, in general, and psychoanalysis, in particular, have been agents of social change for previously disadvantaged populations. I have in mind the particular relationship between psychoanalysis and the offspring of Jewish immigrants in this country during the decades before, during, and after World War II. Psychoanalysis was, for many, a major pathway to becoming American. We learned how to talk the talk and walk the walk, how to leave our parents and their language behind. I remember my analyst being contemptuous of my dreams in Yiddish. (He preferred the Austrian German he had thoroughly superimposed on *his* grandparent's Yiddish.) Assimilation was also Freud's path in Vienna as he left behind the Yiddish of his parents and became thoroughly fluent and brilliant in his adopted German tongue. Psychoanalysis, as a profession, has been a vehicle for socioeconomic upward mobility in which many lose (or repress or suppress or work through) the sounds and smells of their background. Trying to escape *shame*, we plunge into *guilt* as the heavy price of moving beyond our backgrounds, our families, and our early neighborhoods. Guilt, in relation to those we leave behind, has in it, at least, the virtue of *loyalty*.

My wife and colleague, Frances Lippmann, as director of the Williams College Counseling Service, sees the black and Hispanic and Asian students, who fill the seats once filled only by the elite children of the old ruling class, suffer deeply from the ravages of loyalty and its dark twin, guilt, as they are propelled upward. The advantages of a superb education are shadowed by powerful internal conflicts. This is seen in prep schools and colleges across the country where many students begin their voyage upward across socioeconomic boundaries. Luckily, we live in a time when we can more fully embrace our ethnic backgrounds. One's relation to economic class is less often celebrated. The poverty or wealth of one's background are still difficult to acknowledge, albeit for very different reasons. An analyst needs to be aware of all of this in him- or herself as well as in the patient. It can often be most helpful to assist people to feel for and engage with relevant aspects of their history, their people, their soil, or their class membership, and to develop a significant dialogue with their deep background. While such an approach was once frowned upon in our melting-pot rejection of the old world, psychoanalysis can no longer afford to disconnect persons from their deep histories. This was Erikson's message.

In addition to a necessary awareness of the significance of broad sociocultural background, *the times we live in*, the *zeitgeist*, also play a crucial role in shaping both conscious and unconscious experience. The central concerns of the late nineteenth century are not the concerns of today's world. The years surrounding World War II, for example, created ways of thinking, feeling, and relating that were quite different from our experience today. Thus, the times, in their effect on different populations, are a serious participant in private and public psychological life, especially in view of the rapidly changing nature of modern living together with the power of popular culture in affecting us.

As significant as is *zeitgeist* in shaping individual psychological life, it is most difficult for analysts to evaluate the influence of the times within which we, ourselves, operate. Can we, for example, effectively evaluate the impact of the electronic revolution, or the replacement of internal imagery with external sources of imagery (i.e., television, film, computer), or the bottom-line mentality that exists in our market-driven economic world, as they shape feelings, attitudes, and ideas about self, other, and life? It has always been helpful for analysis to exist somewhat to the side of the prevailing culture. To evaluate the culture of which one is a full member is no easy task, since inevitable blind spots exist and our own "social unconscious" contributes to evaluation.

To carry the idea of *zeitgeist* further, we might ask: What will the psychoanalysis of the future look like? Psychoanalysis began as a "Jewish science," as an effort to understand humankind from a historically Jewish perspective, at times with, at times without, awareness of this perspective. Freud attempted to use Jung as the "front man" so the Christian and anti-Semitic world would not destroy his precious discovery. As the central ideas of psychoanalysis spread through the world, each national, religious, or ethnic culture adds its own coloration, its own view of life into the growing mix. American psychoanalysis was shaped in part by escapees from the Holocaust, and in part by the practical, functional, instinctless Sullivan, into an American amalgam focused on the self, on individual life, on personal expression and adaptation. British psychoanalysis survived the wars surrounding the Jewish immigrants—Melanie Klein and Anna Freud—to become finally distinctly British in its emphasis on object relations and the very English schizoid personality. France, at first occupied with an entirely French version of hysteria and sexuality, more recently has been taken with the unconscious shaped in the form of *la langue*, the language—so proudly French. Also, a somewhat Catholic version of life emerged through Lacan. Germany contributed, through Abraham, the anal and obsessive-compulsive personality preoccupied with order and control. Hungary yielded up the passion and creative force, the emotional and intellectual playfulness of Ferenczi and of Balint. Mexican, Italian, Japanese, Argentine, and Spanish psychoanalysis each adds yet other dimensions stemming from the life, history, language, geography, and nature of its people. Each culture puts its stamp on psychoanalysis, that is, on the study of human nature. Within our own American heterogeneity and complexity, what will be the stamp of black culture on psychoanalysis? What will be the stamp of Hispanic culture on psychoanalysis? What will be the view of sex and aggression coming from these cultures? We already see a broader view of sexuality influenced by gay and lesbian analysts. We see a deeper vision of female *and* male development influenced by women analysts. What will be the human face created within psychoanalysis by future generations of analysts from diverse cultures and points of view, as they struggle to understand their own nature and to develop a language that reflects that nature, and also illuminates all of us, as did Freud's Jewish science?

In all these considerations, it is of importance to recognize that we are not referring to a "surrounding" culture, that is, another simplifying idea that suggests that the individual and the culture are conceptually distinct. Often misunderstood, Sullivan and the early Interpersonalists insisted on a thoroughgoing integration of the two. Thus, it would not be correct, from this point of view, to think of the *intrapsychic* as located within the person and the *interpersonal* as between persons. It would make better sense to view the interpersonal to include both the world within together with the interactions between persons. The between-person world *is* intimately implicated in the within-person world. In a more limited sense, object relations theory aims at this same complex view.

In a similar vein, despite their often being spoken of as though in two separate domains, "the culture" and psychoanalysis do not exist as conceptually distinct. To the contrary, the culture is entirely embedded *within* psychoanalysis. We are *of* the culture. While at the same time attempting to stand a bit apart from it, so that we are not fully blinded and merged with its values and its effects on our patients and ourselves, still we are of the culture. Those who for many diverse reasons stand apart from the dominant pull of the culture (e.g., Jews, women, homosexuals, loners, dreamers, blacks, Hispanics, the handicapped, and others of the underclass, along with the very many who identify with them), view manifest life from the latent underside of things, a view absolutely essential for psychoanalysis. It is not an accident that psychoanalysis was first developed by Jews living among the ambivalent welcome and hatred of Central Europe's Christianity. As an inscription on the front page to *The Interpretation of Dreams* (1900), Freud, quoting Virgil, quoting Juno, explicated best by Schorske (1980), writes "*If I cannot bend the higher powers, I shall stir up Hell*," meaning that if we do not have access to the higher realms, we will gain access to power through the lower realms—namely, through knowledge of dreams and the unconscious.

Thus, it is important for us to stand a bit aside from the dominant culture. And yet it is crucial for us to see how thoroughly embedded is the dominant culture within psychoanalysis and is psychoanalysis within the culture. How are we, how is psychoanalysis, *of* the culture?

1. Money moves us. When I make a referral of a prospective patient to a colleague, I can literally hear, in the breathing sound over the telephone, my colleague's pleasure if I say "money is not a problem." I can literally hear my colleague's discomfort if I say "the patient doesn't have much money." Money does move us. Other themes move us too, but money is a big mover in our work. *We are of the culture.* "Show me the money." Success in our field, for many, is measured in how much you can charge. $200 an hour for the successful, $40 an hour for the beginner and the less successful. *We are of the culture.* In this regard, the economic factor joins us more than our psychoanalytic divisions separate us. We have yet to seriously investigate the effect of the business side of our activities on our theories and our practices. I don't believe we will be particularly proud of ourselves on this front, once we are willing to look seriously at how our business interests color our science.
2. We operate on the clock and we are observed to cut the time to make more money. I am not referring here to Lacan's self-serving experiments. More analysts work in 45-minute back-to-back sessions than they did 25 years ago, when most analysts worked in 50-minute sessions with a 10-minute break, which allowed for some spillover, when necessary. In this more rushed way of working, there is no time to

breathe, to think, to reflect, to relax, to waste. Each session, in such a regimen, begins and ends in haste, always a bit late. What values do we practice and what values do we convey in such a system? This pervasive practice goes unchallenged and began well before managed care's nasty influences. It began out of our own greed, I am sorry to say, although usually well rationalized as necessary for one reason or another. *We are of the culture.*

3. We measure success in our work by the success in our patients according to the standards of our culture. Too often have we seen, in clinical presentations, the self-satisfied look on the presenting analyst's and on the audience's faces as the patient is described as "better" with better grades, or a better job, or a steady partner, or a successful book, or a larger apartment. Success in the view of the culture is too often the measure of clinical success. I would once love to hear: "The therapy was successful. She dropped out of school." Or "The therapy was successful and he stayed attached to his elderly parents." Or "The analysis failed in that the patient got a better-paying and more prestigious job at the expense of his soul." More than we ever dream are we tied to our culture.
4. We have little regard, as does our culture, for the significance of the natural and physical world. We run our air conditioners, drive our cars, live in our vacation homes, send our kids to private schools, and gobble up energy while most of the world goes without, with little regard for our ongoing destruction of nature. Our offices are shut off from nature, soundproofed, nature-proofed, shut away in our cities. *We are of the culture.*
5. We do the culture's bidding. We are the "kidneys" of the culture, assisting our patients to get rid of the poisons built up in frantic modern civilization: the unfulfilling jobs, the poor schools, the crowds and the rush, the bottom-line mentality of our culture. We help keep it all going by helping the sufferers better adjust to their conditions. We point attention to early development, to beleaguered mothers and fathers, and not to the society and the system we all cooperate in maintaining. To call attention to our mutual engagement in an often cruel and corrupt social system would be to call attention to our own participation, our own corruption, our own hustle. Better to focus on early development and unempathic mothers. Thus we make it possible to be part of a dangerous world. *We are of the culture.*
6. In this regard, I would like to call attention to a fascinating book, *Hollywood on the Couch*, by Farber and Green (1993). The integration of psychoanalysts in Hollywood filmmaking, of psychoanalysts in Washington politics, of psychoanalysts in the financial and artistic markets of New York, and so on, is a dark and fascinating story of the loss of ethical moorings when money and power, and the allure of the culture's rewards, beckon. The story of psychoanalysis is not a particularly proud one in this regard. *We are of the culture.*

In his psychoanalysis, 100 years ago, at the turn of the century, Freud developed a cogent critique of his culture. His major opus, *The Interpretation of Dreams* (1900), and Schorske's (1980) explication of its inner structure, show the intricate interconnections of personal history, family relations, friendships, ambition, sexuality, social history, politics, economics, and religion interwoven in the experience of dreams and their analyses. As analysts, we need to rekindle that complex view of self and world beyond the narrow confines of our heralded two-person view of the psychoanalytic encounter. Human relations between intimates is not the alpha and omega of all human living, although they are of importance in life and especially in the business of therapy. We need to open to the wider and deeper world of the connection of persons to history, to the life of imagination, to the physical and natural world, to the future. In this regard, psychoanalysis may yet have a relevance in attending to the human situation at the turn of a new century and millennium. The powerful electronic revolution is changing social, political, and economic life. Privacy is an endangered experience. Personal greed expands with the psychology of a global market economy. Family life has been drastically altered. The natural world, including our connection to all living things, is rapidly receding and being replaced by virtual worlds. Medical technology along with genetic research has helped create the possibility of prolonged life including the use of nonhuman body parts. Space travel is near. Who are we becoming? Can psychoanalysis, as the study of human life in depth, open to the enormous impact of these developments? Can psychoanalysis respond to this new world, this twenty-first century, 100 years after Freud opened the door to the twentieth century?

REFERENCES

Bartlett, F. (1938). *Sigmund Freud.* London: Victor Gollancz.

Burston, D. (1991). *The Legacy of Erich Fromm.* Cambridge: Harvard University Press.

Castoriadis, C. (1997). *World in Fragments.* Stanford: Stanford University Press.

Erikson, E. (1950). *Childhood and Society.* New York: W. W. Norton.

Farber, S., & Green, M. (1993). *Hollywood on the Couch.* New York: William Morrow & Co.

Freud, S. (1900). *The Interpretation of Dreams. Standard Edition,* Vols. 4 & 5. London: Hogarth Press.

Hillman, J. (1983). *Inter Views.* New York: Harper & Row.

Jacobi, R. (1983). *The Repression of Psychoanalysis.* New York: Basic Books.

Kagan, J. (1998). *Three Seductive Ideas.* Cambridge: Harvard University Press.

Lippmann, P. (1998). On the Private and Social Nature of Dreams. *Contemporary Psychoanalyis* 34: 195–221.

Lohser, B., & Newton, P. (1996). *Unorthodox Freud.* New York: Guilford Press.

Schorske, C. (1980). *Fin-de-siècle Vienna: Politics and Culture.* New York: Knopf.

CHAPTER 18

Psychoanalysis in a Cold Climate

Robert Prince

A VIGNETTE

I had a few minutes before my first consultation with Mr. Edwards, a very proper gentleman if I could judge anything from his manner over the phone. I was anticipating ending several treatments and, although I was used to the fact that not every person who called actually made a first appointment, I was now being asked different questions over the phone—for example, what HMOs did I belong to and did I "do" cognitive behavioral therapy. The preceding week, a woman had broken her first appointment saying that she had seen her internist who told her that since her problem was anxiety, she should take medication.

While waiting, I decided to go through my mail, first opening a book offer from A.P.A. which, for $39.95, promised to adapt my practice to the new realities of health care. This prompted an association to a medical intern who, after a seminar on psychotherapy, told me that he had been taught in medical school that *id* and *ego* were outmoded terms from the 1960s and another image of an elegantly laid out announcement for a new group practice specializing in psychological consultations for family-owned businesses. Anyway, *if* I bought the book, I could have another one at a discount that would help me automate my office to deal with the increased paperwork resulting from my successful utilization of the first book. After that, I found a brochure from an insurance company, also offering me a discount (this must be my lucky day) to attend a workshop on "solution-oriented" brief therapy which would be taught by a "master clinician" whose photograph was prominently featured.

Fortunately, Mr. Edwards arrived. He complimented my office and apologized for his dress—unnecessarily, to my eye—explaining that he had come straight from his factory. He had come, he said, because of a book, *The Road Less Traveled*, by Scott Peck. He had achieved considerable material success, met many physical challenges, and served in an elite military unit. He regretted his lack of a liberal arts education, but his children would have one. He was proud of his beautiful wife, his large house, and his expensive car (a Mercedes by the way, the big one, which he knew he drove too aggressively). Now Peck's book had helped him realize it was time for him to explore his inner life. He knew it wouldn't be easy, but he was used to facing formidable tasks square on.

By way of background: He was the least-favored middle son of a father who himself had punched his way out of a hard scrabble beginning to achieve considerable material success. Father had never been sympathetic, let alone generous, had sometimes been abusive, and only now was showing some respect for what Mr. Edwards had achieved with his own hands.

What troubled him? He occasionally was reminded of a grizzly experience in combat in which comrades had died horribly and from which he had a permanent physical sequelae—but this was more and more behind him. More immediate, he became irritated with his wife for her occasional refusal to dress to his standards despite her lavish spending on clothes. She complained he was controlling, yet he only saw himself as being this way when he was right. He was worried about his eldest daughter who seemed withdrawn and with whom there was definitely a communication barrier. He thought that some of the problems with his wife and daughter might have something to do with the death of a younger child in a tragic accident that had occurred five years ago that very month. As he told me about this, his deep sadness emerged and it became evident to both of us that he had come to treatment because he had a need to complete his mourning.

I alerted him as we neared the end of our time, and he told me that he found me to be empathic and understanding. He had come hoping I would meet his high expectations, he had not been disappointed, and he would like to begin psychoanalysis with me as soon as possible. There was only one thing more: He had heard that these days psychoanalysts had many unfilled hours and, whereas they had once commanded $150 a session, they were now willing to see patients for $20 a visit, and this was what he would like to pay . . . he would also like to pay in cash.

A Freudian colleague, Linda Gunsberg, upon hearing this material, points out that this treatment begins with a negative transference as Mr. Edwards's fee proposal expresses competitive, contemptuous, and hateful feelings toward his father. She furthermore has a keen ear for the countertransferential themes that greet Mr. Edwards and complement his issues. These include attention taken up by matters that are all too apparent to outside observers but until recently studiously avoided in psychoanalysis. These are the mundane as opposed to the sublime, concerns about competition, status, and, despite Freud's admonition to be frank, money. One of the more dramatic changes in the culture of psychoanalysis is the rapidity with which such concerns have moved from taboo topics to dominant themes of private and public discourse.

This vignette illustrates, in Dolores Morris's wonderful phrase, the *intertwining* of the patient's and analyst's attitudes and those of the cultural context in which they are embedded. While there is a rich cultural heritage in psychoanalytic thought, the emotional valence the term *culture* carries is relatively mild. It is not a sexy word and, ironically, despite our living in a time of millennial upheaval and dramatically changing times, it strikes many ears as tired or warns of an incipient ideological exposition. We still tend to see culture as a product of personal processes or as providing the material for their expression. As analysts, we less often bring it into the treatment as a powerful force in its own right—one that shapes perceptions and values, and determines behavior, emotions, and experience. We tend not to notice that it makes as little sense to talk of interpersonal processes without taking into account a cultural context as it does to talk about intrapsychic processes without taking into account an interpersonal one. Even less than seeing this in our patients, do we see ourselves as caught up both in the surrounding culture and also in the culture (or more precisely one of the many cultures) of psychoanalysis. On occasion, a voice reminds us—although we are all inordinately proud of being "independent" thinkers—just how much of our beliefs, behaviors, and animosities are based on the politics and rhetoric of the particular psychoanalytic school to which we belong. If a psychoanalytic treatment is an interpersonal event, it is also an intergroup event. Thus, I would like this vignette to be a springboard for consideration of the idea that practice of psychoanalysis is profoundly influenced by and given meaning by the cultural context in which it occurs—and that to understand any single session, it is necessary to take into account where it is located in the trajectory of the relation between the analyst, the surrounding culture, and the culture of psychoanalysis. Furthermore, just as the transference must be regarded as reflecting accurate perceptions, it becomes imperative to understand the truth contained in the negative transference the analysis in this vignette begins with.

Clearly Mr. Edwards expresses the general ambivalence about psychotherapy. He needs somewhere to turn to, but that place requires a cultural sanction, which is serendipitously provided by Peck's bestseller. The book, which encompasses Mr. Edwards's respect for education, to say nothing of the status conferred by the title, Doctor, simultaneously gives direction to his personal needs, and it is this that initially legitimizes the analyst's authority. At the same time, Mr. Edwards absorbs and reflects a widespread consensus that there is a crisis in the relationship of psychoanalysis to its surround to the extent that it is in danger of becoming marginalized, if not extinct. His offer of $20 represents themes from his own childhood, a perception of my concerns, and also how the culture confers value. A businessman, he seizes the prerogative of making the first offer in a negotiation. In doing so, he makes a statement about the implicit authority relationship. I, while experiencing the pressure of surrounding attitudes and the balance between my personal needs and the values of my professional class, am nonplused by his omnipotent grandiosity, in interpersonalist terms, his *chutzpa*. However, his behavior is consistent with the industrialization of healthcare, the session becoming, in his mind, a commodity subject to the same market forces as the widgets his factory produces. He, though his numbers are a little low, is more *au courant* than I am.

To be brought up to date requires a historical perspective on the relationship of psychoanalysis to the surrounding culture. Despite the simplification, we can think of this relationship in terms of three broad overlapping phases. The first is the phase of psychoanalysis ascendant. During this phase, Freud gave birth to a new and vibrant set of ideas that attracted brilliant and creative disciples who in turn constituted a discipline that was a magnet for the intellectual leadership of Europe and America. Although what Sulloway (1979) called "the myth of the hero" gained currency, psychoanalysts during this phase were not lonely fighters in the battle against the forces of darkness, comparable to a Semmelweis despised and maligned because of an insistence on the truth. They were aware of their role as explorers of a new and growing field and members of an intellectual elite who existed in the vibrant aura of new ideas. Though they were courageous and bold, though they were often in conflict with the establishment, they also derived power and authority from their medical credentials. If psychoanalysis challenged one system of beliefs, it supported and was supported by a progressive tide. Hale (1995), in his book, *The Rise and Crisis of Psychoanalysis in the United States*, demonstrates that beginning in the 1920s, psychoanalysis became "part of a popular American *Kulturkampf* of cities against the hinterlands, of the new literature against the old, of the religion of science against outmoded tradition, of the modern attack on Victorianism against received standards of sexual behavior" (381).

The second phase can be thought of as the phase of psychoanalysis dominant. It is summed up in the words of W. H. Auden (1991), "Freud, to us he is no more a person / Now but a whole climate of opinion." During these years, many psychoanalysts may have maintained their identity as revolutionaries which was not in the least affected by the fact that the profession brought with it high personal status and financial reward. Hale reports that by 1930, the income of a physician analyst was twice the average of that of American medical doctors. Indeed, the restriction of psychoanalysis to medicine represented a Faustian bargain, which guaranteed the growth and insured the status and influence of psychoanalytic ideas at the cost of their contamination by the culture of American medicine. By the end of the 1940s and the beginning of the 1950s the analytic credential was required for advancement in the psychiatric profession. By the mid-1950s popularization had reached a peak in novels and film, with Freud lionized in the press and extravagant claims for the technique part of the established wisdom. Karl Menninger had access to President Eisenhower who sent his congratulations to the American Psychoanalytic Association, which had hired a public relations firm to help commemorate the event, on the centennial of Freud's birth. A paradox emerged during this phase; namely, while the ego ideals of truth and honesty prevailed, the profession was simultaneously intolerant of deviance, internal as well as external. Heretics were excommunicated. Karen Horney was barred from teaching at New York Psychoanalytic. Sullivan, who left in support, broke with her over her refusal to admit nonmedical analysts to her newly formed society. When the American Psychiatric Association, demonstrating that science is democratic, voted to de-pathologize homosexuality, it was the American Psychoanalytic Association that voiced the most opposition. The avant-garde had become the bulwark of the status quo.

The third phase can be thought of as psychoanalysis beleaguered. At the same time that the scope of the profession was broadening, including new professions, new ideas, and new data, its position began to shift downward. Chairs of the major departments of psychiatry were no longer chosen from the ranks of analysts, and the best and brightest minds were turning toward psychopharmacology, behavior genetics, and neurobiology. The tone of cultural reports, newspaper and magazine articles, movies and fictional portrayals began to turn. For example, a *New Yorker* cartoon portraying a patient on a couch with the caption, "Would it be too much to ask to see some results?" is no longer the good-natured jibe of an earlier era at a respected but anxiety-provoking icon. In contrast to the hagiographic press of the preceding generation, Daniel Goleman, the then psychology reporter for the *New York Times*, responded to an invitation to cover the proceedings of the 1993 Division 39 meetings in New York by writing a piece in the Ideas and Opinions column of that Sunday's Week in Review satirizing "Woody Allen therapy." In the annual *New York Times Book Review* listings of editor's choices, of the hundreds of nonfiction selections, including psychology, philosophy, sociology, biography, genetics, and ornithology, one looks in vain for a single psychoanalytic selection.

However disheartening the "bad press," there has always been a hint of pride in Freud's (1937) declaration of an "impossible profession." More importantly, people, many of them former patients from the time when anybody who was anybody was a patient, were beginning to evince a great deal of anger toward psychoanalysis. Patient reports of their analytic experience became increasingly negative. This "bad word of mouth" has, in the analytic community, been subject to massive selective inattention. The exception of course is the triumph experienced when the failure can be attributed to a competing psychoanalytic orientation. This shortsighted pleasure detracts from the crucial task of addressing the truths contained in the negative transference of not only the culture as a whole but also so many individuals.

Certainly there has always been criticism, but it has always been balanced by support from a strong center and few alternatives. Too little effort, too much of which has been self-serving, has been devoted to understanding this last wave of unmitigated hostility. One set of explanations mirrors Hale's demonstration that the rise of psychoanalysis occurred in tandem with parallel cultural themes. Its decline occurs as the values of the surround diverge. Foremost, psychoanalysis has a predominant value on the individual while the surround is driven by the necessities of a mass society. This includes concern with economies of scale rather than personal fulfillment. Thus the philosophy of care implicit in psychoanalysis is based on a tradition that equates giving with justice. The philosophy of care of the 1990s extends a tradition that attributes the burden of care to those who require it. Where psychoanalysis expects the clinical situation to be designed for the patient, the culture expects all situations to follow the principles of the market. Where psychoanalysis values process, the surround values efficacy and outcome. Where psychoanalysis has a time orientation that blends past, present, and future, the surround is preoccupied by linear time and the rapidity of change. What other intellectual discipline would produce articles with references going back 50 years? Where psychoanalysis values authentic experiences that penetrate appearances, the surround increasingly promotes what the French social critic Jean Beaudrillard (1996) calls simulated experiences which are dependent on the creation of appearances. Psychoanalysis remains analogic while the culture is becoming digitized. The former thrives on associational thinking; the latter demands straightforward, goal-oriented reasoning. Where one common value of all psychoanalytic schools is paradox, the appreciation of which is regarded as evidence of the highest developmental achievement, paradox causes the digital system to crash.

In another work (Prince 1997), I try to examine the implications of Margaret Mead's (1970) distinction between pre- and post-figurative cultures for the psychoanalytic relationship, particularly with regard to authority issues. Freud's mission can be seen as establishing the authority of psychoanalysis by analyzing the authority that pre-figurative culture (that is, cultures in which the younger generation could look to the older for a vision of how life would be) invested in the psychoanalyst. Contemporary culture (post-figurative because the younger generation is actually better equipped than the older to anticipate the future) can be seen as both cynical about authority and yearning for an authority that may no longer exist.

Psychoanalysis, which can claim as a past accomplishment magnificent success in unraveling the mystery of authority, now seems blindsided. For example, the first 1996 issue of *Psychoanalytic Quarterly* is devoted to the issue of authority, and the articles that comprise it are exquisitely sensitive to the psychoanalyst's authority. However, in so doing, these articles affirm the analyst of yesterday who, whatever else was thought, was a formidable figure. Not one article addresses the far more pressing clinical issue of the day, namely, the analyst's loss of authority.

One facet of this loss is the transformation of the medical system in which psychoanalysis has been enmeshed. The contemporary model of the doctor-patient relationship redefines the latter as consumer, the former as provider or vendor, and involves a third party payor. In a variation of a Marxist theme (Groucho not Karl), we nonphysician analysts find ourselves with the dubious achievement of finally belonging to the club that for so long would not have us.

Corresponding to the impact of the changing cultural context is the change in the culture of psychoanalysis. It is inarguable that the rigorous training regime and the group processes of our professional organizations have profoundly shaped our clinical behaviors, often for the better but many times against our better judgment. We fail to acknowledge the scant evidence on which we base our vitriolic criticism of our colleagues who are, to paraphrase Sullivan, all more nearly analytic than otherwise. Group process obscures the degree to which our practice is based on what Spence (1994) has called rhetoric, which we mistake for evidence. We fail to see that our bloody internecine warfare, when it is not based on the narcissism of small differences, derives its intensity from a conflict of values and group socialization disguised as objective standards of emotional health. Lionnels (1998) has pointed out that psychoanalytic culture is plagued by placing impossible and crazy-making demands on its practitioners as word is contradicted by deed. For example, creativity is endorsed in principle only to be condemned when practiced. Paradoxically, it is the change in the culture of psychoanalysis that now permits such perceptions without sanction.

The culture of psychoanalysis also provides the ideals and the inspiration that few of us could achieve on our own. Who of us, on our own, could bring to every session what is provided by 100 years of thought and experience? The loneliness and fear that can be encountered in psychoanalytic spaces would be hard for many of us to endure without the support of what Bion calls the "sentience" provided by the group. But a changing surround has affected psychoanalytic culture. In some venues the wagons have been circled. In others, accommodations have been made and marketing—Fromm forgive us—has been initiated. The nature of psychoanalytic leadership is similarly changing. The power to reward and punish has been attenuated. The narcissistic enhancement of belonging is diminished. As we listen to our patients with one ear, we hear the collective voice of our analytic forebears and contemporaries with the other. The voice was once strong and sharp; increasingly, there is static.

The question, Is analysis done differently in cold climates?, answers itself. The practice of analysis in warmer climates was endangered by the arrogance of power and a group process that reinforced a range of deluded ideas and practices. As the temperature drops, analysts have to monitor their anxiety and security operations. Napoleon (history's first interpersonal general) said "God is in the details," and there are multiple details that inform—from greetings on answering machines that say "Thank you for calling," to how we arrange our schedules, or set fees, or discuss insurance, or answer questions, to say nothing of what we respond to or enact in session. There was a time when we were concerned about being seductive but that was when psychoanalysis was the only game in town. Although I'm a little worried about being quoted as saying anything against empathy, it is hard to avoid noticing the increasing shift from an abstinence to a gratification model across schools as patients become scarcer. Whereas we were once cavalier about our insistence that patients adhere to the basic structure of the situation, we now have to respond to the attributions of the surround that may shape or encourage transference and countertransference.

Analysts and patients belong to groups that are both distinct and overlapping. It may thus be inevitable that every analysis begins with a confrontation of cultures. Ironically, this may be obscured because of the centrality of a personal analysis to an analyst's identity. We forget that approaches that are enhancing to patients who become analysts may be alienating to the group of patients who do not. For example, from the point of view of the patient's culture, the analyst's silence is a violation of a legitimate search for information, guidance, and responsiveness; while from the analyst's point of view, injudicious speech is an unwelcome intrusion into the patient's space that unduly influences the patient and undermines the curative process. Interpreting the resulting confusion of tongues is probably a good way to keep from freezing. We might also find some warmth by remembering Sullivan's plea to be "saved from an analysis that is going well."

REFERENCES

Auden, W. H. (1991). In memory of Freud. In *Collected Poems by W. H. Auden*, ed. Edward Mendelsen. New York: Vintage Books, p. 273.

Beaudrillard, J. (1996). *The perfect crime.* New York: Verso.

Bion, W. R. (1961). *Experiences in groups.* New York: Basic Books.

Freud, S. (1937). Analysis terminable and interminable. *Standard Edition* 23: 209–253.

Goleman, D. (1993). When a long therapy goes a little way. *Ideas & Trends, New York Times*, April 18, p. E6.

Hale, N. (1995). *The rise and crisis of psychoanalysis in the United States.* New York: Oxford.

Lionells, M. (1998). Thanatos is alive and well in psychoanalysis. In R. Prince, ed., *The death of psychoanalysis: Murder, suicide or rumor greatly exaggerated.* Northvale, NJ: Jason Aronson.

Mead, M. (1970). *Culture and commitment: A study of the generation gap.* Garden City, NY: Doubleday.

Prince, R. (1997). Is talk cheap, is silence golden? *Psychoanalytic Inquiry*, 17: 549–558.

Spence, D. (1994). *The rhetorical voice of psychoanalysis: Displacement of evidence by theory.* Cambridge: Harvard University Press.

Sulloway, F. (1979). *Freud: Biologist of the mind.* New York: Basic Books.

Part IV

Psychoanalysis and Religion

CHAPTER 19

Psychoanalysts and the Spiritual Quest: Framing a New Paradigm

Alan Roland

INTRODUCTION

Over the last ten-plus years, a small but growing group of broad Freudian psychoanalysts[1] has been significantly altering the terrain of the relationship of psychoanalysis to the spiritual self.[2] There is now a significant literature on this subject, all by psychoanalysts seriously interested in one or another meditative tradition or who have had spiritual experiences. To appreciate the radical alterations that are taking place, one must take a glance back to what the traditional landscape has been like and, to a large extent, still is. In this survey I am concerned with Freudian and neo-Freudian psychoanalysts, as the Jungian tradition is quite different.

TRADITIONAL PSYCHOANALYTIC VIEWS

Beginning with Freud, psychoanalysis has followed an Enlightenment agenda of rational demystification of religion and spirituality. Freud (1927) was wary of commenting on the spiritual, instead directing his attention to the role of religion within the psyche of the Western common person. He viewed religion as a necessary illusion in which images of a male God are created to compensate for and protect humans from the vulnerability of infantile helplessness and later anxiety in the face of the rigors of nature and civilization.

Romain Rolland, a noted writer and humanist, wrote to Freud in 1927 agreeing in the main with Freud's analysis of the religion of the common person but asserted that Freud should consider spiritual experiences, or the "oceanic feeling,"[3] in his psychology as the sentiment underlying all religion. Freud, who greatly esteemed Rolland, responded that he personally had had no such experience himself. Instead, Freud viewed the essential oneness of spiritual experiences as genetically related to the undifferentiated state of the ego in the infant-mother merger experience (Freud 1930, 64–66).

With but rare exceptions such as Wilfred Bion (1970), Erik Erikson (1969), and Marion Milner (1973/1987), Freudian psychoanalysts have consistently continued to reduce spiritual experiences to regressive, symbiotic merger experiences from an early childhood developmental stage, or to one or another kind of psychopathology. Most fully exemplifying this approach is the Sanskrit scholar, Jeffrey M. Masson (1976, 1980), who became trained in psychoanalysis. He asserted reductionistic strategies *ad absurdum* in the area of Indian studies by drawing upon the full psychoanalytic armamentarium of psychopathology.

The opprobrium attached by Freudian psychoanalysts to mysticism and the spiritual has been so powerful that one of the first Freudian analysts to contribute directly in this area, Marion Milner (1973/1987), delayed publishing her paper on mysticism for a number of years, instead circulating it privately. Another example is a conference in 1994, "The Suffering Self: A Dialogue Between Psychoanalysts and Buddhists," in which a few established psychoanalysts involved in Buddhism were highly reluctant to participate, fearful for their reputation in the field, unless there were other well-recognized analysts on the program. Moreover, the conference itself was sponsored by a small psychoanalytically oriented institute, because most major psychoanalytic institutes would not have touched the subject. Nevertheless, the conference was extremely well attended, attesting to a change of attitude in many psychoanalysts.

More recently, there are three major books by psychoanalysts that critique Freud's views on religion (A. Rizzuto 1979; W. W. Meissner 1984; N. Symington 1994). Rizzuto and Meissner, for instance, contrast Freud's Cartesian dualism of pitting illusion against reality, rational reality being more highly valued, with D. W. Winnicott's view of illusion as central to early childhood development, and to symbolization in all of the realms of culture, including religion. Symington's critique and vision is more far-reaching in his seeing psychoanalysis as a spirituality in the world in its transformation of the inner world of persons from a self-centered, destructive narcissism to more wholesome emotional intimacy relationships, similar to the core values of mature religions. Similar to Freud, they have generally steered away from any detailed considerations of spiritual experiences and spiritual disciplines.

NEO-FREUDIAN PRECURSORS

The true precursors of a new paradigm are not those just mentioned who have written about religion and psychoanalysis, but rather major neo-Freudian psychoanalysts in the 1950s, particularly those in the Karen Horney group (Horney 1945, 1987) and Erich Fromm. Already by 1950, the Horney group was involved in studying Hasadism and Martin Buber through the influence of Antonio Wenkart, a direct descendant of Ba'al Shem, the founder of Hasadism. They also delved into Zen Buddhism through Akahisa Kondo, a Japanese psychiatrist in training at the Horney Institute, who had a background in Zen practice. Kondo played a crucial role in introducing Horney and Fromm to D. T. Suzuki, the noted Zen scholar, Fromm later collaborating with Suzuki (Fromm, Suzuki, & De Martino, 1960). Harold Kelman (1960), another Horney analyst, was also highly influential in recognizing the Eastern spiritual traditions and comparing them with psychoanalysis. However, there does not seem to be any evidence that any of these American analysts were personally involved in an ongoing way with Zen or any other spiritual discipline. Although Suzuki could set forth the tenets of Zen Buddhism, Zen masters had hardly made their appearance on the New York scene.

A FAILED FREUDIAN ATTEMPT

Sudhir Kakar, an Indian psychoanalyst and a disciple of Erik Erikson, is perhaps the first Freudian psychoanalyst to forthrightly challenge the psychoanalytic dismissal of mysticism and to assert its validity in major Indian figures such as Vivekananda (1978, 160–181), Gandhi (1989, 85–128), and Ramakrishna (1991). A close look at his essays, however, reveal that Kakar fully continues the psychoanalytic tradition of reducing spiritual experiences and aspirations to psychopathology or to early childhood emotional states, in spite of his stated intentions to the contrary. One example will suffice.

On Vivekananda, "With the advent of adolescence . . . he found he could not always cope with the claims of archaic grandiosity and the anxiety and guilt associated with its breakthrough. Increasingly he experienced periods of hypomanic excitement; once . . . when he was fifteen . . . Narendra 'spied a large beehive in the cleft of a giant cliff and suddenly his mind was filled with awe and reverence for the Divine Providence. He lost outer consciousness and lay thus in the cart for a long time.'" (Kakar 1978, 178–179). Thus, a spiritual experience is reduced to archaic grandiosity and hypomanic excitement.

Kakar's reductionism stems from problems in his theorizing. In his earlier work, he equates primary process thinking with spiritual realization and knowing (1978, 20, 107), fitting the spiritual self into a Procrustean Bed of Freud psychoanalytic concepts. In his later work, he views spiritual experiences and motivation as essentially a regression to the preverbal, symbiotic experiences of the mother-child relationship, similar to Freud's perspective. He then puts a more positive spin on the regression as one which repairs what Kakar deems is the essential depressive core of life and, in Winnicottian terms, lends itself to creative experiencing. His viewpoint echoes that of an article by Shafi (1973), which Cooper (1998b) rightly comments on as continuing the tradition of psychoanalytic reductionism. Thus, Kakar first takes the Indian position of asserting the validity of its spiritual traditions but then takes the traditional Western psychoanalytic one of reductionism.

FRAMING A NEW PARADIGM

I shall be drawing on the work of Coltart (1992, 1996), Cooper (1998a, 1998b, 1999, 2001), Eigen (1998a, 1998b), Finn (1992), Roland (1988, 1996, 1999), Rubin (1996), and Suler (1993) to focus on common issues to frame the new paradigm. First, a word about their psychoanalytic orientation. Although they all have a background in traditional Freudian psychoanalysis, some more than others, they are all oriented toward the later models of Freudian psychoanalysis where there is a strong emphasis on theories of the self: ego psychology, object relations theory, self psychology, intersubjectivity, and Lacanian theory. They, of course, vary in their leanings toward one or another of these models or toward various combinations thereof; but they are distinctly *not* classical Freudian psychoanalysts, nor are they neo-Freudian.

Most, but not all of them, are seriously involved in one or another of the three main Buddhist meditative traditions that have come to the United States and England: Zen Buddhism from Japan, Vipassana meditation from Burma, and Tibetan Buddhism. While they may follow one meditative tradition, such as Zen Buddhism, they may also draw on the theories of another tradition, such as Tibetan Buddhism. Thus, the growth of the Buddhist movement in Europe and the United States in the 1960s and 1970s has had a profound influence on Coltart, Cooper, Eigen, Finn, Rubin, and Suler; while Eigen is also involved in Hasadism and the Kabbala. Roland, on the other hand, was influenced by the Vedanta movement of the Ramakrishna Mission, which had much earlier roots in the United States, as well as by his research trips to India.

Moreover, because of their interests, they are not infrequently referred patients who are themselves seriously involved in meditation or other spiritual disciplines. For the first time in the psychoanalytic literature, case studies of such patients are reported (Cooper 1998b, 2001; Eigen 1998b; Roland 1988, 1996, 1999; Rubin 1996).

What is this new paradigm? First, all of these analysts reject not only psychoanalytic reductionism, where spiritual experiences are relegated to either regression to some preverbal merger experience with the mother or to some kind of psychopathology, but also the denigration of psychoanalysis that has frequently been voiced by Asian spiritual teachers. Rubin (1996) also critiques the much more sophisticated schema of Wilbur, Engler, and Brown (1986) that states that aspirants must first work out their emotional problems, which are seen at a lower level of development, through some kind of psychotherapy before working on their spiritual evolution. In other words, the psychological level is seen as developmentally inferior to the spiritual.

Similar to Wilbur, Engler, and Brown, the new paradigm recognizes that some people seriously interested in a spiritual quest can also have significant emotional problems. However, the paradigm differs from their view in maintaining that both spiritual practices and psychopathology can and often needs to be addressed simultaneously without privileging one over the other. Psychoanalytic work often frees the person to be more deeply involved in his or her spiritual practices while, simultaneously, meditation or other spiritual practices enables a deeper involvement in the psychoanalytic process (Roland 1988, 1996; Rubin 1996).

Rubin sees the psychoanalytic and Buddhist elaborations on the nature of the self as offering important pathways to transformation but sees both as limited. Psychoanalytic views of the self offer varied understandings of the work of the unconscious and of developmental deficits but neglect the Buddhist meditative approach which helps to develop concentration, inner equanimity, and an awareness of the ever-changing nature of the self. Buddhism, on the other hand, is insufficiently grounded in the effects on the self of unconscious factors and developmental deficits. Experienced Buddhist teachers, both Asian and American, have clearly manifested serious psychopathology in the sexual exploitation of disciples, absconding of monies, and alcoholism. From what is missing in psychoanalysis and Buddhism, Rubin sees that they both have a great deal to offer to each other.

Coltart (1992, 1996) is very much in agreement on the salutary effects that psychoanalysis and Buddhism can have for each other. She sees the eightfold path of Buddhism interpreted in a more modern way as quite similar to the endeavor of psychoanalysis, except for the doctrine of *anatta*, which states that the self has no inherent existence. This, she acknowledges, took her many years of Vipassana meditation to experience. Thus, she emphasizes the congruencies rather than what is missing in each.

Roland (1999) views mental health and the spiritual self as being on two separate continua that can intersect in a number of ways. Thus, a person can be mature, sensitive, productive, and mentally healthy but without any interest whatsoever in a spiritual quest. On the other hand, someone can be quite spiritually realized with significant spiritual experiences but still have emotional problems that cause difficulties in relationships. Or the person who is mentally healthy can also be spiritually realized. The variations are legion.

Roland also sees the effect of culture as playing a major role on the self: The integrations that are taking place between the individualized self of North Americans rooted in the modern Western culture of individualism and the realization of the spiritual self will be significantly different from the centuries-old integrations between the familial self of Asians and the realization of their spiritual self.[4] To discuss this in depth would be another endeavor. Furthermore, Roland points out that although psychoanalysis has sunk roots in Asian cultures such as India and Japan, it has mainly emerged from the modern Western culture of individualism and addresses issues of functioning in such a culture. In Asian cultures such as India and Japan, psychoanalysis becomes relevant to the urban educated who have become more individualized (Roland 1988).

Eigen (1988a, 1998b) posits a paradoxical monism for himself. In part, he is drawn to Zen Buddhist meditation, although not systematically practicing it, as being in touch with the more transcendent part of himself; while he is also involved in a more ecstatic, devotional attitude towards the immanence of God in relationships from his Jewish background. Thus, he sees the practice of psychoanalysis as an integral part of his religio-spiritual orientation and not simply as a profession or discipline.

As part of this new paradigm, these analysts see that psychoanalysis or psychoanalytic therapy can be very helpful to those involved in meditation. When patients are involved in unconsciously using meditation for defensive ways of coping with their inner conflicts, or as some kind of narcissistic compensation, then as they unravel and resolve their emotional problems through psychoanalytic work, their meditation seems to deepen. Or there are others who because of their inner conflicts are undisciplined in their meditation. Again, psychoanalytic therapy seems to help. On the other hand, it is also observed that those involved in meditation are frequently able to tolerate greater anxiety and stay with more difficult material in their psychoanalytic sessions. The one caveat is that when a seriously disturbed person becomes involved in meditation, there is the distinct danger of a breakdown or an open psychosis.

There is an important related issue as to what extent meditation by itself can help resolve significant and/or serious emotional problems. These analysts on the whole regard meditation's ability to do this as definitely limited, in contrast to what some spiritual teachers have said. Coltart (1992) has noted that some people who engage in meditation do so primarily to alleviate emotional distress and would do better to see a therapist. However, these analysts also believe that meditation can contribute a great deal to the equanimity and overall well-being of persons. On the other hand, Walter Odajnik (1998), a contemporary Jungian analyst who also values therapy along with meditation, states that to a significant extent Buddhist meditation can resolve a lot of, if not all, emotional conflicts. He posits that this occurs because the person's psychic energies are channeled to concentration and away from inner conflicts. Coltart (1996) also believes that a great deal of therapeutic value derives from "non-discursive discernment" in Buddhist meditation—that this same process of looking at emotional states in the eye without necessarily talking about them carries a lot of what is therapeutic in psychoanalytic work as well.

Should meditation be taught to patients? Coltart (1992) believes that this is wise only if the patient is interested, and that the analyst should then refer the patient to a qualified teacher. Kondo (1958), however, believed in teaching the basics of zazen (zen meditation) to his patients. Cooper (1999), on the other hand, points out through case material that the analyst encouraging the patient to meditate may involve very subtle transference/countertransference dynamics that become reenacted in the psychoanalytic relationship, and is therefore strongly counterindicated.

Then, there is a most interesting issue concerning the psychoanalyst who is involved in a spiritual discipline. Rubin (1996) emphasizes that psychoanalysts involved in Buddhist meditation are more able to cultivate and enhance their ability to use evenly hovering or free-floating attention in psychoanalytic sessions, which Freud so stressed. That is, that the analyst is able to be more open to the derivatives of the unconscious in the patient's verbal communications. Cooper (1998b, 1999), on the other hand, is much more involved in an object relations approach using the induced countertransference than Rubin is. He, therefore, focuses on the meditating psychoanalyst's greater openness to experiencing and tolerating affects within him- or herself that are profoundly related to the transference reliving or reenactment that is taking place in the psychoanalytic relationship. Both Eigen (1998a) and Roland (1996, 1999) are in agreement over the importance of the enhanced experiential dimension in the analyst. This happens not only with the induced countertransference but also with feelings that the analyst senses the patient has but which the latter is not yet aware of. Roland reports from talks with meditating analysts that they have greater spontaneity in relating to their patients and have an enhanced intuitiveness.

Cooper, who has written more than the others on the use of Buddhist approaches in psychoanalytic work, illustrates how he has patients stay with their own difficult feelings or body images rather than trying to get associations to them as most analysts do. This is a Buddhist meditation method to stay with affect states. When a patient does this, associations to these affect states or body images then spontaneously occur. Of course, the aim of psychoanalysis is different from Buddhist meditation: The former focuses on the psychodynamic meanings of these feeling states to resolve underlying conflicts, whereas the latter focuses on affect states to ascertain that they lack inherent existence.

The question arises as to whether psychoanalysts who meditate are therefore superior in their work to those who don't. The range of clinical astuteness, therapeutic efficacy, and relatedness to patients varies greatly among psychoanalysts although it is rarely written about. One cannot say with any assurance that a given meditating psychoanalyst is superior to one who doesn't meditate. What seems to be the case from self-reports is that those analysts who are involved in some kind of spiritual discipline strongly believe that their abilities as analysts have significantly improved as a result.

PROBLEMATIC ISSUES IN THE NEW PARADIGM

Finally, there are some problematic issues in this new paradigm. The first and easier one relates to psychoanalysts practicing either Zen or Vipassana Buddhist meditation. One easily gets the impression that one size fits all; that is, that Buddhist meditation of the Zen or Vipassana mode is what meditation is all about, especially with their emphasis on mindfulness. Given that there are some 40 different kinds of Buddhist meditation (Lina Gupta, professor of religion and philosophy, personal communication, July 1997) and that there are significantly different meditative traditions in Hinduism, Sufism, the Kabbala, and Christianity, there is a great oversimplification of the meditative tradition and process. I have clearly seen this in working with patients involved in Hindu practices (Roland 1988), as well as with a Sufi meditation teacher, a Christian nun, another deeply involved with Zen Buddhism, and still another in Hassidic practices. Thus, the new paradigm will have to greatly expand the various pathways on the spiritual quest.

Related to this are the attitudes of some of the Buddhist-oriented psychoanalysts to the oceanic feeling that Romain Rolland first broached to Freud. Influenced by Mark Epstein (1995), a gestalt therapist knowledgeable in psychoanalytic theory and deeply involved in Buddhism, they tend either to agree with Epstein that Freud was correct in assessing the oceanic feeling as regressive, or to see it as alien as to what should happen in meditation, or, as with Eigen (1998a, 13, 28–30), that it is shallow and has watered down psychoanalytic discussions on the mystical. Given Romain Rolland's own spiritual experiences and related ones of great Indian spiritual teachers such as Ramakrishna, Vivekananda, and Ramana Maharshi (Parsons 1999), the oceanic feeling must be reconsidered and seriously dealt with in any new paradigm. Perhaps the problem is one of subtle monotheistic attitudes toward Buddhism—as seeing it as the one true religion.

The third problem is a more involved one and mainly emerges from the work of Michael Eigen (1998a). Eigen reports having a deeply significant, unexpected spiritual experience of light and bliss that occurred at a time of intense emotional agony in his twenties. The experience left a lasting impression. He uses the work of Milner, Winnicott, and Bion, who have stressed the deintegration and dedifferentiation necessary for creative work, and who have implied that a certain degree of madness is also valuable. Eigen extends this to spiritual experiences, implying that the deintegration of psychotics may make them more open to such experiences as the one he himself had.

I think this can be seen in a different light. For those persons who are struggling with very serious psychopathology but who also have a capacity for spiritual experiences, they will draw upon the spiritual self to help alleviate their extreme distress. On the other hand, there are deeply disturbed people not so oriented toward the spiritual self who cannot do this. Then, there are stories of people with a well-cultivated and adaptive social self, often, in some part, a false self, who go along in life without embarking on a spiritual quest. Suddenly, after some troubling life experience, there is a complete change. However, from my psychoanalytic experience over the years with over 15 patients seriously involved in a spiritual discipline—a few through their art—most were involved from an early age (teenage or in their twenties), whereas only a couple came to a spiritual quest later in life (in their forties or fifties). Only three of them could be labeled as having severe psychopathology, such as borderline or schizoid, and one was delusional. Thus, access to or awareness of a spiritual self was often present from their teenage years on and, with one exception, seemed quite unrelated to the severity of their psychopathology.

CONCLUSION

It is only in recent years that Freudian psychoanalysts have embarked on a personal spiritual quest with involvement in spiritual disciplines. This has enabled them to develop a new paradigm that integrates this dimension of human experience that a limited but increasing number of North Americans have access to with the psychoanalytic experience. This paradigm is of a different order than had originally prevailed from Freud on—and that still does prevail among the majority of Freudian and neo-Freudian psychoanalysts, and among most who ply the trade of applied psychoanalysis. The new paradigm has had its forerunners among major neo-Freudian psychoanalysts such as Fromm and Horney. It has also had a much longer history among Jung and his followers.[5]

NOTES

1. Freudian psychoanalysis today is a multimodel discipline encompassing classical drive and structural theory, ego psychology, object relations theory, self psychology, intersubjectivity, and Lacanian theory. Jungian analysis has also been integrated with object relations theory, and relational psychoanalysis is an amalgam of interpersonal theory with object relations theory and self psychology.

2. By the spiritual self, I am referring to an underlying ground of being and consciousness in all human beings. This may be experienced by relatively few persons, some referring to it as an immersion in inner light and/or bliss, or to a deeper awareness of the underlying relationships in the universe (Sudarshan 1994). Others, such as Buddhists, refer to emptiness, a powerful ground of being underlying the ever-changing flux of the mind, or to the Bodhi spirit or the Buddha mind (Kondo 1958).

3. The oceanic feeling refers to Romain Rolland's profound spiritual experiences during his adolescence, which he later found mirrored in the experiences of Ramakrishna and Vivekananda, two of the most revered spiritual teachers in the mid- and late-nineteenth-century India. He wrote biographies about both of them. Parsons (1999) evaluates the oceanic feeling as an advanced spiritual state of mystics.

4. The familial self of Indians and Japanese is elaborated at length by Roland (1988,

209–288). The continuity and counterpoint of the spiritual self to the familial self is then discussed (289–311).

5. Jung has not been discussed in this chapter because of the author's lack of familiarity with the Jungian tradition in depth.

REFERENCES

Bion, W. (1970). *Attention and interpretation.* New York: Basic Books.

Coltart, N. (1992). The practice of psychoanalysis and Buddhism. In *Slouching toward Bethlehem.* New York: Guilford Press.

———. (1996). Buddhism and psychoanalysis revisited. In *The baby and the bathwater.* New York: International Universities Press.

Cooper, P. (1998a). Sense and non-sense. *Journal of Religion and Health,* 37: 357–370.

———. (1998b). The disavowal of the spirit: Integration and wholeness in Buddhism and psychoanalysis. In *The couch and the tree: Dialogues in psychoanalysis and Buddhism,* 231–246. Edited by A. Molino. New York: North Point Press, Division of Farrar, Straus and Giroux.

———. (1999). Buddhist meditation and countertransference: A case study. *American Journal of Psychoanalysis,* 59: 71–86.

———. (2001). The gap between being and knowing in Zen Buddhism and psychoanalysis. *American Journal of Psychoanalysis,* 61: 341–362.

Eigen, M. (1998a). *The psychoanalytic mystic.* Binghamton, NY: ESF Publications.

———. (1998b). One reality. In *The couch and the tree: Dialogues in psychoanalysis and Buddhism,* 217–230. Edited by A. Molino. New York: North Point Press, Division of Farrar, Straus and Giroux.

Epstein, M. (1995). *Thoughts without a thinker: Psychotherapy from a Buddhist perspective.* New York: Basic Books.

Erikson, E. (1969). *Gandhi's truth.* New York: W. W. Norton.

Finn, M. (1992). Transitional space and Tibetan Buddhism: The object relations of meditation. In *Object relations theory and religious experience.* Edited by M. Finn and J. Gartner. New York: Praeger.

Freud, S. (1927). The future of an illusion. *Standard Edition,* vol. 21, 1–56. London: Hogarth Press.

———. (1930). Civilization and its discontents. *Standard Edition,* vol. 21, 57–146. London: Hogarth Press.

Fromm, E., D. T. Suzuki, and R. De Martino. (1960). *Zen Buddhism and psychoanalysis.* New York: Harper and Row.

Horney, K. (1945). *Our inner conflicts.* New York: W. W. Norton.

———. (1987). *Final lectures.* New York: W. W. Norton.

Kakar, S. (1978). *The inner world: A psychoanalytic study of childhood and society in India.* Delhi: Oxford University Press.

———. (1989). *Intimate relations: Exploring Indian sexuality.* Chicago: University of Chicago Press.

———. (1991). *The analyst and the mystic: Psychoanalytic reflections on religion and mysticism.* New Delhi: Viking by Penguin Books India.

Kelman, H. (1960). Psychoanalytic thought and Eastern wisdom. In *The history of psychotherapy,* 328–333. Edited by J. Ehrenwald. Northvale, NJ: Jason Aronson.

Kondo, A. (1958). Zen in psychotherapy: The virtue of sitting. In *The couch and the tree: Dialogues in psychoanalysis and Buddhism*, 58–64. Edited by A. Molino. New York: North Point Press, Division of Farrar, Straus and Giroux.

Masson, J. M. (1976). The psychology of the ascetic. *Journal of Asian Studies*, 35: 611–625.

———. (1980). *The oceanic feeling: The origins of religious sentiment in ancient India*. Dordrecht, Holland: D. Reidel.

Meissner, W. W. (1984). *Psychoanalysis and religious experience*. New York: Yale University Press.

Milner, M. (1987). Some notes on psychoanalytic ideas on mysticism. In *The suppressed madness of sane men*. London: Tavistock Publications. (Original work published 1973)

Odajnik, W. (1998). Zen meditation as a way of individuation and healing. In *The couch and the tree: Dialogues in psychoanalysis and Buddhism*, 131–144. Edited by A. Molino. New York: North Point Press, Division of Farrar, Straus and Giroux.

Parsons, W. B. (1999). *The enigma of the oceanic feeling: Revisioning the psychoanalytic theory of mysticism*. New York: Oxford University Press.

Rizzuto, A. (1979). *The birth of the living God: A psychoanalytic study*. Chicago: Chicago University Press.

Roland, A. (1988). *In search of self in India and Japan: Toward a cross-cultural psychology*. Princeton University Press.

———. (1996). *Cultural pluralism and psychoanalysis: The Asian and North American Experience*. New York: Routledge.

———. (1999). The spiritual self and psychopathology: Theoretical reflections and clinical observations. *Psychoanalysis and Psychotherapy*, 16: 211–234.

Rubin, J. B. (1996). *Psychotherapy and Buddhism: Toward an integration*. New York: Plenum Press.

Shafi, M. (1973). Silence in the service of the ego: Psychoanalytic study of meditation. *International Journal of Psychoanalysis*, 54: 431–439.

Sudarshan, N. (1994). *Science as* saksi bhava. Keynote Address at the Fifth International Conference on Vedanta, Miami University, Oxford, OH.

Suler, J. (1993). *Contemporary psychoanalysis and Eastern thought*. Albany, NY: State University of New York Press.

Symington, N. (1994). *Emotion and spirit: Questioning the claims of psychoanalysis and religion*. London: Cassell.

Wilbur, K., J. Engler, and D. Brown. (1986). *Transformations of consciousness: Conventional and contemplative perspectives on development*. Boston: Shambala.

CHAPTER 20

Freedom to Choose between Goodness and Badness: Self-Regulation and the Temptation to Be Evil

Ester Schaler Buchholz

> . . . O God, that men should put an enemy in their mouths to steal away their brains! . . . and transform . . . (themselves) into beasts!
>
> —Shakespeare, *Othello*

When psychology veered away from philosophy and religion, it severed channels vital to a complete understanding of how good, bad, and evil become incorporated into human motivation. Early psychoanalysis, developing in the midst of two world wars, turned its attention toward aggression and away from concepts of good, bad, and evil that seemed to connect back to those disavowed parents of psychology and psychoanalysis. Even the major exception, the contemporary treatment of moral development and pro-social actions, delegates doing good or bad to the cognitive realm rather than that of emotional accomplishments or deficits.[1] In a field concerned with the unconscious, it seemed self-defeating to deal with will, which was thought to portray conscious intentions. Morals and ethics, while connected to character building, did not naturally integrate with psychoanalysis and personality functions. And certainly, knowledge of wrong from right had not curbed maliciously destructive human actions!

A few prescient psychoanalytic thinkers, most notably Otto Rank, took an iconoclastic view. Rank included results of "philosophic, pedagogic, religious and cultural studies" (Rank, 1964, p. 20) into his thinking about human nature; thus he retained an interest in both ethical conflicts and free will (Menaker, 1982). But basically, "good" and "bad" are terms that rarely crop up in the psychoanalytic, psychological, or psychiatric indices. Even in Carl Goldberg's

(1996, 2000) recent attempts to focus on evil psychoanalytically, malevolence is considered primarily only in cases of pathology and genocide.

Thus, the dimensions of good, bad, and evil float in and out of our thinking as abandoned philosophical underpinnings or inner dialogues in cognitive narratives. In our field, goodness and badness remain separated from our attempts to understand emotional motivations. Potential cost to both patient and practitioner is that the analyst may remain ignorant about an individual's spiritual and ethical dilemmas. Recently Siirala wrote that in order to process the horrors in our patients' psyches, it is necessary to develop "a continuous deepening and widening contact with *human universals* (Siirala, 1997, italics in original)." We need to remind ourselves that perhaps while psychoanalysis largely ignores these issues, the average person in his or her day-to-day strivings may be fighting the temptation to be bad and feel helpless and uncertain about how to proceed.

Why should such ideas on good and bad connect me to Esther Menaker? Certainly, evil is not the immediate focus of her work. Rather, because Menaker comments on and adds to psychoanalytic theory as a philosopher-scientist interested in evolutionary antecedents and their influence on motivation, will, feelings, and actions, this particular theme belongs here. It is Menaker who said, "to explain much of human psychology from the relatively narrow vantage point of deviant or neurotic behavior leads, at times, to an obscuring of the broader biologic basis for given human reactions (1979, p. 81)." Thus, she opens up the space to explore unpopular areas of inquiry without trepidation. This chapter concerns the will to be bad and court evil, by interspersing a current psychoanalytic approach with older thoughts, some borrowed back from religion and philosophy.

The following is an example of our free choice to be good or bad. Playing with her father, a three-year old girl named Jennie said, "Go away Daddy. I want to be bad." This child's boldness demonstrates one of Rank's principles about the will and how it operates in conjunction with concern for others. For Rank, the will creates oppositionalism, which many see as evil, but which he saw as part of normal human behavior. Jennie also seems to be requesting a personality distinct from her father. Her desire to be bad on her own may be a desire for "alonetime"[2] for the creative moments to be herself (Buchholz, 1997).

In this exploration of will and its influence on being good, bad, or evil, I ask: How do our experimentations with these different modes add to creativity, energize, and promote healthy identity? If they take us to our darker side, is it a point from which we cannot return?

WILL AND CHOICE: THE RETURN OF A BASIC PERSONAL DILEMMA

In the seminal stages of psychoanalysis—as an upstart in the arena of human behavior—theories grew apart from spiritual, soul-centered practices, and many deemed it less necessary to take an interest in an individual's ethical development. These down-to-earth human characteristics were simply removed from the petri dish in the shift toward a scientific study of behavior. Any discussion of wanting to be good on the part of the analysand required immediate examination for its hidden meanings. The unruly aspects of people's motivations did not just disappear under the power of the new "science," though psychoanalysis and psychology lost touch with understanding and responding to them.

Otto Rank articulated this loss as he described the failure of the psychologies of his day to recognize the full scope of what encompasses personality development. He stressed the significance of continuing to incorporate ethical conflicts into work with patients. Take Rank's discussion of guilt: "Guilt arises . . . from the individual and must continue to produce evil if the individual uses it for the justification of his evil will, when it appears . . . not as a creative guilt which can be atoned for through new creation" (1964, p. 83). Only when guilt is used to understand oneself can it lead to a nonrepetitive cycle of willful desires and willful actions. What stands out is an ongoing decision-making process—acting from will. The individual in conflict has the power of choice. ". . . I want to be good—not like what I have been," said Gwendolen to Daniel Deronda in George Eliot's novel (1986, p. 837). Rank would certainly have accorded Gwendolyn the ability to make good on her words, acknowledging human beings' basic spiritual dilemma.

Whether one reads Rank or George Eliot, one realizes that leaving out the capacity to choose and human will is a significant loss in the psychoanalytic equation throughout the many attempts to analyze actions, thoughts, and fantasies. Without factoring in human will, one does not fully understand why people do the things they do. And certainly destructive and self-destructive behaviors remain unfathomed. Menaker clarifies the necessity, even as we grant respect to the unconscious, of not "los[ing] sight of the importance of consciousness" (1995, p. 175). This has been particularly true in the area of substance abuse, which has been investigated as much outside as inside psychoanalysis.

In fact, nowhere in modern times is the debate between will or compulsion, immoral behavior or illness, and evil or helplessness more prevalent than in current understanding of alcohol abuse (Grinspoon & Bakalar, 1990). On one side are those who recognize that no single cause of alcoholism is scientifically established (Fingarette, 1990). On the other side are those who believe that to treat alcoholics effectively, we need to invoke the medical model, despite the absence of a known biological defect that causes alcoholism (Vaillant, 1990).

Most of the small number of alcoholics who do self-recover in the end do so without medications or therapy (Grinspoon & Bakalar, 1990), suggesting that the use of self-regulation, the influence of individual differences, a person's introspection, and commitment to maintain his or her convictions can be powerful tools. Though this group can be seen as exceptional, it serves to remind us that will is an inextricable part of any kind of recovery.

TWO CASES

Two women who commenced treatment with me within a few months of each other provide a contrasting approach to a similar problem. Belinda (names and other identifying information have been altered to preserve confidentiality), referred by a physician, was a 44-year-old teacher, writer, and poet who had been in long-term treatment for phobias and compulsions on and off since latency. She had been seeing an analyst who also did group work. She had left the group feeling she no longer gained from the interactions, which were beginning to feel preservative. I was the third person with whom Belinda consulted in her quest for individual therapy, and she decided to stick with me. (I tend to think it was the referral by her doctor, whom she idealized, and not my skill, that made her decide to work with me.)

Ardeth, a 46-year-old woman, had never been analyzed personally but was sophisticated about psychoanalytic tenets and practices. Once, she had begun treatment with a therapist well known in music circles but had quickly backed away, saying she could not work with someone whose narcissism outshone hers. Ardeth felt immediately comfortable with me because I happened to recognize a tune she hummed. What is important here is that both patients began with mostly positive reactions (transferences) to me, which were based on idealizations.

Although many aspects of their treatment proved engaging and instructive, I shall focus here on their addictions and the way in which each woman addressed them. Both patients are from the northeastern part of the United States. In their two families, alcohol was a routine part of socializing, and the cocktail hour was mandatory. Neither family thought of alcohol negatively until, in the case of Ardeth, she began to drink at age 12. In an article on the addictive personality, Nathan (1988) declares that antisocial personality is the foremost trait in those subject to addiction and even predicts such behavior. By some outside standards, Ardeth would fit that description because she acted out in school, ran around with a fast, delinquent crowd, defied parental authority, and was considered bad by the community at large. She was sent to boarding school at 13, ran away from there, and, at age 16, ran away from home.

Belinda also attracted teachers' attention, at first because she was exceptionally bright and well behaved. However, by age eight, Belinda had a serious habit of pulling hair off her eyelashes and eyebrows. Until then, her family reacted with "toughness" to Belinda's longstanding fears of separation, flying, and water. But they could no longer ignore the symptoms that gave the lie to her bravado. In treatment, Belinda found that her therapist did help her with these frights and compulsions. She went to college and graduated magna cum laude and Phi Beta Kappa. It was also in college, however, that her drinking career began and she again met with a counselor.

After a series of misadventures, including setting a fire, Ardeth found her way to Oberlin College and then a northeastern music conservatory. On her own and away from her family, her creativity, sociability, and unusual wit and intelligence allowed her to make a great many friends who would later be boosts to her career. Ardeth had never stopped drinking, however, and she added pot, cocaine, and downers to her repertoire. While taking up residence in Dublin, Ireland as a musician, she met her first husband, a talented conductor and composer. Together they had two children. During pregnancy, Ardeth had abandoned drugs, but she was a heavy smoker and drinker when she entered treatment with me.

Ardeth fell in a creative slump. She was a recognized musician with steady performance dates. She had several commissions. But she realized she was not as acclaimed as many of her peers. The money she made and the fame she received dissatisfied her. Money was important to her and to her current partner, a man who tuned instruments for some of the most well-known performers. As a way to make quick supplementary remuneration on the side, she created jingles for advertising. But this was a source of shame to her. The problems of arrested creativity, lack of money, and professional shame caused her to seek therapy.

Belinda felt she was somebody who would always have to be in therapy, as she had rarely functioned out of it. She pictured herself as suffering from life. Shy, with low self-esteem, she experienced bouts of depression. She complained about her relationships—from ones with her sister and cousin, to others with neighbors, co-workers, and friends. She had a love-hate marriage and a fluctuating regard for everyone, especially herself. From the start, I observed strong ups and downs in her mood and self-confidence. She would oscillate between sweet gentleness to uncontrollable angry tirades. After about six months of treatment, I received telephone messages from her that were insulting and disturbing, including one suicide threat. In high school, she had once slit her wrists. However, most of the messages were outbursts of fury filled with suspicion and distrust directed at various people in her life, including me. The honeymoon was over. I cannot say I realized at the time what precipitated these shifts in temperament besides insecurity. Yet, I believed there had to be a chemical or nondisclosed component because many of her resentments were based on the same constructed scenarios.

Initially, neither Ardeth nor Belinda mentioned substances when they described their problems. They did not allude to how they used alcohol as part of their creative process or the fact that on social occasions they could often become inebriated. Belinda did, however, acknowledge the fantasy aspects of her fears and imagined insults. But ultimately it was my physician friend who tipped me off, asking casually one day about Belinda and her drinking.

After this revelation, I began to approach both women differently. In Belinda's case, I brought up the issue as information that had been shared with me. Coincidentally, Ardeth confessed to the problem herself at almost the same time. Before recognizing the use of alcohol as ongoing to these women's existence, I was not privy to the extent of their individual pain, their spiritual struggles, their unique fights to obtain an identity, and their attempts to cure themselves. I also was incorrectly attributing anxiety, depression, insecurity, anger, distrust, and other symptoms to early experiences rather than—as in many cases—to the current effects of liquor. By learning about alcohol and the reasons for heavy drinking in both situations, I became aware of how will and willfulness shape a psyche and contribute to problems, altering the course of treatment. Of equal importance was that until then I was also uninformed about both of their proud but puzzling claims to being bad and their efforts to be good to ease an inner sense of evil.

GOODNESS, BADNESS, AND PSYCHOANALYSIS

I found Menaker's thoughts on moral masochism (1995) most useful in early treatment of these two creative women. For example, Belinda first developed symptoms that separated her from her self. Many of her behaviors could have been seen as narcissistic defenses to maintain a faltering self from overstimulation, as borderline symptoms à la Otto Kernberg, or as masochistic endeavors to maintain connection to a de-idealized mother (Menaker, 1995). And aspects of their behavior could also be explained using Kohut's description of narcissistic injury and its tie to individual rage. Working in those ways did help them both. But it was not until they reevaluated their need for alcohol as a way to self-regulate and promote a will to be bad that each could come to terms with their decision's true folly. When they began to drink, both Belinda and Ardeth believed alcohol use was a sign of their independence from not only family, but also all societal traditions. *Not* drinking was obeying rules—being good in the most obnoxious way.

In theories as diverse as those of Sigmund Freud, Frederick Perls, and B. F. Skinner, psychology and psychoanalysis have long recognized the role of self-mastery, regulation, and control in human makeup. Self psychologists currently incorporate the terms *self-soothing* and *self-regulation* as basic human endeavors (Kohut, 1977). Greenspan (1992) sees the capacity of self-regulation growing from infancy, while I look at self-regulation and the sense of a secure alonetime as having prenatal origins. In any case, both contribute to the strength of an individual's will.

Despite other work about will and disorders in self-regulation (Buchholz, 1997), I had not fully grasped their connection to an inner sense of goodness and badness until faced with problems of addiction. For example, Belinda thought she was obtaining inner power through alcohol, but she was running from loneliness, intimacy, solitude, and her religious background. For a short while she joined Alcoholics Anonymous (AA) and was able to use that connection, in addition to being alone and having quiet time, as arenas for self-rescue. She remembered her early leanings toward religious thought and prayer. And she found a way to reverse her sense of powerlessness and loss of inner regulation when she realized that her dual needs for affection and alone-time were not mutually exclusive. Unfortunately, this period of restraint was temporary. What she failed to see was the strong bond alcohol established with her family.

Belinda had many personality features traditionally described as hysterical—tantrums, part-object identification, and disavowal of her sexuality along with bold flirtations. Inwardly, she struggled to fit between a career-oriented father, who knew how to combine work and drink with some success, and a socially-minded mother, too tired and drunk to find employment. But the split she experienced between the inebriated "Mom" and the nonalcoholic "Mother" further tore her self. In general, Belinda's mother wished her daughter to be stylish and fashionable, creative and arty. When "Mother" was sober, she made it clear that Belinda should keep away from all temptation and be a goody-goody, renouncing sex along with everything else. "Keep away from boys," her mother said; "tell them to stick it in a tree hole." On the other hand, when her divorced "Mom" drank too much, she gave in to sexual abandon. Belinda always saw her drinking as separate and different from her mother's. Her mother used it to be sexual; Belinda to be self-assertive. She also felt defiant and nonconformist when taking a drink. Anytime she was on an upright path, she classified herself as a "nerd."

Thus, for Belinda to find role models and an identity of her own was not easy. In her quest to do the right thing—or the wrong thing, for that matter—she had difficulty choosing and owning a will of her own. She spells this out in her description of what the authority of AA meant to her:

> At first, the idea of AA meetings was sissyish. This may sound awful . . . not even God could make me give away my life. I always thought my drinking was one thing that was solely mine, and I was sticking my tongue out at all the goody-two-shoes. I'm not sure how, but I finally felt things differently. Yes, the group in a way was holding my hand, but I had to do this myself.

Despite fortifying the dual illusion of social ease and being on one's own, addictions inevitably weaken both one's self-reliance and group skills, and leave one feeling impotent and still questing for inner power. Belinda's struggle to find individual space while remaining part of a whole appears often and eloquently as a perplexing dialectic in philosophical and religious writings. The basic dualistic need for a sense of aloneness and connectedness in human nature has come under harsh attack in different guises by those who lobby strongly for one side or the other: "The asserted absolute independence of man, which in the Stoic theory was regarded as man's fundamental virtue, is turned in the Christian theory [which supports community] into his fundamental vice and error (Cassirer, 1944)."

When being by oneself, exercising freedom of choice, and preferring alone moments to social ones are regarded as bad, then one's will can become a negative force. A way in which Ardeth and Belinda dealt with subsequent guilt from such self-denouncement was through their addictions, which obliterated thinking. Both abused substances in order to seek a relief that they had not been able to achieve on their own.

In her first trials with alcohol Ardeth was flaunting her will. It turned out that, from early on, she felt she could care for herself better than her parents could. In part, it was because she felt so different from them and their prosaic tastes. Her parents hated *her* use of alcohol and her risk-taking friends. So she loved both all the more—her "badness" was goodness to her. For Ardeth, alcohol helped her defy all authority and gave her the courage to go her own way.

All forms of abuse share one commonality: Once begun, they are likely to become addictive. People become afraid to let go of what is labeled unfavorable when associations are connected to something deeply desired. They continue abusive behaviors, thoughts, and feelings despite restricting and negative aspects, fearing an unbearable void from their absence. Moreover, abusers believe that their actions will give them control. Drug abusers believe that alcohol will calm them or that the pill will be a quick fix. But the disassociated, out-of-touch, lost-in-space, "fugue" state of "boozing" is actually the opposite of being in charge. Abusers are controlled by their perverse needs far more than they are in charge of them. Each inhalation has them sniffing for more, even though they think, "I am in charge of regulating myself and others."

Both Ardeth and Belinda also felt that they could relate to others better under the influence of alcohol. Each wanted a sense of another's love and tender care and thought it came from the bottle. But after each episode of abuse, the question became: What is alcohol now, soothing or despair? Ardeth tried to obtain relief through peer support, through abusing other substances, and finally through psychoanalysis. Because we all have inborn means for survival by ourselves, Ardeth, who was disappointed by her parents' brand of involvement, preferred to try it alone. But she was not sufficiently prepared.

An idea prevailing among psychotherapists is that an abuser's primary goal is to gain, improve, or restore a sense of relatedness. But this theory is extremely problematic, given the ambivalence many abusers exhibit regarding their relationships. It is as if we were to say that Saturn, the Titan forefather of the Roman gods, who swallowed his children to protect his sovereignty, really just needed to relate. In view of her reactions to her family, it makes much more sense to interpret Ardeth's addictive behavior as a desire for self-control, which she felt her parents resented and denied her.

The relationships between self-regulatory deficits and substance abuse are well documented, and though most researchers support the notion that self-regulation difficulties can lead to substance abuse, they differ as to why. The most generally accepted premise is that people use substances as attempts to cope, exercise their will, and regulate themselves when their natural mechanisms fail them or are unsupported by caretakers.

In the late nineteenth century, Freud first explained the symptoms of amnesia, paralysis, memory lapses, fugue states, and the like seen in patients with hysteria, as a defense against actual trauma, calling it "dissociation." Though it fell out of favor for many years with psychoanalysts, currently, dissociation has regained validity in the psychoanalytic community. Irwin Hirsch, for example, sees it as an ongoing aspect of self-experience throughout development (Hirsch, 1994), and Fischer and Ayoub have described it as part of a normal developmental pathway (Fischer & Ayoub, 1994).

Dissociation, an unconscious device, is both a natural state of need from infancy—the faraway gaze—and a defense mechanism that allows one removal from an emotional event either by numbing feelings or by splitting off the intellectual from the feeling state. Akin to denial, it is another aspect of people's need to tune out, to move away from debilitating situations or emotions that overload the mind and body, and so can serve as a beneficial escape route.

However, true healing from trauma or emotional problems can only take place when the individual begins to regain positive self-regard and empathy. Medications and psychotherapies can be used to provide protection, and certainly some have chosen to "medicate" themselves with alcohol and drugs. But people's inner resources to help themselves are often overlooked. And if we accept will as working unconsciously as well as consciously (Buchholz, 2001a, 2001b), we must see that it is also part of a patient's underlying decision making. "To drink or not to drink?" was the question beneath the surface of Ardeth and Belinda's thoughts. Part of their behavior might be attributable to a form of dissociation, particularly in their youth; but also they were always making a choice—though that choice had become internalized, no longer conscious.

The vice of alcohol became internalized and experienced as a virtue because, for a time, it supported the true selves of Ardeth and Belinda. Originally, their use of alcohol was not conceived as bad or as a wrongdoing but was chosen to assert the self. Drinking allowed each to identify with and rebel against family simultaneously. Pleasing memories of first encounters with the drug, somehow etched in their feelings and thoughts, continued to precipitate its use.

Acute sensitivity to pain was a temperament trait both women shared. Pain and suffering can work to encourage goodness, for how else do we understand the anguish of others? But when our own agonies are ignored, we seek relief elsewhere and may lose some of our empathy for others' hardships and prefer being what society terms "bad." Some continue on this pathway and begin to court evil ways. For Ardeth and Belinda, alcohol helped to numb their unhappiness, as it isolated them from others.

Such isolation, exacerbated by their evolving sense of themselves as outcasts, identified them with the downtrodden. Objectively, these women were good at heart but too difficult to be accepted easily. For them, the sense of being fallen angels through alcohol abuse convinced them that they had more than ordinary gifts of empathy. Thus, their "nonconformity" in using alcohol can be seen as the result of not parental neglect, but of the need to establish a territory they could claim as their creative sphere.

At first alcohol was a "container" giving them a sense of emotional integrity. Belinda used it in an attempt to balance the effects of one of the many symptomological reactions to being emotionally out of control. In short order, that relief will inevitably diminish, so when Ardeth and Belinda were faced with the same—or higher—degrees of anxiety and depression, they increased the substance taking. To admit that they had made a bad choice would have meant acknowledging that their anti-authority actions were purposeless, or even evil. What had been a deliberate bad girl pose became, as the ante raised, a battle with their inner sense of goodness and self-justification. Alcohol was no longer naughty; it became untamable, a malevolent force. The use of alcohol, originally an ethical protest, now became an ethical problem.

As seen, Belinda used drinking to be herself and to be by herself. But she also drank socially. Before she drank, she felt she was going to give herself pleasure, and she was going to do what she pleased. As soon as she drank, her thoughts changed. She became part of the crowd, but not the person she was trying to be. After she slept it off, she realized the insults and assaults, the harm she had done to herself and others. Yet, the pattern repeated often.

Ardeth, when sober, saw alcohol as the root of many of her continuing problems; yet she also retained from young adulthood the belief that giving up alcohol was giving up her will. In considering her childhood drinking, Ardeth ultimately began to differentiate her will from her rebellious acts—part of a child's stubbornness and defiance. When she could accept an adult persona comfortably, she gave up cigarettes and vodka and reconnected with the creative will that had been slipping away.

Prior to this, she also believed her music was dead to her without alcohol and, in fact, steered clear of the composition room fearing she would get the rush in her chest she connected to a desire to booze. When we linked the excitement to her creative force, she felt some of the trepidation dispelled, and she was willing to go to the keyboard, at least tentatively. Risk-taking people pursue excitement, and the timid avoid it. The rest of us, being in the middle, think risk must be bad, not to mention evil—even as we seek it. But Ardeth and I learned something different: Excitement was not from the bottle or external to her. The "buzz" came from inside without any alcohol to ignite it.

If alcohol is the symbol of control over one's life, which hunger receives top priority? Is it the wish for an improved self-image, reduction of anxiety, rest, love or a martini or wine spritzer? Thus, truly taking care of oneself becomes confused with giving oneself a treat. Many of the reasons for drinking are linked either to insufficient or too much time with oneself or for oneself, or to an imbalance in a relationship. Besides the vicious psychological cycles of abuse, a person's system becomes fixated biochemically. We are what we imbibe, to paraphrase the saying; but we are also a mix of what we take in from others, and what we decide upon ourselves. For Belinda and Ardeth, the desire to *be* themselves—their separate wills—got confused with escapes *from* themselves as they unwittingly mirrored parental habits or reactively bucked authority. In their times alone, they lost touch with who they were. Using alcohol as their buffer, they warded off intimacies and solitude.

Within quests for power and people's philosophical and religious struggles is a desire for inner control, sought through both alonetime and relationships. However, one of the steps people invariably take in their search is going against the grain of expectations and obligations. Little Jennie felt sufficient trust to let her father know she wanted to be bad and do her own thing. Belinda and Ardeth could only enact this.

For Belinda, alcohol replaced her other habits and gave her the excuse to exercise her vices, including disavowing her good-girl self, revenge-seeking destructiveness, and all the badness that made her feel evil—yet closer in her experience to her central being. Only recently, a soothing statement made by her sister allowed Belinda to accept a readiness to eliminate alcohol completely from her life. In bemoaning the fact that she was an impossible person with strong dichotomies in her personality, Belinda was surprised to hear her sister respond, "But that's why everyone loves you and some love you in spite of this." Her sister, responding to the subtle request, accepted Belinda's whole self and encouraged Belinda to do the same. Still, Belinda found it hard to completely divorce herself from alcohol because she associated it with that naughty side, of which she is fond, and felt abstinence would make her lose. Her work focused on being able to see her personality as mischievous and merry apart from the booze.

Ardeth knew she flirted with danger, bad things and then worse ones, to proclaim who she was and what she was not. When she realized that she had added shoplifting and other acts of theft to her repertoire, she began to awaken to what she was doing. Suddenly, her being bad came close to being evil in her mind. "I was not doing naughty things," she said, "but making friends with the devil. My bad girl was a 'me' fleeing hypocrisy and other grown-up dishonesties. It was as good as any other part of me. So when I saw myself starting to do things that I found objectionable, I did a double take." From then on, the wellspring for Ardeth fed from her own psychologically replenishing waters, and she turned away from alcohol entirely.

In my own iconoclastic and willful ways, I declare that Jennie's, Ardeth's, and Belinda's bad acts were attempts to be ethical—honorable in commitment to their true selves and in readiness to take the consequences of their willfulness. Menaker has much to say about how costly and creative a process it is to build a self and how it is a neverending and unique task for each person. Ardeth and Belinda had begun their courtship of the bad in an attempt to find truth, but the nutrients these two patients used to "build" identities that seemed most compatible eventually fed only a growing disengagement from their selves. Only when we—patients and therapist—saw the reason behind the alcohol abuse in this light could Ardeth and Belinda reclaim control and the will to find the wisdom and energy to pursue life creatively. In this sense their individual selves were "the center of initiative" engaging in "choice, decision and free will" (Menaker, 1995, p. 27).

NOTES

1. The first psychologist to focus serious attention on children's moral life was Jean Piaget in his work on the moral judgment of children. Intense studies from 1960 to 1980 by Lawrence Kohlberg on moral development were followed by Carol Gilligan's feminist correction (*In a Different Voice*, 1982) emphasizing caring over justice and Robert Coles's investigations on moral intelligence (*The Moral Life of Children*, 1980; *The Moral Intelligence of Children*, 1997).

2. In other works, I use "alonetime" as one word to signify it as an important need, equivalent to the need to attach.

REFERENCES

Buchholz, E. S. (1997). *The call of solitude: Alonetime in a world of attachment.* New York: Simon & Schuster.

Buchholz, E. S. (2001a, April). The child's voice: Will's first encounters with evil. In Feldheim, D., & Levine, M. (Chairs), *The meanings of evil.* Symposium conducted at the Washington Psychoanalytic Foundation, Washington, D.C.

Buchholz, E. S. (2001b, April). *Do all roads lead to Rome? Further travels with will and encounters with evil.* Paper presented at the spring meeting of Division 39 (Psychoanalysis) of the American Psychological Association, Santa Fe, NM.

Cassirer, E. (1944). *An essay on man.* New York: Doubleday.

Eliot, G. (1986). *Daniel Deronda.* London: Penguin Classics.

Fingarette, H. (1990). We should reject the disease concept of alcoholism. *The Harvard Medical School Mental Health Review, 2,* 11–13.

Fischer, K. W., & Ayoub, C. (1994). Affective splitting and dissociation in normal and maltreated children: Developmental pathways for self in relationships. In Cicchetti, D., & Toth, S. (Eds.), *Rochester symposium on developmental psychopathology: Disorders and dysfunctions of the self, Vol. 5,* 149–222.

Goldberg, C. (1996). *Speaking with the devil: A dialogue with evil.* New York: Viking Penguin.

Goldberg, C. (2000). *The evil we do: The psychoanalysis of destructive people.* Amherst, NY: Prometheus Books.

Greenspan, S. I. (1992). *Infancy and early childhood: The practice of clinical assessment and intervention with emotional and developmental challenges.* Madison, CT: International Universities Press

Grinspoon, L., & Bakalar, J. B. (1990). Alcohol abuse and dependence. *The Harvard Medical School Mental Health Review, 1*, 1–10.
Hirsch, Irwin. (1994). Dissociation and the interpersonal self. *Contemporary Psychoanalysis, 30*(4), 777–779. New York: W. A. W. Institute.
Kohut, H. (1977). *The restoration of the self.* New York: International Universities Press.
Menaker, E. (1979). A note on some biologic parallels between certain innate animal behavior and moral masochism. In L. Lerner (Ed.), *Masochism and the emergent ego: Selected papers of Esther Menaker*. New York: Human Sciences Press.
Menaker, E. (1982). *Otto Rank: A rediscovered legacy.* New York: Columbia University Press.
Menaker, E. (1995). *The freedom to inquire: Self psychological perspectives on women's issues, masochism, and the therapeutic relationship.* Northvale, NJ: Jason Aronson.
Nathan, P. E. (1988). The addictive personality is the behavior of the addict. *Journal of Consulting and Clinical Psychology, 56*(2), 183–188.
Rank, O. (1964). *Truth or reality.* New York: W. W. Norton.
Siirala, M. (1997). The myth of man's fall and the basic rule for psychoanalytic therapy discovered by Sigmund Freud: Free association—a program against hubris. *International Forum of Psychoanalysis, 6*, 33–39.
Vaillant, G. E. (1990). We should retain the disease concept of alcoholism. *The Harvard Medical School Mental Health Review, 2*, 13–15.

CHAPTER 21

Kohut and God

Charles B. Strozier

Kohut was deeply interested in religion, though he never wrote a book or even an article specifically on the subject. At a personal level, Kohut regularly attended the Unitarian Church in Hyde Park, near the University of Chicago, where he lived. He became a friend of its minister and even at times spoke to the congregation. He read *Christian Century* for years and seemed particularly concerned with the application of his ideas to what is generally called pastoral counseling. Certainly, many theologians and practitioners sensed in Kohut a kindred spirit striving to define a meaningful relation to God.

Kohut had a restlessly inquisitive mind. He easily broached disciplinary boundaries and refused to be constrained by academic conventions. But Kohut also recognized the limits of his own knowledge. For all his soaring intellect, he was in fact quite modest about what he could really know and understand. Nowhere was this clearer than in his only extended comments on religion, a two-part interview he gave in 1981 to Robert L. Randall. He makes quite clear to Randall, then a young theologian, that it was "your baby" to provide the more complete explanation of the links between self psychology and religion (though Randall has been unable to carry forward that task, he has generously shared the transcripts of his interviews with me). Kohut in those interviews was in no way attempting a kind of self psychological *Future of an Illusion.* He was only providing a framework for such a task, the barest outline that needed completion and fleshing out to be really meaningful. It was not, I think, a falsely modest position. For one thing, he often took such a stance on the relation of self psychological ideas to other realms of human experience. But more importantly, he outlines for Randall just that: a framework and not a completely developed set of ideas. It doesn't make his thoughts less interesting, but it does require us to take them with some caution and to grant them a tentativeness Kohut himself intended. In talking with Randall, Kohut certainly never meant to hand down self psychological dicta that would become dogma.

In his work on religion, Kohut drew his baseline with Freud, especially *The Future of an Illusion.* Freud's error in this work, Kohut feels, was to apply the "yardstick of scientific values to religion." By such criteria religion seems foolish indeed. The story of the "humanoid god" who creates the world in a week is ridiculous as physics. It's pure fairy tale, "abominably poor science." Such tales of origin cannot hope to compete with scientific explorations of the world and its beginnings as well as the workings of the natural world. To consider another example, take the "gimmick" of the afterlife, a place where the virtuous go. That fits beautifully with all the superficial needs of what Kohut derisively called "Guilty Man," or the self Freud imagines. Freud's whole purpose was to unmask (or as we might now say, deconstruct) the completely irrational, fantastical, illusionary nature of religious beliefs that in their deeper understanding are merely projections from our own early experience of infantile helplessness.

But in that very rationalism lies Freud's profound misperception of the true purpose of religion, which is simply in another realm from science. There are three great cultural enterprises for Kohut: science, art, and religion. Science deals with explanations. Art deals with beauty. Religion's unique function is to "shore up, to hold together, sustain, to make harmonious, to strengthen, man's self." For many in the twentieth century, psychoanalysis has robbed religion of those functions and become a substitute religion. Certainly, that has profoundly influenced religion, but it has also placed a terrific burden on psychoanalysis itself, corrupting its true mission to search for psychological truth. The key to the religiosity of psychoanalysis lies in the adoration of and excessive loyalty toward the founder by its followers. No physicist in his right mind would ever place Newton on such a level. We have discovered all kinds of new laws since Newton and yet no one would claim that that represents a rebellion against him. Things move forward, and new giants appear who enhance our understanding of the world and our capacity to explain it.

But there is more to Kohut on religion than a critique of Freud. He also seeks to outline more precisely the "human needs" religion meets. This general topic he addresses in terms of the selfobject experience of idealization, mirroring, and twinship. All these terms need definition and clarification but none more so than *selfobject*, which lies at the heart of his theory. In devising the term selfobject, he sought to capture the way in which we establish and maintain our psychological wholeness through our relationship with primary caretakers and, later, their symbolized substitutes. This relationship is not one of identification, or introjection, or any of the more familiar concepts used in psychoanalysis to describe the more primitive connections between self and objects. Kohut wants to stress that initially, objects as such (and as seen by external observers) are not felt as separate by the self. We take in their functions, indeed their very beings, in the making of our selves. We respond to the caretaking, the feeding, the holding, and the touching of the mother as though she were part of us. We experience her soothing as indistinguishable from our own. The boundaries between self and other are completely permeable; the baby, in fact, is psychologically whole if seen in the context of the maternal matrix. A normal baby is never a baby alone, because the baby "includes the caretakings and responses of [the] selfobject that is empathetically fitted with him." In time, of course, there is a gradually increasing awareness of separateness of the self from the caretaking figure(s), but we never stop turning to the functions of others to meet our deepest self-needs. We are never fully apart, independent, autonomous. Equally significant, selfobject functions, which are never actual people or objects in any event, in time get abstracted and symbolized into various cultural forms. That's where an institution like religion enters in.

Issues of idealization lie at the heart of any effort to understand religion from a self psychological point of view. Kohut would never fall prey to simple reductionism. "I would have no doubt that anything as encompassing and broad and basic as religion is to man . . . could not possibly relate to just one dimension of the self." That said, he recognizes the centrality of idealization in his reflections about religion and returns to them often. And for good reason. Idealizing needs are perhaps the most conspicuous aspects of religion. We can hardly dispense with a concept of God, "because there must be something idealizeable, something that nears perfection or that is perfect, something that one wants to live up to, something that lifts one up." The fragmenting self, he notes, is weak, chaotic, and disharmonious. In religion one searches for and often finds a sense of uplift from and healing of that fragmentation. This may come from a particularly inspiring sermon, which lifts one out of the humdrum of everyday existence and gives meaning where there had been emptiness. The service itself, with its familiar rituals and words and song, may inspire and soothe. Even the rhythms of the church year can be significant in this regard. "The mere unrolling of specific holidays in the course of a twelve month period . . . the gradual decline with winter, and the rebirth with Easter spring, appeals to something deep in all of us."

Such experiences touch the psychological core of our first encounters with the majestic mother who uplifted us as babies and held us close to her. That baby alone is "frightened, disheveled, fragmented." The mother, on the other hand, is "calm, big, powerful." Uplifted, we merged into the mother's greatness and calmness. Later, Kohut says, we all suffer various kinds of narcissistic blows, which can be powerfully disorienting. Some find soothing by going into a church and sitting there. Others might experience a similar kind of healing in a more abstracted spiritual form, such as climbing to the top of a mountain, or looking down into the Grand Canyon, or walking in the woods. Still others find uplift in listening to great and beautiful music. But whatever the form, such spiritual uplift is a central part of how we understand the role of religion in our lives. And this sense we have of God's purpose evokes our earliest encounter with the maternal selfobject matrix. Kohut here offers no simplistic causal relation between God and our earliest selfobject experiences. We don't merely seek uplift from God because our mothers once picked us up to hold and feed and soothe us. Religion is not, as it was basically for Freud, a rather mundane human institution but rather a complex interplay of human psychological needs and the deeper workings of the Divine. Unlike Freud, one might say, Kohut grants a God and then tries to understand our psychological relation to him or her.

In the Randall interviews, one of the more interesting themes Kohut pursues about idealization and uplift (a theme he also took up in his contemporaneous interviews with me in *Self Psychology and the Humanities*), is his discussion of death. At the time of the conversation he was in fact dying, which he talked about only with family and a handful of intimate friends, and was in increasing amounts of pain. Kohut's key idea is that a healthy individual is not afraid of death. It is too natural a part of the curve of life, "of being born, of growing, of reaching some flowering of the program that's laid down in us early in life," that inevitably involves death as part of its course. It's the same with a rose.

> There is a seed, there is a flowering, there is a wilting, there is a death and the next generation of roses takes over. I think that one isn't really fully alive if one doesn't somehow down deep in one's bones feel this eternal rhythm of life, this coming and going of which one is only a link in a chain. To me this is an uplifting thought, not a discouraging thought. It goes beyond my individuality to something broader and more enduring than this little me that is common, hasn't been here during Plato's time and will not be here in a thousand years when there's another Plato or maybe nothing. Who knows? Why do I have to be around and have been around? I wasn't and I won't. That doesn't disturb me.

In this sense of what one might call a theology of the rose he sometimes half-jokingly called himself an atheist. Toward the end when he was very sick he told a colleague a dream. In it a large airplane was dropping out of the sky. He was clinging to it like a bird to a falling plane. Kohut commented: "I was afraid but yet I remain a strong atheist." I actually think Kohut was much too spiritual himself to take this self-designation seriously. It was like a rationalist defense showing through. But it is true that his main concern was with dying rather than death itself. And here the point is that in the actual process of dying, selfobjects are vital. People tend to withdraw from the dying person. But if someone can connect at that stage and convey genuine feelings such as, "You're dying. I will also cross that threshold one of these days. The way you handle this is an inspiration to me. I will get a great deal of strength from watching how you do this," that dying person will feel confirmed.

Religion supports the dying person in a myriad of idealizing selfobject ways quite aside from the hope for an afterlife. There are enduring issues in the world, Kohut says, like the great mystery of creation, both of the world and the complexity and beauty of human culture. None of that is accidental but it will in some way endure, whether or not we observe it. That is more accurately what we mean by eternal life rather than the fairy tale of heaven with winged angels singing hallelujah. That "doesn't particularly send me," Kohut said. It sounds rather "boring." In fact, "the greatness of experience is timeless." It has intrinsic value, even should the human race become extinct someday. That's what the God concept is all about at its most idealized and philosophical level. "There is something about this world in our experience that does lift us up beyond the simplicity of an individual existence, that lifts us into something higher, enduring, or, as I would rather say, timeless."

This uplift had long interested Kohut in terms of what he called in the mid-1960s "cosmic narcissism." At the end of life it is possible to revive the earliest psychological union with the mother in a new and creative form. The illusion of the eternal life of the self must be given up in the face of the certainty of death. In its place one invests (at least the potential for such investment exists as a human potential) the ideals one cherishes. This shift is not a mystical one but a "sad and realistic goodbye to oneself." The "most perfect" artistic representation of this process, Kohut says, is the end of Beethoven's Piano Sonata op. 111. [to Raymond Prince, May 4, 1967, Curve 168]

The second self need that religion meets has to do with what Kohut called mirroring. We all have a need for "responsiveness to our own vitality," as well as powerful ambitions and a "sense of innate greatness." One of Kohut's favorite examples to illustrate these self needs and how they are best met by the selfobject is when the young child first starts walking. He struggles to his feet (to use the example of a little boy) and totters off very precariously across the room. He feels buoyed and excited by his own accomplishment, and yet terribly insecure that he might fall and lose it all. He looks back at the mother and sees her smiling with confidence and joy at what he is doing. That "gleam in the mother's eye" in turn firms his own faltering confidence and steadies his step. The gleam is himself reflected or mirrored back. Neither she nor that smile is experienced for the most part as at all separate from himself. Through the gleam he knows at the deepest level her trust and presence, and that as a result he can trust himself to be capable of making it to the table, and from there to almost any other challenge he will face in life.

Such mirroring needs, Kohut says, are met in religion through what is usually called grace, or the idea that "there is something given to you, some innate perception of your right to be here and to assert yourself, and that somebody will smile at you and will respond to you and will be in turn with your worthwhileness. . . ." In the Old Testament, a crucial text that defines the idea of grace is Psalm 84:11: "For the Lord God *is* a sun and shield; the

Lord will give grace and glory. No good *thing* will be withhold from them that walk uprightly." That basic idea runs through the Christian sacred texts, though it is added, of course, that Jesus becomes the medium through which the grace of God flows. In Acts 20:24, for example: "But none of these things move me, neither count I my life dear unto myself, so that I might finish my course with joy, and the ministry, which I have received of the Lord Jesus, to testify the gospel of the grace of God." Kohut's favorite text on grace is secular—the line from Eugene O'Neill's *Great God Brown:* "Man is born broken. He lives by mending. The grace of God is the glue." The psychological point is that God's grace is available for us to heal our wounds and to mirror our needs simply for the asking, in the same way the protective, secure mother, especially the gleam in her eye, provided cohesion for ourselves through all the vagaries of development. But if that mother, as in *Long Day's Journey into Night,* is drug addicted, there is no grace and the family degenerates into drunken brawling.

Life and creativity in general, Kohut felt, emerge out of this fall from grace, which is a kind of self psychological version of original sin. At best we have a glimmer of the mother's gleam. But we are spurred on by the very "shortcomings of that early grace," which in religious terms is the perfect mirroring and calmness of God. To elaborate his point Kohut considers music, which was a lifelong interest of his, and notes that the perfect chord is not what makes great music appealing. It is rather the "deviation into dissonance" and the complex ways the music returns to consonance. The tunes and harmonies reach out through structures of movements, creating tensions that express the unease, until there is at last a return to balance, or at least an illusion of harmony and peace. That process is what Kohut meant by the "curve of life." He even ironically thanks God for the scars and trauma of life. They spur us on to new ways of solving problems. "If life were perfect, man would never have created religion or art or science."

The third specific selfobject need Kohut discusses as being met in religion is what he called alter ego or twinship. Even in theory, the distinction between mirroring and twinship is somewhat blurred. In his first formulation of twinship (1971) Kohut considers it as a subtopic of mirroring, though a decade later he granted it rather more autonomy. In using this concept, Kohut is trying to explain the dreams and fantasies that often appear in self analysis of a twin or alter, as well as the regressive idea that the analyst is actually quite like the patient. In trying to meet twinship needs, Kohut felt, we often search out others as selfobjects bearing some resemblance to us in reality or in fantasy. Their value lies precisely in their similarity to us. The origin of such self needs appears to lie in our interactions with siblings, peers, and others of our size and of our insignificance. Twinship is thus a somewhat later emergent self need (later, that is, than mirroring or idealization) and often associated with the *period* Freud called "oedipal," as opposed to the famous complex that Kohut believed was by no means universal or necessary.

Kohut felt that religion satisfies twinship needs in the locale of the church or sacred environment and especially in one's participation in the congregation. Religion, of course, is both a solitary and communal experience. Much of what religion does in meeting idealizing and mirroring needs is solitary. Something goes on in private between you and your concept of God. But religion is also communal. Church surrounds you with worshipers like yourself who have made common faith commitments. However different your lives might be in other respects, in church you and they are joined in a common spiritual quest before a God you jointly recognize and conceive and to whom you direct your prayers in a shared and utterly familiar liturgy. Week after week, year after year, you return to the same pews and sing the same songs and listen together to the sermons. Such intensely experienced rituals tend to flatten out what might be otherwise felt as significant differences between people in terms of personality, background, wealth, profession, or even appearance. Within the sacred space of the church you become more like your neighbor. You abandon the extraneous and emphasize the essential. The human bonds deepen in this circle of reflected sameness. And that is enormously reassuring. You become one of God's children in a powerfully shared experience.

Within these three realms—idealization, mirroring, and twinship—religion meets the deepest needs of the self. The apparent neatness of the distinctions between the three forms of selfobject experience, however, is quite misleading at both theoretical and applied levels. At the level of theory, as noted, twinship at best stands in some kind of dependent relationship to mirroring. But mirroring is itself quite protean in its expression and alternates easily between a variety of forms of extension of the grandiose self and twinship, and may blend with forms of idealization. What matters, Kohut stresses, is not the specific mode of the transference, "but the fact that the transference brings about the (re)establishment of a cohesive and durable narcissistic object relationship. . . ." Furthermore, in our actual clinical work, it can be difficult to distinguish modes of transference. There may be rapid oscillations between idealization and mirroring and/or the transference may be mixed. All of this overlap and apparent confusion begins in the earliest self needs of the baby who experiences the mother simultaneously as both a secure and wonderful figure with whom to merge and as an extension of the baby's grandiosity that gets reflected back in that gleam.

In terms of religion, Kohut's discursive conversation with Randall conveys just these complications. He never lets his categories of analysis overwhelm and destroy the complexity of his data. He thus emphasizes the importance of idealization in the construction of a God concept and images of perfection, but in talking about mirroring he notes that it is the grace of God that is at work to meet this self need. The uplift of religion, which primarily meets the needs of idealization, is at work just as much in the mirroring experience of God's grace as it is in the twinship of choir practice. These kinds of subtleties hardly muddy the waters. There are real differences between the modes of self-experience and the ways in which religion meets them. To sort out the forms of overlap in the way in which an individual experiences religion would require the full-scale work that Kohut challenges theologians sensitive to self psychology to undertake. He does stress that one can hardly determine in advance or in theory within a topological scheme the ways in which different individuals will bring their varied self needs into their spiritual life within an institution as complex as religion.

At another level, however, there is a contradiction in Kohut's approach to religion. It is striking in the Randall interviews how "Christian" a stance Kohut assumes. He talks of churches and ministers and the rhythms of the holidays from Christmas to Easter. At one point he has a long disquisition on Catholicism, at another on the meaning of the search (especially Albert Schweitzer's, which he clearly knew well) for the historical Jesus, and so on. In his correspondence throughout his life, Kohut often returned to religious themes. He clearly knew the Bible, commenting once that Daniel was a great interpreter of dreams, though he is not as widely known as Joseph. Kohut, his son firmly believes, considered himself a Christian by faith. Kohut's whole discourse is Christian. In talking to Randall, Kohut offers no qualifications that enlarge the dialogue to include other religions, even Judaism. Now it is true that Kohut, for example, turns to the historical Jesus in his conversations with Randall because he is asked about it. Kohut also knew Randall was a Christian theologian and granted the interview partly because he knew Randall was concerned with the "soteriological" or salvational aspects of self psychology (based on an article Randall wrote in the late 1970s). Kohut held to Christian themes in part, in other words, out of empathic respect for the person sitting across from him in his study.

But Kohut's Christian discourse may also reflect a much deeper ambivalence about his own Jewishness, which he obscured all his life. There is in fact no question he was Jewish on both sides of his family and had been for generations, though he was born into a cultured, well-off, and highly assimilated Viennese family. But Kohut's relationship to his Jewishness was not at all like that of that other assimilated Viennese Jew, Sigmund Freud. Many of Kohut's close friends at the University of Vienna during the 1930s had no idea he was Jewish. He never told Jewish jokes, or used Yiddish expressions, or made any reference to Jewish cultural traditions (and looked baffled whenever anyone did any of these in his presence). Kohut's best friend in medical school was still wondering 40 years later when I interviewed him why Kohut had to leave Vienna after the Anschluss in 1938. In Chicago colleagues whispered that his mother was Jewish, or maybe his father, or maybe both, or maybe neither. Some wild (and incorrect) rumors floated about that he had crosses on his mantle. One patient, who was himself in psychoanalytic training and concerned about his own ethnicity, asked Kohut directly at the beginning of his treatment if he was Jewish. Kohut said, "Well, who's Jewish anyway," and this and that. The patient, himself an analyst, was never quite clear about what Kohut had said. Another patient, also an analyst, asked Kohut once from the couch if he was Jewish. There was no answer, so he moved onto another subject. And Mr. W. (from *The Restoration of the Self*), whom I interviewed separately, himself a German Jewish immigrant, always thought Kohut was Christian. Kohut once told his son, who had said "schmuck," that he thought that was a Yiddish word, just as he led his best friend, Robert Wadsworth, to believe he did not know what a *bris* was. And all that from a man who was given a Yiddish name–Wolf Hersh–at his own *bris* in 1913 and was bar mitzvahed at the Mullnergasse synagogue in 1926.

Kohut's ambivalence about his Jewishness spilled over directly to his work. In his last lecture at the self psychology meetings on the Berkeley campus a few days before he died, Kohut said some truly incredible things about the Nazis. The context was a general discussion about empathy. The general point he was making was that empathy in and of itself heals. The mere act of being empathic with someone else has beneficial effects. Empathy is a therapeutic action in the broadest sense. Even if nothing else happens with a patient, if there is empathy from the analyst, healing occurs. Kohut was fully aware of the radical implications of such an idea for someone like himself who was so deeply ingrained in the Freudian tradition. It muddied the waters of inquiry. "I wish I could just simply bypass it," he said shrugging. But "since it is true, and I know it is true" it is an aspect of his topic that deserved the closest attention. He had to mention it. Nor did Kohut shirk from stating the point in the strongest and most general of terms. "The presence of empathy in the surrounding milieu—whether used for compassionate, well-intentioned, therapeutic, and, now listen, even for utterly destructive purposes—is still an admixture of something positive."

Kohut's theory of empathy is of the greatest significance for the theory and practice of psychoanalysis, and it was to be elegantly elaborated in the rest of the lecture. But Kohut's first few sentences, which attempted to clarify his challenging thesis, remain the most problematic of all he wrote in his entire life that has survived, or of anything he said for attribution (as in this lecture on the Berkeley campus, which he knew was being videotaped by a professional company and, as with previous conferences, would be sold and widely distributed):

In other words, there is a step beyond an empathy-informed hatred that wants to destroy you; and an empathyless environment that just brushes you off the face of the earth. The dreadful experiences of prolonged stays in concentration camps during the Nazi era in Germany were just that. It was not cruelty on the whole. (The Nazis were not sadistic or cruel in those camps. There were exceptions of course, it couldn't be otherwise, there are always some exceptions; but that was clearly punished, that was clearly frowned on.) They totally disregarded the humanness of the victims. They were not human, either fully not human, or almost not human (there was a little shift between, I think, the Jews and the Poles, or something like that, in that respect). That was the worst.

It is hard to imagine a more absurd or offensive view of the Nazi concentration camps. Even Paul Ornstein, the editor of *Search* and a longtime friend and colleague of Kohut's, added a footnote after the first passage in parentheses which says, gratuitously, that neither a "search of the literature" nor "any eye-witness accounts" could validate the idea that the Nazis were not sadistic, or that they were regularly punished for breaches of the rules. Should this point even have to be made? Nazi sadism should hardly require scholarly documentation for Heinz Kohut, most of whose relatives died in the Holocaust.

Contradictions, however, I would argue, spur creativity. Kohut's own confusions about his Jewish identity led him to think more deeply about the nature of religion itself. He refused to fall back on the secure, if somewhat mindless, rationalism of Freud's view of religion that has always dominated psychoanalysis. Kohut remained concerned with ultimate issues and sought to locate self psychology in the broadest possible sense within human concerns, traditions, and learning. Perhaps if Kohut had been more at ease with himself and his Jewishness he would not have struggled so intensely with these issues. As Erikson said of Luther, one might say that Kohut lifted his own patienthood to a universal level and tried to solve for all what he could not solve for himself alone.

These "solutions" are richly varied. Kohut's is truly a potential psychology of religion. What he left was only a sketch or outline, it is true, but it is there ready for much larger elaboration. In that work he clarified the specific needs, in terms of idealization, mirroring, and twinship, that religion meets. Such a perspective captures the most significant psychological purposes of religion and shows that uncovering the "illusions" of faith are the beginning, rather than the end, of wisdom.

But I would also note in conclusion that Kohut's deeper understanding of religion carried over into his theorizing about the self. His is a psychology with empathy at its core. No aspect of the psychoanalytic encounter makes sense except in terms of empathy. It is a theory about connectedness and the ways we seek to recover traumatically disrupted union. That quest can and often does fail miserably. Kohut talked of "Tragic Man" in opposition to Freud's "Guilty Man." And yet his theory is ultimately full of hope, in contrast to the brooding pessimism of Freud. There is redemption in the selfobject.

There is also an ethical dimension to the very idea of a holistic self. Freud's model divides the self into warring factions that at best work in tandem, if not quite in cooperation, to keep a human organism thriving. There are higher and lower functions and an elaborate set of ideas about the transformations of desire from one system to another. Defenses keep the structures apart and clearly demarcate the boundaries. There is no larger unity, and he could only sneer with disdain behind his cigar at the idea of life as anything but ultimately a lonely journey by autonomous beings on a detour toward death. We bear no real psychological responsibility for others who are merely objects in our internalized world. In such a view of human nature, a passionate commitment to help others and become involved in their lives and try to heal their wounds and alter the destructive institutions of society becomes suspect. Psychoanalysis for good reason has fed the solipsism of the contemporary self.

Kohut's ideas move in an entirely different direction. In the end, he completely rejected drive theory as meaningless, while recognizing the psychological experience of feeling driven. His notion of the self is a holistic one, not one built on contending pieces. Everything centers on connection and reconnection, growth from disruption (what he called "optimal frustration"), movement from stasis. We are only human in unities and in union with others. That's what the idea of the selfobject is all about. We are and become through others. We are never autonomous, though our selfobject involvements may be more or less primitive, more or less mature, and so on. And as we get so much from others, we implicitly carry an obligation to give back. It is a powerful ethics of the self. God is the glue.

CHAPTER 22

Mysticism and Negative Presence

Barry Ulanov

Language is a constant source of defeat for the mystic, a temptation to despair, a sign that what he has experienced is beyond communication, which is at the very least frustrating—or, worse, an indication that he may not have achieved the hoped-for illumination at all. The weakness of language in general or his grasp of it in particular imparts to the mystic's writing a sometimes becoming, occasionally maddening tentativeness. He speaks apologetically; he warns us against accepting anything he says literally; and when he speaks *figuraliter* he takes refuge in an obliqueness that can only be penetrated by an elevation of spirit equal to his own.

For our time, the locus classicus of these difficulties is T. S. Eliot in the *Four Quartets*, or, more precisely in the concluding sections, the fifth, of each of the first three *Quartets*. The end of "Burnt Norton" bursts with the terror of a poet seeking utterance for what at least approximates mystical experience and finding no suitable language.

> Words strain
> Crack and sometimes break, under the burden
> Under the tension, slip, slide, perish,
> Decay with imprecision, will not stay in place,
> Will not stay still. Shrieking voices
> Scolding, mocking, or merely chattering
> Always assail them.[1]

At the end of his second attempt, "East Coker," the most personal of the *Quartets*, he confesses a further emptiness, the result of two decades of disappointment and defeat, the "middle" of his "way," the shabbiest of parallels to that midpoint in the journey of his life at which Dante begins the *Commedia*, leaving Eliot still

> Trying to learn to use words, and every attempt
> Is a wholly new start, and a different kind of failure
> Because one has only learnt to get the better of words
> For the thing one no longer has to say, or the way in which
> One is no longer disposed to say it.[2]

He calls his equipment "shabby," sees it "always deteriorating," and in the service of an understanding and an articulation that other men, "whom one cannot hope to emulate," have managed far better. One is left only with "the trying," for the terrible fact is, as he says at the end of "The Dry Salvages," that

> to apprehend
> The point of intersection of the timeless
> With time, is an occupation for the saint—
> No occupation either, but something given
> And taken, in a lifetime's death in love,
> Ardour and selflessness and self surrender.[3]

The virtues, then, are negative and the insights inverted. If there is something to be said of these events, these experiences, these terrors, it is something that is self-deprecating, self-denying, self-emptying. To make the point as clear as a fitful, untrustworthy language will permit, Eliot seizes upon a passage at the end of Chapter 13 of Book I of St. John of the Cross's *Ascent of Mount Carmel.* There, John elaborates the advice he had inscribed in his diagram of the mystical way, the ascent of the mountain of perfection which ends at "the summit union." It is a dialectic of the *via negativa:* In order to arrive at having pleasure in everything, at possessing everything, at knowing everything, one must desire to have pleasure in nothing, to possess nothing, to be nothing, to know nothing. And equally, in order to arrive at these supreme points of dispossession one must go by the ways of dispossession: "In order to arrive at that which you are, you must go through that which you are not." And finally, says John, "in order to pass from the all to the All, you must deny yourself all in all [totally]. And when you come to possess it totally, you must possess it without desiring anything."[4]

Is this a kind of self-denial that a poet can practice? Can anyone practice it and still seek to explain anything, even the way of perfection, the ascent of Mount Carmel, which is the way of self-denial? Obviously, John thought something could be said about the nature of self-denial without giving up the practice of self-denial, for he lived the life of the Carmelites of the reform under the tutelage of the reformer herself, Teresa of Avila. He found in the newly ordained austerities a sufficient sweetness to produce his extraordinary poetry, and not only the poetry but that elaborate commentary upon it which makes up his mystical theology. His negations are in the form of counsels and exercises of denial and withdrawal, of purification and denudation, at first active and then passive, moving from the senses to the spirit, but never, even at the highest pitch of his preaching of detachment, altogether separated from a rhetoric of the body. There is, in fact, a sensuality in John, as in all the great mystics who have found their figurative language in the Song of Songs, that only a person as cauterized (to use a central figure of John's) in the service of the spirit could lift beyond the world of the flesh.[5] But then John never goes beyond anything without going through that thing itself. It is his flesh that is cauterized with a branding iron—however obliquely one understands the burning—to permit him to go with the flesh, through the flesh, beyond it.[6] This much Eliot understands very well, from his own experience, from John's experience: "Only through time time is conquered," he concludes at the finish of the long meditation which is part two of "Burnt Norton;" "Not fare well," he says in his extraordinary appropriation of the exhortation of Krishna to Arjuna in the *Bhagavad-Gita*, which is part three of "The Dry Savages;" "Not fare well," he says, "But fare forward, voyagers."[7]

As one goes through the flesh to get beyond the flesh, and through time to overcome time, so must one use language to transcend language. The procedure is almost exactly that which Wittgenstein sums up in the penultimate proposition of the *Tractatus Logico-Philosophicus:*

> My propositions are elucidatory in this way: he who understands me finally recognizes them as senseless, when he has climbed out through them, on them, over them. (He must, so to speak, throw away the ladder after he has climbed up on it.)
>
> He must surmount these propositions; then he sees the world rightly. (6.54)

Any mystic who has written about what purports to be mystical experience must accept the good sense of this dark saying: One climbs up on the language, through it, with it, and then throws it away. One may even accept some of the underlying propositions of Wittgenstein in the *Tractatus:*

> *How* the world is, is completely indifferent for what is higher. God does not reveal himself *in* the world. (6.432)

Or:

> The contemplation of the world *sub specie aeterni* is its contemplation as a limited whole.
>
> The feeling of the world as a limited whole is the mystical feeling. (6.45)

Or, most important for an understanding of the *via negativa* functions of language:

There is indeed the inexpressible. This *shows* itself; it is the mystical. (6.522)

and thus the final negation, with which the *Tractatus* exhausts the logic of language:

Whereof one cannot speak, thereof one must be silent.[8]

To achieve that silence, however, one must not merely talk; one must be garrulous. The inexpressible—Wittgenstein's *Unaussprechliches*—requires, to begin with, a speaking out. One never discovers the ineffable until one has exhausted the affable; the point of the limitless is limitation. Thus Dante stops at the end of the *Purgatorio* because the space—the actual pieces of paper—ordained for the second part of the *Commedia* is full and the limitations of art will not allow him to go further:

ma perchè piene son tutte le carte
ordite a questa cantica seconda,
non mi lascia più ir lo fren dell'arte. (*Purg.* XXXIII, 139–41)

Having achieved the powers of this asceticism, knowing the limits of art, he can transcend them; he can notate his silences and make his soundless litany of light entirely audible to the ear that can hear. When he says, at the end of that litany, in the last lines of the *Paradiso* and of the *Commedia* itself, that at this point, the still point in a turning universe, power failed the great vision, we believe him. We have approached the limits with him, we have seen the limits, and we have all but crossed them. We have no difficulty believing, in exactly the way one believes in a religious doctrine, that his desire and will, turning round and round like a wheel going at a fixed speed, were set in perfect motion by the love that moves the sun and the other stars:

All'alta fantasia qui mancò possa;
ma gia volgeva il mio disio e 'l velle,
sì come rota ch' igualmente è mossa
l'amor che move il sole e l'altre stelle. (*Par.* XXXIII, 142–45)

Dante's *Paradiso* is a voyage to the limits, the limits of art, the limits of human experience, and the limits of language as a means of expressing the experience. Like Wittgenstein in the *Tractatus* and St. John of the Cross in the counsels of perfection of the *Ascent*, Dante has discovered mystical feeling in his apprehension of the world as a limited whole (*als begrenztes Ganzes*). What he discovers at that point is not a void, not the absurd in the modern sense, but a presence—a negative presence. The appropriate conclusion for the *Commedia* is an open—but not empty—space, a blank page as the printer might see it, but not an unfilled page as the mystic would understand it or as a reader who has gone beyond the letter, the allegory, and the tropological direction of the *Paradiso* should understand it. For this is *anagoge;* this is the elevation of the spirit promised by Dante in his dedication of the third cantica to Can Grande della Scala.[9]

We can see the elevation as the result of grace, if we want to make merely doctrinal discriminations about the *Commedia* and thus reduce the number of those who achieve it to the ranks of those in a state of grace. We can gather some sense of the presence that closes off speech and gathers Dante, and presumably those who follow him, into the motions of eternity and the stillness of the *Unaussprechliches*, with the aid of the systematizers of the mystical, such as St. John of the Cross, and the grammarians of epistemology, such as Wittgenstein. In either case, our understanding would be truncated if we made the leap, or, more precisely, attempted the leap into the universe, or the universal, without a very long pause at the level of the concrete. We must find ourselves in that concrete negative presence, which is the only certain presence, at the end of the *Paradiso;* or at the top of Mount Carmel; or at point seven in the *Tractatus;* or even in the language-game speculations of Wittgenstein's *Philosophical Investigations*, though they may seem to be diametrically opposed in concept and performance to the method and content of the *Tractatus*. Certainly it is the concrete with which the mystics leave us at the end of their bouts with language and negative presence. The concrete presence that we know—and that we know we know—in the works of the mystics is always the negative, and that seems to be true whether the mystic is a self-proclaiming kind of person who pushes and pushes at himself to the very bounds of self-assertion, or a self-demeaning type whose struggles take him to the outside limits of abnegation.

The extreme point of negation is the point of transformation. At that point the concrete is exhausted. One has reached the apogee of contemplation of oneself-in-the-world or of an object-in-the-world. Surely that is what "presentness" means in Plotinus, where the *nous* becomes accessible to us and all sense of spatial and temporal dimension falls away. Plotinus brings us, as human beings, into full contemplation of the immutable Intelligence (*nous*) by means of our ecstatic exploration of the world of our senses. We see, hear, touch, taste, and smell everything in order to pass beyond things, to leave them behind, even as the *nous* must eventually in its own ecstasy get beyond itself, leave itself, negate itself (in a manner of speaking), if it is to get hold of the One, from which it emanates.

The same point is reached in the paradoxical language of Pascal in his *Mémorial*. There he specifies as exactly as he can the time of the remarkable experience the document commemorates—complete as to clock time, calendar day, and place in the Roman Martyrology, both the feast day just ending and the one being anticipated.

In the year of grace 1654
Monday 23 November, feast of St. Clement, Pope and Martyr,
and others in the Martyrology.
Vigil of St. Chrysogonus, Martyr, and others.
From about half past ten in the evening until about half
past twelve.
Fire
God of Abraham, God of Issac, God of Jacob,
not of the philosophers and scholars.
Certitude, certitude; feeling, joy, peace.
God of Jesus Christ.
My God and Thy God.
Thy God shall be my God.
Forgetfulness of the world and of all save God.
He is to be found only by the means taught in the Gospel.
Greatness of the human soul.[10]

In the great "Fire," which must stand by itself as the mark of the experience, all is consumed. The concrete moment when Pascal attained "Forgetfulness of the world and of all save God" and perceived the "Greatness of the human soul" is memorialized. That occurrence of negative presence meant so much to Pascal as concrete evidence of what had happened that he sewed into the lining of his doublet both his first quick notation of the *Mémorial* and a fine copy of it on parchment.

We may not always examine our knowledge of mystical experience, or of the way in which mystical experience is presented as a kind of knowledge, in terms of the negative. We may reserve for the categories of the negative those mystics, or putative mystics, who deliberately affect the rhetoric and the logic of the *via negativa.* But sooner or later we must come to formulate our understanding of what we call the mystical, or our understanding of someone else's understanding, in this way. To some extent, all the problems that turn upon the language of mysticism turn upon the negative. All that we can say—all that can be said—is what we cannot say—what cannot be said. What we seek is the unutterable, and if we find it, what we say we have found is—unutterable. What is more, we can only approach the positive, the affirmative, can only achieve some sense of an ultimate reality, through the negative, whether we start by affirming and wind down to negation or move from the lowest level of the negative—of denial—up to some adumbration, at least, of the meaning of—and here again we must use negative terms to say anything worth saying—the opposite of meaninglessness. The language (slightly modernized) of the fourteenth-century English paraphrase of the Pseudo-Dionysius, *Denis Hid Divinity*, is incomparable here:

And eftsoons by the means, from the highest to the last, and from the last to the highest again, we fold all together and do them away, that we may clearly know that unknowing the which is walled about from all knowable powers in all these being things; and that we may see that sovereign-substantial darkness, privily hid from all light in these being things.[11]

Eventually, in this context with language in which light can only be found in darkness and knowledge in a cloud of unknowing, one must come to the compendious summation of the Pseudo-Dionysius in his *Mystical Theology*, that marvelously brief and quick-witted but not unsolemn assertion of what Divinity is not. The central points are made in the concluding litany of the concluding chapter, the fifth, which is no more than a medium-length paragraph *in toto* and comes to its breathtaking last words as quickly as possible in order to make clear that what is most clear is that nothing can be altogether clear in this area, including these words:

It is not knowledge or truth; nor is It kingship or wisdom; nor is It One, nor is It unity, nor is It Godhead or Goodness; nor is It a Spirit, as we understand the term, since It is not Sonship or Fatherhood; nor is It any other thing such as we or any other being can have knowledge of; nor does It belong to the category of nonexistence or to that of existence; nor do existent beings know It as It actually is, nor does It know them as they actually are; nor can the reason attain to It to name It or to know It; nor is It darkness, nor is It light, or error, or truth; nor can any affirmation or negation apply to It; for while applying affirmations or negations to those orders of being that come next to It, we apply not unto It either affirmation or negation, inasmuch as It transcends all negation by the pre-eminence of Its simple and absolute nature—free from every limitation and beyond them all.[12]

The fourteenth-century language of *Denis Hid Divinity* says it best of all, perhaps, in its simple, blunt, colloquial way:

For the perfect and singular Cause of all must needs be without compensation of the most high height above all, both setting and doing away. And his not-understandable overpassing is understandably above all affirming and denying.[13]

Of course, the precision of the sixth-century Dionysius's understanding and the recension of the grounds of imprecision in the language and thought of mystical theology did not keep him from attempting some statement of what cannot really be stated. Nor did it preclude an attempt at an angelology, with which the world has been enlarging and diminishing its imagination ever since. For it is the Pseudo-Dionysius whose ghostly wit fixed the medieval ununderstanding with the fleshly images of the Seraphim and the Cherubim, the Angels and the Archangels, the Thrones and the Dominations, the Principalities and the Powers.

If one accepts the Dionysian imagination at face value, one sees only the most sentimental values in things, attractive values, entertaining values, but inevitably superficial ones—literally on the surface—and therefore without concreteness. For the great strength of the Pseudo-Areopagite's use of figurative language, as in his angelic hierarchy, is to lead his reader by excess and defect, by inversion and subversion, away from surfaces, away from universals, away from abstractions, to concrete particulars. His mystical language is a language that comes from experience and reaches out to experience. One takes what one has—an image, a conception, a name, a counter for an experience—and goes beyond it, transcends it, which is to say, negates it, turns it into something quite different from itself, something quite *other*.

Otherness will not long tolerate abstractions, however much it may demand a vocabulary that is generalized into categories and classes of being. We do not know otherness until it has passed from categorical essence into existing being, until its name has been fleshed out and its image been brought to earth. Thus Dionysius proceeds and so does John. Thus Dante invents and Jacob Boehme formulates his doctrine of counterstroke and efflux.[14] Thus are produced the extravagances, to the point of a gland-tickling voluptuousness, of the mystics in the Song of Songs tradition. These mystics, in their spectacular concretions, are the original masters of sublimation. But theirs is a sublimation with a reach and an intensity, an awareness of the process of sublimation and an acceptance of it that Sigmund Freud's use of the term does not contemplate.

Sublimation in the language and in the experience of the mystics is a matter of negative presence, not of mere negation or transformation from a lower to a higher plane. It is not the conversion of, say, sexual energy from the flesh to the spirit that is accomplished, but rather that spiritualization of the flesh which for the first time permits the flesh—as the mystic understands it—to be itself wholly and truly. Now the flesh, in this category, is no longer merely in a category; it is particularized, concretized; it has been fully infused, wholly informed with being. And so it is, the mystics seem to be saying, with each of the experiences of concretization: What has been merely one of a multifarious kind, an example, just one more thing in a class of things, now exists for the particularizing, concretizing mystic as something entirely in and of itself; its class ties have been cut, its categorical essence has been forgotten or destroyed in the ritual of inspiriting which is mystical experience; it is entirely present; it has presence. One would not be out of order, perhaps, if one inflected Wittgenstein's words in the *Tractatus* in a special way here: It is not simply the feeling of the world as a *limited* whole that is the mystical feeling, but, more importantly, the feeling of the world as a limited *whole*. Concreteness that comes as a result of mystical inquiry is exhaustive, a decisive totality. It consumes everything by accounting for everything. Such concreteness is a kind of burnt offering, and in the figurative language of the mystics it is perhaps allowable to say that the burning occurs because a fire that descends from the heavens consumes everything by its total identification of a thing, by its radical particularity, by its presenting the mystic with nothing less than the *Ding an sich*. And like all burnt offerings of this sort, it gives glory to God.[15] That is the point of St. Thérèse of Lisieux's late-nineteenth-century

"Act of Oblation as Victim of Holocaust to God's Merciful Love." Thérèse goes far beyond the conventional language of self-mortification to identify herself with all victims, past and present, to particularize suffering with love and somehow make it acceptable, to God and man, in its most extravagant particularizations.[16]

The Buddhist configuration of reality offers the same concentration on the particular, on the concrete, though it asserts more openly the distrust of abstractions, of universals, of names as anything more than counters for perceptions that names can never, in themselves, evoke. Thus, in the dialogue between a Buddhist and a Realist, both so called by the ninth-century Nepalese Buddhist Vācaspatimiśra, the point is made tersely enough by the Buddhist:

> . . . a (Universal) has never been (really) perceived (by the senses). On the contrary, the thing (really) perceived is the particular, the (extreme concrete and) particular which is alone the ultimate reality (it is the thing in itself shorn of all its extensions). Therefore it (alone) is the efficient cause of sensation, but not the Universal. The (Universal) is bare of any kind of efficiency, it is a spurious (reality).[17]

Names, we are told, do not stand for reality but only for logical constructions; sensations are "unutterable," for if we could really communicate a sensation "we would know what heat is from its name, just as we know it by actual experience, and if we could feel it from its name, cold would disappear (as soon as the word 'heat' would be pronounced)."

What keeps the mystic from being caught up in the Kantian search for the thing-in-itself is his apprehension of negative presence. His achievement of the concrete is ultimately a triumph, with and through the concrete, over the concrete. He comes now to his blank page. Words are finished. Things have receded. There is nothing left to say, for everything has been said. Nonetheless, he will say something; he will say that he has no more to say. Sometimes he will say it by explaining how defeated he is by the inadequacies of language and how close to despair these inadequacies leave him. Sometimes he will say it by narrating the great journey into silence, by inscribing, at whatever length, in whatever degree of obliqueness, his *Commedia*. Sometimes, depending upon the depth of his experience of the concrete, of particularity, of negative presence, he will systematize his own approach to that point of exhaustion where energy really begins by offering a methodology of language, or logic, or the ascent of the ascetical mountain. In every case, he will come at last to that passivity in which it is no longer necessary to complain, to confess, to systematize, to allegorize, or to make sure by the appropriate noises that everyone realizes that he has become silent. He has attained the highest point of passivity, that degree of submission at which even hope is a meaningless term, for what one has attained one no longer needs to hope for, and love and faith are terms as useless as knowledge and truth and wisdom and all the others in the Pseudo-Dionysius's negative litany. For one who has really experienced the immanence of the transcendent, language must be a constant source of defeat, only now it is no temptation to despair, but the very opposite: Everything in it that defeats this mystic is a badge of this triumph.

NOTES

1. T. S. Eliot, *Collected Poems 1909–1962* (New York: Harcourt Brace & World, Inc. 1966), 180.

2. Ibid., 188–89.

3. Ibid., 198.

4. See St. John of the Cross, "Ascent of Mount Carmel," Book I, chapter 13, 10–13, in *The Complete Works of Saint John of the Cross*, E. Allison Peers, trs. (Westminster, MD: 1953), 59–60. Westminster Press.

5. The examples are innumerable; two of the best are the figures of the nursing mother in Book I, chapter 1, of *Dark Night of the Soul*, and the elaboration of his allegorization of Song of Songs 1:1 in the Vulgate, *Osculetur me osculo oris sui*, in Book II, chapter 23, 12. See *Complete Works*, 452–53.

6. See poem III (in the Sanlucar Codex numbering), preferably in the Spanish, which makes the strength and thoroughness of the branding clear in a way none of the translations into English quite reproduces. Most of the translations are available in bilingual editions, for example, those by Willis Barnstone, Roy Campbell, and John Frederick Nims; the Peers, in *Complete Works*, is without the original text.

7. See Eliot, *Collected Poems*, 178, 195–97.

8. See Ludwig Wittgenstein, *Tractatus-Logico-Philosophicus* (London: Cambridge University Press, 1955), 186–87, 188–89, with the German and English on facing pages.

9. See *Le Opere di Dante Alighierei*, Paget Toynbee, ed. (Oxford: 1924), *Epistola* X, 414–20. Oxford University Press.

10. This is about half the text of the *Mémorial*. For the complete text, see *Oeuvres de Blaise Pascale*, Leon Brunschvicg, ed. (Paris: 1904–14), xii, 5.

11. See "Denis Hid Divinity," in *The Cloud of Unknowing and Other Treatises by an English Mystic of the Fourteenth Century*, Dom Justin McCann, ed. (London: 1936), 268. Burns, Oates, and Washbourne Publishers.

12. See Dionysius the Areopagite, *On the Divine Names and the Mystical Theology*, C. E. Rolt, trs. (London: 1951), 200–1. SPCK Publishers.

13. See McCann, *Denis Hid Divinity*, 282.

14. See Jacob Boehme, "On the Divine Intuition," chapter 3, in *Six Theosophic Points and Other Writings*, J. R. Earle, trs. (Ann Arbor: 1970), with an excellent introduction by Nicholas Berdyaev. Ann Arbor: Kessinger Publishing Co., 1992.

15. For some of the special meanings "burnt offering" can have for a writer with mystical inclinations, see R. Abraham b. Isaac ha-Levi TaMaKH, *Commentary on the Song of Songs*, Leon A. Feldman, ed. and trs. (Assen: 1970), 102–3, original text and translation. The passage deals with Song of Songs 3:10.

16. See Barry Ulanov, *The Making of a Modern Saint: A Biographical Study of Thérèse of Lisieux* (New York, 1966), 227–37. Doubleday Press.

17. See "Vācaspatimišra on the Buddhist Theory of Perception," in *Buddhist Logic*, Theodore Stcherbatsky, ed. (The Hague: 1958), Vol. 2, 263–64. See also Vol. 1, part 2, chapter 4, "Ultimate Reality" (*paramārtha-sat*).

Afterword: A Few Remarks on Authenticity

Esther Menaker

Let me begin by thanking all of you for the very authentic contributions that you have made to this volume. I feel honored and grateful, for, in the professional world of psychoanalysis in which I spent a big part of my professional life, I was not often appreciated. Maverick that I am, my divergent views were regarded with suspicion, if not contempt. And I lacked the talent to couch my views in ways that would make them less abrasive, less deviant. Thus, it is little wonder that I am thankful for your appreciation of my attempt to preserve and express my authenticity.

What do we mean when we characterize someone as "authentic?" We usually are referring to the fact that the individual has retained something of the simplicity of childhood; that societal pressures have not impinged too much on the original self structure, character, and values.

Very early in childhood, the child's needs and wishes begin to be expressed—this results in the "willing" of an independent entity, the individual self, and the child. In the interaction with parental figures, important processes take place, processes which are sometimes in harmony with those of the particular individual and sometimes in opposition to them. Through this constant interaction, the individual self is formed. This is the groundwork for the development of the authentic self.

Yet it would be inaccurate to speak of the simplicity of childhood. From the beginning of life, the individual is unique in constitution and in temperament in response to the outside world, especially as it relates to his or her needs as they are conveyed in the interaction with the outside world—uniquely in every case depending on the original disposition and the nature of the original parental environment. This is the first encounter with the outer social environment, and it is unique in every case. It is this uniqueness that lies at the root of authenticity. Otto Rank emphasized the uniqueness of individuals and the importance of affirming it in the therapeutic process.

The authenticity of an individual begins with the ability to retain and express with others the earliest products of the earliest internalizations, which are the result of the interactions within the first social environment, the family. The expression of an individual's authenticity begins when he or she can express to others the precipitates of the earliest internalizations—those derivatives which are the product of interactions within the first social environment, the family.

It is within the family that the socialization process begins. Sometimes there are conflicts between the will of the growing child and that of parents or caretakers. For the child, these conflicts often precipitate fear and shame, and the self-esteem of the child is threatened. It is the beginning of the effect of social pressure on the freedom of self-expression and is therefore a threat to the individual's authenticity.

What is it, then, in the movement of human history that threatens the authenticity of the individual? Every individual is not only unique but is embedded in a social situation, beginning with family and then continuing with the larger community—school, church, neighborhood, community.

The opportunity for uniqueness, that is, for the differentiation of one individual from another from the beginning of each and every life, I think, is a product of evolution. It is on individual difference that the continuing evolution of human beings depends.

But human beings are not born to live alone. From the beginning of life we are embedded in the social structure. The family almost always is part of a larger community. Although the ideals and values of the family are the primary source, through processes of identification, for the growing child's ego, superego, and ego ideal, and could be said to be the prime source of authenticity—the attitudes, values, and ideals of the larger community are of great importance. An individual, to be authentic in adult life, must have had a relationship to parents that resulted in adequate self-esteem. Insufficient self-esteem makes the individual vulnerable to social and community pressures. The wish to be well thought of by the community, if it becomes overpowering, may easily result in fraudulence, which represents a failed attempt to avoid fear and shame. Authenticity is sacrificed in this attempt.

The power of the community's standards and requirements and criticisms over a growing child is great. Self-esteem is easily injured. One way to combat the loss of self-esteem is by taking on the standards of the social group, but by doing this, the individual gives up a piece of authenticity.

On a more optimistic note, however, creativity is the antidote to the threat of danger to authenticity. Social pressures, as they appear in the form of rigid social codes, or ethical values, or prescribed social etiquette, or absolute belief in political or social points of view, or even so-called scientific systems of thought, are a danger to the maintenance of authenticity.

It is in this spirit of support for your authenticity that I thank you again for your creative efforts in venturing into the realms of dissent.

Index

Contributors

JUDITH L. ALPERT is professor of applied psychology, and faculty and supervisor, Postdoctoral Program in Psychotherapy and Psychoanalysis, New York University.

CLAUDE BARBRE is executive director of The Harlem Family Institute and associate editor of the *Journal of Religion and Health*.

DORIS BROTHERS is co-founder, faculty, and training analyst, the Training and Research Institute for Self Psychology.

JULIE JOSLYN BROWN is co-founder, faculty member, and training analyst, the Training and Research Institute for Self Psychology.

ESTER SCHALER BUCHHOLZ is a professor, Applied Psychology Department, and founder and director, Psychology of Parenthood Masters Program, New York University; and co-director of psychoanalytic training, Institute of Child, Adolescent, and Family Studies.

ROSEMARIE PEREZ FOSTER is an associate professor, Ehrenkranz School of Social Work; and faculty, Postdoctoral Program in Psychotherapy and Psychoanalysis, New York University.

PETER L. GIOVACCHINI is faculty and training analyst, Chicago Psychoanalytic Institute.

LUDWIG JANUS is faculty and training analyst, Heidelberg Psychoanalytic Institute, and editor of the *Journal of Psychohistory*.

BRIGITTE JANUS-STANEK is faculty and training analyst, Heidelberg Psychoanalytic Institute.

R. G. K. KAINER is faculty and training analyst, Washington School of Psychiatry.

S. KAINER is a physicist, novelist, and playwright, and was formerly director of drama, Chestnut Lodge Hospital.

ROBERT KRAMER is Distinguished Adjunct Professor and director of executive education programs, School of Public Affairs, American University, Washington D.C.

E. JAMES LIEBERMAN is a clinical professor, Department of Psychiatry and Behavioral Sciences, George Washington University.

DANIEL LIECHTY is faculty, School of Social Work, Illinois State University.

PAUL LIPPMANN is faculty and training analyst, William Alanson White Institute; and faculty, Postdoctoral Program in Psychotherapy and Psychoanalysis, New York University.

ESTHER MENAKER, deceased, was a co-founder, faculty, and training analyst, Postdoctoral Program in Psychoanalysis and Psychotherapy, New York University; and faculty and training analyst, National Psychological Association for Psychoanalysis, and the Training and Research Institute for Self Psychology.

DOLORES O. MORRIS is a supervisor, Postdoctoral Program in Psychotherapy and Psychoanalysis, New York University, New Hope Guild Centers, and New York Institute for Psychotherapy Training in Infancy, Childhood, and Adolescence.

SPYROS D. ORFANOS is co-director of the Manhattan Institute for Psychoanalysis; and adjunct professor, Clinical Psychology Program, Long Island University and the Center for Byzantine and Modern Greek Studies, Queens College, City University of New York.

ROBERT PRINCE is faculty, Postdoctoral Program in Psychoanalysis and Psychotherapy, New York University.

ARNOLD WM. RACHMAN is a training and supervising analyst, Postgraduate Center for Mental Health, and clinical professor of psychology, Adelphi University Postdoctoral Program in Psychoanalysis.

PAUL ROAZEN was a professor, Department of Government, Harvard University; and a professor of political science, York University, Toronto.

ALAN ROLAND is faculty and training analyst, National Psychological Association for Psychoanalysis, and Institute for Expressive Analysis; and an adjunct instructor, Psychiatry and Religion Department, Union Theological Seminary.

JEFFREY B. RUBIN has taught at the Postgraduate Center for Mental Health, the Object Relations Institute, the C. G. Jung Foundation, and Yeshiva University.

CHARLES B. STROZIER is a professor of history and director of the Center on Terrorism and Public Safety, John Jay College, City University of New York; faculty and training analyst, the Training and Research Institute for Self Psychology; and founding editor of the *Psychohistory Review.*

BARRY ULANOV, deceased, was McIntosh Professor of Literature, emeritus, Barnard College, Columbia University; faculty, Union Theological Seminary; and editor of the *Journal of Religion and Health.*